WEBSTER'S

INSTANT WORD GUIDE

Webster's
INSTANT
WORD
GUIDE

A Merriam-Webster ®

M E R R I A M - W E B S T E R   I N C.

Springfield, Massachusetts

A GENUINE MERRIAM-WEBSTER

The name *Webster* alone is no guarantee of excellence. It is used by a number of publishers and may serve mainly to mislead an unwary buyer.

A Merriam-Webster® is the registered trademark you should look for when you consider the purchase of dictionaries or other fine reference books. It carries the reputation of a company that has been publishing since 1831 and is your assurance of quality and authority.

Copyright © 1980 by Merriam-Webster Inc.

Philippines Copyright 1980 by Merriam-Webster Inc.

Library of Congress Cataloging in Publication
Main entry under title:

Webster's instant word guide.

    1. Spellers.
PE1145.2.W4   428'.1   79-20748
ISBN 0-87779-273-9

MADE IN THE UNITED STATES OF AMERICA

2930313233IB898887

CONTENTS

PREFACE

The major feature of Webster's Instant Word Guide is an alphabetical word list which is intended for the use of writers, secretaries, and typists as a handy guide to spelling and to the division of words at the end of lines. The word divisions in this book have been revised to agree with those shown in Webster's New Collegiate Dictionary, copyright 1979. Variant spellings are shown for many words, as are irregular inflections of verbs, adjectives, and nouns. Short identifying glosses and cross-references are provided to help distinguish words of similar sound or spelling that might otherwise be confused, such as *allusive, elusive,* and *illusive* or *straight* and *strait.*

The division of words in English dictionaries has a long, somewhat complicated history, and the traditions upon which such division is based have developed gradually, not to say haphazardly, over a period of about a century and a half. It is commonly thought that word division is based primarily on pronunciation. In actuality, spelling, etymology (the history of a word), common sense, and occasionally arbitrary choice also play important roles. The question of end-of-line division occurs only in written contexts, and it is perhaps unreasonable to expect the spoken form of the language to dictate a workable set of principles to solve a largely mechanical problem. For one thing, there are many words with perfectly acceptable variant pronunciations. Let us take *homicide* as an example. Those who pronounce the first syllable of *homicide* to rhyme with *home* may prefer an end-of-line division before the *m,* while those who rhyme it with *bomb* may prefer a division after the *m.* Both divisions are correct, but in this book only one of them is shown since an entry such as *ho·m·i·cide* would be confusing to many. In order to be consistent in the large number of cases which fall into this category it was decided to show only the leftmost division in each instance. Thus, the entry *ho·mi·cide* appears in this book. Etymology is taken into account in the division of such words as *accordance* and *dictionary.* These

vi

words were not formed by adding suffixes to the English words *accord* and *diction;* rather they are derived from the early French *acordance* and medieval Latin *dictionarium* respectively. Thus, in the present book we show the divisions *ac·cor·dance* and *dic·tio·nary* rather than *ac·cord·ance* and *dic·tion·ary.* Common sense and the established practice of most typists and printers are followed in this book in that a single letter at the beginning or end of a word is not separated from the rest of the word.

The adoption of the above and other principles allows us to achieve a greater degree of consistency of division than in the past and accounts for many differences between this and some of our earlier books. Our general recommendation to those concerned about end-of-line division is to choose a reliable up-to-date dictionary or word guide such as this and to rely upon it without worrying about divisions shown elsewhere. Other books may not be wrong, just different. Greater consistency of division will result from the regular use of a single work. While there are acceptable alternative end-of-line divisions just as there are acceptable variant spellings and pronunciations, we recognize that the purpose of showing divisions in this book is to save the user the time and trouble of making a choice in what is essentially a minor matter.

Variant spellings preceded by *or* are found in frequent use. Those preceded by *also* are found less frequently though often enough to be included in this book. All of the variant spellings given are acceptable in standard English writing. The following labels and abbreviations are used in the glosses and cross-references which distinguish between entries:

adj (adjective)	*masc* (masculine)
adverb	*math* (mathematics)
biol (biology)	*noun*
chem (chemistry)	*pl* (plural)
comp (comparative)	*prep* (preposition)
conj (conjunction)	*var* (variant)
fem (feminine)	*verb*

For ease of reference guide words are printed in boldface type at the top left and right hand corners of each two page spread. The guide words are the alphabetically first and last words on the spread, including variants and inflected forms. A few exceptions result from the proviso that consecutive guide words themselves must be in alphabetical order. Following the A to Z vocabulary list this book also contains a list of abbreviations, a brief discussion of punctuation, and a table of weights and measures.

All of the features just enumerated make the editors confident that users of Webster's Instant Word Guide will find it to be a convenient and reliable reference tool.

J. K. Bollard
Editor

A

aard·vark
aba·cus
 pl aba·ci *or*
  aba·cus·es

ab·a·lo·ne
aban·don
aban·doned
aban·don·ment
abase
abase·ment
abash
abate
abate·ment
ab·a·tis
 pl ab·a·tis *or*
  ab·a·tis·es

ab·at·toir
ab·ax·i·al
ab·ba·cy
ab·bé
ab·bess
ab·bey
ab·bot
ab·bre·vi·ate
ab·bre·vi·a·tion
ab·di·cate
ab·di·ca·tion
ab·do·men
ab·dom·i·nal
ab·duct
ab·duc·tion
ab·duc·tor
abe·ce·dar·i·an
abed

ab·er·rant
ab·er·ra·tion
abet
 abet·ted
 abet·ting
abet·tor
 or abet·ter

abey·ance
ab·hor
 ab·horred
 ab·hor·ring
ab·hor·rence
ab·hor·rent
abide
abil·i·ty
 pl abil·i·ties

ab·ject
ab·jec·tion
ab·ject·ly
ab·ject·ness
ab·ju·ra·tion
ab·jure
ab·late
ab·la·tion
ab·la·tive
ablaze
able
able-bod·ied
ab·lu·tion
ab·ne·gate
ab·ne·ga·tion
ab·nor·mal
ab·nor·mal·i·ty
ab·nor·mal·ly
aboard

abode
aboil
abol·ish
ab·o·li·tion
ab·o·li·tion·ist
A-bomb
abom·i·na·ble
abom·i·nate
abom·i·na·tion
ab·orig·i·nal
ab·orig·i·ne
aborn·ing
abort
abor·tion
abor·tion·ist
abor·tive
abound
about
about-face
above
above·board
ab·ra·ca·dab·ra
abrade
abra·sion
abra·sive
ab·re·act
abreast
abridge
abridg·ment
 or abridge·ment

abroad
ab·ro·gate
ab·ro·ga·tion
abrupt
ab·scess

1

ab·scis·sa
ab·scis·sion
ab·scond
ab·sence
ab·sent
ab·sen·tee
ab·sen·tee·ism
ab·sent·mind·ed
ab·sinthe
  or ab·sinth

ab·so·lute
ab·so·lute·ly
ab·so·lu·tion
ab·so·lut·ism
ab·solve
ab·sorb
ab·sor·ben·cy
ab·sor·bent
ab·sorp·tion
ab·sorp·tive
ab·stain
ab·ste·mi·ous
ab·sten·tion
ab·sti·nence
ab·stract
ab·strac·tion
ab·struse
ab·surd
ab·sur·di·ty
abun·dance
abun·dant
abuse
abu·sive
abut
  abut·ted

abut·ting
abut·ment
abut·tals
abys·mal
abys·mal·ly
abyss
abys·sal
aca·cia
ac·a·deme
ac·a·dem·ic
  also ac·a·dem·i·cal

ac·a·dem·i·cal·ly
ac·a·de·mi·cian
ac·a·dem·i·cism
acad·e·my
acan·thus
a cap·pel·la
  also a ca·pel·la

ac·cede
  agree (see exceed)

ac·ce·le·ran·do
ac·cel·er·ate
ac·cel·er·a·tion
ac·cel·er·a·tor
ac·cent
ac·cen·tu·al
ac·cen·tu·ate
ac·cen·tu·a·tion
ac·cept
  receive (see except)

ac·cept·abil·i·ty
ac·cept·able
ac·cep·tance
ac·cep·ta·tion

ac·cess
  approach (see **excess**)

ac·ces·si·bil·i·ty
ac·ces·si·ble
ac·ces·sion
ac·ces·so·ry
  also ac·ces·sa·ry
  pl ac·ces·so·ries
    also ac·ces·sa·ries

ac·ci·dence
ac·ci·dent
ac·ci·den·tal
ac·ci·den·tal·ly
  also ac·ci·dent·ly

ac·claim
ac·cla·ma·tion
ac·cli·mate
ac·cli·ma·ti·za·
  tion
ac·cli·ma·tize
ac·cliv·i·ty
ac·co·lade
ac·com·mo·date
ac·com·mo·dat·
  ing
ac·com·mo·da·
  tion
ac·com·pa·ni·
  ment
ac·com·pa·nist
ac·com·pa·ny
ac·com·plice
ac·com·plish
ac·com·plished
ac·com·plish·
  ment

ac·cord
ac·cor·dance
ac·cor·dant
ac·cord·ing·ly
ac·cor·di·on
ac·cost
ac·count
ac·count·abil·i·ty
ac·count·able
ac·coun·tan·cy
ac·coun·tant
ac·count·ing
ac·cou·tre
  or ac·cou·ter

ac·cou·tre·ment
  or ac·cou·ter·ment

ac·cred·it
ac·cred·i·ta·tion
ac·cre·tion
ac·cru·al
ac·crue
ac·cru·ing
ac·cul·tur·ate
ac·cul·tur·a·tion
ac·cu·mu·late
ac·cu·mu·la·tion
ac·cu·mu·la·tor
ac·cu·ra·cy
ac·cu·rate
ac·cu·rate·ly
ac·cu·rate·ness
ac·cursed
ac·cus·al
ac·cu·sa·tion
ac·cu·sa·tive

ac·cuse
ac·cus·er
ac·cus·tom
ac·cus·tomed
acer·bi·ty
ac·et·al·de·hyde
ac·et·an·i·lide
  or ac·et·an·i·lid
ace·tate
ace·tic
  chem (*see* ascetic)

ace·tone
acet·y·lene
ache
achieve
achieve·ment
ach·ing
ach·ro·mat·ic
ac·id
acid·ic
acid·i·fi·ca·tion
acid·i·fy
acid·i·ty
ac·i·do·sis
acid·u·late
acid·u·lous
ack-ack
ac·knowl·edge
ac·knowl·edg·
    ment
  also ac·knowl·edge·
    ment

ac·me
ac·ne
ac·o·lyte
ac·o·nite

acorn
acous·tic
acous·ti·cal
acous·ti·cal·ly
acous·tics
ac·quaint
ac·quain·tance
ac·quain·tance·
    ship
ac·qui·esce
ac·qui·es·cence
ac·qui·es·cent
ac·quire
ac·quire·ment
ac·qui·si·tion
ac·quis·i·tive
ac·quis·i·tive·ness
ac·quit
  ac·quit·ted
  ac·quit·ting
ac·quit·tal
acre
acre·age
ac·rid
acrid·i·ty
ac·ri·mo·ni·ous
ac·ri·mo·ny
ac·ro·bat
ac·ro·bat·ic
ac·ro·nym
ac·ro·pho·bia
acrop·o·lis
across
across-the-board
acros·tic
ac·ry·late

acryl·ic
act·ing
ac·tin·ic
ac·tin·i·um
ac·tion
ac·tion·able
ac·ti·vate
ac·ti·va·tion
ac·tive
ac·tive·ly
ac·tiv·ism
ac·tiv·ist
ac·tiv·i·ty
ac·tor
ac·tress
ac·tu·al
ac·tu·al·i·ty
ac·tu·al·ize
ac·tu·al·ly
ac·tu·ar·i·al
ac·tu·ary
ac·tu·ate
ac·tu·a·tor
acu·ity
acu·men
acu·punc·ture
acute
acute·ly
acute·ness
ad·age
ada·gio
pl ada·gios

ad·a·mant
ad·a·man·tine
ad·a·mant·ly

adapt
to fit (see adept, adopt)

adapt·abil·i·ty
adapt·able
ad·ap·ta·tion
adapt·er
also adapt·or

ad·dend
ad·den·dum
pl ad·den·da

ad·der
snake

add·er
one that adds

ad·dict
ad·dic·tion
ad·dic·tive
ad·di·tion
ad·di·tion·al
ad·di·tion·al·ly
ad·di·tive
ad·dle
ad·dress
ad·dress·ee
ad·duce
ad·e·noid
ad·e·noi·dal
ad·ept
an expert

adept
proficient (see adapt, adopt)

adept·ly
adept·ness

ad·e·qua·cy
ad·e·quate
ad·e·quate·ly
ad·here
ad·her·ence
ad·her·ent
ad·he·sion
ad·he·sive
ad·he·sive·ness
ad hoc
adi·a·bat·ic
adieu
pl adieus *or* adieux

ad in·fi·ni·tum
ad in·ter·im
adi·os
ad·i·pose
ad·i·pos·i·ty
ad·ja·cent
ad·jec·ti·val
ad·jec·ti·val·ly
ad·jec·tive
ad·join
ad·join·ing
ad·journ
ad·journ·ment
ad·judge
ad·ju·di·cate
ad·ju·di·ca·tion
ad·junct
ad·ju·ra·tion
ad·jure
ad·just
ad·just·able
ad·just·er
also ad·jus·tor

ad·just·ment
ad·ju·tant
ad·ju·vant
ad-lib
  ad·libbed
  ad·lib·bing
ad lib
  adverb

ad li·bi·tum
ad·man
ad·min·is·ter
ad·min·is·tra·ble
ad·min·is·trant
ad·min·is·trate
ad·min·is·tra·tion
ad·min·is·tra·tive
ad·min·is·tra·tor
ad·mi·ra·ble
ad·mi·ra·bly
ad·mi·ral
ad·mi·ral·ty
ad·mi·ra·tion
ad·mire
ad·mir·er
ad·mis·si·bil·i·ty
ad·mis·si·ble
ad·mis·sion
ad·mit
  ad·mit·ted
  ad·mit·ting
ad·mit·tance
ad·mit·ted·ly
ad·mix
ad·mix·ture
ad·mon·ish

ad·mo·ni·tion
ad·mon·i·to·ry
ad nau·se·am
ado
ado·be
ad·o·les·cence
ad·o·les·cent
adopt
  to accept (see adapt, adept)

adop·tion
adop·tive
ador·able
ad·o·ra·tion
adore
adorn
adorn·ment
ad·re·nal
adren·a·line
adrift
adroit
adroit·ly
adroit·ness
ad·sorb
ad·sor·bent
ad·sorp·tion
ad·sorp·tive
ad·u·late
ad·u·la·tion
adult
adul·ter·ant
adul·ter·ate
adul·ter·a·tion
adul·ter·er
adul·ter·ess
adul·ter·ous

adul·tery
adult·hood
ad·um·brate
ad·um·bra·tion
ad va·lo·rem
ad·vance
ad·vance·ment
ad·van·tage
ad·van·ta·geous
ad·vent
ad·ven·ti·tious
ad·ven·ture
ad·ven·tur·er
ad·ven·ture·some
ad·ven·tur·ess
ad·ven·tur·ous
ad·verb
ad·ver·bi·al
ad·ver·bi·al·ly
ad·ver·sary
ad·ver·sa·tive
ad·ver·sa·tive·ly
ad·verse
  unfavorable (see averse)

ad·verse·ly
ad·ver·si·ty
ad·vert
ad·ver·tise
ad·ver·tise·ment
ad·ver·tis·er
ad·ver·tis·ing
ad·vice
  noun (see advise)

ad·vis·abil·i·ty
ad·vis·able

ad·vise
verb (see advice)

ad·vis·er
or ad·vi·sor

ad·vise·ment

ad·vi·sory

ad·vo·ca·cy

ad·vo·cate

ae·gis
or egis

ae·o·lian

ae·on

aer·ate

aer·a·tion

ae·ri·al
adj

aer·i·al
noun

ae·ri·al·ist

ae·rie

aero

aer·o·bat·ics

aer·obe

aer·o·bic

aero·drome

aero·dy·nam·i·
cal·ly

aero·dy·nam·ics

aer·o·log·i·cal

aer·ol·o·gist

aer·ol·o·gy

aero·naut

aero·nau·ti·cal
or aero·nau·tic

aero·nau·tics

aer·o·nom·ic
or aer·o·nom·i·cal

aer·on·o·mist

aer·on·o·my

aero·pause

aero·sol

aero·space

aery

aes·thete
or es·thete

aes·thet·ic
or es·thet·ic

aes·thet·i·cal·ly

aes·thet·i·cism

aes·thet·ics
or es·thet·ics

aes·ti·vate

aes·ti·va·tion

af·fa·bil·i·ty

af·fa·ble

af·fa·bly

af·fair

af·fect
to influence (see
effect)

af·fec·ta·tion

af·fect·ed

af·fect·ing

af·fec·tion

af·fec·tion·ate

af·fer·ent

af·fi·ance

af·fi·da·vit

af·fil·i·ate

af·fil·i·a·tion

af·fin·i·ty

af·firm

af·fir·ma·tion

af·fir·ma·tive

af·fix

af·fla·tus

af·flict

af·flic·tion

af·flic·tive

af·flu·ence

af·flu·ent

af·ford

af·fray

af·fright

af·front

af·ghan

af·ghani

Af·ghan·i·stan

afi·cio·na·do
pl afi·cio·na·dos

afield

afire

aflame

afloat

aflut·ter

afoot

afore·men·tioned

afore·said

afore·thought

a for·ti·o·ri

afraid

afresh

Af·ri·can

Af·ri·kaans

Af·ro

af·ter
af·ter·birth
af·ter·burn·er
af·ter·care
af·ter·deck
af·ter·ef·fect
af·ter·glow
af·ter·life
af·ter·math
af·ter·noon
af·ter·taste
af·ter·tax
af·ter·thought
af·ter·ward
   or af·ter·wards

again
against
Aga·na
agape
   adj, gaping

aga·pe
   noun, love

ag·ate
ag·ate·ware
aga·ve
age·less
agen·cy
agen·da
agent
age-old
ag·gior·na·men·to
   pl ag·gior·na·men·
   tos
ag·glom·er·ate
ag·glom·er·a·tion
ag·glu·ti·nate

ag·glu·ti·na·tion
ag·gran·dize
ag·gran·dize·ment
ag·gra·vate
ag·gra·va·tion
ag·gre·gate
ag·gre·ga·tion
ag·gres·sion
ag·gres·sive
ag·gres·sive·ness
ag·gres·sor
ag·grieve
aghast
ag·ile
agil·i·ty
ag·i·tate
ag·i·ta·tion
ag·i·ta·tor
agleam
aglit·ter
aglow
ag·nos·tic
ag·nos·ti·cism
ago
agog
ag·o·nize
ag·o·niz·ing·ly
ag·o·ny
ag·o·ra
   marketplace, pl ag·o·
   ras
   or ag·o·rae

ago·ra
   coin, pl ago·rot

ag·o·ra·pho·bia
ag·o·ra·pho·bic

agrar·i·an
agree
agree·abil·i·ty
agree·able
agree·able·ness
agree·ably
agree·ment
ag·ri·cul·tur·al
ag·ri·cul·ture
ag·ri·cul·tur·ist
ag·ro·nom·ic
   or ag·ro·nom·i·cal

ag·ro·nom·i·cal·
   ly
agron·o·mist
agron·o·my
aground
ague
ahead
ahoy
aid
   help

aide
   assistant

aide-de-camp
   pl aides-de-camp

ai·grette
ail
   to be ill (see ale)

ai·le·ron
ail·ment
aim·less
aim·less·ness
air
   gas (see heir)

air·borne
air·brush
air·bus
air-con·di·tion
air-cool
air·craft
air·crew
air·drome
air·drop
air-dry
air·field
air·flow
air·foil
air·frame
air·glow
air·lift
air·line
air·lin·er
air·mail
air·man
air mile
air-mind·ed
air·mo·bile
air·plane
air·port
air·post
air·ship
air·sick
air·sick·ness
air·space
air·speed
air·stream
air·strip
air·tight
air-to-air
air·wave

air·way
air·wor·thi·ness
air·wor·thy
airy
aisle
    passage (see isle)

ajar
akim·bo
Ak·ron
Al·a·bama
al·a·bas·ter
a la carte
alac·ri·ty
a la mode
alarm
    also ala·rum

alarm·ist
Alas·ka
al·ba·core
Al·ba·nia
Al·ba·nian
Al·ba·ny
al·ba·tross
al·be·it
Al·ber·ta
al·bi·nism
al·bi·no
al·bum
al·bu·men
    egg white

al·bu·min
    protein

al·bu·min·ous
Al·bu·quer·que
al·cal·de

al·ca·zar
al·che·mist
al·che·my
al·co·hol
al·co·hol·ic
al·co·hol·ism
al·cove
al·der
al·der·man
ale
    beverage (see ail)

ale·a·tor·ic
ale·house
ale·wife
alert
alert·ness
Al·ex·an·dria
al·ex·an·drine
al·fal·fa
al·fres·co
al·ga
    pl al·gae *also* al·gas

al·ge·bra
al·ge·bra·ic
Al·ge·ria
Al·ge·ri·an
al·go·rithm
alias
al·i·bi
alien
alien·able
alien·ate
alien·ation
alien·ist
alight

align
  also aline

align·ment
  also aline·ment

alike
al·i·ment
al·i·men·ta·ry
al·i·mo·ny
al·i·quot
alive
al·ka·li
al·ka·line
al·ka·lin·i·ty
al·ka·lin·ize
al·ka·loid
al·kyd
all
  the whole (see awl)

Al·lah
all-Amer·i·can
all-around
al·lay
al·le·ga·tion
al·lege
al·leg·ed·ly
Al·le·ghe·ny
al·le·giance
al·le·gor·i·cal
al·le·go·ry
al·le·gro
al·le·lu·ia
Al·len·town
al·ler·gen
al·ler·gen·ic
al·ler·gic

al·ler·gist
al·ler·gy
al·le·vi·ate
al·le·vi·a·tion
al·ley
  passage (see ally)

al·ley·way
All·hal·lows
al·li·ance
al·lied
al·li·ga·tor
al·lit·er·ate
al·lit·er·a·tion
al·lit·er·a·tive
al·lo·cate
al·lo·ca·tion
al·lo·ge·ne·ic
al·lot
  al·lot·ted
  al·lot·ting
al·lot·ment
al·lot·tee
all-out
all·over
al·low
al·low·able
al·low·ance
al·loy
all-round
All Saints' Day
All Souls' Day
all·spice
al·lude
  to refer (see elude)

al·lure

al·lure·ment
al·lu·sion
  reference (see illusion)

al·lu·sive
  suggestive (see
    elusive, illusive)

al·lu·sive·ness
al·lu·vi·al
al·lu·vi·um
al·ly
  to unite, friend (see
    alley)

al·ma ma·ter
al·ma·nac
al·mighty
al·mond
al·mo·ner
al·most
alms
alms·house
al·ni·co
al·oe
aloft
alo·ha
alone
along
along·shore
along·side
aloof
aloof·ness
aloud
al·paca
al·pen·stock
al·pha
al·pha·bet

al·pha·bet·ic
  or al·pha·bet·i·cal

al·pha·bet·ize
al·pha·nu·mer·ic
  also al·pha·nu·mer·
    i·cal

Al·pine
al·ready
al·so
al·so·ran
al·tar
  noun (*see* alter)

al·tar·piece
al·ter
  verb (*see* altar)

al·ter·ation
al·ter·cate
al·ter·ca·tion
al·ter ego
al·ter·nate
al·ter·nate·ly
al·ter·nat·ing
al·ter·na·tion
al·ter·na·tive
al·ter·na·tor
al·though
  also al·tho

al·tim·e·ter
al·ti·tude
al·to
  pl al·tos

al·to·geth·er
al·tru·ism
al·tru·ist
al·tru·is·tic

al·um
alu·mi·na
alu·mi·num
alum·na
  pl alum·nae

alum·nus
  pl alum·ni

al·ways
amal·gam
amal·gam·ate
amal·gam·ation
aman·u·en·sis
  pl aman·u·en·ses

am·a·ranth
am·a·ran·thine
Am·a·ril·lo
am·a·ryl·lis
amass
am·a·teur
am·a·to·ry
amaze
amaze·ment
amaz·ing·ly
am·a·zon
am·a·zo·nian
am·bas·sa·dor
am·bas·sa·do·ri·
  al

am·bas·sa·dress
am·ber
am·ber·gris
am·bi·dex·trous
am·bi·ence
  or am·bi·ance

am·bi·ent

am·bi·gu·ity
am·big·u·ous
am·bi·tion
am·bi·tious
am·biv·a·lence
am·biv·a·lent
am·ble
am·bro·sia
am·bro·sial
am·bu·lance
am·bu·lant
am·bu·la·to·ry
am·bus·cade
am·bush
ame·ba
  var of amoeba

ame·ban
  var of amoeban

ame·bic
  var of amoebic

ame·lio·rate
ame·lio·ra·tion
ame·na·ble
amend
  to change (*see* emend)

amend·ment
ame·ni·ty
amerce
amerce·ment
Amer·i·can
Amer·i·ca·na
Amer·i·can·ism
Amer·i·can·iza·
  tion

Amer·i·can·ize

am·er·i·ci·um
Am·er·ind
Am·er·in·di·an
am·e·thyst
ami·a·bil·i·ty
ami·a·ble
ami·a·bly
am·i·ca·bil·i·ty
am·i·ca·ble
am·i·ca·bly
amid
  or amidst

amid·ships
ami·no
amiss
am·i·ty
am·me·ter
am·mo
am·mo·nia
am·mo·nite
am·mo·ni·um
am·mu·ni·tion
am·ne·sia
am·ne·si·ac
  or am·ne·sic

am·nes·ty
amoe·ba
  or ame·ba
  pl amoe·bas *or*
    amoe·bae *or*
    ame·bas

amoe·bic
  or ame·bic *also*
    amoe·ban *also*
    ame·ban

amoe·boid
amok

among
  also amongst

amon·til·la·do
  pl amon·til·la·dos

amor·al
amor·al·ly
am·o·rous
amor·phous
am·or·ti·za·tion
am·or·tize
amount
amour
amour pro·pre
am·per·age
am·pere
am·per·sand
am·phet·amine
am·phib·i·an
am·phib·i·ous
am·phi·the·ater
am·pho·ra
  pl am·pho·rae *or*
    am·pho·ras

am·ple
am·pli·fi·ca·tion
am·pli·fi·er
am·pli·fy
am·pli·tude
am·ply
am·pul
  or am·pule *or* am·poule

am·pul·la
  pl am·pul·lae

am·pu·tate
am·pu·ta·tion

am·pu·tee
am·u·let
amuse
amuse·ment
anach·ro·nism
anach·ro·nis·tic
an·a·con·da
an·a·dem
anae·mia
  var of anemia

anae·mic
  var of anemic

an·aer·o·bic
an·aes·the·sia
  var of anesthesia

an·aes·thet·ic
  var of anesthetic

ana·gram
An·a·heim
anal
an·al·ge·sia
an·al·ge·sic
anal·o·gous
an·a·logue
  or an·a·log

anal·o·gy
anal·y·sis
  pl anal·y·ses

an·a·lyst
  one who analyzes (*see*
    annalist)

an·a·lyt·ic
  or an·a·lyt·i·cal

an·a·lyze
an·a·pest

an·a·pes·tic
an·ar·chic
an·ar·chism
an·ar·chist
an·ar·chis·tic
an·ar·chy
an·astig·mat·ic
anath·e·ma
anath·e·ma·tize
an·a·tom·ic
  or an·a·tom·i·cal

anat·o·mist
anat·o·mize
anat·o·my
an·ces·tor
an·ces·tral
an·ces·try
an·chor
an·chor·age
an·cho·ress
  or an·cress

an·cho·rite
an·cho·vy
an·cien ré·gime
an·cient
an·cil·lary
an·dan·te
and·iron
and/or
An·dor·ra
An·dor·ran
an·dro·gen
an·ec·dote
ane·mia
  or anae·mia

ane·mic
  or anae·mic
an·e·mom·e·ter
anem·o·ne
an·er·oid
an·es·the·sia
  or an·aes·the·sia

an·es·the·si·ol·o·gist
an·es·the·si·ol·o·gy
an·es·thet·ic
  or an·aes·thet·ic
anes·the·tist
anes·the·tize
an·gel
  spiritual being (see angle)

an·gel·ic
  or an·gel·i·cal
an·gel·i·cal·ly
An·ge·lus
an·ger
an·gi·na
an·gle
  math (see angel)

an·gler
an·gle·worm
An·gli·can
an·gli·cism
an·gli·ci·za·tion
an·gli·cize
an·gling
an·glo·phile
an·glo·probe

An·glo-Sax·on
An·go·la
an·go·ra
an·gri·ly
an·gry
angst
ang·strom
an·guish
an·gu·lar
an·gu·lar·i·ty
an·hy·drous
an·i·line
an·i·mad·ver·sion
an·i·mad·vert
an·i·mal
an·i·mal·cule
  or an·i·mal·cu·lum
  pl an·i·mal·cules *or*
  an·i·mal·cu·la

an·i·mal·ism
an·i·mate
an·i·mat·ed
an·i·ma·tion
an·i·mism
an·i·mist
an·i·mis·tic
an·i·mos·i·ty
an·i·mus
an·ion
an·ise
an·is·ette
ankh
an·kle
an·klet
an·nal·ist
  recorder of events (see
  analyst)

An·nap·o·lis
an·neal
an·nex
an·nex·ation
an·ni·hi·late
an·ni·hi·la·tion
an·ni·ver·sa·ry
an·no Do·mi·ni
an·no·tate
an·no·ta·tion
an·no·ta·tor
an·nounce
an·nounce·ment
an·nounc·er
an·noy
an·noy·ance
an·nu·al
an·nu·al·ly
an·nu·itant
an·nu·ity
an·nul
an·nu·lar
an·nul·ment
an·nun·ci·ate
an·nun·ci·a·tion
an·nun·ci·a·tor
an·ode
an·od·ize
an·o·dyne
anoint
anom·a·lous
anom·a·ly
an·o·nym·i·ty
anon·y·mous
anoph·e·les
an·oth·er

an·ovu·lant
an·ovu·la·to·ry
an·swer
an·swer·able
ant·ac·id
an·tag·o·nism
an·tag·o·nist
an·tag·o·nis·tic
an·tag·o·nize
ant·arc·tic
Ant·arc·ti·ca
an·te
ant·eat·er
an·te·bel·lum
an·te·ced·ent
an·te·cham·ber
an·te·date
an·te·di·lu·vi·an
an·te·lope
an·te me·ri·di·em
an·te·mor·tem
an·te·na·tal
an·ten·na
  pl an·ten·nae *or*
    an·ten·nas

an·te·pe·nult
an·te·pen·ul·ti·
  mate
an·te·ri·or
an·te·room
an·them
an·ther
ant·hill
an·thol·o·gy
an·thra·cite
an·thrax

an·thro·po·cen·
  tric
an·thro·poid
an·thro·po·log·i·
  cal
an·thro·pol·o·gist
an·thro·pol·o·gy
an·thro·po·mor·
  phic
an·thro·po·mor·
  phism
an·ti
an·ti·air·craft
an·ti·bac·te·ri·al
an·ti·bal·lis·tic
  mis·sile
an·ti·bi·ot·ic
an·ti·body
an·tic
An·ti·christ
an·tic·i·pate
an·tic·i·pa·tion
an·tic·i·pa·to·ry
an·ti·cli·mac·tic
an·ti·cli·max
an·ti·de·pres·sant
an·ti·dote
an·ti·freeze
an·ti·gen
an·ti·grav·i·ty
an·ti·his·ta·mine
an·ti·knock
an·ti·log·a·rithm
an·ti·ma·cas·sar
an·ti·mag·net·ic
an·ti·mis·sile

an·ti·mo·ny
an·ti·pas·to
an·ti·pa·thet·ic
an·tip·a·thy
an·ti·per·son·nel
an·ti·phon
an·tiph·o·nal
an·tip·o·dal
an·ti·pode
  pl an·tip·o·des

an·ti·pov·er·ty
an·ti·quar·i·an
an·ti·quary
an·ti·quat·ed
an·tique
an·tiq·ui·ty
an·ti-Se·mit·ic
an·ti-Sem·i·tism
an·ti·sep·sis
an·ti·sep·tic
an·ti·sep·ti·cal·ly
an·ti·so·cial
an·tith·e·sis
  pl an·tith·e·ses

an·ti·thet·i·cal
an·ti·thet·i·cal·ly
an·ti·tox·in
an·ti·trust
ant·ler
ant·lered
ant·onym
an·trum
anus
an·vil
anx·i·ety

anx·ious
any·body
any·how
any·more
any·one
any·place
any·thing
any·way
any·where
any·wise
aor·ta
aor·tic
apace
apart
apart·heid
apart·ment
ap·a·thet·ic
ap·a·thet·i·cal·ly
ap·a·thy
aper·i·tif
ap·er·ture
apex
  pl apex·es *or*
  api·ces

apha·sia
aph·elion
  pl aph·elia
aphid
aphis
  pl aphi·des
aph·o·rism
aph·o·ris·tic
aph·ro·dis·i·ac
api·a·rist
api·ary
api·cal

apiece
aplomb
apoc·a·lypse
apoc·a·lyp·tic
apoc·ry·pha
apoc·ry·phal
apo·gee
apo·lit·i·cal
apol·o·get·ic
apol·o·get·i·cal·ly
ap·o·lo·gia
apol·o·gist
apol·o·gize
ap·o·logue
apol·o·gy
ap·o·plec·tic
ap·o·plexy
apos·ta·sy
apos·tate
a pos·te·ri·o·ri
apos·tle
apos·to·late
ap·os·tol·ic
apos·tro·phe
apos·tro·phize
apoth·e·cary
ap·o·thegm
apo·the·o·sis
Ap·pa·la·chian
ap·pall
  also ap·pal
ap·pa·nage
ap·pa·ra·tus
  pl ap·pa·ra·tus·es
  or ap·pa·ra·tus

ap·par·el

ap·par·ent
ap·pa·ri·tion
ap·peal
ap·pear
ap·pear·ance
ap·pease
ap·pease·ment
ap·pel·lant
ap·pel·late
ap·pel·la·tion
ap·pel·lee
ap·pend
ap·pend·age
ap·pen·dec·to·my
ap·pen·di·ci·tis
ap·pen·dix
   pl ap·pen·dix·es *or*
    ap·pen·di·ces

ap·per·cep·tion
ap·per·tain
ap·pe·tite
ap·pe·tiz·er
ap·pe·tiz·ing
ap·plaud
ap·plause
ap·ple
ap·ple·jack
ap·pli·ance
ap·pli·ca·bil·i·ty
ap·pli·ca·ble
ap·pli·cant
ap·pli·ca·tion
ap·pli·ca·tor
ap·plied
ap·pli·qué
ap·ply

ap·point
ap·poin·tee
ap·point·ive
ap·point·ment
ap·por·tion
ap·por·tion·ment
ap·po·site
ap·po·si·tion
ap·pos·i·tive
ap·prais·al
ap·praise
  value (see apprise*)*

ap·prais·er
ap·pre·cia·ble
ap·pre·ci·ate
ap·pre·ci·a·tion
ap·pre·cia·tive
ap·pre·hend
ap·pre·hen·sion
ap·pre·hen·sive
ap·pren·tice
ap·pren·tice·ship
ap·prise
  inform (see appraise*)*

ap·proach
ap·proach·able
ap·pro·ba·tion
ap·pro·pri·ate
ap·pro·pri·ate·ly
ap·pro·pri·ate·
  ness
ap·pro·pri·a·tion
ap·prov·al
ap·prove
ap·prox·i·mate

ap·prox·i·mate·ly
ap·prox·i·ma·tion
ap·pur·te·nance
ap·pur·te·nant
apri·cot
April
a pri·o·ri
apron
ap·ro·pos
ap·ti·tude
apt·ly
apt·ness
aqua·cade
aqua·ma·rine
aqua·naut
aqua·plane
aquar·i·um
  pl aquar·i·ums *or*
   aquar·ia

aquat·ic
aq·ue·duct
aque·ous
aq·ui·line
ar·a·besque
Ara·bi·an
Ar·a·bic
ar·a·ble
ar·ba·lest
  or ar·ba·list
ar·bi·ter
ar·bit·ra·ment
ar·bi·trari·ly
ar·bi·trari·ness
ar·bi·trary
ar·bi·trate
ar·bi·tra·tion ·

ar·bi·tra·tor
ar·bor
ar·bo·re·al
ar·bo·re·tum
  pl ar·bo·re·tums *or*
    ar·bo·re·ta

ar·bor·vi·tae
ar·bu·tus
arc
  curve (see ark)

ar·cade
ar·cane
ar·chae·o·log·i·
  cal
ar·chae·ol·o·gist
ar·chae·ol·o·gy
ar·cha·ic
ar·cha·i·cal·ly
arch·an·gel
arch·bish·op
arch·bish·op·ric
arch·dea·con
arch·di·o·cese
arch·duch·ess
arch·duke
arch·en·e·my
ar·cher
ar·chery
ar·che·type
arch·fiend
ar·chi·epis·co·pal
ar·chi·pel·a·go
  pl ar·chi·pel·a·goes
    or ar·chi·pel·a·gos

ar·chi·tect
ar·chi·tec·ton·ic

ar·chi·tec·tur·al
ar·chi·tec·ture
ar·chi·trave
ar·chive
ar·chi·vist
arch·ly
arch·ness
arch·way
arc·tic
ar·dent
ar·dor
ar·du·ous
ar·ea
  space (see aria)

area·way
are·na
Ar·gen·ti·na
Ar·gen·tine
ar·gon
ar·go·sy
ar·got
ar·gu·able
ar·gue
ar·gu·ment
ar·gu·men·ta·tion
ar·gu·men·ta·tive
  also ar·gu·men·tive

ar·gyle
aria
  song (see area)

ar·id
arid·i·ty
arise
arose
aris·en

aris·ing
ar·is·toc·ra·cy
aris·to·crat
aris·to·crat·ic
arith·me·tic
  noun

ar·ith·met·ic
  or ar·ith·met·i·cal
  adj

arith·me·ti·cian
Ar·i·zo·na
ark
  boat (see arc)

Ar·kan·sas
ar·ma·da
ar·ma·dil·lo
Ar·ma·ged·don
ar·ma·ment
ar·ma·ture
arm·chair
Ar·me·nian
arm·hole
ar·mi·stice
arm·let
ar·mor
ar·mored
ar·mor·er
ar·mo·ri·al
ar·mory
arm·pit
arm·rest
ar·my
ar·ni·ca
aro·ma
ar·o·mat·ic
ar·o·mat·i·cal·ly

around
arous·al
arouse
ar·peg·gio
ar·raign
ar·raign·ment
ar·range
ar·range·ment
ar·rant
ar·ras
   pl ar·ras

ar·ray
ar·rears
ar·rest
ar·ri·ère-pen·sée
ar·riv·al
ar·rive
ar·ro·gance
ar·ro·gant
ar·ro·gate
ar·row
ar·row·head
ar·row·root
ar·royo
ar·se·nal
ar·se·nic
   noun

ar·sen·ic
   adj

ar·son
ar·te·fact
   var of artifact

ar·te·ri·al
ar·te·ri·ole

ar·te·rio·scle·ro·
   sis
ar·te·rio·scle·rot·
   ic
ar·tery
ar·te·sian well
art·ful
art·ful·ly
ar·thrit·ic
ar·thri·tis
   pl ar·thrit·i·des

ar·thro·pod
ar·ti·choke
ar·ti·cle
ar·tic·u·lar
ar·tic·u·late
ar·tic·u·late·ly
ar·tic·u·la·tion
ar·ti·fact
   or ar·te·fact

ar·ti·fice
ar·ti·fi·cer
ar·ti·fi·cial
ar·ti·fi·ci·al·i·ty
ar·ti·fi·cial·ly
ar·til·lery
art·i·ly
art·i·ness
ar·ti·san
art·ist
ar·tiste
ar·tis·tic
ar·tis·ti·cal·ly
art·ist·ry
art·less

arty
ar·um
Ary·an
as·bes·tos
   also as·bes·tus

as·cend
as·cen·dan·cy
   also as·cen·den·cy

as·cen·dant
   also as·cen·dent

as·cen·sion
as·cent
   upward slope (see
   assent)

as·cer·tain
as·cet·ic
   austere (see acetic)

as·cet·i·cism
ascor·bic acid
as·cot
as·crib·able
as·cribe
as·crip·tion
asep·tic
asex·u·al
ashamed
ash·en
ash·lar
ashore
ashy
Asian
aside
as·i·nine
as·i·nin·i·ty
askance

askew
aslant
asleep
aso·cial
as·par·a·gus
as·pect
as·pen
as·per·i·ty
as·per·sion
as·phalt
as·phyx·ia
as·phyx·i·ate
as·phyx·i·a·tion
as·pic
as·pi·dis·tra
as·pi·rant
as·pi·rate
as·pi·ra·tion
as·pire
as·pi·rin
as·sail
as·sail·ant
as·sas·sin
as·sas·si·nate
as·sas·si·na·tion
as·sault
as·say
  to try (see essay)

as·sem·blage
as·sem·ble
as·sem·bly
as·sem·bly·man
as·sent
  agree (see ascent)

as·sert

as·ser·tion
as·sert·ive
as·sess
as·sess·ment
as·ses·sor
as·set
as·sev·er·ate
as·sev·er·a·tion
as·si·du·ity
as·sid·u·ous
as·sign
as·sign·able
as·sig·na·tion
as·sign·ment
as·sim·i·late
as·sim·i·la·tion
as·sist
as·sis·tance
as·sis·tant
as·size
as·so·ci·ate
  verb

as·so·ci·ate
  adj, noun

as·so·ci·a·tion
as·so·cia·tive
as·so·nance
as·so·nant
as·sort
as·sort·ed
as·sort·ment
as·suage
as·sume
as·sump·tion
as·sur·ance

as·sure
as·sured
  pl as·sured or
    as·sureds

as·ta·tine
as·ter
as·ter·isk
as·ter·oid
asth·ma
asth·mat·ic
as·tig·mat·ic
as·tig·mat·i·cal·
  ly
astig·ma·tism
as·ton·ish
as·ton·ish·ment
as·tound
astrad·dle
as·tra·khan
  or as·tra·chan

as·tral
astride
as·trin·gen·cy
as·trin·gent
as·tro·bi·ol·o·gist
as·tro·bi·ol·o·gy
as·tro·labe
as·trol·o·ger
as·tro·log·i·cal
as·trol·o·gy
as·tro·naut
as·tro·nau·tic
  or as·tro·nau·ti·cal

as·tro·nau·tics
as·tron·o·mer

as·tro·nom·i·cal
  or as·tro·nom·ic

as·tron·o·my
as·tro·phys·i·cist
as·tro·phys·ics
as·tute
asun·der
asy·lum
asym·met·ric
  or asym·met·ri·cal

at
  coin, pl at

at·a·vism
at·a·vis·tic
ate·lier
athe·ism
athe·ist
athe·is·tic
ath·e·nae·um
  or ath·e·ne·um

ath·lete
ath·let·ic
ath·let·i·cal·ly
ath·let·ics
athwart
At·lan·ta
At·lan·tic
at·las
at·mo·sphere
at·mo·spher·ic
at·mo·spher·ics
atoll
at·om
atom·ic
atom·ics

at·om·ize
at·om·iz·er
aton·al
ato·nal·i·ty
aton·al·ly
atone
atone·ment
atri·um
  pl atria *also*
  atri·ums

atro·cious
atroc·i·ty
at·ro·phy
at·ro·pine
at·tach
at·ta·ché
at·tach·ment
at·tack
at·tain
at·tain·abil·i·ty
at·tain·able
at·tain·der
at·tain·ment
at·taint
at·tar
at·tempt
at·tend
at·ten·dance
at·ten·dant
at·ten·tion
at·ten·tive
at·ten·u·ate
at·ten·u·a·tion
at·test
at·tes·ta·tion
at·tic

at·tire
at·ti·tude
at·ti·tu·di·nize
at·tor·ney
at·tract
at·trac·tion
at·trac·tive
at·trib·ut·able
at·tri·bute
  noun

at·trib·ute
  verb

at·tri·bu·tion
at·trib·u·tive
at·tri·tion
at·tune
atyp·i·cal
au·burn
au cou·rant
auc·tion
auc·tion·eer
auc·to·ri·al
au·da·cious
au·dac·i·ty
au·di·bil·i·ty
au·di·ble
au·di·bly
au·di·ence
au·dio
au·dio·phile
au·dio·vi·su·al
au·dit
au·di·tion
au·di·tor
au·di·to·ri·um

au·di·to·ry
au·ger
   tool (see augur*)*

aught
   zero (see ought*)*

aug·ment
aug·men·ta·tion
au gra·tin
au·gur
   foretell (see auger*)*

au·gu·ry
au·gust
Au·gust
Au·gus·ta
auk
au·ra
au·ral
   hearing (see oral*)*

au·re·ate
au·re·ole
   or au·re·o·la

au re·voir
au·ri·cle
   heart chamber (see
   oracle*)*

au·ric·u·lar
au·rif·er·ous
au·ro·ra
   pl au·ro·ras *or*
   au·ro·rae

au·ro·ra aus·tra·
   lis
au·ro·ra bo·re·al·
   is
aus·pice

aus·pi·cious
aus·tere
aus·ter·i·ty
Aus·tin
aus·tral
Aus·tra·lia
Aus·tra·lian
Aus·tria
Aus·tri·an
au·then·tic
au·then·ti·cal·ly
au·then·ti·cate
au·then·ti·ca·tion
au·then·tic·i·ty
au·thor
au·thor·ess
au·thor·i·tar·i·an
au·thor·i·ta·tive
au·thor·i·ty
au·tho·ri·za·tion
au·tho·rize
au·thor·ship
au·to
au·to·bahn
au·to·bi·og·ra·
   pher
au·to·bio·graph·i·
   cal
   also auto·bio·graph·
   ic

au·to·bi·og·ra·
   phy
au·toch·tho·nous
au·toc·ra·cy
au·to·crat
au·to·crat·ic

au·to·crat·i·cal·ly
au·to·graph
au·to·in·tox·i·ca·
   tion
au·to·mate
au·to·mat·ic
au·to·mat·i·cal·ly
au·to·ma·tion
au·tom·a·ti·za·
   tion
au·tom·a·tize
au·tom·a·ton
   pl au·tom·a·tons
   or au·tom·a·ta

au·to·mo·bile
au·to·mo·bil·ist
au·to·mo·tive
au·ton·o·mous
au·ton·o·my
au·top·sy
au·to·stra·da
au·tumn
au·tum·nal
aux·il·ia·ry
aux·in
avail
avail·abil·i·ty
avail·able
av·a·lanche
avant-garde
av·a·rice
av·a·ri·cious
avenge
aveng·er
av·e·nue
aver

averred
aver·ring
av·er·age
averse
  reluctant (see adverse)

aver·sion
avert
avi·an
avi·ary
avi·a·tion
avi·a·tor
avi·a·trix
av·id
avid·ity
av·id·ly
av·o·ca·do
av·o·ca·tion
avoid
avoid·able
avoid·ance
av·oir·du·pois
avow
avow·al
avun·cu·lar
await
awake
  awoke
  awak·en
award
aware
aware·ness
awash
away
  from this place

aweigh
  raised

awe·some
awe·strick·en
  or awe·struck

aw·ful
  objectionable (see offal)

aw·ful·ly
awhile
awhirl
awk·ward
awk·ward·ness
awl
  tool (see all)

aw·ning
awry
ax
  or axe

ax·i·al
  or ax·al

ax·i·om
ax·i·om·at·ic
ax·is
  pl ax·es

ax·le
axle·tree
aza·lea
az·i·muth
Az·tec
azure

B

bab·bitt
bab·ble
ba·bel

ba·boon
ba·bush·ka
ba·by
ba·by-sit
ba·by-sit·ter
bac·ca·lau·re·ate
bac·ca·rat
bac·cha·nal
bac·cha·na·lia
bac·cha·na·lian
bach·e·lor
ba·cil·lus
  pl ba·cil·li

back·ache
back-bench·er
back·bite
back·bit·er
back·board
back·bone
back·drop
back·er
back·field
back·fire
back·gam·mon
back·ground
back·hand
back·hand·ed
back·ing
back·lash
back·log
back·rest
back·side
back·slap
back·slap·per
back·slide

back·slid·er
back·spin
back·stage
back·stairs
back·stop
back·stretch
back·stroke
back talk
back·track
back·up
  noun

back·ward
  or back·wards

back·ward·ness
back·wash
back·wa·ter
back·woods
ba·con
bac·te·ri·al
bac·te·ri·cid·al
bac·te·ri·o·log·ic
  or bac·te·ri·o·log·i·
  cal
bac·te·ri·ol·o·gist
bac·te·ri·ol·o·gy
bac·te·ri·um
  pl bac·te·ria

badge
bad·ger
ba·di·nage
bad·land
bad·min·ton
bad·ness
Bae·de·ker
baf·fle

bag
  bagged
  bag·ging
bag·a·telle
ba·gel
bag·gage
bag·gy
ba·gnio
  pl ba·gnios

bag·pipe
ba·guette
Ba·ha·ma
Bah·rain
  or Bah·rein

baht
  pl bahts *or* baht

bail
  security (see bale)

bai·liff
bai·li·wick
bails·man
bait
  lure (see bate)

bai·za
baize
bak·er
bak·er's doz·en
bak·ery
bak·sheesh
bal·a·lai·ka
bal·ance
bal·boa
bal·brig·gan
bal·co·ny

bal·da·chin
  or bal·da·chi·no

bal·der·dash
bald·ness
bale
  bundle (see bail)

bal·er
bale·ful
balk
Bal·kan
balky
ball
  rounded body (see
  bawl)

bal·lad
bal·last
ball·car·ri·er
bal·le·ri·na
bal·let
bal·let·o·mane
bal·lis·tic
bal·lis·tics
bal·loon
bal·loon·ist
bal·lot
ball-point pen
ball·room
bal·ly·hoo
  pl bal·ly·hoos

balmy
bal·sa
bal·sam
Bal·tic
Bal·ti·more
bal·us·ter

bal·us·trade
bam·boo
bam·boo·zle
ban
  prohibit (see band)

  banned
  ban·ning
ban
  pl ba·ni
  coin

ba·nal
ba·nal·i·ty
ba·nana
band
  strip (see ban)

ban·dage
ban·dan·na
  or ban·dana

band box
ban·de·role
  or ban·de·rol

ban·dit
ban·dit·ry
band·mas·ter
ban·do·lier
  or ban·do·leer

band·stand
band·wag·on
ban·dy
bane·ful
Ban·gla·desh
ban·gle
bang·tail
bang-up
  adj

bang up
  verb

ban·ish
ban·ish·ment
ban·is·ter
  also ban·nis·ter

ban·jo
  pl ban·jos

ban·jo·ist
bank·book
bank·er
bank·roll
bank·rupt
bank·rupt·cy
ban·ner
ban·nock
banns
  marriage

ban·quet
ban·quette
ban·shee
ban·tam
ban·ter
Ban·tu
Ban·tu·stan
ban·yan
ban·zai
bao·bab
bap·tism
bap·tis·mal
Bap·tist
bap·tis·tery
  or bap·tis·try

bap·tize

bar
  exclude (see bard)

  barred
  bar·ring
Bar·ba·di·an
Bar·ba·dos
bar·bar·ian
bar·bar·ic
bar·ba·rism
bar·bar·i·ty
bar·ba·rous
bar·be·cue
bar·bell
bar·ber
bar·ber·shop
bar·ber·ry
bar·bi·tal
bar·bi·tu·rate
bar·ca·role
  or bar·ca·rolle

bard
  poet (see bar)

bare
  naked (see bear)

bare·back
  or bare·backed

bare·faced
bare·foot
  or bare·foot·ed

bare-hand·ed
bare·head·ed
bare·ly
bar·gain
barge·man
bari·tone

bar·i·um
bar·keep·er
bark·er
bar·ley
bar·maid
bar·man
bar mitz·vah
bar·na·cle
barn·storm
barn·yard
baro·graph
ba·rom·e·ter
baro·met·ric
bar·on
   a noble (*see* barren)

bar·on·age
bar·on·ess
bar·on·et
bar·on·et·cy
ba·ro·ni·al
bar·ony
ba·roque
ba·rouche
bar·rack
bar·ra·cu·da
bar·rage
bar·ra·try
bar·rel
bar·ren
   sterile (*see* baron)

bar·ren·ness
bar·rette
bar·ri·cade
bar·ri·er
bar·ris·ter

bar·room
bar·row
bar·tend·er
bar·ter
bas·al
ba·salt
ba·sal·tic
base
   foundation (*see* bass)

base·ball
base·board
base·born
base·less
base·ly
base·ment
base·ness
base·run·ning
bash·ful
bash·ful·ness
ba·sic
ba·si·cal·ly
ba·sil
ba·sil·i·ca
bas·i·lisk
ba·sin
ba·sis
   pl ba·ses

bask
bas·ket
bas·ket·ball
bas·ket·work
bas mitz·vah
Basque
bas-re·lief

bass
   fish, deep voice (*see* base)

bas·si·net
bas·so
   pl bas·sos *or* bas·si

bas·soon
bass·wood
bas·tard
bas·tard·ize
baste
bas·tion
bas·tioned
bat
   bat·ted
   bat·ting

batch
bate
   restrain (*see* bait)

ba·teau
   pl ba·teaux

bath
bathe
bath·er
ba·thet·ic
bath·house
ba·thos
bath·robe
bath·room
bath·tub
bathy·scaphe
   also bathy·scaph

bathy·sphere
ba·tik
ba·tiste

bat·man
ba·ton
Bat·on Rouge
bats·man
bat·tal·ion
bat·ten
bat·ter
bat·tery
bat·ting
bat·tle
bat·tle-ax
bat·tle·field
bat·tle·ment
bat·tle·ship
bau·ble
baux·ite
Ba·var·i·an
bawd·i·ly
bawd·i·ness
bawdy
bawl
    cry (see ball)

bay·ber·ry
bay·o·net
    bay·o·net·ed
    also bay·o·net·ted

    bay·o·net·ing
    also bay·o·net·
        ting

bay·ou
ba·zaar
    marketplace (see
        bizarre)

ba·zoo·ka
beach
    shore (see beech)

beach·comb·er
beach·head
bea·con
bead
bead·ing
bea·dle
beady
bea·gle
bea·ker
bean·ie
bear
    animal, carry (see
        bare, born)

    bore

    borne
        also born

    bear·ing
bear·able
beard·less
bear·er
bear·ish
bé·ar·naise
    sauce
bear·skin
beast·ly
beat
    to strike (see beet)

    beat
    beat·en
        or beat

    beat·ing
be·atif·ic
be·at·i·fi·ca·tion
be·at·i·fy
be·at·i·tude
beat·nik

beau
    pl beaux or
        beaus
    suitor (see bow)

Beau·jo·lais
beau monde
Beau·mont
beau·te·ous
beau·ti·cian
beau·ti·fi·ca·tion
beau·ti·fi·er
beau·ti·ful
beau·ti·ful·ly
beau·ti·fy
beau·ty
bea·ver
be·calm
be·cause
beck·on
be·cloud
be·come
    be·came
    be·come
    be·com·ing
    be·com·ing·ly
bed
    bed·ded
    bed·ding
be·daz·zle
be·daz·zle·ment
bed·bug
bed·clothes
bed·ding
be·deck
be·dev·il
bed·fel·low

bed·lam
bed·ou·in
  or bed·u·in
be·drag·gled
bed·rid·den
  or bed·rid
bed·rock
bed·roll
bed·room
bed·side
bed·sore
bed·spread
bed·stead
bed·time
beech
  tree (see beach)
beech·nut
beef
  pl beefs *or* beeves
beef·steak
beefy
bee·hive
bee·keep·er
bee·keep·ing
bee·line
beer
  beverage (see bier)
beery
bees·wax
beet
  vegetable (see beat)
bee·tle
be·fall
  be·fell
  be·fall·en
be·fit

be·fog
be·fore
be·fore·hand
be·friend
be·fud·dle
beg
  begged
  beg·ging
be·get
  be·got
  be·got·ten
    or be·got
  be·get·ting
beg·gar
beg·gar·ly
be·gin
  be·gan
  be·gun
  be·gin·ning
be·gin·ner
be·gone
be·go·nia
be·grime
be·grudge
be·guile
be·guine
be·gum
be·half
be·have
be·hav·ior
be·hav·ior·al
be·hav·ior·ism
be·hav·ior·ist
be·head
be·he·moth
be·hest

be·hind
be·hind·hand
be·hold
  be·held
  be·hold·ing
be·hold·en
be·hold·er
be·hoove
  or be·hove
  be·hooved
    or be·hoved
  be·hoov·ing
    or be·hov·ing
beige
be·ing
be·la·bor
be·lat·ed
be·lay
belch
be·lea·guer
bel·fry
Bel·gian
Bel·gium
be·lie
  be·lied
  be·ly·ing
be·lief
be·liev·able
be·lieve
be·liev·er
be·lit·tle
bel·la·don·na
bell·boy
belles let·tres
bell·hop
bel·li·cose
bel·li·cos·i·ty

bel·lig·er·ence
bel·lig·er·en·cy
bel·lig·er·ent
bel·low
bel·lows
bell·weth·er
bel·ly
be·long
be·long·ings
be·loved
be·low
belt·way
be·mire
be·moan
be·muse
bend
  bent
  bend·ing
ben·day
be·neath
ben·e·dict
bene·dic·tion
bene·fac·tion
bene·fac·tor
bene·fac·tress
ben·e·fice
be·nef·i·cence
be·nef·i·cent
ben·e·fi·cial
ben·e·fi·cial·ly
ben·e·fi·cia·ry
ben·e·fit
  ben·e·fit·ed
    or ben·e·fit·ted
  ben·e·fit·ing
    or ben·e·fit·ting

be·nev·o·lence
be·nev·o·lent
be·night·ed
be·nign
be·nig·nant
be·nig·ni·ty
be·nign·ly
ben·i·son
Be·nin
ben·thic
  or ben·thal

ben·thos
be·numb
Ben·ze·drine
ben·zene
ben·zine
ben·zo·ic acid
ben·zo·in
ben·zol
be·queath
be·quest
be·rate
Ber·ber
ber·ceuse
be·reave
  be·reaved
    or be·reft

  be·reav·ing
be·reave·ment
be·ret
beri·beri
Berke·ley
Ber·mu·da
Ber·mu·di·an
  or Ber·mu·dan

ber·ry
  fruit (see bury)

ber·serk
berth
  distance, bed (see birth)

ber·yl
be·ryl·li·um
be·seech
  be·sought
    or be·seeched

  be·seech·ing
be·set
be·set·ting
be·side
be·sides
be·siege
be·sieg·er
be·smirch
be·sot·ted
bes·tial
bes·ti·al·i·ty
bes·ti·ary
be·stir
be·stow
bet
  bet
    also bet·ted

  bet·ting
be·ta
bête noire
  pl bêtes noires

be·tray
be·tray·al
be·tray·er

be·troth
be·troth·al
be·trothed
bet·ter
  comp of good, well
  (*see* bettor)

bet·ter·ment
bet·tor
  or bet·ter
  one that bets
  (*see* better)

be·tween
be·twixt
bev·el
  bev·eled
    or bev·elled

  bev·el·ing
    or bev·el·ling

bev·er·age
bevy
be·wail
be·ware
be·wil·der
be·wil·der·ment
be·witch
be·yond
be·zel
bi·an·nu·al
bi·as
  bi·ased
    or bi·assed

  bi·as·ing
    or bi·as·sing

bi·be·lot
bi·ble
bib·li·cal

bib·li·og·ra·pher
bib·lio·graph·ic
bib·lio·graph·i·cal
bib·li·og·ra·phy
bib·lio·phile
bib·u·lous
bi·cam·er·al
bi·car·bon·ate
bi·cen·te·na·ry
bi·cen·ten·ni·al
bi·ceps
bi·chlo·ride
bick·er
bi·cus·pid
bi·cy·cle
bid
  bade
    or bid

  bid·den
    or bid *also* bade

  bid·ding
bid·da·ble
bid·der
bide
  bode
    or bid·ed

  bid·ed
  bid·ing
bi·en·ni·al
bi·en·ni·al·ly
bi·en·ni·um
  pl bi·en·ni·ums *or*
  bi·en·nia

bier
  coffin stand (*see* beer)

bi·fo·cals
bi·fur·cate
bi·fur·ca·tion
big·a·mist
big·a·mous
big·a·my
big·horn
bight
big·ness
big·ot
big·ot·ed
big·ot·ry
big·wig
bi·jou
  pl bi·joux

bike·way
bi·ki·ni
bi·lat·er·al
bi·lat·er·al·ly
bilge
bi·lin·gual
bil·ious
bill·board
bil·let
bil·let-doux
  pl bil·lets-doux

bill·fold
bill·head
bil·liards
bill·ing
bil·lings·gate
bil·lion
bil·lionth
bil·low
bil·lowy

bil·ly
bil·ly goat
bi·met·al·lism
bi·month·ly
bi·na·ry
bin·au·ral
bind
  bound
  bind·ing
bind·er
binge
bin·na·cle
bin·oc·u·lar
bi·no·mi·al
bio·as·tro·nau·
  tics
bio·chem·i·cal
bio·chem·ist
bio·chem·is·try
bio·de·grad·abil·
  i·ty
bio·de·grad·able
bio·geo·graph·ic
bio·ge·og·ra·phy
bi·og·ra·pher
bio·graph·i·cal
bi·og·ra·phy
bi·o·log·i·cal
bi·ol·o·gist
bi·ol·o·gy
bio·med·i·cal
bio·med·i·cine
bi·on·ics
bio·phys·ics
bi·op·sy
bio·sphere

bio·syn·thet·ic
bio·syn·thet·i·
  cal·ly
bio·syn·the·sis
bi·ot·ic
bi·o·tin
bi·par·ti·san
bi·par·tite
bi·ped
bi·plane
bi·ra·cial
bird·bath
bird·house
bird·ie
bird·lime
bird·seed
bird's-eye
bi·ret·ta
Bir·ming·ham
birth
  nativity (see berth)
birth·day
birth·mark
birth·place
birth·rate
birth·right
birth·stone
bis·cuit
bi·sect
bi·sex·u·al
bish·op
bish·op·ric
Bis·marck
bis·muth
bi·son
  pl bi·son

bisque
bis·tro
  pl bis·tros
bitch
bite
  bit
  bit·ten
    also bit
  bit·ing
bit·ter
bit·tern
bit·ter·ness
bit·ter·sweet
bi·tu·men
bi·tu·mi·nous
bi·valve
  also bi·valved
biv·ouac
  biv·ouacked
  biv·ouack·ing
bi·week·ly
bi·zarre
  odd (see bazaar)
bi·zarre·ly
bi·zon·al
blab
  blabbed
  blab·bing
black·a·moor
black·ball
black·ber·ry
black·bird
black·board
black·en
black·guard

black·head
black·jack
black·list
black·mail
black·out
black·smith
black·thorn
black·top
blad·der
blame·less
blame·wor·thi·ness
blame·wor·thy
blanc·mange
blan·dish·ment
blan·ket
blar·ney
bla·sé
blas·pheme
blas·phe·mous
blas·phe·my
blast off
bla·tan·cy
bla·tant
blath·er
blaz·er
bla·zon
bleach·ers
bleak·ly
bleed
   bled
   bleed·ing
blem·ish
bless·ed·ness
blight
blind·fold

blink·er
blin·tze
   or blintz
bliss·ful
bliss·ful·ly
blis·ter
blithe·ly
blithe·some
blitz
blitz·krieg
bliz·zard
bloat·er
bloc
   group
block
   solid piece
block·ade
block·bust·er
block·head
block·house
blond
   or blonde
blood·cur·dling
blood·hound
blood·less
blood·mo·bile
blood·shed
blood·shot
blood·stain
blood·stone
blood·stream
blood·suck·er
blood·thirst·i·ly
blood·thirsty
bloody

bloop·er
blos·som
blot
   blot·ted
   blot·ting
blotch
blot·ter
blouse
blow-by-blow
blow·gun
blow·out
blow·pipe
blow·sy
   also blow·zy

blow·torch
blowy
blub·ber
blu·cher
blud·geon
blue·bell
blue·ber·ry
blue·bird
blue·fish
blue·grass
blue·nose
blue·point
blue·print
blue·stock·ing
blu·et
bluff·er
blu·ing
   or blue·ing

blu·ish
blun·der
blun·der·buss

blunt·ly
blunt·ness
blur
  blurred
  blur·ring
blur·ry
blus·ter
blus·tery
boa
boar
  animal (see bore)
board·er
  lodger (see border)
board·ing·house
board·walk
boast·ful
boast·ful·ly
boat hook
boat·man
boat·swain
  or bo·s'n *or* bo'·s'n
  or bo·sun *or* bo'·
  sun
bob
  bobbed
  bob·bing
bob·bin
bob·ble
bob·by-sox·er
bob·cat
bob·o·link
bob·sled
bob·white
boc·cie
  or boc·ci *or* boc·ce
bode

bod·ice
bodi·less
bodi·ly
bod·kin
body·guard
Boer
bog
  bogged
  bog·ging
bo·gey
  also bo·gy *or* bo·gie
  pl bo·geys
  also bo·gies
bo·gey·man
bo·gus
Bo·he·mi·an
boil·er
boil·er·mak·er
Boi·se
bois·ter·ous
bold·face
bold-faced
bold·ly
bold·ness
bo·le·ro
bo·li·var
  pl bo·li·vars *or*
  bo·li·va·res
Bo·liv·ia
Bo·liv·i·an
bo·lo
  pl bo·los
bo·lo·gna
Bol·she·vik
bol·she·vism
bol·ster

bo·lus
bom·bard
bom·bar·dier
bom·bard·ment
bom·bast
bom·bas·tic
bom·ba·zine
bomb·er
bomb·proof
bomb·shell
bomb·sight
bo·na fide
bo·nan·za
bon·bon
bond·age
bond·hold·er
bonds·man
bone·less
bon·er
bon·fire
bon·go
  pl bon·gos *also*
  bon·goes
bon·ho·mie
bo·ni·to
  pl bo·ni·tos *or*
  bo·ni·to
bon mot
  pl bons mots *or*
  bon mots
bon·net
bon·ny
bon·sai
  pl bon·sai
bo·nus

bon vi·vant
  pl bons vi·vants *or*
  bon vi·vants

bon voy·age
bony
  or bon·ey

boo·by
boo·dle
book·case
book·end
book·ie
book·ish
book·keep·er
book·keep·ing
book·let
book·mak·er
book·mak·ing
book·mark
book·mo·bile
book·plate
book·sell·er
book·shelf
boo·mer·ang
boon·dog·gle
boor·ish
boost·er
boot·black
boo·tee
  or boo·tie
  baby's sock (see booty)

booth
  pl booths

boot·leg
boo·ty
  loot (see bootee)

booze

boozy
bo·rac·ic acid
bo·rax
bor·der
  edge (see boarder)

bor·der·land
bor·der·line
bore
  drill, tire (see boar)

bo·re·al
bore·dom
bor·er
bo·ric
born
  given birth to (see bear)

bo·ron
bor·ough
  town (see burro, burrow)

bor·row
borscht
  or borsch

bo·s'n, bo'·s'n
  var of boatswain

bo·som
boss·i·ness
bossy
Bos·ton
Bos·to·nian
bo·sun, bo'·sun
  var of boatswain

bo·tan·i·cal
bot·a·nist
bot·a·ny

botch
both·er
both·er·some
Bo·tswa·na
bot·tle
bot·tle·neck
bot·tom
bot·tom·less
bot·u·lism
bou·doir
bouf·fant
bough
  tree branch (see bow)

bought
bouil·lon
  soup (see bullion)

boul·der
bou·le·vard
bounce
bounc·er
bound
bound·a·ry
bound·en
bound·less
boun·te·ous
boun·ti·ful
boun·ti·ful·ly
boun·ty
bou·quet
bour·bon
bour·geois
  pl bour·geois

bour·geoi·sie
bourse
bou·tique

bou·ton·niere
bo·vine
bow
   submit (see bough)

bow
   knot (see beau)

bowd·ler·ize
bow·el
bow·er
bowl·ful
bow·legged
bowl·er
   one that bowls

bow·ler
   hat

bowl·ing
bow·man
bow·sprit
bow·string
box·car
box·er
box·ing
box·wood
boy
   male child (see buoy)

boy·cott
boy·hood
boy·ish
boy·sen·ber·ry
brace·let
brack·en
brack·et
brack·ish
brag
   bragged

brag·ging
brag·ga·do·cio
brag·gart
Brah·man
   or Brah·min

braid
braille
brain·child
brain·less
brain·storm
brain·wash·ing
brainy
braise
   cook (see braze)

brake
   slow (see break)

brake·man
bram·ble
bran·dish
brand-new
bran·dy
bras·siere
brassy
bra·va·do
   pl bra·va·does *or*
   bra·va·dos

brave·ly
brav·ery
bra·vo
   pl bra·vos *or*
   bra·voes

bra·vu·ra
brawl
brawl·er
brawny

braze
   solder (see braise)

bra·zen
bra·zen·ness
bra·zier
Bra·zil
Bra·zil·ian
breach
   break (see breech)

bread·bas·ket
bread·board
breadth
   width (see breath)

bread·win·ner
break
   rupture (see brake)

   broke
   bro·ken
   break·ing
break·able
break·age
break·down
break·er
break·fast
break·front
break·out
break·through
break·wa·ter
breast·bone
breast·plate
breast·stroke
breast·work
breath
   air (see breadth)

breathe

breath·er
breath·less
breath·tak·ing
breech
  trousers, rear part (see breach)

breed
  bred
  breed·ing
breed·er
breeze·way
breezy
breth·ren
bre·vet
  bre·vet·ted
  or brev·et·ed

  bre·vet·ting
  or brev·et·ing

bre·via·ry
brev·i·ty
brew·ery
brib·ery
bric-a-brac
brick·bat
brick·lay·er
brid·al
  wedding (see bridle)

bride·groom
brides·maid
bridge·head
Bridge·port
bridge·work
bri·dle
  restrain (see bridal)

brief·case

bri·er
  or bri·ar

bri·gade
brig·a·dier
brig·and
brig·an·tine
bright·en
bright·ly
bright·ness
bril·liance
bril·lian·cy
bril·liant
bril·lian·tine
brim·ful
brim·stone
brin·dled
bring
  brought
  bring·ing
briny
bri·oche
bri·quette
  or bri·quet

bris·ket
brisk·ly
bris·ling
  or bris·tling
  herring (see bristle)

bris·tle
  bris·tled
  bris·tling
  stand erect (see brisling)

bris·tly
Brit·ain
  country (see Briton)

Bri·tan·nic
Brit·ish
Brit·on
  person (see Britain)

brit·tle
broach
  to open (see brooch)

broad·band
broad·cast
  broad·cast
  also broad·cast·ed

  broad·cast·ing
broad·cloth
broad·en
broad-mind·ed
broad·side
broad·sword
bro·cade
broc·co·li
  or broc·o·li

bro·chette
bro·chure
bro·gan
brogue
broil·er
bro·ken
bro·ken·heart·ed
bro·ker
bro·ker·age
bro·mide
bro·mid·ic
bro·mine
bron·chi·al
bron·chi·tis

bron·chus
  pl bron·chi

bron·co
  pl bron·coes

brooch
  ornament (*see* broach)

brood·er
brook·let
Brook·lyn
broom·stick
broth·el
broth·er
broth·er·hood
broth·er-in-law
  pl broth·ers-in-law

broth·er·li·ness
broth·er·ly
brougham
brought
brou·ha·ha
brow·beat
brown·ie
brown·stone
browse
bru·in
bruise
bruis·er
bru·net
  or bru·nette

brush-off
brush·wood
brusque
  also brusk

brusque·ly
brus·sels sprout

bru·tal
bru·tal·i·ty
bru·tal·ly
brut·ish
bub·ble
bub·bly
bu·bon·ic
buc·ca·neer
buck·board
buck·et
buck·et·ful
buck·le
buck·ler
buck·ram
buck·saw
buck·shot
buck·skin
buck·wheat
bu·col·ic
bud
  bud·ded
  bud·ding

Bud·dha
Bud·dhism
Bud·dhist
bud·dy
budge
bud·get
Buf·fa·lo
buf·fa·lo
  pl buf·fa·lo *or*
  buf·fa·loes

buff·er
buf·fet
buf·foon
buf·foon·ery

bug·a·boo
bug·bear
bug·gy
bu·gle
bu·gler
build
  built
  build·ing

build·er
build·ing
built-in
bul·bous
Bul·gar·ia
Bul·gar·i·an
bulge
bulg·ing
bulk·head
bulk·i·ly
bulk·i·ness
bulky
bull·dog
bull·doze
bull·doz·er
bul·let
bul·le·tin
bul·let·proof
bull·fight
bull·finch
bull·frog
bull·head·ed
bul·lion
  precious metal (*see*
  bouillon)

bull·ish
bul·lock
bul·ly

bul·rush
also bull·rush

bul·wark

bum
bummed
bum·ming

bum·ble·bee

bump·er

bump·kin

bump·tious

bumpy

bun·co
or bun·ko
pl bun·cos *or* bun·kos

bun·dle

bun·ga·low

bung·hole

bun·gle

bun·gler

bun·ion

bun·ker

bun·kum
or bun·combe

bun·ting

buoy
float (see boy)

buoy·an·cy

buoy·ant

buq·sha

bur·den

bur·den·some

bur·dock

bu·reau
pl bu·reaus *also*
bu·reaux

bu·reau·cra·cy

bu·reau·crat

bu·reau·crat·ic

bur·geon

bur·gess

bur·gher

bur·glar

bur·glar·ize

bur·gla·ry

bur·go·mas·ter

Bur·gun·dy

buri·al

bur·lap

bur·lesque

bur·ly

Bur·ma

Bur·man

Bur·mese

burn
burned
or burnt

burn·ing

burn·er

bur·nish

bur·noose
or bur·nous

burn·out

burr

bur·ro
donkey (see burrow,
borough)

bur·row
hole (see burro,
borough)

bur·sar

bur·si·tis

burst
burst
or burst·ed

burst·ing

Bu·run·di

Bu·run·di·an

bury
to inter (see berry)

bus
pl bus·es *or* bus·ses
vehicle (see buss)

bus·boy

bus·by

bush·el

bush·ing

bush·whack

busi·ly

busi·ness

busi·ness·man

bus·ing
or bus·sing

bus·kin

buss
kiss (see bus)

bus·tle

busy

busy·body

but
conj, prep (see butt)

butch·er

butch·ery

but·ler

butt
strike (see but)

but·ter

but·ter·cup
but·ter·fat
but·ter·fin·gered
but·ter·fin·gers
but·ter·fly
but·ter·milk
but·ter·nut
but·ter·scotch
but·tery
but·tocks
but·ton
but·ton·hole
but·ton·hook
but·tress
bu·tut
bux·om
buy
  bought
  buy·ing
buy·er
buz·zard
buzz·er
by·gone
by·law
  or bye·law

by-line
by·pass
by·path
by·play
by-prod·uct
by·stand·er
byte
by·way
by·word
Byz·an·tine

C

ca·bal
  ca·balled
  ca·bal·ling
ca·bana
cab·a·ret
cab·bage
cab·by
  or cab·bie

cab·in
cab·i·net
cab·i·net·mak·er
cab·i·net·mak·ing
cab·i·net·work
ca·ble
ca·ble·gram
cab·man
cab·o·chon
ca·boose
cab·ri·o·let
cab·stand
ca·cao
  pl ca·caos

cache
ca·chet
cack·le
ca·coph·o·nous
ca·coph·o·ny
cac·tus
  pl cac·ti or
  cac·tus·es

ca·dav·er
ca·dav·er·ous

cad·die
  or cad·dy
  golf (see caddy)

cad·dish
cad·dish·ness
cad·dy
  small box (see caddie)

ca·dence
ca·den·za
ca·det
cadge
cad·mi·um
cad·re
ca·du·ceus
  pl ca·du·cei

Cae·sar
cae·su·ra
ca·fé
  also ca·fe

ca·fé au lait
caf·e·te·ria
caf·feine
caf·tan
ca·gey
  also ca·gy

ca·gi·ly
ca·gi·ness
  also ca·gey·ness

ca·hoot
cais·son
cai·tiff
ca·jole
ca·jole·ment
ca·jol·ery

Ca·jun
also Ca·jan

cal·a·bash

cal·a·boose

cal·a·mine

ca·lam·i·tous

ca·lam·i·ty

cal·car·e·ous

cal·ci·fi·ca·tion

cal·ci·fy

cal·ci·mine

cal·ci·na·tion

cal·cine

cal·ci·um

cal·cu·la·ble

cal·cu·late

cal·cu·lat·ing

cal·cu·la·tion

cal·cu·la·tor

cal·cu·lus

cal·dron
or caul·dron

cal·en·dar
time (*see* calender)

cal·en·der
press (*see* calendar)

cal·ends

calf
pl calves *also* calfs

calf·skin

Cal·ga·ry

cal·i·ber
or cal·i·bre

cal·i·brate

cal·i·bra·tion

cal·i·co
pl cal·i·coes *or*
cal·i·cos

Cal·i·for·nia

cal·i·per
or cal·li·per

ca·liph
or ca·lif

ca·liph·ate

cal·is·then·ics

calk

cal·la

call·back

call-board

call·er

cal·lig·ra·pher

cal·lig·ra·phy

call·ing

cal·li·o·pe

cal·lous
unfeeling (*see* callus)

cal·low

cal·lus
skin (*see* callous)

calm·ly

cal·o·mel

ca·lo·ric

cal·o·rie
also cal·o·ry

cal·o·rim·e·ter

cal·u·met

ca·lum·ni·ate

ca·lum·ni·a·tion

ca·lum·ni·a·tor

ca·lum·ni·ous

cal·um·ny

calve

Cal·vin·ism

Cal·vin·is·tic

ca·lyp·so

ca·lyx

ca·ma·ra·de·rie

cam·ber

cam·bi·um

Cam·bo·dia

Cam·bo·di·an

cam·bric

Cam·bridge

Cam·den

cam·el

ca·mel·lia
also ca·me·lia

Cam·em·bert

cam·eo
pl cam·eos

cam·era

Cam·er·oon

Cam·er·oo·nian

cam·i·sole

cam·o·mile
var of chamomile

cam·ou·flage

cam·paign

cam·pa·nile

camp·er

cam·phor

cam·phor·ate

camp·o·ree

camp·stool

cam·pus

cam·shaft
can
  canned
  can·ning
Can·a·da
Ca·na·di·an
ca·naille
ca·nal
can·a·li·za·tion
can·a·lize
can·a·pé
  food (see canopy*)*

ca·nard
ca·nary
ca·nas·ta
can·can
can·cel
  can·celed
   or can·celled

  can·cel·ing
   or can·cel·ling

can·cel·la·tion
  also can·cel·ation

can·cel·lous
can·cer
can·cer·ous
can·de·la·bra
can·de·la·brum
  pl can·de·la·bra *also*
  can·de·la·brums

can·des·cence
can·des·cent
can·did
candi·da·cy
can·di·date

can·died
can·dle
can·dle·light
Can·dle·mas
can·dle·pin
can·dle·stick
can·dle·wick
can·dor
can·dy
cane·brake
ca·nine
can·is·ter
  also can·nis·ter

can·ker
can·ker·ous
can·ker·worm
can·nel coal
can·nery
can·ni·bal
can·ni·bal·ism
can·ni·bal·is·tic
can·ni·bal·ize
can·ni·ly
can·ni·ness
can·non
  gun (see canon*)*

can·non·ade
can·non·ball
can·non·eer
can·not
can·ny
ca·noe
can·on
  principle (see cannon*)*

ca·non·i·cal

can·on·iza·tion
can·on·ize
can·o·py
  shelter (see canapé*)*

can·ta·bi·le
can·ta·loupe
can·tan·ker·ous
can·ta·ta
can·teen
can·ter
  gallop (see cantor*)*

can·ti·cle
can·ti·le·ver
can·to
  pl can·tos

Can·ton
can·ton
can·ton·al
can·ton·ment
can·tor
  singer (see canter*)*

can·vas
  also can·vass
  cloth (see canvass*)*

can·vas·back
can·vass
  also can·vas
  solicit (see canvas*)*

can·yon
caou·tchouc
cap
  capped
  cap·ping
ca·pa·bil·i·ty
ca·pa·ble
ca·pa·bly

ca·pa·cious
ca·pac·i·tance
ca·pac·i·tor
ca·pac·i·ty
ca·par·i·son
ca·per
cape·skin
Cape Verde
cap·il·lar·i·ty
cap·il·lary
cap·i·tal
  city, wealth (*see* capitol)

cap·i·tal·ism
cap·i·tal·ist
cap·i·tal·is·tic
cap·i·tal·is·ti·cal·ly
cap·i·tal·iza·tion
cap·i·tal·ize
cap·i·tal·ly
cap·i·ta·tion
cap·i·tol
  building (*see* capital)

ca·pit·u·late
ca·pit·u·la·tion
ca·pon
ca·pric·cio
  pl ca·pric·cios

ca·price
ca·pri·cious
cap·ri·ole
cap·size
cap·stan
cap·su·lar

cap·su·late
  or cap·su·lat·ed

cap·sule
cap·tain
cap·tain·cy
cap·tion
cap·tious
cap·ti·vate
cap·ti·va·tion
cap·tive
cap·tiv·i·ty
cap·tor
cap·ture
Cap·u·chin
car·a·bao
car·a·cole
ca·rafe
car·a·mel
car·a·pace
car·at
  weight (*see* caret, carrot, karat)

car·a·van
car·a·van·sa·ry
  or car·a·van·se·rai

car·a·vel
car·a·way
car·bide
car·bine
car·bo·hy·drate
car·bol·ic acid
car·bon
car·bon·ate
car·bon·ation
car·bon·ic
car·bon·if·er·ous

car·bon·iza·tion
car·bon·ize
Car·bo·run·dum
car·boy
car·bun·cle
car·bu·re·tor
car·cass
car·cin·o·gen
car·cin·o·gen·ic
car·ci·no·ma
car·da·mom
card·board
card-car·ry·ing
car·di·ac
car·di·gan
car·di·nal
car·di·nal·i·ty
car·dio·gram
car·dio·graph
car·di·og·ra·phy
car·di·ol·o·gy
car·dio·vas·cu·lar
ca·reen
ca·reer
care·free
care·ful
care·ful·ly
care·less
ca·ress
car·et
  insert mark (*see* carat, carrot, karat)

care·tak·er
care·worn
car·fare

car·go
   pl car·goes *or*
     car·gos

car·hop
Ca·rib·be·an
car·i·bou
car·i·ca·ture
car·i·ca·tur·ist
car·ies
car·il·lon
car·load
car·mi·na·tive
car·mine
car·nage
car·nal
car·nal·i·ty
car·nal·ly
car·na·tion
car·nau·ba
car·ne·lian
car·ni·val
car·ni·vore
car·niv·o·rous
car·ol
   song (*see* carrel)

car·om
car·o·tene
ca·rot·id
ca·rous·al
   revel (*see* carousel)

ca·rouse
ca·rou·sel
   or car·rou·sel
   merry-go-round (*see*
    carousal)

car·pel

car·pen·ter
car·pen·try
car·pet
car·pet·bag
car·pet·bag·ger
car·pet·ing
car·port
car·rel
   library study (*see*
    carol)

car·riage
car·ri·er
car·ri·on
car·rot
   vegetable (*see* carat,
    caret, karat)

car·rou·sel
   var of carousel

car·ry
car·ry·all
car·ry·on
car·ry-over
car·sick
Car·son City
cart·age
carte blanche
car·tel
car·ti·lage
car·ti·lag·i·nous
car·to·gram
car·tog·ra·pher
car·tog·raph·ic
car·tog·ra·phy
car·ton
car·toon
car·toon·ist

car·tridge
cart·wheel
carv·er
carv·ing
cary·at·id
   pl cary·at·ids *or*
    cary·at·i·des

ca·sa·ba
cas·cade
cas·cara
ca·sein
case·ment
ca·shew
cash·ier
cash·mere
cas·ing
ca·si·no
   also cas·si·no
   pl ca·si·nos *also* cas·
    si·nos

cas·ket
cas·sa·va
cas·se·role
cas·sette
   or ca·sette

cas·sia
cas·sock
cast
   throw (*see* caste)

cast
cast·ing
cas·ta·net
cast·away
caste
   class (*see* cast)

cas·tel·lat·ed

cast·er
  or cas·tor

cas·ti·gate
cas·ti·ga·tion
cast·ing
cast iron
cas·tle
cast-off
  adj

cast·off
  noun

cas·tor
cas·trate
cas·tra·tion
ca·su·al
ca·su·al·ly
ca·su·al·ty
ca·su·ist
ca·su·is·tic
ca·su·is·ti·cal
ca·su·ist·ry
ca·sus bel·li
cat·a·clysm
cat·a·clys·mal
  or cat·a·clys·mic

cat·a·comb
cat·a·falque
Cat·a·lan
cat·a·lep·sy
cat·a·lep·tic
cat·a·log
  or cat·a·logue

cat·a·log·er
  or cat·a·logu·er

ca·tal·pa

ca·tal·y·sis
cat·a·lyst
cat·a·ma·ran
cat·a·pult
cat·a·ract
ca·tarrh
ca·tarrh·al
ca·tas·tro·phe
cat·a·stroph·ic
cat·call
catch
  caught
  catch·ing
catch·all
catch·er
catch·ing
catch·ment
catch·pen·ny
catch·word
catchy
cat·e·chism
cat·e·chist
cat·e·chize
cat·e·chu·men
cat·e·gor·i·cal
  also cat·e·gor·ic

cat·e·gor·i·cal·ly
cat·e·go·rize
cat·e·go·ry
ca·ter
cat·er·cor·ner
  or cat·er-cor·nered
  or cat·ty·cor·ner
  or cat·ty·cor·nered
  or kit·ty·cor·ner
  or kit·ty·cor·nered

ca·ter·er

cat·er·pil·lar
cat·er·waul
cat·fish
cat·gut
ca·thar·sis
ca·thar·tic
ca·the·dral
cath·e·ter
cath·ode
ca·thod·ic
cath·o·lic
Ca·thol·i·cism
cath·o·lic·i·ty
cat·ion
cat·kin
cat·like
cat·nap
cat·nip
cat-o'-nine-tails
  pl cat-o'-nine-tails

cat's-paw
cat·sup
  or ketch·up

cat·tail
cat·ti·ly
cat·ti·ness
cat·tle
cat·ty
cat·ty-cor·ner
  or cat·ty-cor·nered
  var of catercorner

cat·walk
Cau·ca·sian
Cau·ca·soid
cau·cus
cau·dal

caul·dron
var of caldron

cau·li·flow·er

caulk
or calk

caus·al

cau·sal·i·ty

caus·al·ly

cau·sa·tion

caus·ative

cause cé·lè·bre
pl causes cé·lè·bres

cau·se·rie

cause·way

caus·tic

caus·ti·cal·ly

cau·ter·i·za·tion

cau·ter·ize

cau·tion

cau·tion·ary

cau·tious

cav·al·cade

cav·a·lier

cav·al·ry

cav·al·ry·man

ca·ve·at

cave-in

cave·man

cav·ern

cav·ern·ous

cav·i·ar
or cav·i·are

cav·il
cav·iled
or cav·illed

cav·il·ing
or cav·il·ling

cav·i·ty

ca·vort

ca·vy

cay·enne

cay·use

cease-fire

cease·less

ce·cum
pl ce·ca

ce·dar

Ce·dar Rap·ids

ce·di

ce·dil·la

ceil·ing

cel·an·dine

cel·e·brant

cel·e·brate

cel·e·brat·ed

cel·e·bra·tion

ce·leb·ri·ty

ce·ler·i·ty

cel·ery

ce·les·ta

ce·les·tial

ce·li·ac

cel·i·ba·cy

cel·i·bate

cel·lar

cel·lar·age

cel·lar·ette
or cel·lar·et

cel·list

cel·lo

cel·lo·phane

cel·lu·lar

cel·lu·loid

cel·lu·lose

Cel·sius

Celt·ic

cem·ba·lo
pl cem·ba·li
or cem·ba·los

ce·ment

ce·men·ta·tion

cem·e·tery

cen·o·bite

cen·o·bit·ic

ceno·taph

cen·ser
vessel (see censor)

cen·sor
suppressor (see censer)

cen·so·ri·al

cen·so·ri·ous

cen·sor·ship

cen·sur·able

cen·sure

cen·sur·er

cen·sus

cent
coin (see send)

cen·taur

cen·ta·vo

cen·te·nar·i·an

cen·te·na·ry

cen·ten·ni·al

cen·ten·ni·al·ly

cen·ter

cen·ter·board
cen·ter·piece
cen·tes·i·mal
cen·tes·i·mo
   pl cen·tes·i·mi

cen·ti·grade
cen·ti·gram
cen·time
cen·ti·me·ter
cen·ti·mo
cen·ti·pede
cen·tral
cen·tral·iza·tion
cen·tral·ize
cen·trif·u·gal
cen·tri·fuge
cen·trip·e·tal
cen·trist
cen·tu·ri·on
cen·tu·ry
ce·phal·ic
ce·ram·ic
ce·ra·mist
   or ce·ram·i·cist

ce·re·al
   grain (see serial)

cer·e·bel·lum
ce·re·bral
cer·e·brate
cer·e·bra·tion
ce·re·brum
cer·e·mo·ni·al
cer·e·mo·ni·al·ly
cer·e·mo·ni·ous
cer·e·mo·ny

ce·rise
ce·ri·um
cer·met
cer·tain
cer·tain·ly
cer·tain·ty
cer·tif·i·cate
cer·ti·fi·ca·tion
cer·ti·fy
cer·ti·tude
ce·ru·le·an
cer·vi·cal
cer·vix
   pl cer·vi·ces

ce·sar·e·an
   also ce·sar·i·an

ce·si·um
ces·sa·tion
ces·sion
   a yielding (see session)

cess·pool
ces·ta
Cha·blis
cha-cha
Chad
Chad·ian
chafe
   rub (see chaff)

chaff
   husks (see chafe)

chaf·finch
chaf·ing
cha·grin
   cha·grined

cha·grin·ing
chain-re·act
chair·man
chaise longue
chal·ced·o·ny
cha·let
chal·ice
chalk·board
chalky
chal·lenge
chal·lis
cham·ber
cham·ber·lain
cham·ber·maid
cham·bray
cha·me·leon
cham·fer
cham·ois
   also cham·my
   or sham·my

cham·o·mile
   or cam·o·mile

cham·pagne
   wine (see champaign)

cham·paign
   open country (see champagne)

cham·pi·on
cham·pi·on·ship
chan·cel
chan·cel·lery
   or chan·cel·lory

chan·cel·lor
chan·cery
chan·cre
chancy

chan·de·lier
chan·dler
change·able
change·ful
change·less
change·ling
chang·er
chan·nel
  chan·neled
    or chan·nelled

  chan·nel·ing
    or chan·nel·ling

chan·nel·iza·tion
chan·nel·ize
chan·son
chan·teuse
chan·tey
  or chan·ty

chan·ti·cleer
chan·try
Cha·nu·kah
  var of Hanukkah

cha·os
cha·ot·ic
cha·ot·i·cal·ly
chap
  chapped
  chap·ping
chap·book
chap·el
chap·er·on
  or chap·er·one

chap·fall·en
chap·lain
chap·let

chap·ter
char
  charred
  char·ring
char·ac·ter
char·ac·ter·is·tic
char·ac·ter·is·ti·
  cal·ly
char·ac·ter·iza·
  tion
char·ac·ter·ize
cha·rade
char·coal
charge·able
charge-a-plate
  or charge plate

char·gé d'af·faires
  pl char·gés d'af·
  faires

char·ger
cha·ri·ly
char·i·ness
char·i·ot
char·i·o·teer
cha·ris·ma
char·is·mat·ic
char·i·ta·ble
char·i·ty
char·la·tan
Charles·ton
char·ley horse
Char·lotte
charm·er
charm·ing
char·nel
char·ter

char·treuse
char·wom·an
chary
chase
  pursue (see chaste)

  chased
  chas·ing
chas·er
chasm
chas·sis
chaste
  virtuous (see chase)

chas·ten
chas·tise
chas·tise·ment
chas·ti·ty
cha·su·ble
châ·teau
  pl châ·teaus *or*
  châ·teaux

chat·e·laine
Chat·ta·noo·ga
chat·tel
chat·ter
chat·ter·box
chat·ty
chauf·feur
chau·vin·ism
chau·vin·ist
chau·vin·is·tic
chau·vin·is·ti·
  cal·ly
cheap
  inexpensive (see
  cheep)

cheap·en

cheap·skate
cheat·er
check·book
check·er
check·er·board
check·ers
check·list
check·mate
check·off
check·out
check·point
check·room
check·up
ched·dar
cheek·bone
cheek·i·ly
cheek·i·ness
cheeky
cheep
 peep (see cheap)

cheer·ful
cheer·ful·ly
cheer·i·ly
cheer·i·ness
cheer·lead·er
cheer·less
cheery
cheese·burg·er
cheese·cake
cheese·cloth
cheesy
chee·tah
chef d'oeu·vre
 pl chefs d'oeu·vre

chem·i·cal

chem·i·cal·ly
che·mise
chem·ist
chem·is·try
che·mo·ther·a·py
chem·ur·gy
che·nille
cher·ish
che·root
cher·ry
cher·ub
 pl cher·ubs *or*
  cher·u·bim

ches·ter·field
chest·nut
che·va·lier
chev·i·ot
chev·ron
chewy
Chey·enne
Chi·an·ti
chiao
 pl chiao
 coin (see ciao)

chiar·oscu·ro
chic
 stylish (see chick)

Chi·ca·go
chi·ca·nery
chi·chi
chick
 young bird (see chic)

chick·a·dee
chick·en
chick·en·heart·ed
chick·weed

chic·o·ry
chide
 chid
  or chid·ed

 chid
  or chid·den *or*
   chid·ed

 chid·ing
chief·ly
chief·tain
chif·fon
chif·fo·nier
chig·ger
chi·gnon
chil·blain
child
 pl chil·dren

child·birth
child·hood
child·like
Chi·le
Chil·ean
chill·er
chill·i·ness
chilly
chi·me·ra
 or chi·mae·ra

chi·me·ri·cal
chim·ney
chim·pan·zee
chin
 chinned
 chin·ning
Chi·na
chi·na

chin·chil·la
Chi·nese
chi·no
chintz
chip
  chipped
  chip·ping
chip·munk
chip·per
chi·rog·ra·pher
chi·ro·graph·ic
chi·rog·ra·phy
chi·ro·man·cy
chi·rop·o·dist
chi·rop·o·dy
chi·ro·prac·tic
chi·ro·prac·tor
chis·el
  chis·eled
    or chis·elled
  chis·el·ing
    or chis·el·ling
chis·el·er
chit·chat
chit·ter·lings
  or chit·lings or
  chit·lins
chi·val·ric
chiv·al·rous
chiv·al·ry
chlo·ral
chlor·dane
chlo·ric
chlo·ride
chlo·ri·nate
chlo·ri·na·tion

chlo·rine
chlo·ro·form
chlo·ro·phyll
chock·a·block
chock-full
choc·o·late
choir
  singers (see quire)
choir·boy
choir·mas·ter
cho·ler
chol·era
cho·ler·ic
cho·les·ter·ol
chon
  pl chon
choose
  chose
  cho·sen
  choos·ing
choos·er
choosy
  or choos·ey
chop
  chopped
  chop·ping
chop·house
chop·per
chop·pi·ly
chop·pi·ness
chop·py
chop·stick
chop su·ey
cho·ral
  of a choir
    (see chorale, coral)

cho·rale
  also cho·ral
  hymn (see choral,
    coral)
cho·ral·ly
chord
  music (see cord)
chore
cho·rea
cho·reo·graph
cho·re·og·ra·pher
cho·reo·graph·ic
cho·reo·graph·i·
    cal·ly
cho·re·og·ra·phy
cho·ris·ter
chor·tle
chorus
cho·sen
chow·chow
  relish (see chow chow)
chow chow
  dog (see chowchow)
chow·der
chow mein
chrism
chris·ten
Chris·ten·dom
chris·ten·ing
Chris·tian
chris·ti·ania
Chris·tian·i·ty
Chris·tian·ize
chris·tie
  or chris·ty
Christ·mas

Christ·mas·tide
chro·mat·ic
chro·ma·tic·i·ty
chro·mato·graph·
  ic
chro·mato·graph·
  i·cal·ly
chro·ma·tog·ra·
  phy
chrome
chro·mic
chro·mite
chro·mi·um
chro·mo·som·al
chro·mo·some
chron·ic
chron·i·cal·ly
chron·i·cle
chron·i·cler
chro·no·graph
chro·no·log·i·cal
chro·nol·o·gist
chro·nol·o·gy
chro·nom·e·ter
chrys·a·lis
chry·san·the·
  mum
chrys·o·lite
chub·bi·ness
chub·by
chuck·hole
chuck·le
chug
  chugged
  chug·ging
chuk·ka
  boot (see chukker)

chuk·ker
  or chuk·kar
  or chuk·ka
  polo (see chukka)

chum
  chummed
  chum·ming
chum·mi·ness
chum·my
chunky
church·go·er
church·less
church·man
church·war·den
church·yard
churl
churl·ish
churn
chute
  slide (see shoot)

chut·ney
chutz·pah
  or chutz·pa

ciao
  greeting (see chiao)

ci·ca·da
cic·a·trix
  pl cic·a·tri·ces

ci·ce·ro·ne
ci·der
ci·gar
cig·a·rette
  also cig·a·ret

cin·cho·na
Cin·cin·nati
cinc·ture

cin·der
cin·e·ma
cin·e·mat·ic
cin·e·mat·o·graph
cin·e·ma·tog·ra·
  pher
cin·e·mat·o·
  graph·ic
cin·e·ma·tog·ra·
  phy
cin·er·ar·i·um
  pl cin·er·ar·ia

cin·na·bar
cin·na·mon
ci·pher
cir·ca
cir·cle
cir·clet
cir·cuit
cir·cu·itous
cir·cuit·ry
cir·cu·ity
cir·cu·lar
cir·cu·lar·i·ty
cir·cu·lar·iza·tion
cir·cu·lar·ize
cir·cu·late
cir·cu·la·tion
cir·cu·la·to·ry
cir·cum·am·bi·
  ent
cir·cum·am·bu·
  late
cir·cum·cise
cir·cum·ci·sion

cir·cum·fer·ence
cir·cum·flex
cir·cum·lo·cu·tion
cir·cum·lu·nar
cir·cum·nav·i·gate
cir·cum·nav·i·ga·tion
cir·cum·po·lar
cir·cum·scribe
cir·cum·scrip·tion
cir·cum·spect
cir·cum·spec·tion
cir·cum·stance
cir·cum·stan·tial
cir·cum·stan·tial·ly
cir·cum·vent
cir·cum·ven·tion
cir·cus
cir·rho·sis
cir·ro·cu·mu·lus
cir·ro·stra·tus
cir·rus
cis·lu·nar
cis·tern
cit·a·del
ci·ta·tion
cite
   quote (*see* sight, site)

citi·fy
cit·i·zen
cit·i·zen·ry
cit·i·zen·ship
ci·trate

cit·ric acid
cit·ron
cit·ro·nel·la
cit·rus
city
city-state
civ·et
civ·ic
civ·ics
civ·il
ci·vil·ian
ci·vil·i·ty
civ·i·li·za·tion
civ·i·lize
civ·il·ly
claim·ant
clair·voy·ance
clair·voy·ant
clam·bake
clam·ber
clam·mi·ness
clam·my
clam·or
clam·or·ous
clam·shell
clan·des·tine
clan·gor
clan·gor·ous
clan·nish
clans·man
clap
   clapped
      also clapt
   clap·ping
clap·board
clap·per

clap·trap
claque
clar·et
clar·i·fi·ca·tion
clar·i·fy
clar·i·net
clar·i·net·ist
clar·i·on
clar·i·ty
clas·sic
clas·si·cal
clas·si·cal·ly
clas·si·cism
clas·si·cist
clas·si·fi·able
clas·si·fi·ca·tion
clas·si·fy
   clas·si·fied
   clas·si·fy·ing
class·mate
class·room
clat·ter
clause
claus·tro·pho·bia
clav·i·chord
clav·i·cle
cla·vier
clay·ey
clay·more
clean-cut
clean·er
clean·li·ness
clean·ly
clean·ness
cleanse
cleans·er

clear·ance
clear-cut
clear·head·ed
clear·ing
clear·ing·house
cleav·age
cleave
cling

cleaved
or clove
also clave

cleav·ing
cleave
split

cleaved
also cleft *or* clove

cleaved
also cleft *or* clo·ven

cleav·ing
cleav·er
cle·ma·tis
clem·en·cy
clem·ent
clere·sto·ry
or clear·sto·ry

cler·gy
cler·gy·man
cler·ic
cler·i·cal
cler·i·cal·ism
Cleve·land
clev·er
clev·er·ness
clew
or clue

cli·ché
cli·ent
cli·en·tele
cliff-hang·er
cli·mac·tic
of a climax (see climatic)
cli·mate
cli·mat·ic
weather (see climactic)
cli·ma·to·log·i·cal
cli·ma·tol·o·gist
cli·ma·tol·o·gy
cli·max
climb·er
clinch·er
cling
clung
cling·ing
clin·ic
clin·i·cal
clin·i·cal·ly
cli·ni·cian
clin·ker
clip
clipped
clip·ping
clip·board
clip·per
clip·ping
clip·sheet
clique
cli·to·ral
or cli·tor·ic
cli·to·ris
cloche

clock·wise
clock·work
clod·hop·per
clog
clogged
clog·ging
cloi·son·né
clois·ter
closed-end
close·fist·ed
close·ly
close·mouthed
close·ness
clos·et
close-up
clo·sure
clot
clot·ted
clot·ting
cloth
fabric (see clothe)
clothe
to dress (see cloth)
clothed
or clad
cloth·ing
clothes·horse
clothes·line
clothes·pin
clothes·press
cloth·ier
cloth·ing
clo·ture
cloud·burst
cloud·i·ness

clo·ver
clo·ver·leaf
  pl clo·ver·leafs
   or clo·ver·leaves

clown·ish
club
  clubbed
  club·bing
club·foot
club·house
clue
  var of clew

clum·si·ly
clum·si·ness
clum·sy
clus·ter
clut·ter
coach·er
coach·man
co·ad·ju·tor
co·ag·u·lant
co·ag·u·late
co·ag·u·la·tion
co·ag·u·lum
  pl co·ag·u·la

co·alesce
co·ales·cence
coal·field
co·ali·tion
coarse
  rough (see course)

coars·en
coarse·ness
coast·al
coast·er

coast guard
coast·line
coat·ing
co·au·thor
co·ax·i·al
co·balt
cob·ble
cob·bler
cob·ble·stone
co·bra
cob·web
co·ca
co·caine
coc·cus
  pl coc·ci

coc·cyx
  pl coc·cy·ges *also*
   coc·cyx·es

coch·i·neal
co·chlea
  pl co·chle·as *or*
   co·chle·ae

cock·ade
cock·a·too
cock·crow
cock·er·el
cock·eyed
cock·fight
cock·i·ly
cock·i·ness
cock·le
cock·le·shell
cock·ney
cock·pit
cock·roach
cock·sure

cock·tail
cocky
co·coa
co·co·nut
co·coon
co·da
cod·dle
co·deine
co·dex
  pl co·di·ces

cod·fish
cod·ger
cod·i·cil
cod·i·fi·ca·tion
cod·i·fy
co·ed·u·ca·tion
co·ed·u·ca·tion·al
co·ef·fi·cient
co·equal
co·erce
co·er·cion
co·er·cive
co·eval
co·ex·ist
co·ex·is·tence
co·ex·ten·sive
cof·fee
cof·fee·house
cof·fee·pot
cof·fer
cof·fer·dam
cof·fin
co·gen·cy
co·gent
cog·i·tate

cog·i·ta·tion
co·gnac
cog·nate
cog·ni·tion
cog·ni·tive
cog·ni·zance
cog·ni·zant
cog·no·men
cog·wheel
co·hab·it
co·hab·i·ta·tion
co·heir
co·here
co·her·ence
co·her·ent
co·he·sion
co·he·sive
co·hort
coif·feur
coin·age
co·in·cide
co·in·ci·dence
co·in·ci·dent
co·in·ci·den·tal
co·ition
co·itus
co·la
col·an·der
cold-blood·ed
cold·ly
cold·ness
cole·slaw
col·ic
col·i·se·um
  or col·os·se·um
  arena (see Colosseum)

co·li·tis
col·lab·o·rate
col·lab·o·ra·tion
col·lab·o·ra·tor
col·lage
col·lapse
col·laps·ible
col·lar
col·lar·bone
col·lard
col·late
col·lat·er·al
col·la·tion
col·la·tor
col·league
col·lect
col·lect·ed
col·lect·ible
  or col·lect·able

col·lec·tion
col·lec·tive
col·lec·tive·ly
col·lec·tiv·ism
col·lec·tiv·is·tic
col·lec·tiv·ize
col·lec·tor
col·leen
col·lege
col·le·gi·al·i·ty
col·le·gian
col·le·giate
col·le·gi·um
col·lide
col·lie
col·lier

col·liery
col·li·sion
col·lo·ca·tion
col·lo·di·on
col·loid
col·loi·dal
col·lo·qui·al
col·lo·qui·al·ism
col·lo·qui·um
col·lo·quy
col·lu·sion
col·lu·sive
co·logne
Co·lom·bia
Co·lom·bi·an
co·lon
  biol, punctuation

co·lon
  pl co·lo·nes
  currency

col·o·nel
  military (see kernel)

co·lo·ni·al
co·lo·nial·ism
col·o·nist
col·o·ni·za·tion
col·o·nize
col·o·niz·er
col·on·nade
col·o·ny
col·o·phon
col·or
Col·o·ra·do
col·or·ation
col·or·a·tu·ra
col·or-blind

col·or·cast
col·ored
col·or·fast
col·or·fast·ness
col·or·ful
col·or·less
co·los·sal
Col·os·se·um
  or Col·i·se·um
  amphitheater in
  Rome
  (*see* coliseum)

co·los·sus
Co·lum·bia
col·um·bine
Co·lum·bus
col·umn
co·lum·nar
col·um·nist
co·ma
  unconsciousness (*see*
  comma)

co·ma·tose
com·bat
com·bat·ant
com·bat·ive
comb·er
com·bi·na·tion
com·bine
comb·ings
com·bo
  pl com·bos

com·bus·ti·ble
com·bus·tion
come
  came
  come

com·ing
come·back
co·me·di·an
co·me·di·enne
come·down
com·e·dy
come·li·ness
come·ly
come-on
co·mes·ti·ble
com·et
come·up·pance
com·fit
com·fort
com·fort·able
com·fort·ably
com·fort·er
com·ic
com·i·cal
com·i·ty
com·ma
  punctuation (*see*
  coma)

com·mand
com·man·dant
com·man·deer
com·mand·er
com·mand·ment
com·man·do
  pl com·man·dos *or*
  com·man·does

com·mem·o·rate
com·mem·o·ra·
  tion
com·mem·o·ra·
  tive

com·mence
com·mence·ment
com·mend
com·mend·able
com·men·da·tion
com·men·su·ra·
  bil·i·ty
com·men·su·ra·
  ble
com·men·su·rate
com·ment
com·men·tary
com·men·ta·tor
com·merce
com·mer·cial
com·mer·cial·ism
com·mer·cial·iza·
  tion
com·mer·cial·ize
com·mer·cial·ly
com·mi·na·tion
com·mi·na·to·ry
com·min·gle
com·mis·er·ate
com·mis·er·a·tion
com·mis·sar
com·mis·sar·i·at
com·mis·sary
com·mis·sion
com·mis·sion·er
com·mit
  com·mit·ted
  com·mit·ting
com·mit·ment
com·mit·tal
com·mit·tee

com·mit·tee·man
com·mit·tee·
 wom·an
com·mode
com·mo·di·ous
com·mod·i·ty
com·mo·dore
com·mon
com·mon·al·i·ty
 commonness

com·mon·al·ty
 common people

com·mon·er
com·mon·ly
com·mon·ness
com·mon·place
com·mon·weal
com·mon·wealth
com·mo·tion
com·mu·nal
com·mune
com·mu·ni·ca·ble
com·mu·ni·cant
com·mu·ni·cate
com·mu·ni·ca·
 tion
com·mu·ni·ca·
 tive
com·mu·nion
com·mu·ni·qué
com·mu·nism
com·mu·nist
com·mu·nis·tic
com·mu·nis·ti·
 cal·ly

com·mu·ni·ty
com·mu·nize
com·mut·able
com·mu·ta·tion
com·mu·ta·tive
com·mu·ta·tor
com·mute
com·mut·er
Com·o·ro
com·pact
com·pac·tor
 or com·pact·er

com·pan·ion
com·pan·ion·able
com·pan·ion·ship
com·pan·ion·way
com·pa·ny
com·pa·ra·ble
com·par·a·tive
com·par·a·tive·ly
com·pare
com·par·i·son
com·part·ment
com·part·men·
 tal·ize
com·pass
com·pas·sion
com·pas·sion·ate
com·pat·i·bil·i·ty
com·pat·i·ble
com·pa·tri·ot
com·peer
com·pel
 com·pelled
 com·pel·ling

com·pen·di·um
 pl com·pen·di·ums
 or com·pen·di·a

com·pen·sate
com·pen·sa·tion
com·pen·sa·to·ry
com·pete
com·pe·tence
com·pe·ten·cy
com·pe·tent
com·pe·ti·tion
com·pet·i·tive
com·pet·i·tor
com·pi·la·tion
com·pile
com·pil·er
com·pla·cence
com·pla·cen·cy
com·pla·cent
 self-satisfied (see
  complaisant)

com·plain
com·plain·ant
com·plaint
com·plai·sance
com·plai·sant
 affable (see
  complacent)

com·ple·ment
 full quantity (see
  compliment)

com·ple·men·ta·
 ry
com·plete
com·plete·ness
com·ple·tion
com·plex

com·plex·ion
com·plex·i·ty
com·pli·ance
com·pli·an·cy
com·pli·ant
com·pli·cate
com·pli·cat·ed
com·pli·ca·tion
com·plic·i·ty
com·pli·er
com·pli·ment
flattery (see
  complement)

com·pli·men·ta·
  ry
com·ply
com·po·nent
com·port
com·port·ment
com·pose
com·posed
com·pos·er
com·pos·ite
com·po·si·tion
com·pos·i·tor
com·post
com·po·sure
com·pote
com·pound
com·pre·hend
com·pre·hen·si·
  ble
com·pre·hen·sion
com·pre·hen·sive
com·press
com·pressed

com·pres·sion
com·pres·sor
com·prise
com·pro·mise
comp·trol·ler
com·pul·sion
com·pul·sive
com·pul·so·ry
com·punc·tion
com·pu·ta·tion
com·pute
com·put·er
com·put·er·iz·
  able
com·put·er·iza·
  tion
com·put·er·ize
com·rade
con
  conned
  con·ning
con brio
con·cat·e·na·tion
con·cave
con·cav·i·ty
con·ceal
con·ceal·ment
con·cede
con·ceit
con·ceit·ed
con·ceiv·able
con·ceiv·ably
con·ceive
con·cel·e·brant
con·cen·trate
con·cen·tra·tion

con·cen·tric
con·cept
con·cep·tion
con·cep·tu·al
con·cep·tu·al·iza·
  tion
con·cep·tu·al·ize
con·cep·tu·al·ly
con·cern
  con·cerned
  con·cern·ing
con·cern·ment
con·cert
con·cert·ed
con·cer·ti·na
con·cert·mas·ter
  or con·cert·meis·ter

con·cer·to
  pl con·cer·ti *or*
    con·cer·tos

con·ces·sion
con·ces·sion·aire
con·ces·sive
conch
  pl conchs *or*
    conch·es

con·cierge
con·cil·i·ate
con·cil·i·a·tion
con·cil·ia·to·ry
con·cise
con·cise·ness
con·ci·sion
con·clave
con·clude
con·clu·sion

con·clu·sive
con·coct
con·coc·tion
con·com·i·tant
con·cord
con·cor·dance
con·cor·dant
con·cor·dat
con·course
con·cres·cence
con·cres·cent
con·crete
con·cre·tion
con·cu·bi·nage
con·cu·bine
con·cu·pis·cence
con·cur
  con·curred
  con·cur·ring
con·cur·rence
con·cur·rent
con·cus·sion
con·demn
con·dem·na·tion
con·dem·na·to·ry
con·den·sa·tion
con·dense
con·dens·er
con·de·scend
con·de·scend·ing·ly
con·de·scen·sion
con·dign
con·di·ment
con·di·tion
con·di·tion·al

con·di·tioned
con·dole
con·do·lence
con·do·min·i·um
con·do·na·tion
con·done
con·dor
con·duce
con·du·cive
con·duct
con·duc·tance
con·duc·tion
con·duc·tive
con·duc·tiv·i·ty
con·duc·tor
con·duit
Con·es·to·ga
co·ney
con·fab·u·la·tion
con·fec·tion
con·fec·tion·er
con·fec·tion·ery
con·fed·er·a·cy
con·fed·er·ate
con·fed·er·a·tion
con·fer
  con·ferred
  con·fer·ring
con·fer·ee
con·fer·ence
con·fess
con·fessed·ly
con·fes·sion
con·fes·sion·al
con·fes·sor
con·fet·ti

con·fi·dant
  friend (see confident)

con·fide
con·fi·dence
con·fi·dent
  assured (see confidant)

con·fi·den·tial
con·fi·den·tial·ly
con·fid·ing
con·fig·u·ra·tion
con·fine
con·fine·ment
con·fin·er
con·firm
con·fir·ma·tion
con·fir·ma·to·ry
con·firmed
con·fis·cate
con·fis·ca·tion
con·fis·ca·to·ry
con·fla·gra·tion
con·flict
con·flu·ence
con·flu·ent
con·flux
con·form
con·form·able
con·for·mance
con·for·ma·tion
con·form·ist
con·for·mi·ty
con·found
con·fra·ter·ni·ty
con·frere
con·front

con·fron·ta·tion
Con·fu·cian·ism
con·fuse
con·fus·ed·ly
con·fu·sion
con·fu·ta·tion
con·fute
con·ga
con·geal
con·ge·nial
con·gen·i·tal
con·ger
con·ge·ries
con·gest
con·ges·tion
con·glom·er·ate
con·glom·er·a·
  tion
Con·go
Con·go·lese
con·grat·u·late
con·grat·u·la·tion
con·grat·u·la·to·
  ry
con·gre·gate
con·gre·ga·tion
con·gre·ga·tion·al
con·gre·ga·tion·
  al·ism
con·gre·ga·tion·
  al·ist
con·gress
con·gres·sio·nal
con·gress·man
con·gress·wom·an
con·gru·ence

con·gru·en·cy
con·gru·ent
con·gru·ity
con·gru·ous
con·ic
con·i·cal
co·ni·fer
co·nif·er·ous
con·jec·tur·al
con·jec·ture
con·join
con·joint
con·ju·gal
con·ju·gate
con·ju·ga·tion
con·junct
con·junc·tion
con·junc·tive
con·junc·ti·vi·tis
con·junc·ture
con·ju·ra·tion
con·jure
con·jur·er
  or con·ju·ror

con·nect
Con·nect·i·cut
con·nec·tion
con·nec·tive
con·nec·tor
  also con·nect·er

con·nip·tion
con·niv·ance
con·nive
con·nois·seur
con·no·ta·tion

con·no·ta·tive
con·note
con·nu·bi·al
con·quer
con·quer·or
con·quest
con·quis·ta·dor
  pl con·quis·ta·do·res
  or con·quis·ta·
    dors

con·san·guin·e·
  ous
con·san·guin·i·ty
con·science
con·sci·en·tious
con·scious
con·scious·ness
con·script
con·scrip·tion
con·se·crate
con·se·cra·tion
con·sec·u·tive
con·sen·sus
con·sent
con·se·quence
con·se·quent
con·se·quen·tial
con·se·quent·ly
con·ser·va·tion
con·ser·va·tion·
  ist
con·ser·va·tism
con·ser·va·tive
con·ser·va·tor
con·ser·va·to·ry
con·serve

con·sid·er
con·sid·er·able
con·sid·er·ably
con·sid·er·ate
con·sid·er·ation
con·sid·ered
con·sid·er·ing
con·sign
con·sign·ee
con·sign·ment
con·sign·or
con·sist
con·sis·tence
con·sis·ten·cy
con·sis·tent
con·sis·to·ry
con·so·la·tion
con·so·la·to·ry
con·sole
con·sol·i·date
con·sol·i·da·tion
con·som·mé
con·so·nance
con·so·nant
con·so·nan·tal
con·sort
con·sor·tium
con·spec·tus
con·spic·u·ous
con·spir·a·cy
con·spir·a·tor
con·spire
con·sta·ble
con·stab·u·lary
con·stan·cy
con·stant

con·stel·la·tion
con·ster·na·tion
con·sti·pate
con·sti·pa·tion
con·stit·u·en·cy
con·stit·u·ent
con·sti·tute
con·sti·tu·tion
con·sti·tu·tion·al
con·sti·tu·tion·al·
  i·ty
con·sti·tu·tion·al·
  ly
con·sti·tu·tive
con·strain
con·straint
con·strict
con·stric·tion
con·stric·tive
con·stric·tor
con·struct
con·struc·tion
con·struc·tion·ist
con·struc·tive
con·struc·tor
con·strue
con·sub·stan·ti·a·
  tion
con·sul
con·sul·ar
con·sul·ate
con·sult
con·sul·tant
con·sul·ta·tion
con·sul·ta·tive
con·sume

con·sum·er
con·sum·er·ism
con·sum·mate
con·sum·ma·tion
con·sump·tion
con·sump·tive
con·tact
con·ta·gion
con·ta·gious
con·tain
con·tain·er
con·tain·er·iza·
  tion
con·tain·er·ize
con·tain·ment
con·tam·i·nant
con·tam·i·nate
con·tam·i·na·tion
con·temn
con·tem·plate
con·tem·pla·tion
con·tem·pla·tive
con·tem·po·ra·
  ne·ous
con·tem·po·rary
con·tempt
con·tempt·ible
con·temp·tu·ous
con·tend
con·tend·er
con·tent
con·tent·ed
con·ten·tion
con·ten·tious
con·tent·ment
con·ter·mi·nous

con·test
con·tes·tant
con·text
con·tex·tu·al
con·ti·gu·ity
con·tig·u·ous
con·ti·nence
con·ti·nent
con·ti·nen·tal
con·tin·gen·cy
con·tin·gent
con·tin·u·al
con·tin·u·al·ly
con·tin·u·ance
con·tin·u·a·tion
con·tin·ue
con·ti·nu·ity
con·tin·u·ous
con·tin·u·um
   pl con·tin·ua *or*
   con·tin·u·ums

con·tort
con·tor·tion
con·tor·tion·ist
con·tour
con·tra·band
con·tra·cep·tion
con·tra·cep·tive
con·tract
con·trac·tile
con·trac·til·i·ty
con·trac·tion
con·trac·tor
con·trac·tu·al
con·trac·tu·al·ly
con·tra·dict

con·tra·dic·tion
con·tra·dic·to·ry
con·tra·dis·tinc·
   tion
con·trail
con·tral·to
   pl con·tral·tos

con·trap·tion
con·tra·pun·tal
con·tra·ri·ety
con·trari·ly
con·trari·wise
con·trary
con·trast
con·tra·vene
con·tra·ven·tion
con·tre·temps
con·trib·ute
con·tri·bu·tion
con·trib·u·tor
con·trib·u·to·ry
con·trite
con·tri·tion
con·triv·ance
con·trive
con·triv·er
con·trol
   con·trolled
   con·trol·ling
con·trol·ler
con·tro·ver·sial
con·tro·ver·sy
con·tro·vert
con·tro·vert·ible
con·tu·ma·cious

con·tu·ma·cy
con·tu·me·li·ous
con·tu·me·ly
con·tuse
con·tu·sion
co·nun·drum
con·ur·ba·tion
con·va·lesce
con·va·les·cence
con·va·les·cent
con·vec·tion
con·vene
con·ve·nience
con·ve·nient
con·vent
con·ven·ti·cle
con·ven·tion
con·ven·tion·al
con·ven·tion·al·i·
   ty
con·ven·tion·al·
   ize
con·ven·tu·al
con·verge
con·ver·gence
con·ver·gent
con·ver·sant
con·ver·sa·tion
con·ver·sa·tion·al
con·verse
con·verse·ly
con·ver·sion
con·vert
con·vert·er
   or con·ver·tor

con·vert·ible
con·vex
con·vex·i·ty
con·vey
con·vey·ance
con·vey·er
  or con·vey·or

con·vict
con·vic·tion
con·vince
con·vinc·ing
con·viv·ial
con·viv·i·al·i·ty
con·viv·ial·ly
con·vo·ca·tion
con·voke
con·vo·lut·ed
con·vo·lu·tion
con·voy
con·vulse
con·vul·sion
con·vul·sive
cook·book
cook·ery
cook·ie
  or cooky

cook·out
cool·ant
cool·er
coo·lie
  laborer (see coolly)

cool·ly
  also cooly
  chillily (see coolie)

cool·ness

co-op
coo·per
coo·per·age
co·op·er·ate
co·op·er·a·tion
co·op·er·a·tive
co·op·er·a·tor
co-opt
co·or·di·nate
co·or·di·na·tion
co·or·di·na·tor
co·part·ner
copi·er
co·pi·lot
cop·ing
co·pi·ous
cop·per
cop·per·as
cop·per·head
cop·pice
co·pra
cop·u·la
cop·u·late
cop·u·la·tion
cop·u·la·tive
copy·book
copy·boy
copy·cat
copy·desk
copy·ist
copy·read·er
copy·right
co·quet
  or co·quette
    co·quet·ted
    co·quet·ting

co·que·try
co·quette
  noun

co·quett·ish
co·qui·na
cor·a·cle
cor·al
  marine skeleton
  (see choral,
  chorale)

cor·bel
cord
  string (see chord)

cord·age
cor·dial
cor·dial·i·ty
cor·dial·ly
cor·dil·le·ra
cord·less
cor·do·ba
cor·don
cor·do·van
cor·du·roy
core
  center (see corps)

co·re·spon·dent
  law (see correspondent)

co·ri·an·der
cork
cork·screw
cor·mo·rant
corn·cob
corn·crib
cor·nea
cor·ner

cor·ner·stone
cor·net
corn·flow·er
cor·nice
corn·meal
corn·stalk
corn·starch
cor·nu·co·pia
corny
co·rol·la
cor·ol·lary
co·ro·na
cor·o·nary
cor·o·na·tion
cor·o·ner
cor·o·net
cor·po·ral
cor·po·rate
cor·po·ra·tion
cor·po·ra·tive
cor·po·re·al
corps
  group (see core,
    corpse)

corpse
  dead body (see corps)

cor·pu·lence
cor·pu·lent
cor·pus
cor·pus·cle
cor·pus de·lic·ti
Cor·pus Chris·ti
cor·ral
cor·rect
cor·rec·tion
cor·rec·tive

cor·re·late
cor·re·la·tion
cor·rel·a·tive
cor·re·spond
cor·re·spon·dence
cor·re·spon·dent
  writer (see
    corespondent)

cor·ri·dor
cor·ri·gen·dum
cor·rob·o·rate
cor·rob·o·ra·tion
cor·rob·o·ra·tive
cor·rob·o·ra·to·ry
cor·rode
cor·ro·sion
cor·ro·sive
cor·ru·gate
cor·ru·ga·tion
cor·rupt
cor·rupt·ible
cor·rup·tion
cor·sair
cor·set
cor·tege
  also cor·tège

cor·tex
  pl cor·ti·ces *or*
    cor·tex·es

cor·ti·cal
cor·ti·sone
co·run·dum
cor·us·cate
cor·us·ca·tion
cor·vette
co·ry·za

co·sig·na·to·ry
cos·met·ic
cos·me·tol·o·gist
cos·me·tol·o·gy
cos·mic
  also cos·mi·cal

cos·mog·o·ny
cos·mo·log·i·cal
cos·mol·o·gy
cos·mo·naut
cos·mo·pol·i·tan
cos·mop·o·lite
cos·mos
cos·sack
Cos·ta Ri·ca
Cos·ta Ri·can
cost·li·ness
cost·ly
cos·tume
cos·tum·er
cos·tu·mi·er
co·te·rie
co·ter·mi·nous
co·til·lion
  also co·til·lon

cot·tage
cot·ter
cot·ton
cot·ton·seed
cot·ton·tail
cot·ton·wood
cot·y·le·don
couch·ant
cou·gar
cough

cou·lomb
coun·cil
   assembly (see counsel)

coun·cil·lor
   or coun·cil·or
   council member
    (see counselor)

coun·cil·man
coun·sel
   advice (see council)

coun·sel
  coun·seled
   or coun·selled

  coun·sel·ing
   or coun·sel·ling

coun·sel·or
  or coun·sel·lor
  adviser
   (see councillor)

count·able
count·down
coun·te·nance
count·er
coun·ter·act
coun·ter·ac·tive
coun·ter·at·tack
coun·ter·bal·ance
coun·ter·claim
coun·ter·clock·
  wise
coun·ter·es·pi·o·
  nage
coun·ter·feit
coun·ter·feit·er
coun·ter·in·tel·li·
  gence

coun·ter·in·sur·
  gen·cy
count·er·man
coun·ter·mand
coun·ter·mea·sure
coun·ter·of·fen·
  sive
coun·ter·pane
coun·ter·part
coun·ter·point
coun·ter·poise
coun·ter·rev·o·lu·
  tion
coun·ter·sig·na·
  ture
coun·ter·sign
coun·ter·sink
coun·ter·ten·or
coun·ter·weight
count·ess
count·less
coun·tri·fied
  also coun·try·fied

coun·try
coun·try·man
coun·try·side
coun·ty
coup de grace
coup d'etat
cou·pé
  or coupe

cou·ple
cou·plet
cou·pling
cou·pon

cour·age
cou·ra·geous
cou·ri·er
course
  track (see coarse)

cours·er
cour·te·ous
cour·te·san
cour·te·sy
court·house
court·ier
court·li·ness
court·ly
court-mar·tial
  pl courts-martial

court·room
court·ship
court·yard
cous·in
cov·en
cov·e·nant
cov·er
cov·er·age
cov·er·all
cov·er·let
co·vert
cov·et
cov·et·ous
cov·ey
cow·ard
cow·ard·ice
cow·ard·li·ness
cow·bell
cow·boy
cow·er

cow·hide
cow·lick
cowl·ing
co-work·er
cow·poke
cow·punch·er
cow·slip
cox·comb
cox·swain
coy·ly
coy·ness
coy·ote
coz·en
co·zi·ly
co·zi·ness
co·zy
crab·bed
crab·by
crack·down
crack·er
crack·er·jack
  also crack·a·jack

crack·le
crack·pot
crack-up
cra·dle
craft·i·ness
crafts·man
crafty
crag·gy
cram
  crammed
  cram·ming
cran·ber·ry
cra·ni·al

cra·ni·um
  pl cra·ni·ums *or*
    cra·nia
crank·case
crank·i·ly
crank·i·ness
crank·shaft
cranky
cran·ny
crap·shoot·er
crash-land
crass·ly
cra·ter
cra·vat
cra·ven
crav·ing
craw·fish
cray·fish
cray·on
cra·zi·ly
cra·zi·ness
cra·zy
creak
  squeak (see creek)

creaky
cream·ery
creamy
cre·ate
cre·ation
cre·ative
cre·ativ·i·ty
cre·ator
crea·ture
crèche
cre·dence
cre·den·tial

cred·i·bil·i·ty
cred·i·ble
cred·it
cred·it·able
cred·it·ably
cred·i·tor
cre·do
  pl cre·dos
cre·du·li·ty
cred·u·lous
creek
  stream (see creak)

creel
creep
  crept
  creep·ing
creep·er
creepy
cre·mate
cre·ma·tion
cre·ma·to·ry
cren·el·late
  or cren·el·ate

cren·el·la·tion
Cre·ole
cre·o·sote
crepe
  or crêpe

cre·pus·cu·lar
cre·scen·do
  pl cre·scen·dos
    or cre·scen·does

cres·cent
crest·fall·en
cre·ta·ceous

cre·tin
cre·tonne
cre·vasse
crev·ice
crib
  cribbed
  crib·bing
crib·bage
crick·et
cri·er
crim·i·nal
crim·i·nal·i·ty
crim·i·nal·ly
crim·i·no·log·i·cal
crim·i·nol·o·gist
crim·i·nol·o·gy
crim·son
cringe
crin·kle
crin·kly
crin·o·line
crip·ple
cri·sis
crisp·ly
crisp·ness
crispy
criss·cross
cri·te·ri·on
  pl cri·te·ria

crit·ic
crit·i·cal
crit·i·cal·ly
crit·i·cism
crit·i·cize

cri·tique
crit·ter
croak
cro·chet
crock·ery
croc·o·dile
cro·cus
  pl cro·cus·es *also*
  cro·ci
crois·sant
cro·ny
crook·ed
croon·er
crop
  cropped
  crop·ping
crop·land
crop·per
cro·quet
  game (see croquette)
cro·quette
  food (see croquet)
cro·sier
cross·bar
cross·bow
cross·breed
cross-coun·try
cross-cur·rent
cross-cut
cross-ex·am·i·na·tion
cross-ex·am·ine
cross-eye
cross-eyed
cross·hatch
cross·ing

cross·over
cross·piece
cross-pol·li·nate
cross-pol·li·na·tion
cross-pur·pose
cross-ques·tion
cross-re·fer
cross-ref·er·ence
cross·road
cross·walk
cross·wise
crotch
crotch·et
crotch·et·i·ness
crotch·ety
crou·pi·er
crou·ton
crow·bar
crow·foot
cru·cial
cru·ci·ble
cru·ci·fix
cru·ci·fix·ion
cru·ci·form
cru·ci·fy
crude·ly
cru·el
cru·el·ly
cru·el·ty
cru·et
cruis·er
crul·ler
crum·ble
crum·bly
crum·pet

crum·ple

cru·sade

cru·sad·er

crus·ta·cean

crust·al

crusty

crutch

crux
   pl crux·es
     also cru·ces

cru·zei·ro
   pl cru·zei·ros

cry·ba·by

cryo·bi·o·log·i·cal

cryo·bi·ol·o·gist

cryo·bi·ol·o·gy

cryo·gen·ic

cryo·gen·i·cal·ly

cryo·gen·ics

cryo·sur·gery

crypt

cryp·tic

cryp·to·gram

cryp·tog·ra·pher

cryp·tog·ra·phy

crys·tal

crys·tal·line

crys·tal·li·za·tion

crys·tal·lize

Cu·ba

Cu·ban

cub·by·hole

cu·bic

cu·bi·cal
   like a cube (see
    cubicle)

cu·bi·cle
   compartment (see
    cubical)

cu·bit

cuck·old

cuck·oo
   pl cuck·oos

cu·cum·ber

cud·dle

cud·gel

cue
   signal (see queue)

cui·sine

cul-de-sac
   pl culs-de-sac *also*
    cul-de-sacs

cu·li·nary

cull

cul·mi·nate

cul·mi·na·tion

cul·pa·ble

cul·prit

cult·ist

cul·ti·va·ble

cul·ti·vat·able

cul·ti·vate

cul·ti·va·tion

cul·ti·va·tor

cul·tur·al

cul·tur·al·ly

cul·ture

cul·tured

cul·vert

cum·ber·some

cum·brous

cum·mer·bund

cu·mu·la·tive

cu·mu·lus

cu·ne·i·form

cun·ning

cup·bear·er

cup·board

cup·cake

cup·ful

cu·pid

cu·pid·i·ty

cu·po·la

cur·able

cu·rate

cu·ra·tive

cu·ra·tor

curb·ing

cur·dle

cu·ré

cure-all

cur·few

cu·ria

cu·rio
   pl cu·ri·os

cu·ri·os·i·ty

cu·ri·ous

cu·ri·ous·ly

cu·ri·um

curl·er

curli·cue

curly

cur·rant
   berry (see current)

cur·ren·cy

cur·rent
   present, stream (see
    currant)

cur·ric·u·lum
pl cur·ric·u·la *also*
cur·ric·u·lums

cur·ry
cur·ry·comb
cur·sive
cur·so·ri·ly
cur·so·ry
cur·tail
cur·tain
curt·ly
curt·sy
or curt·sey

cur·va·ture
curve
cush·ion
cus·pi·dor
cus·tard
cus·to·di·al
cus·to·di·an
cus·to·dy
cus·tom
cus·tom·ari·ly
cus·tom·ary
cus·tom-built
cus·tom·er
cus·tom·house
cus·tom-made
cut
  cut
  cut·ting
cut-and-dried
cu·ta·ne·ous
cut·back
cu·ti·cle
cut·lass

cut·lery
cut·let
cut·off
cut·ter
cut·throat
cut·ting
cut·tle·bone
cut·tle·fish
cut·up
cut·worm
cy·a·nide
cy·ber·nat·ed
cy·ber·na·tion
cy·ber·net·ics
cy·cla·mate
cy·cla·men
cy·cle
cy·clic
cy·cli·cal
cy·clist
cy·clom·e·ter
cy·clone
cy·clon·ic
cy·clo·pe·dia
  or cy·clo·pae·dia
cy·clo·tron
cyg·net
cyl·in·der
cy·lin·dri·cal
  or cy·lin·dric

cym·bal
  musical instrument
  (*see* symbol)

cyn·ic
cyn·i·cal
cyn·i·cism

cy·no·sure
cy·press
Cyp·ri·ot
  or Cyp·ri·ote

Cy·prus
cyst
cys·tic
cy·to·plasm
czar
  or tsar *or* tzar

cza·ri·na
czar·ism
czar·ist
Czech
Czecho·slo·vak
Czecho·slo·va·kia
Czecho·slo·va·ki·
  an

D

dab
  dabbed
  dab·bing
dab·ble
dab·bler
dachs·hund
dac·tyl
dac·tyl·ic
dad·dy
daf·fo·dil
daf·fy
dag·ger
da·guerre·o·type
dahl·ia

dai·ly
dain·ti·ly
dain·ti·ness
dain·ty
dai·qui·ri
dairy
dairy·maid
dairy·man
da·is
dai·sy
da·la·si
Dal·las
dal·li·ance
dal·ly
  dal·lied
  dal·ly·ing
dal·ma·tian
dam
  stop up (see damn)

  dammed
  dam·ming
dam·age
dam·a·scene
dam·ask
damn
  condemn (see dam)

dam·na·ble
dam·na·bly
dam·na·tion
damp·en
damp·en·er
damp·er
damp·ness
dam·sel
dam·son

danc·er
dan·de·li·on
dan·der
dan·di·fy
dan·dle
dan·druff
dan·dy
dan·dy·ish
dan·ger
dan·ger·ous
dan·gle
Dan·ish
dan·seuse
dap·per
dap·ple
dare·dev·il
dar·ing
dark·en
dark·room
dar·ling
dash·board
dash·ing
das·tard·ly
da·ta
date·less
date·line
da·tive
da·tum
  pl da·ta *or* da·tums

daugh·ter
daugh·ter-in-law
  pl daugh·ters-in-law

daunt·less
dau·phin
dav·en·port

da·vit
daw·dle
daw·dler
day·bed
day·book
day·break
day·dream
day·light
day·time
Day·ton
daz·zle
daz·zling·ly
dea·con
dea·con·ess
de·ac·ti·vate
de·ac·ti·va·tion
dead·beat
dead·en
dead·line
dead·li·ness
dead·lock
dead·ly
dead·pan
dead·weight
dead·wood
deaf·en
deaf-mute
deaf·ness
deal
  dealt
  deal·ing
dean·ery
Dear·born
dear·ly
dearth
death·bed

death·blow
death·less
death·ly
death's-head
death·watch
de·ba·cle
de·bar
de·bark
de·bar·ka·tion
de·base
de·bat·able
de·bate
de·bat·er
de·bauch
de·bauch·ery
de·ben·ture
de·bil·i·tate
de·bil·i·ta·tion
de·bil·i·ty
deb·it
deb·o·nair
de·bouch
de·brief
de·bris
   pl de·bris

debt·or
de·bunk
de·but
deb·u·tante
de·cade
dec·a·dence
dec·a·dent
de·cal
de·cal·co·ma·nia
deca·logue

de·camp
de·cant
de·cant·er
de·cap·i·tate
de·cap·i·ta·tion
deca·syl·lab·ic
de·cath·lon
de·cay
de·cease
de·ceased
de·ce·dent
de·ceit
de·ceit·ful
de·ceit·ful·ly
de·ceive
de·ceiv·er
de·cel·er·ate
de·cel·er·a·tion
de·cel·er·a·tor
De·cem·ber
de·cen·cy
de·cen·ni·al
de·cen·ni·al·ly
de·cent
   proper (*see* descent, dissent)

de·cen·tral·iza·
  tion
de·cen·tral·ize
de·cep·tion
de·cep·tive·ly
deci·bel
de·cide
de·cid·ed
de·cid·u·ous
dec·i·mal

dec·i·mal·ize
dec·i·mal·ly
dec·i·mate
de·ci·pher
de·ci·pher·able
de·ci·sion
de·ci·sive
de·ci·sive·ness
deck·hand
deck·le
de·claim
dec·la·ma·tion
de·clam·a·to·ry
dec·la·ra·tion
de·clar·a·tive
de·clar·a·to·ry
de·clare
de·clar·er
de·clas·si·fy
de·clen·sion
de·clin·able
dec·li·nate
dec·li·na·tion
de·cline
de·cliv·i·ty
de·code
dé·col·le·tage
dé·col·le·té
de·col·o·ni·za·
  tion
de·com·mis·sion
de·com·pose
de·com·po·si·tion
de·com·press
de·com·pres·sion

de·con·tam·i·nate
de·con·tam·i·na·
    tion
de·con·trol
de·cor
    or dé·cor

dec·o·rate
dec·o·ra·tion
dec·o·ra·tive
dec·o·ra·tor
dec·o·rous
de·co·rum
de·coy
de·crease
de·cree
dec·re·ment
de·crep·it
de·crep·i·tate
de·crep·i·tude
de·cre·scen·do
de·cry
ded·i·cate
ded·i·ca·tion
ded·i·ca·to·ry
de·duce
de·duc·ible
de·duct
de·duct·ible
de·duc·tion
de·duc·tive
deep·en
deep·ly
deep-root·ed
deep-sea
deep-seat·ed

deer·skin
de-es·ca·late
de-es·ca·la·tion
de·face
de·face·ment
de fac·to
de·fal·cate
de·fal·ca·tion
de·fal·ca·tor
def·a·ma·tion
de·fam·a·to·ry
de·fame
de·fault
de·fault·er
de·feat
de·feat·ism
de·feat·ist
def·e·cate
def·e·ca·tion
de·fect
de·fec·tion
de·fec·tive
de·fec·tor
de·fend
de·fen·dant
de·fend·er
de·fense
    or de·fence

de·fense·less
de·fen·si·ble
de·fen·sive
de·fer
    de·ferred
    de·fer·ring
def·er·ence
    respect (*see* difference)

def·er·en·tial
de·fer·ment
de·fer·ra·ble
de·fi·ance
de·fi·ant
de·fi·cien·cy
de·fi·cient
def·i·cit
de·file
de·file·ment
de·fin·able
de·fine
de·fin·er
def·i·nite
def·i·ni·tion
de·fin·i·tive
de·flate
de·fla·tion
de·fla·tion·ary
de·flect
de·flec·tion
de·flec·tor
de·fo·li·ant
de·fo·li·ate
de·fo·li·a·tion
de·for·es·ta·tion
de·form
de·for·ma·tion
de·for·mi·ty
de·fraud
de·fray
de·fray·al
de·frost
deft·ly
de·funct
de·fy

de·gen·er·a·cy
de·gen·er·ate
de·gen·er·a·tion
de·gen·er·a·tive
de·grad·able
deg·ra·da·tion
de·grade
de·gree
de·gree-day
de·hu·man·iza·
   tion
de·hu·man·ize
de·hu·mid·i·fy
de·hy·drate
de·hy·dra·tion
de·hy·dro·ge·nate
de·hy·dro·ge·na·
   tion
de·ice
de·ic·er
de·i·fi·ca·tion
de·i·fy
deign
de·ism
de·is·tic
de·i·ty
de·ject·ed
de·jec·tion
de ju·re
Del·a·ware
de·lay
de·le
de·lec·ta·ble
de·lec·ta·tion
del·e·gate
del·e·ga·tion

de·lete
del·e·te·ri·ous
de·le·tion
delft·ware
de·lib·er·ate
de·lib·er·ate·ness
de·lib·er·a·tion
de·lib·er·a·tive
del·i·ca·cy
del·i·cate
del·i·cate·ly
del·i·ca·tes·sen
de·li·cious
de·light
de·light·ed
de·light·ful·ly
de·lim·it
de·lin·eate
de·lin·ea·tion
de·lin·quen·cy
de·lin·quent
del·i·quesce
del·i·ques·cent
de·lir·i·ous
de·lir·i·um tre·
   mens
de·liv·er
de·liv·er·ance
de·liv·er·er
de·liv·ery
de·louse
del·phin·i·um
del·ta
de·lude
del·uge
de·lu·sion

de·lu·sive
de·luxe
delve
de·mag·ne·tize
dem·a·gog·ic
dem·a·gogue
   or dem·a·gog

dem·a·gogu·ery
dem·a·gogy
de·mand
de·mar·cate
de·mar·ca·tion
de·marche
de·mean
de·mean·or
de·ment·ed
de·men·tia
de·mer·it
de·mesne
demi·god
demi·john
de·mil·i·tar·i·za·
   tion
de·mil·i·ta·rize
de·mi·monde
de·mise
demi·tasse
de·mo·bi·li·za·
   tion
de·mo·bi·lize
de·moc·ra·cy
dem·o·crat
dem·o·crat·ic
dem·o·crat·i·cal·
   ly

Dem·o·crat·ic
  Kam·pu·chea
de·moc·ra·ti·za·
  tion
de·moc·ra·tize
de·mog·ra·pher
de·mo·graph·ic
de·mo·graph·i·
  cal·ly
de·mog·ra·phy
de·mol·ish
de·mo·li·tion
de·mon
  or dae·mon

de·mon·e·ti·za·
  tion
de·mon·e·tize
de·mo·ni·ac
de·mo·ni·a·cal·ly
de·mon·ic
de·mon·i·cal·ly
de·mon·ol·o·gy
dem·on·strate
dem·on·stra·tion
dem·on·stra·tive
dem·on·stra·tor
de·mor·al·iza·tion
de·mor·al·ize
de·mote
de·mot·ic
de·mo·tion
de·mul·cent
de·mur
  object (see demure)

de·murred
de·mur·ring
de·mure
  prim (see demur)

de·mur·rage
de·mur·rer
de·na·tion·al·iza·
  tion
de·na·tion·al·ize
de·nat·u·ral·iza·
  tion
de·nat·u·ral·ize
de·na·tur·ant
de·na·ture
den·dri·form
den·dro·chron·o·
  log·i·cal·ly
den·dro·chro·nol·
  o·gy
den·dro·log·ic
den·drol·o·gist
den·drol·o·gy
den·gue
de·ni·al
de·ni·er
  one that denies

de·nier
  coin

den·i·grate
den·im
den·i·zen
Den·mark
de·nom·i·nate
de·nom·i·na·tion
de·nom·i·na·tor

de·no·ta·tion
de·no·ta·tive
de·note
de·noue·ment
de·nounce
dense·ly
den·si·ty
den·tal
den·tal·ly
den·ti·frice
den·tin
  or den·tine

den·tist
den·tist·ry
den·ti·tion
den·ture
de·nu·da·tion
de·nude
de·nun·ci·a·tion
Den·ver
de·ny
de·odor·ant
de·odor·ize
de·odor·iz·er
de·ox·i·dize
de·ox·i·diz·er
de·oxy·ri·bo·nu·
  cle·ic acid
de·part
de·part·ment
de·part·men·tal
de·part·men·tal·
  ize
de·par·ture
de·pend

de·pend·abil·i·ty
de·pend·able
de·pen·dence
  also de·pen·dance

de·pen·den·cy
de·pen·dent
de·per·son·al·iza·
  tion
de·per·son·al·ize
de·pict
de·pic·tion
de·pil·a·to·ry
de·plane
de·plete
de·ple·tion
de·plor·able
de·plore
de·ploy
de·po·lar·iza·tion
de·po·lar·ize
de·po·nent
de·pop·u·late
de·pop·u·la·tion
de·port
de·por·ta·tion
de·por·tee
de·port·ment
de·pose
de·pos·it
de·po·si·tion
de·pos·i·tor
de·pos·i·to·ry
de·pot
de·pra·va·tion
  corruption (see
  deprivation)

de·prave
de·praved
de·prav·i·ty
dep·re·cate
dep·re·ca·tion
dep·re·ca·to·ry
de·pre·ci·ate
de·pre·ci·a·tion
dep·re·da·tion
de·press
de·pres·sant
de·pres·sion
dep·ri·va·tion
  loss (see depravation)

de·prive
depth
dep·u·ta·tion
de·pute
dep·u·tize
dep·u·ty
de·rail
de·range
de·range·ment
der·by
der·e·lict
der·e·lic·tion
de·ride
de ri·gueur
de·ri·sion
de·ri·sive
der·i·va·tion
de·riv·a·tive
de·rive
der·ma·ti·tis
der·ma·tol·o·gist

der·ma·tol·o·gy
der·mis
der·o·gate
der·o·ga·tion
de·rog·a·to·ri·ly
de·rog·a·to·ry
der·rick
der·ri·ere
  or der·ri·ère

der·ring-do
der·rin·ger
der·vish
de·sal·i·nate
de·sal·i·na·tion
de·sal·i·ni·za·tion
de·sal·i·nize
de·salt
des·cant
de·scend
de·scen·dant
  or de·scen·dent

de·scent
  decline (see decent,
  dissent)

de·scrib·able
de·scribe
de·scrip·tion
de·scrip·tive
de·scrip·tor
de·scry
des·e·crate
des·e·cra·tion
de·seg·re·gate
de·seg·re·ga·tion
de·sen·si·ti·za·
  tion

de·sen·si·tize
de·sen·si·tiz·er
des·ert
  barren area (see
    dessert)

de·sert
  leave (see dessert)

de·sert·er
de·ser·tion
de·serve
de·served·ly
de·serv·ing
des·ic·cant
des·ic·cate
des·ic·ca·tion
des·ic·ca·tor
de·sid·er·a·tum
  pl de·sid·er·a·ta

de·sign
des·ig·nate
des·ig·na·tion
de·sign·er
de·sign·ing
de·sir·abil·i·ty
de·sir·able
de·sire
de·sir·ous
de·sist
Des Moines
des·o·late
des·o·late·ly
des·o·la·tion
des·oxy·ri·bo·nu·
  cle·ic acid
de·spair
de·spair·ing·ly

des·patch
  var of dispatch

des·per·a·do
  pl des·per·a·does *or*
    des·per·a·dos

des·per·ate
  hopeless (see
    disparate)

des·per·ate·ly
des·per·a·tion
de·spi·ca·ble
des·pi·ca·bly
de·spise
de·spite
de·spoil
de·spoil·ment
de·spo·li·a·tion
de·spond
de·spon·den·cy
de·spon·dent
des·pot
des·pot·ic
des·pot·i·cal·ly
des·po·tism
des·sert
  sweet food (see desert)

des·ti·na·tion
des·tine
des·ti·ny
des·ti·tute
des·ti·tu·tion
de·stroy
de·stroy·er
de·struct
de·struc·ti·bil·i·
  ty

de·struc·ti·ble
de·struc·tion
de·struc·tive
de·struc·tive·ness
de·struc·tor
de·sue·tude
des·ul·to·ry
de·tach
de·tach·able
de·tached
de·tach·ment
de·tail
de·tain
de·tain·ee
de·tect
de·tect·able
de·tec·tion
de·tec·tive
de·tec·tor
dé·tente
de·ten·tion
de·ter
  de·terred
  de·ter·ring
de·ter·gent
de·te·ri·o·rate
de·te·ri·o·ra·tion
de·ter·min·able
de·ter·min·ably
de·ter·mi·na·cy
de·ter·mi·nant
de·ter·mi·nate
de·ter·mi·na·tion
de·ter·mine
de·ter·mined
de·ter·mined·ly

de·ter·mined·ness
de·ter·min·ism
de·ter·min·ist
de·ter·rence
de·ter·rent
de·test
de·test·able
de·test·ably
de·tes·ta·tion
de·throne
de·throne·ment
det·o·nate
det·o·na·tion
det·o·na·tor
de·tour
de·tract
de·trac·tion
de·trac·tor
de·train
det·ri·ment
det·ri·men·tal·ly
de·tri·tus
De·troit
deuce
deu·te·ri·um
deut·sche mark
de·val·u·a·tion
de·val·ue
dev·as·tate
dev·as·ta·tion
de·vel·op
de·vel·op·er
de·vel·op·ment
de·vel·op·men·
  tal·ly
de·vi·ant

de·vi·ate
de·vi·a·tion
de·vice
  mechanism (see
  devise)

dev·il
  dev·iled
    or dev·illed

  dev·il·ing
    or dev·il·ling

dev·il·ish
dev·il·ment
dev·il·ry
  or dev·il·try

de·vi·ous
de·vis·able
de·vise
  invent (see device)

de·vi·tal·ize
de·vit·ri·fy
de·void
de·vo·lu·tion
de·volve
de·vote
de·vot·ed
dev·o·tee
de·vo·tion
de·vo·tion·al
de·vour
de·vour·er
de·vout
de·vout·ness
dew
dew·ber·ry
dew·drop

dew·lap
dewy
dex·ter·i·ty
dex·ter·ous
  or dex·trous

dex·trose
dhow
di·a·be·tes
di·a·bet·ic
di·a·bol·ic
  or di·a·bol·i·cal

di·a·bol·i·cal·ly
di·a·crit·ic
di·a·crit·i·cal
di·a·dem
di·aer·e·sis
  or di·er·e·sis
  pl di·aer·e·ses
    or di·er·e·ses

di·ag·nose
di·ag·no·sis
  pl di·ag·no·ses

di·ag·nos·tic
di·ag·nos·ti·cal·ly
di·ag·nos·ti·cian
di·ag·o·nal
di·ag·o·nal·ly
di·a·gram
  di·a·gramed
    or di·a·grammed

  di·a·gram·ing
    or di·a·gram·ming

di·a·gram·mat·ic
di·a·gram·mat·i·
  cal·ly
di·al

di·aled
  or di·alled

di·al·ing
  or di·al·ling

di·a·lect
di·a·lec·tic
di·a·logue
  or di·a·log

di·am·e·ter
di·a·met·ri·cal·ly
di·a·mond
di·a·mond·back
di·a·pa·son
di·a·per
di·aph·a·nous
di·a·phragm
di·a·phrag·mat·ic
di·a·rist
di·ar·rhea
  or di·ar·rhoea

di·a·ry
di·as·to·le
di·a·stroph·ic
di·as·tro·phism
dia·ther·my
dia·ton·ic
dia·ton·i·cal·ly
di·a·tribe
dib·ble
dice
di·chot·o·my
dick·er
dick·ey
  or dicky

di·cot·y·le·don

di·cot·y·le·don·
  ous
Dic·ta·phone
dic·tate
dic·ta·tion
dic·ta·tor
dic·ta·to·ri·al
dic·ta·tor·ship
dic·tion
dic·tio·nary
Dic·to·graph
dic·tum
  pl dic·ta *also*
  dic·tums

di·dac·tic
di·dac·ti·cal·ly
di·dac·ti·cism
die
  expire (see dye)

died
dy·ing
die
  pl dice *or* dies
  spotted cube, tool
  (*see* dye)

die·hard
di·elec·tric
di·er·e·sis
  var of diaeresis

die·sel
di·et
di·etary
di·etet·ic
di·etet·ics
di·eti·tian
  or di·eti·cian

dif·fer
dif·fer·ence
  unlikeness (*see*
  deference)

dif·fer·ent
dif·fer·en·tial
dif·fer·en·ti·ate
dif·fer·en·ti·a·
  tion
dif·fi·cult
dif·fi·cul·ty
dif·fi·dence
dif·fi·dent
dif·frac·tion
dif·fuse
dif·fu·sion
dig
  dug
  dig·ging
di·gest
di·gest·ibil·i·ty
di·gest·ible
di·ges·tion
di·ges·tive
dig·ger
dig·it
dig·i·tal
dig·i·tal·is
dig·i·tal·ly
dig·ni·fied
dig·ni·fy
dig·ni·tary
dig·ni·ty
di·gress
di·gres·sion
di·gres·sive

di·lap·i·dat·ed
di·lap·i·da·tion
di·la·ta·tion
di·late
di·la·tion
dil·a·to·ry
di·lem·ma
dil·et·tante
 pl dil·et·tantes *or*
 dil·et·tan·ti

dil·i·gence
dil·i·gent
dil·ly·dal·ly
dil·u·ent
di·lute
di·lu·tion
dim
 dimmed
 dim·ming
di·men·sion
di·men·sion·al
di·min·ish
di·min·u·en·do
dim·i·nu·tion
di·min·u·tive
dim·i·ty
dim·ly
dim·mer
dim·out
dim·ple
di·nar
din·er
 one that dines (see
 dinner)

di·nette

din·ghy
 boat (see dingy)

din·gi·ness
din·gy
 shabby (see dinghy)

din·ky
din·ner
 meal (see diner)

din·ner·ware
di·no·saur
di·oc·e·san
di·o·cese
di·o·ra·ma
di·ox·ide
dip
 dipped
 dip·ping
diph·the·ria
diph·thong
di·plo·ma
di·plo·ma·cy
dip·lo·mat
dip·lo·mat·ic
dip·lo·mat·i·cal·
 ly
di·plo·ma·tist
dip·per
dip·so·ma·nia
dip·so·ma·ni·ac
dip·stick
dip·ter·an
dip·ter·ous
di·rect
di·rec·tion
di·rec·tion·al

di·rec·tive
di·rect·ly
di·rec·tor
di·rec·tor·ate
di·rec·tor·ship
di·rec·to·ry
dire·ful
dirge
dir·ham
di·ri·gi·ble
dirndl
dirt·i·ness
dirty
dis·abil·i·ty
dis·able
dis·abuse
dis·ad·van·tage
dis·ad·van·ta·
 geous
dis·af·fect
dis·af·fec·tion
dis·agree
dis·agree·able
dis·agree·ably
dis·agree·ment
dis·al·low
dis·al·low·ance
dis·ap·pear
dis·ap·pear·ance
dis·ap·point
dis·ap·point·ment
dis·ap·pro·ba·tion
dis·ap·prov·al
dis·ap·prove
dis·arm
dis·ar·ma·ment

dis·ar·range
dis·ar·range·ment
dis·ar·ray
dis·as·sem·ble
dis·as·so·ci·ate
di·sas·ter
di·sas·trous
dis·avow
dis·avow·al
dis·band
dis·bar
dis·bar·ment
dis·be·lief
dis·be·lieve
dis·be·liev·er
dis·bur·den
dis·burse
   pay out (see disperse)

dis·burse·ment
disc
   var of disk

dis·card
dis·cern
dis·cern·ible
dis·cern·ing
dis·cern·ment
dis·charge
dis·charge·able
dis·ci·ple
dis·ci·pli·nar·i·an
dis·ci·plin·ary
dis·ci·pline
dis·claim
dis·claim·er
dis·close

dis·clo·sure
dis·cog·ra·pher
dis·cog·ra·phy
dis·col·or
dis·col·or·ation
dis·com·bob·u·
   late
dis·com·fit
dis·com·fi·ture
dis·com·fort
dis·com·mode
dis·com·pose
dis·com·po·sure
dis·con·cert
dis·con·nect
dis·con·nect·ed
dis·con·so·late
dis·con·tent
dis·con·tinu·ance
dis·con·tin·ue
dis·con·ti·nu·ity
dis·con·tin·u·ous
dis·co·phile
dis·cord
dis·cor·dant
dis·co·theque
dis·count
dis·count·able
dis·coun·te·nance
dis·cour·age
dis·cour·age·ment
dis·course
dis·cour·te·ous
dis·cour·te·sy
dis·cov·er
dis·cov·er·er

dis·cov·ery
dis·cred·it
dis·cred·it·able
dis·creet
   prudent (see discrete)

dis·crep·an·cy
dis·crep·ant
dis·crete
   distinct (see discreet)

dis·cre·tion
dis·cre·tion·ary
dis·crim·i·nate
dis·crim·i·nat·ing
dis·crim·i·na·tion
dis·crim·i·na·to·
   ry
dis·cur·sive
dis·cus
   disk (see discuss)

dis·cuss
   argue (see discus)

dis·cus·sant
dis·cus·sion
dis·dain
dis·dain·ful·ly
dis·ease
dis·em·bark
dis·em·bar·ka·
   tion
dis·em·body
dis·em·bow·el
dis·em·bow·el·
   ment
dis·en·chant
dis·en·cum·ber

dis·en·gage
dis·en·tan·gle
dis·es·tab·lish
dis·es·tab·lish·
  ment
dis·es·teem
dis·fa·vor
dis·fig·ure
dis·fig·ure·ment
dis·fran·chise
dis·gorge
dis·grace
dis·grace·ful·ly
dis·grun·tle
dis·guise
dis·gust
dis·gust·ed·ly
dis·ha·bille
dis·har·mo·ny
dish·cloth
dis·heart·en
di·shev·el
  di·shev·eled
  or di·shev·elled

  di·shev·el·ing
  or di·shev·el·ling

dis·hon·est
dis·hon·es·ty
dis·hon·or
dis·hon·or·able
dis·hon·or·ably
dish·rag
dish·wash·er
dish·wa·ter
dis·il·lu·sion

dis·il·lu·sion·
  ment
dis·in·cli·na·tion
dis·in·cline
dis·in·fect
dis·in·fec·tant
dis·in·fec·tion
dis·in·gen·u·ous
dis·in·her·it
dis·in·te·grate
dis·in·te·gra·tion
dis·in·ter
dis·in·ter·est·ed
dis·in·ter·est·ed·
  ness
dis·join
dis·joint
dis·joint·ed
disk
  or disc

dis·like
dis·lo·cate
dis·lo·ca·tion
dis·lodge
dis·loy·al
dis·loy·al·ty
dis·mal
dis·mal·ly
dis·man·tle
dis·may
dis·mem·ber
dis·mem·ber·
  ment
dis·miss
dis·miss·al

dis·mount
dis·obe·di·ence
dis·obe·di·ent
dis·obey
dis·or·der
dis·or·der·ly
dis·or·ga·ni·za·
  tion
dis·or·ga·nize
dis·own
dis·par·age
dis·par·age·ment
dis·par·ag·ing·ly
dis·pa·rate
  dissimilar (see
  desperate)

dis·par·i·ty
dis·pas·sion·ate
dis·pas·sion·ate·
  ly
dis·patch
  or des·patch

dis·patch·er
dis·pel
  dis·pelled
  dis·pel·ling
dis·pens·able
dis·pen·sa·ry
dis·pen·sa·tion
dis·pense
dis·pens·er
dis·pers·al
dis·perse
  spread (see disburse)

dis·per·sion
dispir·it

distortion

dis·place
dis·place·ment
dis·play
dis·please
dis·plea·sure
dis·port
dis·pos·able
dis·pos·al
dis·pose
dis·pos·er
dis·po·si·tion
dis·pos·sess
dis·pos·ses·sion
dis·proof
dis·pro·por·tion
dis·pro·por·tion·
  ate
dis·prove
dis·pu·ta·ble
dis·pu·tant
dis·pu·ta·tion
dis·pu·ta·tious
dis·pute
dis·put·er
dis·qual·i·fi·ca·
  tion
dis·qual·i·fy
dis·qui·et
dis·qui·etude
dis·qui·si·tion
dis·re·gard
dis·re·gard·ful
dis·re·pair
dis·rep·u·ta·ble
dis·rep·u·ta·bly
dis·re·pute

dis·re·spect
dis·re·spect·ful
dis·robe
dis·rupt
dis·rup·tion
dis·rup·tive
dis·sat·is·fac·tion
dis·sat·is·fy
dis·sect
dis·sect·ed
dis·sec·tion
dis·sem·ble
dis·sem·bler
dis·sem·i·nate
dis·sem·i·na·tion
dis·sen·sion
  also dis·sen·tion

dis·sent
  *disagree (see decent,
  descent)*

dis·sent·er
dis·sen·tient
dis·ser·ta·tion
dis·ser·vice
dis·sev·er
dis·si·dence
dis·si·dent
dis·sim·i·lar
dis·sim·i·lar·i·ty
dis·sim·u·late
dis·sim·u·la·tion
dis·si·pate
dis·si·pat·ed
dis·si·pa·tion
dis·so·ci·ate
dis·so·ci·a·tion

dis·sol·u·ble
dis·so·lute
dis·so·lute·ness
dis·so·lu·tion
dis·solve
dis·so·nance
dis·so·nant
dis·suade
dis·sua·sion
dis·taff
dis·sym·me·try
dis·tance
dis·tant
dis·taste
dis·taste·ful
dis·tem·per
dis·tend
dis·ten·sion
  or dis·ten·tion

dis·tich
dis·ti·chous
dis·till
  also dis·til

dis·til·late
dis·til·la·tion
dis·till·er
dis·till·ery
dis·tinct
dis·tinc·tion
dis·tinc·tive
dis·tin·guish
dis·tin·guish·able
dis·tin·guish·ably
dis·tort
dis·tor·tion

dis·tract
dis·trac·tion
dis·train
dis·trait
dis·traught
dis·tress
dis·tress·ful·ly
dis·trib·ute
dis·tri·bu·tion
dis·trib·u·tive
dis·trib·u·tor
dis·trict
Dis·trict of Co·
  lum·bia
dis·trust
dis·trust·ful·ly
dis·turb
dis·tur·bance
dis·turbed
dis·union
dis·unite
dis·uni·ty
dis·use
ditch
dith·er
dit·to
  pl dit·tos

dit·ty
di·uret·ic
di·ur·nal
di·va
  pl di·vas *or* di·ve

di·va·gate
di·va·ga·tion
di·van

dive
  dived
    or dove

  dived
  div·ing
div·er
di·verge
di·ver·gence
di·ver·gent
di·vers
  various (*see* diverse)

di·verse
  unlike (*see* divers)

di·ver·si·fi·ca·
  tion
di·ver·si·fy
di·ver·sion
di·ver·sion·ary
di·ver·si·ty
di·vert
di·vest
di·vide
div·i·dend
di·vid·er
div·i·na·tion
di·vine
di·vin·er
di·vin·i·ty
di·vis·i·bil·i·ty
di·vis·i·ble
di·vi·sion
di·vi·sion·al
di·vi·sive
di·vi·sor
di·vorce

di·vor·cée
div·ot
di·vulge
diz·zi·ly
diz·zi·ness
diz·zy
Dji·bou·ti
do
  did
  done
  do·ing
  does
dob·bin
do·cent
doc·ile
do·cil·i·ty
dock·age
dock·et
dock·hand
dock·yard
doc·tor
doc·tor·al
doc·tor·ate
doc·tri·naire
doc·trin·al
doc·trine
doc·u·ment
doc·u·men·ta·ry
doc·u·men·ta·tion
dod·der
dodge
do·do
  pl do·does *or* do·dos

doe·skin
doff

dog
 hunt (see dogged)

 dogged
 dog·ging
dog·cart
dog·catch·er
doge
dog-ear
dog·fight
dog·fish
dog·ged
 determined (see dog)

dog·ger·el
dog·house
dog·ma
dog·mat·ic
dog·mat·i·cal·ly
dog·ma·tism
dog·ma·tist
dog·trot
doi·ly
do·ing
do-it-your·self
dol·drums
dole·ful
dole·ful·ly
dol·lar
dol·lop
dol·ly
dol·men
do·lor
do·lor·ous
dol·phin
dolt·ish
do·main

do·mes·tic
do·mes·ti·cal·ly
do·mes·ti·cate
do·mes·ti·ca·tion
do·mes·tic·i·ty
do·mi·cile
do·mi·cil·i·ary
dom·i·nance
dom·i·nant
dom·i·nate
dom·i·na·tion
dom·i·neer
Dom·in·i·ca
Do·min·i·can Re·
 pub·lic
do·min·ion
dom·i·no
 pl dom·i·noes *or*
 dom·i·nos

don
 donned
 don·ning
do·nate
do·na·tion
dong
don·key
don·ny·brook
do·nor
doo·dad
doo·dle
doo·dler
dooms·day
door·jamb
door·keep·er
door·knob
door·man

door·mat
door·plate
door·step
door·way
door·yard
dop·ant
dor·man·cy
dor·mant
dor·mer
dor·mi·to·ry
dor·mouse
 pl dor·mice

dor·sal
do·ry
dos·age
dos·sier
dot
 dot·ted
 dot·ting
dot·age
dot·ard
dot·ing
dou·ble
dou·ble-cross
dou·ble-cross·er
dou·ble-deal·er
dou·ble-deal·ing
dou·ble-deck·er
dou·ble en·ten·
 dre
dou·ble·head·er
dou·ble-park
dou·ble-quick
dou·ble-space
dou·blet

dou·ble-talk
dou·ble·think
dou·bloon
dou·bly
doubt
doubt·ful
doubt·ful·ly
doubt·less
douche
dough
dough·boy
dough·nut
dough·ty
doughy
dour
douse
dove·cote
 or dove·cot

Do·ver
dove·tail
dow·a·ger
dowd·i·ly
dowd·i·ness
dowdy
dow·el
dow·er
down·beat
down·cast
down·fall
down·fall·en
down·grade
down·heart·ed
down·hill
down·pour
down·range

down·right
down·stage
down·stairs
down·stream
down·stroke
down·swing
down-to-earth
down·town
down·trod·den
down·turn
down·ward
 or down·wards
down·wind
downy
dow·ry
dox·ol·o·gy
doze
doz·en
doz·enth
drach·ma
dra·co·ni·an
draft·ee
drafts·man
drafty
drag
 dragged
 drag·ging
drag·net
drag·o·man
 pl drag·o·mans or
 drag·o·men
drag·on
drag·on·fly
dra·goon
drain·age
drain·pipe

dra·ma
dra·mat·ic
dra·mat·i·cal·ly
dra·ma·tist
dra·ma·ti·za·tion
dra·ma·tize
dra·ma·tur·gy
drap·er
drap·ery
dras·tic
dras·ti·cal·ly
draw
 drew
 drawn
 draw·ing
draw·back
draw·bridge
draw·er
draw·ing
drawl
draw·string
dread·ful
dread·ful·ly
dread·nought
dream
 dreamed
 or dreamt
 dream·ing
dream·er
dream·i·ly
dream·land
dream·like
dream·world
dreamy
drea·ri·ly
drea·ry

dredge
dredg·er
dress·mak·er
dress·mak·ing
dres·sage
dress·er
dress·ing
dressy
drib·ble
drib·let
dri·er
 or dry·er
 noun (see dry)

drift·er
drift·wood
drill·er
drill·mas·ter
drily
drink
 drank
 drunk
  or drank

drink·ing
drink·able
drip
 dripped
 drip·ping
drip-dry
drive
 drove
 driv·en
 driv·ing
drive-in
driv·el
 driv·eled
  or driv·elled

driv·el·ing
 or driv·el·ling

driv·el·er
 or driv·el·ler

driv·er
drive·way
driz·zle
droll·ery
drol·ly
drom·e·dary
drop
 dropped
 drop·ping
drop·kick
drop·let
drop·out
drop·per
drop·sy
dross
drought
 or drouth

drov·er
drowse
drows·i·ly
drows·i·ness
drowsy
drub
 drubbed
 drub·bing
drudge
drudg·ery
drug
 drugged
 drug·ging
drug·gist

drug·store
dru·id
drum
 drummed
 drum·ming
drum·beat
drum·mer
drum·stick
drunk·ard
drunk·en·ness
dry
 adj (see drier)

dri·er
dri·est
dry-clean
dry·er
 noun, var of drier

dry·ly
dry·ness
dry-rot
du·al
 double (see duel)

du·al·ism
du·al·i·ty
du·al·ly
dub
 dubbed
 dub·bing
du·bi·ety
du·bi·ous
du·bi·ous·ness
du·cal
duc·at
duch·ess
duchy

duck·bill
duck·board
duck·ling
duck·pin
duc·tile
duc·til·i·ty
duct·less
dud·geon
du·el
　combat (see dual)

du·el·ist
du·en·de
du·et
duf·fel
　or duf·fle

duf·fer
dug·out
duke·dom
dul·cet
dul·ci·mer
dull·ard
dull·ness
　or dul·ness

dul·ly
Du·luth
du·ly
dumb·bell
dumb·found
　or dum·found

dumb·ly
dumb·wait·er
dum·dum
dum·my
dump·ling
dumpy

dun
　dunned
　dun·ning
dun·der·head
dun·ga·ree
dun·geon
dung·hill
du·o·de·nal
du·o·de·num
　pl du·o·de·na *or*
　du·o·de·nums

du·plex
du·pli·cate
du·pli·ca·tion
du·pli·ca·tor
du·plic·i·ty
du·ra·bil·i·ty
du·ra·ble
du·rance
du·ra·tion
du·ress
dur·ing
dusk·i·ly
dusk·i·ness
dusky
dust·er
dust·i·ly
dust·i·ness
dust·less
dust·pan
dusty
Dutch
du·te·ous
du·ti·able
du·ti·ful
du·ti·ful·ly

du·ty
dwarf
　pl dwarfs *or*
　dwarves

dwarf·ish
dwell
　dwelt
　　or dwelled

dwell·ing
dwin·dle
dyb·buk
　pl dyb·bu·kim *also*
　dyb·buks

dye
　color (see die)

dyed
dye·ing
dye·stuff
dy·nam·ic
dy·nam·i·cal·ly
dy·na·mism
dy·na·mite
dy·na·mo
　pl dy·na·mos

dy·nast
dy·nas·tic
dy·nas·ty
dyne
dy·node
dys·en·tery
dys·pep·sia
dys·pep·tic
dys·pep·ti·cal·ly
dys·tro·phic
dys·tro·phy

E

ea·ger
ea·ger·ly
ea·ger·ness
ea·gle
ea·glet
ear·ache
ear·drum
ear·li·ness
ear·lobe
ear·ly
ear·mark
ear·muff
ear·nest
ear·nest·ly
ear·nest·ness
earn·ings
ear·phone
ear·ring
ear·shot
ear·split·ting
earth·en
earth·en·ware
earth·i·ness
earth·ling
earth·ly
earth·quake
earth·shak·ing
earth·work
earth·worm
earthy
ear·wax
ea·sel
ease·ment
eas·i·ly

eas·i·ness
east·er·ly
east·ern
East·ern·er
east·ward
easy
easy·go·ing
eat
  ate
  eat·en
  eat·ing
eat·able
eat·er
eau de co·logne
  pl eaux de co·logne

eaves
eaves·drop
eaves·drop·per
eb·o·ny
ebul·lience
ebul·lient
eb·ul·li·tion
ec·cen·tric
ec·cen·tri·cal·ly
ec·cen·tric·i·ty
ec·cle·si·as·tic
ec·cle·si·as·ti·cal
ech·e·lon
echo
  pl ech·oes

echo·lo·ca·tion
éclair
éclat
eclec·tic
eclec·ti·cism

eclipse
eclip·tic
ec·logue
eco·log·i·cal
  also eco·log·ic

eco·log·i·cal·ly
ecol·o·gist
ecol·o·gy
eco·nom·ic
eco·nom·i·cal
eco·nom·i·cal·ly
eco·nom·ics
econ·o·mist
econ·o·mize
econ·o·my
eco·sphere
eco·sys·tem
eco·tone
ecru
ec·sta·sy
ec·stat·ic
ec·stat·i·cal·ly
Ec·ua·dor
Ec·ua·dor·an
Ec·ua·dor·ian
ec·u·men·i·cal
ec·u·men·i·cal·ly
ec·u·me·nic·i·ty
ec·ze·ma
ec·zem·a·tous
Edam
ed·dy
edel·weiss
ede·ma
edem·a·tous

edge
edge·ways
edge·wise
edg·i·ness
edg·ing
edgy
ed·i·bil·i·ty
ed·i·ble
edict
ed·i·fi·ca·tion
ed·i·fice
ed·i·fy
ed·it
edi·tion
ed·i·tor
ed·i·to·ri·al
ed·i·to·ri·al·iza·
 tion
ed·i·to·ri·al·ize
ed·i·to·ri·al·iz·er
ed·i·to·ri·al·ly
ed·i·tor·ship
Ed·mon·ton
ed·u·ca·ble
ed·u·cate
ed·u·ca·tion
ed·u·ca·tion·al·ly
ed·u·ca·tor
educe
educ·ible
educ·tion
ee·rie
 also ee·ry

ee·ri·ly
ef·face

ef·face·able
ef·face·ment
ef·fect
 result (see affect*)*

ef·fec·tive
ef·fec·tive·ly
ef·fec·tive·ness
ef·fec·tu·al
ef·fec·tu·al·ly
ef·fec·tu·ate
ef·fem·i·na·cy
ef·fem·i·nate
ef·fer·ent
ef·fer·vesce
ef·fer·ves·cence
ef·fer·ves·cent
ef·fete
ef·fi·ca·cious
ef·fi·ca·cy
ef·fi·cien·cy
ef·fi·cient
ef·fi·cient·ly
ef·fi·gy
ef·flo·resce
ef·flo·res·cence
ef·flu·ence
ef·flu·ent
ef·flu·vi·um
 pl ef·flu·via *or*
 ef·flu·vi·ums

ef·fort
ef·fort·less·ly
ef·fron·tery
ef·ful·gence
ef·ful·gent
ef·fuse

ef·fu·sion
ef·fu·sive
egal·i·tar·i·an
egal·i·tar·i·an·
 ism
egg·beat·er
egg·head
egg·nog
egg·plant
egg·shell
egis
 var of aegis

ego
 pl egos

ego·cen·tric
ego·cen·tric·i·ty
ego·ism
ego·ist
ego·is·tic
 also ego·is·ti·cal

ego·is·ti·cal·ly
ego·tism
ego·tist
ego·tis·tic
 or ego·tis·ti·cal

ego·tis·ti·cal·ly
egre·gious
egress
egret
Egypt
Egyp·tian
ei·der
eigh·teen
eigh·teenth
eighth

eight·i·eth
eighty
ei·ther
ejac·u·late
ejac·u·la·tion
eject
ejec·tion
ejec·tor
eke
ekis·tics
elab·o·rate
elab·o·rate·ly
elab·o·rate·ness
elab·o·ra·tion
élan
elapse
elas·tic
elas·tic·i·ty
elate
ela·tion
el·bow
el·bow·room
el·der·ber·ry
el·der·ly
el·dest
El Do·ra·do
elect·able
elec·tion
elec·tion·eer
elec·tive
elec·tor
elec·tor·al
elec·tor·ate
elec·tric
elec·tri·cal
elec·tri·cal·ly

elec·tri·cian
elec·tric·i·ty
elec·tri·fi·ca·tion
elec·tri·fy
elec·tro·anal·y·sis
elec·tro·an·a·lyt·ic
elec·tro·car·dio·gram
elec·tro·car·dio·graph
elec·tro·car·di·og·ra·phy
elec·tro·chem·i·cal·ly
elec·tro·chem·is·try
elec·tro·cute
elec·tro·cu·tion
elec·trode
elec·tro·en·ceph·a·lo·gram
elec·tro·en·ceph·a·lo·graph
elec·trol·y·sis
elec·tro·lyte
elec·tro·lyt·ic
elec·tro·lyze
elec·tro·mag·net
elec·tro·mag·net·ic
elec·tro·mag·ne·tism
elec·trom·e·ter
elec·tro·mo·tive force

elec·tron
elec·tron·ic
elec·tron·i·cal·ly
elec·tron·ics
elec·tro·plate
elec·tro·shock
elec·tro·ther·a·py
elec·tro·ther·mal
   or elec·tro·ther·mic

elec·tro·type
el·ee·mos·y·nary
el·e·gance
el·e·gant
ele·gi·ac
   also el·e·gi·a·cal

el·e·gize
el·e·gy
el·e·ment
el·e·men·tal
el·e·men·ta·ry
el·e·phant
el·e·phan·ti·a·sis
el·e·phan·tine
el·e·vate
el·e·va·tion
el·e·va·tor
elev·en
elev·enth
elf
   pl elves

elf·in
elf·ish
elic·it
   draw out (see illicit)
elide

el·i·gi·bil·i·ty
el·i·gi·ble
elim·i·nate
elim·i·na·tion
eli·sion
elite
elit·ism
elit·ist
elix·ir
Eliz·a·beth
Eliz·a·be·than
el·lipse
el·lip·sis
   pl el·lip·ses
el·lip·tic
   or el·lip·ti·cal
el·o·cu·tion
el·o·cu·tion·ist
elon·gate
elon·ga·tion
elope
elope·ment
el·o·quence
el·o·quent
El Paso
El Sal·va·dor
else·where
elu·ci·date
elu·ci·da·tion
elude
   evade (see alude)
elu·sive
   evasive (see allusive)
elu·sive·ly
elu·sive·ness

ely·sian
Ely·si·um
ema·ci·ate
ema·ci·a·tion
em·a·nate
em·a·na·tion
eman·ci·pate
eman·ci·pa·tion
eman·ci·pa·tor
emas·cu·late
emas·cu·la·tion
em·balm
em·balm·er
em·bank
em·bank·ment
em·bar·go
   pl em·bar·goes
em·bark
em·bar·ka·tion
em·bar·rass
em·bar·rass·ment
em·bas·sy
em·bat·tle
em·bed
   or im·bed
em·bel·lish
em·bel·lish·ment
em·ber
em·bez·zle
em·bez·zle·ment
em·bez·zler
em·bit·ter
em·bla·zon
em·blem
em·blem·at·ic
   also em·blem·at·i·cal

em·bodi·ment
em·body
em·bold·en
em·bol·ic
em·bo·lism
em·boss
em·bou·chure
em·brace
em·brace·able
em·bra·sure
em·bro·cate
em·bro·ca·tion
em·broi·der
em·broi·dery
em·broil
em·broil·ment
em·bryo
   pl em·bry·os
em·bry·o·log·ic
   or em·bry·o·log·i·cal
em·bry·ol·o·gist
em·bry·ol·o·gy
em·bry·on·ic
em·cee
emend
   correct (see amend)
emen·da·tion
em·er·ald
emerge
emer·gence
emer·gen·cy
emer·gent
emer·i·ta
emer·i·tus
   pl emer·i·ti

em·ery
emet·ic
em·i·grant
em·i·grate
  leave one's country
  (see immigrate)
em·i·gra·tion
émi·gré
  or emi·gré

em·i·nence
em·i·nent
  outstanding (see
  immanent,
  imminent)

emir
em·is·sary
emis·sion
emis·siv·i·ty
emit
  emit·ted
  emit·ting
emol·lient
emol·u·ment
emote
emo·tion
emo·tion·al
emo·tion·al·ly
emo·tive
em·path·ic
em·pa·thy
em·pen·nage
em·per·or
em·pha·sis
  pl em·pha·ses

em·pha·size
em·phat·ic

em·phat·i·cal·ly
em·phy·se·ma
em·pire
em·pir·i·cal
  also em·pir·ic
em·pir·i·cal·ly
em·pir·i·cism
em·pir·i·cist
em·place·ment
em·ploy
em·ploy·abil·i·ty
em·ploy·able
em·ploy·ee
  or em·ploye
em·ploy·er
em·ploy·ment
em·po·ri·um
  pl em·po·ri·ums *also*
  em·po·ria
em·pow·er
em·press
emp·ti·ness
emp·ty
emp·ty-hand·ed
em·py·re·an
emu
em·u·late
em·u·la·tion
em·u·lous
emul·si·fi·able
emul·si·fi·ca·tion
emul·si·fi·er
emul·si·fy
emul·sion
en·able
  en·abled

en·abling
en·act
en·act·ment
enam·el
  enam·eled
  or enam·elled
  enam·el·ing
  or enam·el·ling
enam·el·ware
en·am·or
en bloc
en·camp
en·camp·ment
en·cap·su·late
en·case
en·ceph·a·lit·ic
en·ceph·a·li·tis
en·ceph·a·lo·my·
  eli·tis
en·chain
en·chant
en·chant·er
en·chant·ment
en·chant·ress
en·chi·la·da
en·ci·pher
en·cir·cle
en·cir·cle·ment
en·clave
en·close
en·clo·sure
en·code
en·co·mi·um
  pl en·co·mi·ums *or*
  en·co·mia

en·com·pass

en·core
en·coun·ter
en·cour·age
en·cour·age·ment
en·croach
en·croach·ment
en·crust
   or in·crust

en·cum·ber
en·cum·brance
en·cyc·li·cal
en·cy·clo·pe·dia
   also en·cy·clo·pae·dia
en·cy·clo·pe·dic
   also en·cy·clo·pae·dic

en·cyst
en·dan·ger
en·dear
en·dear·ment
en·deav·or
en·dem·ic
end·ing
en·dive
end·less
end·most
en·do·crine
en·do·cri·nol·o·gy
en·dog·a·mous
en·dog·a·my
en·dorse
   or in·dorse

en·dorse·ment
en·do·scope
en·do·scop·ic

en·dos·co·py
en·dow
en·dow·ment
en·dur·able
en·dur·ance
en·dure
end·ways
en·e·ma
en·e·my
en·er·get·ic
en·er·get·i·cal·ly
en·er·gize
en·er·giz·er
en·er·gy
en·er·vate
en·er·va·tion
en·fee·ble
en·fee·ble·ment
en·fi·lade
en·fold
en·force
en·force·able
en·force·ment
en·fran·chise
en·fran·chise·
  ment
en·gage
  en·gaged
  en·gag·ing
en·gage·ment
en·gen·der
en·gine
en·gi·neer
En·gland
En·glish
en·graft

en·grave
  en·graved
  en·grav·ing
en·grav·er
en·gross
en·gulf
en·hance
en·hance·ment
enig·ma
enig·mat·ic
   also enig·mat·i·cal

enig·mat·i·cal·ly
en·jamb·ment
   or en·jambe·ment

en·join
en·joy
en·joy·able
en·joy·ably
en·joy·ment
en·large
en·large·ment
en·larg·er
en·light·en
en·light·en·ment
en·list
en·list·ment
en·liv·en
en masse
en·mesh
en·mi·ty
en·no·ble
en·no·ble·ment
en·nui
enor·mi·ty
enor·mous

enough
en·plane
en·quire
en·qui·ry
en·rage
en·rap·ture
en·rich
en·rich·ment
en·roll
   or en·rol

  en·rolled
  en·roll·ing
en·roll·ment
en route
en·sconce
en·sem·ble
en·sheathe
en·shrine
en·shroud
en·sign
en·si·lage
en·slave
en·slave·ment
en·snare
en·sue
en·sure
en·tail
en·tan·gle
en·tan·gle·ment
en·tente
en·ter
en·ter·i·tis
en·ter·prise
en·ter·pris·ing
en·ter·tain
en·ter·tain·er

en·ter·tain·ment
en·thrall
   or en·thral

  en·thralled
  en·thrall·ing
en·throne
en·thuse
en·thu·si·asm
en·thu·si·ast
en·thu·si·as·tic
en·thu·si·as·ti·
  cal·ly
en·tice
en·tice·ment
en·tire
en·tire·ly
en·tire·ty
en·ti·tle
en·ti·ty
en·tomb
en·tomb·ment
en·to·mo·log·i·cal
en·to·mol·o·gist
en·to·mol·o·gy
en·tou·rage
en·tr'acte
en·trails
en·train
en·trance
en·trant
en·trap
en·trap·ment
en·treat
en·treaty
en·trée
   or en·tree

en·trench
en·trench·ment
en·tre·pre·neur
en·tro·py
en·trust
en·try
en·twine
enu·mer·ate
enu·mer·a·tion
enu·mer·a·tive
enu·mer·a·tor
enun·ci·ate
enun·ci·a·tion
enun·ci·a·tor
en·ure·sis
en·vel·op
en·ve·lope
en·vel·op·ment
en·ven·om
en·vi·able
en·vi·ably
en·vi·ous
en·vi·ous·ly
en·vi·ous·ness
en·vi·ron·ment
en·vi·ron·men·tal
en·vi·rons
en·vis·age
en·voy
en·vy
en·wreathe
en·zy·mat·ic
  also en·zy·mic

en·zyme
eon

ep·au·let
 also ep·au·lette

epergne
ephed·rine
ephem·er·al
ephem·er·on
 pl ephem·era *also*
 ephem·er·ons

ep·ic
 poem (see epoch*)*

epi·cen·ter
ep·i·cure
ep·i·cu·re·an
ep·i·dem·ic
epi·der·mal
 also epi·der·mic

epi·der·mis
epi·glot·tis
ep·i·gram
ep·i·gram·mat·ic
ep·i·gram·mat·i·
 cal·ly
ep·i·graph
epig·ra·pher
ep·i·graph·ic
 also ep·i·graph·i·cal

epig·ra·phy
ep·i·lep·sy
ep·i·lep·tic
ep·i·logue
epiph·a·ny
epis·co·pa·cy
epis·co·pal
Epis·co·pa·lian
epis·co·pate

ep·i·sode
ep·i·sod·ic
 also epi·sod·i·cal

ep·i·sod·i·cal·ly
epis·tle
epis·to·lary
ep·i·taph
ep·i·tha·la·mi·
 um
 or ep·i·tha·la·mi·on
 pl ep·i·tha·la·mi·
 ums
 or ep·i·tha·la·mia

ep·i·the·li·al
ep·i·the·li·um
ep·i·thet
epit·o·me
epit·o·mize
ep·och
 era (see epic*)*

ep·och·al
ep·oxy
eq·ua·bil·i·ty
equa·ble
equa·bly
equal
 equaled
 or equalled

 equal·ing
 or equal·ling

equal·i·ty
equal·iza·tion
equal·ize
equal·iz·er
equal·ly
equa·nim·i·ty

equate
equa·tion
equa·tor
equa·to·ri·al
Equa·to·ri·al
 Guin·ea
equer·ry
eques·tri·an
eques·tri·enne
equi·an·gu·lar
equi·dis·tant
equi·lat·er·al
equil·i·brate
equil·i·bra·tion
equi·lib·ri·um
 pl equi·lib·ri·ums *or*
 equi·lib·ria

equine
equi·noc·tial
equi·nox
equip
 equipped
 equip·ping

eq·ui·page
equip·ment
equi·poise
eq·ui·ta·ble
eq·ui·ta·bly
eq·ui·ta·tion
eq·ui·ty
equiv·a·lence
equiv·a·lent
equiv·o·cal
equiv·o·cal·ly
equiv·o·cate
equiv·o·ca·tion

equiv·o·ca·tor
era
erad·i·ca·ble
erad·i·cate
erad·i·ca·tion
erad·i·ca·tor
eras·able
erase
eras·er
era·sure
erect
erec·tion
erec·tor
ere·long
Erie
er·mine
erode
erog·e·nous
  also er·o·gen·ic

ero·sion
ero·sive
erot·ic
erot·i·ca
erot·i·cal·ly
erot·i·cism
er·ran·cy
er·rand
er·rant
er·ra·ta
er·rat·ic
er·rat·i·cal·ly
er·ra·tum
  pl er·ra·ta

er·ro·ne·ous
er·ror

er·satz
erst·while
er·u·dite
er·u·di·tion
erupt
  to force out (see
  irrupt)

erup·tion
erup·tive
er·y·sip·e·las
es·ca·late
es·ca·la·tion
es·ca·la·tor
es·cal·lop
es·ca·pade
es·cape
es·cap·ee
es·cap·ism
es·cap·ist
es·ca·role
es·carp
es·carp·ment
es·char
es·cha·rot·ic
es·cha·to·log·i·
  cal·ly
es·cha·tol·o·gy
es·cheat
es·chew
es·cort
es·cri·toire
es·crow
es·cu·do
es·cutch·eon
Es·ki·mo
esoph·a·ge·al

esoph·a·gus
es·o·ter·ic
es·o·ter·i·cal·ly
es·pa·drille
es·pal·ier
es·pe·cial
es·pe·cial·ly
Es·pe·ran·to
es·pi·o·nage
es·pla·nade
es·pous·al
es·pouse
espres·so
es·prit de corps
es·py
es·quire
es·say
  attempt (see assay)

es·say·ist
es·sence
es·sen·tial
es·sen·tial·ly
es·tab·lish
es·tab·lish·ment
es·tate
es·teem
es·ter
es·thete
  var of aesthete

es·thet·ic
  var of aesthetic

es·thet·ics
  var of aesthetics

es·ti·ma·ble
es·ti·mate

es·ti·ma·tion
es·ti·ma·tor
Es·to·nia
Es·to·ni·an
es·trange
es·trange·ment
es·tro·gen
es·tu·ary
etch
etch·er
etch·ing
eter·nal
eter·nal·ly
eter·ni·ty
eth·ane
ether
ethe·re·al
ethe·re·al·ly
eth·i·cal
   also eth·ic

eth·i·cal·ly
eth·ics
Ethi·o·pia
Ethi·o·pi·an
eth·nic
eth·ni·cal·ly
eth·no·cen·tric
eth·no·cen·tri·cal·ly
eth·no·cen·trism
eth·nog·ra·pher
eth·no·graph·ic
eth·no·graph·i·cal·ly
eth·nog·ra·phy

eth·no·log·ic
eth·no·log·i·cal·ly
eth·nol·o·gist
eth·nol·o·gy
etho·log·i·cal
ethol·o·gist
ethol·o·gy
ethos
eth·yl
eti·o·log·ic
eti·ol·o·gy
et·i·quette
étude
et·y·mo·log·i·cal
et·y·mol·o·gist
et·y·mol·o·gy
eu·ca·lyp·tus
Eu·cha·rist
eu·cha·ris·tic
eu·chre
eu·gen·ic
eu·gen·i·cal·ly
eu·gen·ics
eu·lo·gis·tic
eu·lo·gize
eu·lo·gy
eu·nuch
eu·phe·mism
eu·phe·mis·tic
eu·phe·mis·ti·cal·ly
eu·phon·ic
eu·pho·ni·ous
eu·pho·ny
eu·pho·ria

eu·phor·ic
Eur·asian
eu·re·ka
Eu·ro·bond
Eu·ro·dol·lar
Eu·rope
Eu·ro·pe·an
eu·sta·chian
   tube
eu·tha·na·sia
eu·then·ics
evac·u·ate
evac·u·a·tion
evac·u·ee
evade
eval·u·ate
eval·u·a·tion
ev·a·nes·cence
ev·a·nes·cent
evan·gel·i·cal
   also evan·gel·ic

Evan·gel·i·cal·ism
evan·gel·i·cal·ly
evan·ge·lism
evan·ge·list
evan·ge·lis·tic
evan·ge·lis·ti·cal·ly
evan·ge·lize
Ev·ans·ville
evap·o·rate
evap·o·ra·tion
evap·o·ra·tor
eva·sion

eva·sive
even·hand·ed
eve·ning
even·ly
even·ness
even·song
event
event·ful
even·tide
even·tu·al
even·tu·al·i·ty
even·tu·al·ly
even·tu·ate
ev·er
ev·er·bloom·ing
ev·er·glade
ev·er·green
ev·er·last·ing
ev·er·more
ev·ery
ev·ery·body
ev·ery·day
ev·ery·one
ev·ery·thing
ev·ery·where
evict
evic·tion
ev·i·dence
ev·i·dent
ev·i·den·tial
ev·i·den·tial·ly
evil·do·er
evil·ly
evil-mind·ed
evince
evis·cer·ate

evis·cer·a·tion
evo·ca·tion
evoke
evo·lu·tion
evo·lu·tion·ary
evo·lu·tion·ist
evolve
ewe
 female sheep (see
 yew)

ew·er
ex·ac·er·bate
ex·ac·er·ba·tion
ex·act
ex·act·ing
ex·ac·tion
ex·ac·ti·tude
ex·act·ly
ex·act·ness
ex·ag·ger·ate
ex·ag·ger·a·tion
ex·ag·ger·a·tor
ex·alt
ex·al·ta·tion
ex·am·i·na·tion
ex·am·ine
ex·am·in·er
ex·am·ple
ex·as·per·ate
ex·as·per·a·tion
ex·ca·vate
ex·ca·va·tion
ex·ca·va·tor
ex·ceed
 surpass (see accede)

ex·ceed·ing·ly

ex·cel
ex·celled
ex·cel·ling
ex·cel·lence
ex·cel·len·cy
ex·cel·lent
ex·cel·si·or
ex·cept
 also ex·cep·ting
 leave out (see accept)

ex·cep·tion
ex·cep·tion·able
ex·cep·tion·al
ex·cep·tion·al·ly
ex·cerpt
ex·cerp·tion
ex·cess
 surplus (see access)

ex·ces·sive
ex·ces·sive·ly
ex·change
ex·change·able
ex·che·quer
ex·cis·able
ex·cise
ex·ci·sion
ex·cit·abil·i·ty
ex·cit·able
ex·ci·tant
ex·ci·ta·tion
ex·cite
ex·cit·ed·ly
ex·cite·ment
ex·claim
ex·cla·ma·tion
ex·clam·a·to·ry

ex·clude
ex·clu·sion
ex·clu·sive
ex·clu·sive·ness
ex·clu·siv·i·ty
ex·com·mu·ni·
cate
ex·com·mu·ni·ca·
tion
ex·co·ri·ate
ex·co·ri·a·tion
ex·cre·ment
ex·cres·cence
ex·cres·cent
ex·crete
ex·cre·tion
ex·cre·to·ry
ex·cru·ci·at·ing
ex·cul·pate
ex·cul·pa·tion
ex·cul·pa·to·ry
ex·cur·sion
ex·cur·sion·ist
ex·cur·sive
ex·cus·able
ex·cus·ably
ex·cuse
ex·e·cra·ble
ex·e·crate
ex·e·cra·tion
ex·e·cute
ex·e·cu·tion
ex·e·cu·tion·er
ex·ec·u·tive
ex·ec·u·tor
ex·ec·u·trix

ex·e·ge·sis
pl ex·e·ge·ses

ex·e·gete
ex·em·plar
ex·em·pla·ry
ex·em·pli·fi·ca·
tion
ex·em·pli·fy
ex·empt
ex·emp·tion
ex·er·cis·able
ex·er·cise
exert (see exorcise)

ex·er·cis·er
ex·ert
ex·er·tion
ex·ha·la·tion
ex·hale
ex·haust
ex·haust·ibil·i·ty
ex·haust·ible
ex·haus·tion
ex·haus·tive
ex·haust·less
ex·hib·it
ex·hi·bi·tion
ex·hi·bi·tion·ism
ex·hib·i·tor
ex·hil·a·rate
ex·hil·a·ra·tion
ex·hort
ex·hor·ta·tion
ex·hu·ma·tion
ex·hume
ex·i·gen·cy

ex·i·gent
ex·i·gu·i·ty
ex·ig·u·ous
ex·ile
ex·ist
ex·is·tence
ex·is·tent
ex·is·ten·tial
ex·is·ten·tial·ism
ex·it
ex·o·dus
ex of·fi·cio
ex·og·a·mous
ex·og·a·my
ex·og·e·nous
ex·on·er·ate
ex·on·er·a·tion
ex·or·bi·tant
ex·or·cise
expel (see exercise)

ex·or·cism
ex·or·cist
ex·o·ter·ic
ex·o·ter·i·cal·ly
ex·ot·ic
ex·ot·i·cal·ly
ex·ot·i·cism
also ex·o·tism

ex·pand
ex·pand·able
ex·pand·er
ex·panse
ex·pan·sion
ex·pan·sive
ex par·te

ex·pa·ti·ate
ex·pa·ti·a·tion
ex·pa·tri·ate
ex·pa·tri·a·tion
ex·pect
ex·pect·able
ex·pect·ably
ex·pec·tan·cy
ex·pec·tant
ex·pec·ta·tion
ex·pec·to·rant
ex·pec·to·rate
ex·pec·to·ra·tion
ex·pe·di·ence
ex·pe·di·en·cy
ex·pe·di·ent
ex·pe·dite
ex·pe·dit·er
also ex·pe·di·tor

ex·pe·di·tion
ex·pe·di·tion·ary
ex·pe·di·tious
ex·pel
  ex·pelled
  ex·pel·ling
ex·pend
ex·pend·abil·i·ty
ex·pend·able
ex·pen·di·ture
ex·pense
ex·pen·sive
ex·pen·sive·ly
ex·pe·ri·ence
ex·pe·ri·enced
ex·pe·ri·en·tial

ex·pe·ri·en·tial·ly
ex·per·i·ment
ex·per·i·men·tal
ex·per·i·men·tal·
  ly
ex·per·i·men·ta·
  tion
ex·per·i·ment·er
ex·pert
ex·per·tise
ex·pert·ly
ex·pert·ness
ex·pi·a·ble
ex·pi·ate
ex·pi·a·tion
ex·pi·a·tor
ex·pi·a·to·ry
ex·pi·ra·tion
ex·pire
ex·plain
ex·plain·able
ex·pla·na·tion
ex·plan·a·to·ry
ex·ple·tive
ex·pli·ca·ble
ex·pli·cate
ex·pli·ca·tion
ex·pli·ca·tor
ex·pli·ca·to·ry
ex·plic·it
ex·plode
ex·ploit·able
ex·ploi·ta·tion
ex·ploit·ative
ex·ploit·er

ex·plo·ra·tion
ex·plor·ato·ry
ex·plore
ex·plor·er
ex·plo·sion
ex·plo·sive
ex·po·nent
ex·po·nen·tial
ex·port
ex·por·ta·tion
ex·port·er
ex·pose
ex·po·sé
ex·po·si·tion
ex·pos·i·tor
ex·pos·i·to·ry
ex post fac·to
ex·pos·tu·late
ex·pos·tu·la·tion
ex·po·sure
ex·pound
ex·press
ex·press·ible
ex·pres·sion
ex·pres·sion·ism
ex·pres·sion·ist
ex·pres·sion·is·tic
ex·pres·sive
ex·press·man
ex·press·way
ex·pro·pri·ate
ex·pro·pri·a·tion
ex·pul·sion
ex·punge
ex·pur·gate
ex·pur·ga·tion

ex·qui·site
ex·tant
existent (see extent)

ex·tem·po·ra·ne·
ous
ex·tem·po·rary
ex·tem·po·re
ex·tem·po·rize
ex·tend
ex·ten·sion
ex·ten·sive
ex·tent
size (see extant)

ex·ten·u·ate
ex·ten·u·a·tion
ex·te·ri·or
ex·ter·mi·nate
ex·ter·mi·na·tion
ex·ter·mi·na·tor
ex·tern
ex·ter·nal
ex·ter·nal·ly
ex·ter·ri·to·ri·al
ex·ter·ri·to·ri·al·
i·ty
ex·tinct
ex·tinc·tion
ex·tin·guish
ex·tin·guish·able
ex·tin·guish·er
ex·tir·pate
ex·tir·pa·tion
ex·tol
also ex·toll

ex·tolled

ex·tol·ling
ex·tort
ex·tor·tion
ex·tor·tion·ate
ex·tor·tion·er
ex·tor·tion·ist
ex·tra
ex·tract
ex·tract·able
or ex·tract·ible

ex·trac·tion
ex·trac·tive
ex·trac·tor
ex·tra·cur·ric·u·
lar
ex·tra·dit·able
ex·tra·dite
ex·tra·di·tion
ex·tra·ga·lac·tic
ex·tra·le·gal
ex·tra·le·gal·ly
ex·tral·i·ty
ex·tra·mar·i·tal
ex·tra·mu·ral
ex·tra·ne·ous
ex·traor·di·nari·
ly
ex·traor·di·nary
ex·trap·o·late
ex·trap·o·la·tion
ex·tra·sen·so·ry
ex·tra·ter·res·tri·
al
ex·tra·ter·ri·to·
ri·al

ex·tra·ter·ri·to·
ri·al·i·ty
ex·trav·a·gance
ex·trav·a·gant
ex·trav·a·gan·za
ex·tra·ve·hic·u·
lar
ex·tra·ver·sion
or ex·tro·ver·sion

ex·tra·vert
or ex·tro·vert

ex·tra·vert·ed
or ex·tro·vert·ed

ex·treme
ex·treme·ly
ex·trem·ism
ex·trem·ist
ex·trem·i·ty
ex·tri·cate
ex·tri·ca·tion
ex·trin·sic
ex·trin·si·cal·ly
ex·trude
ex·tru·sion
ex·u·ber·ance
ex·u·ber·ant
ex·u·da·tion
ex·ude
ex·ult
ex·ul·tant
ex·ul·ta·tion
ex·urb
ex·ur·ban·ite
ex·ur·bia
eye

eyed
eye·ing
  or ey·ing

eye·ball
eye·brow
eye·ful
eye·glass
eye·lash
eye·let
  hole (see islet)

eye·lid
eye-open·er
eye·piece
eye·sight
eye·sore
eye·spot
eye·strain
eye·tooth
eye·wash
eye·wit·ness
ey·rir
  pl au·rar

F

Fa·bi·an
Fa·bi·an·ism
fa·ble
fa·bled
fab·ric
fab·ri·cate
fab·ri·ca·tion
fab·ri·ca·tor
fab·u·lous
fa·cade
  also fa·çade

face·down
face-lift·ing
fac·et
fa·ce·tious
fa·ce·tious·ness
fa·cial
fac·ile
fa·cil·i·tate
fa·cil·i·ty
fac·ing
fac·sim·i·le
fac·tion
fac·tion·al·ism
fac·tion·al·ly
fac·tious
fac·ti·tious
  artificial (see
  fictitious)

fac·tor
fac·tor·able
fac·to·ri·al
fac·to·ry
fac·to·tum
fac·tu·al
fac·tu·al·ly
fac·ul·ty
fad·dish
fad·dist
fade·less
fag
  fagged
  fag·ging
fag·ot
  or fag·got
fag·ot·ing
  or fag·got·ing

Fahr·en·heit
fa·ience
  or fa·ïence

fail·ing
faille
  silk (see file)

fail-safe
fail·ure
faint
  weak (see feint)

faint·heart·ed
faint·ness
fair·ground
fair·ing
fair·ly
fair-mind·ed
fair·ness
fair-spok·en
fair-trade
fair·way
fair-weath·er
fairy
fairy·land
fait ac·com·pli
  pl faits ac·com·plis

faith·ful
faith·ful·ly
faith·ful·ness
faith·less
faith·less·ness
fak·er
  imposter (see fakir)

fa·kir
  dervish (see faker)

fal·con

fal·con·er
fal·con·ry
fall
  fell
  fall·en
  fall·ing
fal·la·cious
fal·la·cy
fal·li·bil·i·ty
fal·li·ble
fal·li·bly
fall·ing-out
  pl fall·ings-out
  or fall·ing-outs

fal·lo·pi·an tube
fall·out
fal·low
false·hood
false·ly
false·ness
fal·set·to
  pl fal·set·tos

fal·si·fi·ca·tion
fal·si·fi·er
fal·si·fy
fal·si·ty
fal·ter
fal·ter·ing·ly
fa·mil·ial
fa·mil·iar
fa·mil·iar·i·ty
fa·mil·iar·iza·tion
fa·mil·iar·ize
fam·i·ly
fam·ine
fam·ish

fa·mous
fa·mous·ly
fan
  fanned
  fan·ning
fa·nat·ic
  or fa·nat·i·cal

fa·nat·i·cal·ly
fa·nat·i·cism
fan·ci·er
fan·ci·ful
fan·ci·ful·ly
fan·ci·ly
fan·cy
fan·cy-free
fan·cy·work
fan·dan·go
  pl fan·dan·gos

fan·fare
fan-jet
fan·light
fan·tail
fan·ta·sia
fan·tas·tic
fan·tas·ti·cal
fan·tas·ti·cal·ly
fan·ta·sy
far·ad
far·a·day
far·away
far·ceur
far·ci·cal
far·ci·cal·ly
fare·well
far·fetched

far-flung
fa·ri·na
far·i·na·ceous
farm·er
farm·hand
farm·house
farm·ing
farm·land
farm·stead
farm·yard
far-off
far-out
far·ra·go
  pl far·ra·goes

far-reach·ing
far·row
far·see·ing
far·sight·ed
far·sight·ed·ness
far·ther
far·thest
far·thing
fas·ci·cle
fas·ci·nate
fas·ci·na·tion
fas·ci·na·tor
fas·cism
fas·cist
fas·cis·tic
fash·ion
fash·ion·able
fash·ion·ably
fast·back
fas·ten
fas·ten·er

fas·ten·ing
fas·tid·i·ous
fas·tid·i·ous·ness
fast·ness
fast-talk
fa·tal
fa·tal·ism
fa·tal·ist
fa·tal·is·tic
fa·tal·is·ti·cal·ly
fa·tal·i·ty
fa·tal·ly
fat·back
fat·ed
fate·ful
fate·ful·ly
fa·ther
fa·ther·hood
fa·ther-in-law
   pl fa·thers-in-law

fa·ther·land
fa·ther·less
fa·ther·li·ness
fa·ther·ly
fath·om
fath·om·able
fath·om·less
fa·tigue
fat·ten
fat·ty
fa·tu·ity
fat·u·ous
fau·ces
fau·cet
fault·find·er

fault·find·ing
fault·i·ly
fault·less
faulty
faun
   deity (see fawn)

fau·na
   pl fau·nas *also*
   fau·nae

faux pas
   pl faux pas

fa·vor
fa·vor·able
fa·vor·ably
fa·vored
fa·vor·ite
fa·vor·it·ism
fawn
   grovel, deer (see faun)

faze
   daunt (see phase)

fe·al·ty
fear·ful
fear·ful·ly
fear·less
fear·less·ness
fear·some
fea·si·bil·i·ty
fea·si·ble
fea·si·bly
feat
   deed (see foot)

feath·er
feath·er·bed
feath·er·bed·ding

feath·ered
feath·er·edge
feath·er·weight
feath·ery
fea·ture
   fea·tured
   fea·tur·ing
fea·ture·less
feb·ri·fuge
fe·brile
Feb·ru·ary
fe·cal
fe·ces
feck·less
fe·cund
fec·un·date
fec·un·da·tion
fe·cun·di·ty
fed·er·al
fed·er·al·ism
fed·er·al·ist
fed·er·al·iza·tion
fed·er·al·ize
fed·er·ate
fed·er·a·tion
fed·er·a·tive
fe·do·ra
fee·ble
fee·ble·mind·ed
fee·ble·mind·ed·
   ness
fee·ble·ness
fee·bly
feed
   fed
   feed·ing

feed·back
feed·er
feel
  felt
  feel·ing
feel·er
feel·ing·ly
feign
feint
  feigned (see faint)

fe·lic·i·tate
fe·lic·i·ta·tion
fe·lic·i·tous
fe·lic·i·ty
fe·line
fel·lah
  pl fel·la·hin *or*
    fel·la·heen

fel·low
fel·low·man
fel·low·ship
fel·on
fe·lo·ni·ous
fel·o·ny
fe·male
fem·i·nine
fem·i·nin·i·ty
fem·i·nism
fem·i·nist
fe·mur
  pl fe·murs *or*
    fem·o·ra

fen
  pl fen

fenc·er
fenc·ing

fend·er
fen·es·tra·tion
fen·nel
fer·ment
fer·men·ta·tion
fe·ro·cious
fe·ro·cious·ness
fe·roc·i·ty
fer·ret
fer·ric
Fer·ris wheel
fer·rous
fer·rule
  metal ring (see ferule)

fer·ry
fer·ry·boat
fer·tile
fer·til·i·ty
fer·til·iza·tion
fer·til·ize
fer·til·iz·er
fer·ule
  rod (see ferrule)

fer·ven·cy
fer·vent
fer·vid
fer·vor
fes·tal
fes·ter
fes·ti·val
fes·tive
fes·tiv·i·ty
fes·toon
fe·tal
fetch

fetch·ing
fete
  or fête

fet·id
fe·tish
  also fe·tich

fe·tish·ism
fe·tish·ist
fet·lock
fet·ter
fet·tle
fe·tus
feu·dal
feu·dal·ism
feu·dal·is·tic
feu·da·to·ry
fe·ver
fe·ver·ish·ly
fez
  pl fez·zes

fi·an·cé
  masc

fi·an·cée
  fem

fi·as·co
  pl fi·as·coes

fi·at
fib
  fibbed
  fib·bing
fib·ber
fi·ber
  or fi·bre

fi·ber·board
fi·ber·glass

fi·bril·late
fi·bril·la·tion
fi·brin
fi·bri·nous
fi·broid
fi·brous
fib·u·la
  pl fib·u·lae *or*
  fib·u·las

fib·u·lar
fiche
fick·le
fick·le·ness
fic·tion
fic·tion·al
fic·ti·tious
  imaginary (see
  factitious)

fid·dle
fid·dler
fid·dle·stick
fi·del·i·ty
fid·get
fid·gety
fi·du·cia·ry
field·er
field·piece
fiend·ish
fierce·ly
fierce·ness
fi·ery
fi·es·ta
fif·teen
fif·teenth
fifth
fif·ti·eth

fif·ty
fif·ty-fif·ty
fight
  fought
  fight·ing
fight·er
fig·ment
fig·u·ra·tion
fig·u·ra·tive
fig·ure
fig·ure·head
fig·u·rine
Fi·ji
fil·a·ment
fil·a·men·tous
fil·bert
filch
file
  tool, cabinet (see
  faille)

fi·let
  lace (see fillet)

fi·let mi·gnon
  pl fi·lets mi·gnons

fil·ial
fil·i·bus·ter
fil·i·bus·ter·er
fil·i·gree
fil·ing
Fil·i·pi·no
fill·er
  one that fills

fil·ler
  pl fil·lers *or* fil·ler
  coin

fil·let
  also fi·let
  strip, slice (see filet)

fill·ing
fil·lip
fil·ly
film·card
film·dom
film·strip
filmy
fils
  pl fils

fil·ter
  strainer (see philter)

fil·ter·able
  also fil·tra·ble

filth·i·ness
filthy
fil·trate
fil·tra·tion
fi·na·gle
fi·na·gler
fi·nal
fi·na·le
fi·nal·ist
fi·nal·i·ty
fi·nal·ize
fi·nal·ly
fi·nance
fi·nan·cial
fi·nan·cial·ly
fi·nan·cier
find
  found
  find·ing

find·er
fin de siè·cle
find·ing
fine·ly
fine·ness
fin·ery
fine·spun
fi·nesse
fin·ger
fin·ger·board
fin·gered
fin·ger·ing
fin·ger·nail
fin·ger·post
fin·ger·print
fin·ger·tip
fin·i·al
fin·i·cal
fin·i·cal·ly
fin·ick·i·ness
fin·ick·ing
fin·icky
fi·nis
fin·ish
fin·ished
fin·ish·er
fi·nite
Fin·land
Fin·land·er
Finn
fin·nan had·die
Finn·ish
fiord
    var of fjord
fir
    tree (see fur)

fire·arm
fire·ball
fire·boat
fire·box
fire·brand
fire·break
fire·brick
fire·bug
fire·clay
fire·crack·er
fire·damp
fire-eat·er
fire·fly
fire·house
fire·light
fire·man
fire·place
fire·plug
fire·pow·er
fire·proof
fire·side
fire·stone
fire·trap
fire·wa·ter
fire·wood
fire·work
fir·ing
fir·ma·ment
firm·ly
firm·ness
first·born
first·fruits
first·hand
first·ly
first-rate
first-string

firth
fis·cal
fis·cal·ly
fish
    pl fish *or* fish·es
fish-and-chips
fish·er
fish·er·man
fish·ery
fish·hook
fish·ing
fish·mong·er
fish·tail
fish·wife
fishy
fis·sion
fis·sion·able
fis·sure
fist·i·cuffs
fis·tu·la
    pl fis·tu·las *or*
    fis·tu·lae
fis·tu·lous
fit
    fit·ted
        also fit
    fit·ting
fit·ful
fit·ful·ly
fit·ly
fit·ness
fit·ter
fit·ting
fix·a·tion
fix·a·tive
fixed·ly

fixed·ness
fix·i·ty
fix·ture
fiz·zle
fjord
　or fiord

flab·ber·gast
flab·bi·ly
flab·bi·ness
flab·by
flac·cid
fla·con
flag
　flagged
　flag·ging
fla·gel·lant
flag·el·late
flag·el·la·tion
fla·gel·lum
　pl fla·gel·la also
　fla·gel·lums

fla·geo·let
flag·ging
flag·on
flag·pole
fla·gran·cy
fla·grant
fla·gran·te
　de·lic·to
fla·grant·ly
flag·ship
flag·staff
flag·stone
flag-wav·ing
flair
　aptitude (see flare)

flak·i·ness
flaky
flam·beau
　pl flam·beaux or
　flam·beaus

flam·boy·ance
flam·boy·an·cy
flam·boy·ant
fla·men·co
flame-out
flame·proof
flam·er
flame·throw·er
flam·ing
fla·min·go
　pl fla·min·gos also
　fla·min·goes

flam·ma·bil·i·ty
flam·ma·ble
flange
flang·er
flank·er
flan·nel
flan·nel·ette
flap
　flapped
　flap·ping
flap·jack
flap·per
flap·py
flare
　flame (see flair)

flare·back
flar·ing
flare-up
flash·back

flash·bulb
flash·cube
flash·gun
flash·i·ly
flash·i·ness
flash·ing
flash·light
flashy
flask
flat
　flat·ted
　flat·ting
flat·bed
flat·boat
flat·car
flat·fish
flat-foot·ed
flat·iron
flat·ly
flat·ness
flat·ten
flat·ter
flat·ter·er
flat·tery
flat·top
flat·u·lence
flat·u·lent
fla·tus
flat·ware
flat·work
flat·worm
flaunt
flau·tist
fla·vor
fla·vored
fla·vor·ful

fla·vor·ing
fla·vor·less
fla·vor·some
flaw
flaw·less
flax·en
flea-bit·ten
fledg·ling
flee
  fled
  flee·ing
fleecy
fleet·ing
fleet·ly
fleet·ness
Flem·ing
Flem·ish
flesh·i·ness
flesh·ly
flesh·pot
fleshy
fleur-de-lis
  or fleur-de-lys
  pl fleurs-de-lis *or*
    fleur-de-lis *or*
    fleurs-de-lys *or*
    fleur-de-lys

flex·i·bil·i·ty
flex·i·ble
flex·i·bly
flex·or
flex·ure
flick·er
fli·er
  or fly·er

flight·i·ness
flight·less

flighty
flim·flam
flim·si·ly
flim·si·ness
flim·sy
fling
  flung
  fling·ing
Flint
flint·i·ly
flint·i·ness
flint·lock
flinty
flip
  flipped
  flip·ping
flip-flop
flip·pan·cy
flip·pant
flip·per
flir·ta·tion
flir·ta·tious
flit
  flit·ted
  flit·ting
flit·ter
fliv·ver
float·er
float·ing
flock·ing
floe
  ice (see flow)

flog
  flogged
  flog·ging

flog·ger
flood·gate
flood·light
flood·plain
flood·wa·ter
flood·way
floor·board
floor·ing
floor-length
floor·walk·er
floo·zy
  or floo·zie
flop
  flopped
  flop·ping
flop·py
flo·ra
  pl flo·ras *also* flo·rae
flo·ral
flo·res·cence
  flourishing (see
    fluorescence)
flo·res·cent
flo·ri·cul·ture
flor·id
Flor·i·da
Flo·rid·i·an
flo·rin
flo·rist
flossy
flo·ta·tion
flo·til·la
flot·sam
flounc·ing
flouncy
floun·der

flour·ish
flout
flow
stream (see floe)

flow·chart
flow·er
flow·ered
flow·er·i·ness
flow·er·pot
flow·ery
flu
influenza (see flue)

flub
flubbed
flub·bing
fluc·tu·ate
fluc·tu·a·tion
flue
chimney (see flu)

flu·en·cy
flu·ent
fluff·i·ness
fluffy
flu·id
flu·id·ic
flu·id·i·ty
flu·id·ounce
flu·idram
flum·mox
flun·ky
or flun·key

flu·o·resce
flu·o·res·cence
light (see florescence)

flu·o·res·cent

flu·o·ri·date
flu·o·ri·da·tion
flu·o·ride
flu·o·ri·nate
flu·o·ri·na·tion
flu·o·rine
flu·o·ro·scope
flu·o·ros·co·py
flur·ry
flus·ter
flut·ed
flut·ing
flut·ist
flut·ter
flut·tery
fly
move in air

flew
flown
fly·ing
fly
hit a fly ball

flied
fly·ing
fly·able
fly·blown
fly·by
fly-by-night
fly·catch·er
fly·er
var of flier

fly·leaf
fly·over
fly·pa·per
fly·speck

fly·weight
fly·wheel
foam·i·ly
foam·i·ness
foamy
fob
fobbed
fob·bing
fo·cal
fo·cal·ly
fo·cal·iza·tion
fo·cal·ize
fo·cus
pl fo·cus·es *or* fo·ci

fo·cus
fo·cused
also fo·cussed

fo·cus·ing
also fo·cus·sing

fod·der
foe
foe·tal
var of fetal

foe·tus
var of fetus

fog
fogged
fog·ging
fog·bound
fog·gi·ly
fog·gi·ness
fog·gy
fog·horn
fo·gy
also fo·gey

foi·ble
fold·away
fold·er
fol·de·rol
fo·liage
fo·li·ate
fo·li·at·ed
fo·li·a·tion
fo·lio
   pl fo·li·os

folk·lore
folk·lor·ist
folksy
folk·way
fol·li·cle
fol·low
fol·low·er
fol·low·ing
fol·low-through
fol·low-up
fol·ly
fo·ment
fo·men·ta·tion
fon·dant
fon·dle
fond·ly
fond·ness
fon·due
   also fon·du

food·stuff
fool·har·di·ly
fool·har·di·ness
fool·har·dy
fool·ish
fool·ish·ly

fool·ish·ness
fool·proof
fools·cap
   or fool's cap

foot
   (*see* feat)
   pl feet
   also foot

foot·age
foot·ball
foot·board
foot·bridge
foot·can·dle
foot·ed
foot·fall
foot·hill
foot·hold
foot·ing
foot·lights
foot·lock·er
foot·loose
foot·man
foot·mark
foot·note
foot·pad
foot·path
foot-pound
foot·print
foot·race
foot·rest
foot·sore
foot·step
foot·stool
foot·wear
foot·work
fop·pery

fop·pish
for·age
for·ag·er
for·ay
for·bear
   abstain (*see* forebear)

   for·bore
   for·borne
   for·bear·ing
for·bear·ance
for·bid
   for·bade
      or for·bad

   for·bid·den
   for·bid·ding
force·ful
force·ful·ly
for·ceps
   pl for·ceps

forc·ible
forc·ibly
fore-and-aft
fore·arm
fore·bear
   or for·bear
   ancestor (*see* forebear)

fore·bode
   also for·bode

fore·bod·ing
fore·cast
   fore·cast
      or fore·cast·ed

   fore·cast·ing
fore·cast·er
fore·cas·tle

fore·close
fore·clo·sure
fore·deck
fore·doom
fore·fa·ther
fore·fin·ger
fore·foot
fore·front
fore·go
  precede (see forgo)

fore·went
fore·gone
fore·go·ing
fore·ground
fore·hand
fore·hand·ed
fore·head
for·eign
for·eign·er
fore·know
fore·knowl·edge
fore·la·dy
fore·land
fore·leg
fore·limb
fore·lock
fore·man
fore·mast
fore·most
fore·name
fore·named
fore·noon
fo·ren·sic
fo·ren·si·cal·ly
fore·or·dain

fore·or·di·na·tion
fore·play
fore·quar·ter
fore·run·ner
fore·sad·dle
fore·said
fore·sail
fore·see
  fore·saw
  fore·seen
  fore·see·ing
fore·see·able
fore·shad·ow
fore·sheet
fore·shore
fore·short·en
fore·sight
fore·sight·ed·ness
fore·skin
for·est
fore·stall
for·es·ta·tion
for·est·ed
for·est·er
for·est·ry
fore·taste
fore·tell
  fore·told
  fore·tell·ing
fore·thought
fore·to·ken
fore·top
for·ev·er
for·ev·er·more
fore·warn
fore·wom·an

fore·word
  preface (see
   forward)
for·feit
for·fei·ture
for·gath·er
  or fore·gath·er

forg·er
forg·ery
for·get
  for·got
  for·got·ten
   or for·got

for·get·ting
for·get·ful
for·get·ta·ble
forg·ing
for·giv·able
for·give
  for·gave
  for·giv·en
  for·giv·ing
for·give·ness
for·giv·ing
for·go
  or fore·go
  renounce (see forego)

for·went
  or fore·went

for·gone
  or fore·gone

for·go·ing
  or fore·go·ing

fo·rint
forked

fork·lift
for·lorn
for·mal
form·al·de·hyde
for·mal·ism
for·mal·i·ty
for·mal·iza·tion
for·mal·ize
for·mal·ly
for·mat
for·ma·tion
for·ma·tive
for·mer
for·mer·ly
form·fit·ting
for·mi·da·ble
for·mi·da·bly
form·less
For·mo·sa
For·mo·san
for·mu·la
for·mu·late
for·mu·la·tion
for·mu·la·tor
for·ni·cate
for·ni·ca·tion
for·ni·ca·tor
for·sake
 for·sook
 for·sak·en
 for·sak·ing
for·sooth
for·swear
 or fore·swear

 for·swore
  or fore·swore

for·sworn
 or fore·sworn

for·swear·ing
 or fore·swear·ing

for·syth·ia
fort
 fortified place

forte
 special skill

for·te
 loudly

forth·com·ing
forth·right
forth·with
for·ti·eth
for·ti·fi·ca·tion
for·ti·fi·er
for·ti·fy
for·tis·si·mo
 pl for·tis·si·mos *or*
  for·tis·si·mi

for·ti·tude
Fort Lau·der·dale
fort·night·ly
for·tress
for·tu·itous
for·tu·ity
for·tu·nate
for·tune
for·tune-tell·er
for·tune-tell·ing
Fort Wayne
Fort Worth
for·ty
forty-five

for·ty-nin·er
fo·rum
 pl fo·rums *also* fo·ra

for·ward
 brash, toward the
 front
 (see foreword)

for·ward·er
for·ward·ing
fos·sil
fos·sil·ize
fos·ter
foul
 dirty (see fowl)

fou·lard
foul·ly
foul·mouthed
foul·ness
foun·da·tion
foun·der
 verb, collapse

found·er
 noun, establisher

found·ling
found·ry
foun·tain
foun·tain·head
four-flush·er
four-fold
four-foot·ed
four-hand·ed
four-in-hand
four-post·er
four·score
four·some
four·square

four·teen
four·teenth
fourth
four-wheel·er
fowl
 bird (see foul)
fox
 pl fox·es *or* fox
fox·glove
fox·hole
fox·hound
fox·i·ly
fox·i·ness
fox-trot
foxy
foy·er
fra·cas
frac·tion
frac·tion·al
frac·tion·al·ize
frac·tion·al·ly
frac·tious
frac·ture
frag·ile
fra·gil·i·ty
frag·ment
frag·men·tal·ly
frag·men·tary
frag·men·ta·tion
frag·men·tize
fra·grance
fra·grant
frail·ty
fram·er
frame-up

frame·work
franc
 currency (see frank)
France
fran·chise
fran·chi·see
fran·gi·bil·i·ty
fran·gi·ble
frank
 forthright (see franc)
Fran·ken·stein
Frank·fort
frank·furt·er
 or frank·fort·er *or*
 frank·furt *or*
 frank·fort
frank·in·cense
fran·tic
fran·ti·cal·ly
frap·pé
 or frappe
fra·ter·nal
fra·ter·nal·ly
fra·ter·ni·ty
frat·er·ni·za·tion
frat·er·nize
frat·ri·cide
fraud·u·lence
fraud·u·lent
fraught
fray·ing
fraz·zle
freak·ish
freck·le
free·bie
 or free·bee

free·boo·ter
free·born
freed·man
free·dom
freed·wom·an
free-fall
free-for-all
free·hand
free·hold
free-lance
free·ly
free·man
Free·ma·son
free·stand·ing
free·stone
free·style
free·think·er
free·way
free·wheel
freeze
 chill (see frieze)
froze
fro·zen
freez·ing
freeze-dry
freez·er
freight·age
freight·er
Fre·mont
French
French·man
French·wom·an
fre·net·ic
fre·net·i·cal·ly
fren·zied
fren·zy

fre·quen·cy
fre·quent
fres·co
  pl fres·coes *or*
    fres·cos

fresh·en
fresh·et
fresh·ly
fresh·man
fresh·ness
fresh·wa·ter
Fres·no
fret
  fret·ted
  fret·ting
fret·ful
fret·ful·ly
fret·ful·ness
fret·work
fri·a·ble
fri·ar
  monk (see fryer)

fric·as·see
fric·tion
fric·tion·al·ly
Fri·day
friend·less
friend·li·ness
friend·ly
friend·ship
fri·er
  var of fryer

frieze
  ornament (see
    freeze)

frig·ate

fright·en
fright·ful
fright·ful·ly
frig·id
fri·gid·i·ty
frilly
frip·pery
frisk·i·ly
frisk·i·ness
frisky
frit·ter
fri·vol·i·ty
friv·o·lous
frizz·i·ly
frizz·i·ness
friz·zle
friz·zly
frizzy
frog·man
frol·ic
  frol·icked
  frol·ick·ing
frol·ic·some
front·age
fron·tal
fron·tier
fron·tiers·man
fron·tis·piece
frost·bite
frost·ed
frost·i·ly
frost·i·ness
frost·ing
frosty
froth·i·ly
froth·i·ness

frothy
frou·frou
fro·ward
frown
frow·sy
  also frow·zy

fro·zen
fruc·ti·fi·ca·tion
fruc·ti·fy
fruc·tose
fruc·tu·ous
fru·gal
fru·gal·i·ty
fru·gal·ly
fruit·cake
fruit·ful·ly
fru·ition
fruit·less
fruity
frump·ish
frumpy
frus·trate
frus·tra·tion
fry
  fried
  fry·ing
fry·er
  or fri·er
  one that fries (see
    friar)

fuch·sia
fud·dle
fudge
fu·el
  fu·eled
    or fu·elled

fu·el·ing
  or fu·el·ling

fu·gi·tive

fugue

füh·rer
  or fueh·rer

ful·crum
  pl ful·crums *or*
  ful·cra

ful·fill
  or ful·fil

ful·filled

ful·fill·ing

ful·fill·ment

full·back

full-blood·ed

full-blown

full-bod·ied

full·er
  one that fulls cloth

ful·ler
  blacksmith's hammer

full-fash·ioned

full-fledged

full-length

full·ness
  also ful·ness

full-scale

ful·ly

ful·mi·nate

ful·mi·na·tion

ful·mi·na·tor

ful·some

fu·ma·role

fum·ble

fu·mi·gant

fu·mi·gate

fu·mi·ga·tion

fu·mi·ga·tor

func·tion

func·tion·al

func·tion·al·ism

func·tion·al·ly

func·tion·ary

func·tion·less

fun·da·men·tal

fun·da·men·tal·
  ism

fun·da·men·tal·
  ist

fun·da·men·tal·ly

fu·ner·al

fu·ner·ary

fu·ne·re·al

fun·gi·cid·al

fun·gi·cide

fun·gus
  pl fun·gi *also*
  fun·gus·es

fu·nic·u·lar

funky

fun·nel

fun·neled
  also fun·nelled

fun·nel·ing
  also fun·nel·ling

fun·ni·ly

fun·ni·ness

fun·ny

fur
  hair (see fir*)*

fur·be·low

fur·bish

fu·ri·ous

furl

fur·long

fur·lough

fur·nace

fur·nish

fur·nish·ings

fur·ni·ture

fu·ror
  rage, vogue, uproar

fu·rore
  vogue, uproar

fur·ri·er

fur·row

fur·ry

fur·ther

fur·ther·ance

fur·ther·more

fur·ther·most

fur·thest

fur·tive

fur·tive·ness

fu·ry

fu·se·lage

fus·ibil·i·ty

fus·ible

fu·sil·lade

fu·sion

fuss·bud·get

fuss·i·ly

fuss·i·ness

fussy

fus·tian

fus·ti·ly
fus·ti·ness
fus·ty
fu·tile
fu·til·i·ty
fu·ture
fu·tur·ism
fu·tur·ist
fu·tur·is·tic
fu·tu·ri·ty
fuzz·i·ly
fuzz·i·ness
fuzzy

G

gab
  gabbed
  gab·bing
gab·ar·dine
  or gab·er·dine

gab·ble
gab·by
gab·fest
ga·ble
ga·bled
Ga·bon
Gab·o·nese
gad
  gad·ded
  gad·ding
gad·about
gad·fly
gad·get
gad·get·ry

Gael·ic
gaff
  spear, hook
gaffe
  blunder
gaf·fer
gag
  gagged
  gag·ging
gage
  pledge (see gauge)
gag·gle
gag·man
gag·ster
gai·ety
  or gay·ety
gai·ly
  or gay·ly
gain·er
gain·ful
gain·ful·ly
gain·say
  gain·said
  gain·say·ing
gain·say·er
gait
  walk (see gate)
gai·ter
ga·la
ga·lac·tic
Gal·a·had
gal·axy
gal·lant
gal·lant·ry
gall·blad·der

gal·le·on
gal·ler·ied
gal·lery
gal·ley
Gal·lic
gall·ing
gal·li·vant
gal·lon
gal·lop
gal·lop·er
gal·lows
gall·stone
ga·lore
ga·losh
gal·van·ic
gal·va·nism
gal·va·ni·za·tion
gal·va·nize
gal·va·nom·e·ter
Gam·bia
Gam·bi·an
gam·bit
gam·ble
  wager (see gambol)
gam·bler
gam·bol
  leap about (see gamble)
  gam·boled
  or gam·bolled
  gam·bol·ing
  or gam·bol·ling
gam·brel
game·cock
game·keep·er

game·ly
game·ster
ga·mete
gam·in
gam·i·ness
gam·ma glob·u·lin
gam·ut
gamy
  or gam·ey

gan·der
gan·dy danc·er
gang·land
gan·gling
gan·gli·on
  pl gan·glia *also*
  gan·gli·ons

gang·plank
gan·grene
gan·gre·nous
gang·ster
gang·way
gant·let
gan·try
ga·rage
ga·rage·man
gar·bage
gar·ble
gar·çon
gar·den
gar·den·er
Gar·den Grove
gar·de·nia
gar·gan·tuan
gar·gle
gar·goyle

gar·ish
gar·land
gar·lic
gar·licky
gar·ment
gar·ner
gar·net
gar·nish
gar·nish·ee
gar·nish·eed
gar·nish·ment
gar·ni·ture
gar·ret
gar·ri·son
gar·rote
  or ga·rotte

gar·ru·li·ty
gar·ru·lous
gar·ru·lous·ness
gar·ter
Gary
gas·eous
gas·ket
gas·light
gas·o·line
  also gas·o·lene

gas·ser
gas·si·ness
gas·sy
gas·tric
gas·tri·tis
gas·tro·en·ter·ol·o·gist
gas·tro·en·ter·ol·o·gy

gas·tro·in·tes·ti·nal
gas·tro·nom·ic
gas·tron·o·my
gas·works
gate
  door (see gait)

gate-crash·er
gate·post
gate·way
gath·er
gath·er·er
gauche
  crude (see gouache)

gau·che·rie
gau·cho
  pl gau·chos

gaud·i·ly
gaud·i·ness
gaudy
gauge
  measure (see gage)

gaunt
gaunt·let
  or gant·let

gauze
gauzy
gav·el
ga·votte
gawk·ish
gawky
gay·ety
  var of gaiety

gay·ly
  var of gai·ly

ga·ze·bo
  pl ga·ze·bos

ga·zelle
gaz·er
ga·zette
gaz·et·teer
gear·box
gear·ing
gear·shift
gee·zer
Gei·ger
gei·sha
  pl gei·sha *or* gei·shas

gel
  gelled
  gel·ling
gel·a·tin
  also gel·a·tine

ge·la·ti·ni·za·tion
ge·la·ti·nize
ge·lat·i·nous
geld·ing
gel·id
ge·lid·i·ty
gel·ig·nite
gem·i·nate
gem·i·na·tion
gem·stone
gen·darme
gen·dar·mer·ie
  or gen·dar·mery

gen·der
ge·ne·a·log·i·cal
ge·ne·a·log·i·cal·
  ly

ge·ne·al·o·gist
ge·ne·al·o·gy
gen·er·a·ble
gen·er·al
gen·er·a·lis·si·mo
gen·er·al·i·ty
gen·er·al·iza·tion
gen·er·al·ize
gen·er·al·ly
gen·er·al·ship
gen·er·ate
gen·er·a·tion
gen·er·a·tive
gen·er·a·tor
ge·ner·ic
ge·ner·i·cal·ly
gen·er·os·i·ty
gen·er·ous
gen·e·sis
  pl gen·e·ses

ge·net·ic
  also ge·net·i·cal

ge·net·i·cal·ly
ge·net·ics
ge·nial
ge·nial·i·ty
ge·nial·ly
gen·ic
ge·nie
  pl ge·nies *also* ge·nii

gen·i·tal
gen·i·ta·lia
gen·i·tals
gen·i·tive
gen·i·to·uri·nary

ge·nius
  pl ge·nius·es *or*
    ge·nii

geno·cid·al
geno·cide
genre
gens
  pl gen·tes

gen·teel
gen·tian
gen·tile
gen·til·i·ty
gen·tle
gen·tle·folk
  also gen·tle·folks

gen·tle·man
gen·tle·man·ly
gen·tle·wom·an
gen·tly
gen·try
gen·u·flect
gen·u·flec·tion
gen·u·ine
gen·u·ine·ly
gen·u·ine·ness
ge·nus
  pl gen·era

geo·cen·tric
geo·cen·tri·cal·ly
geo·chem·i·cal
geo·chem·i·cal·ly
geo·chem·is·try
geo·chro·no·log·i·
  cal
geo·chro·nol·o·gy

giggly

geo·de·sic
ge·od·e·sy
geo·det·ic
geo·det·i·cal·ly
geo·graph·ic
  or geo·graph·i·cal

ge·o·graph·i·cal·
  ly
ge·og·ra·phy
geo·log·ic
  or geo·log·i·cal

geo·log·i·cal·ly
ge·ol·o·gist
ge·ol·o·gy
geo·mag·net·ic
geo·mag·ne·tism
ge·o·met·ric
  or ge·o·met·ri·cal

ge·o·met·ri·cal·ly
geo·me·tri·cian
ge·om·e·try
geo·phys·i·cal
geo·phys·i·cist
geo·phys·ics
geo·po·lit·i·cal
geo·po·lit·i·cal·ly
geo·pol·i·ti·cian
geo·pol·i·tics
Geor·gia
geo·ther·mal
ge·ra·ni·um
ger·i·at·ric
ger·i·at·rics
Ger·man
ger·mane

Ger·man·ic
Ger·ma·ny
ger·mi·cid·al
ger·mi·cide
ger·mi·nal
ger·mi·nate
ger·mi·na·tion
ger·on·tol·o·gist
ger·on·tol·o·gy
ger·ry·man·der
ger·und
ge·sta·po
  pl ges·ta·pos

ges·tate
ges·ta·tion
ges·tic·u·late
ges·tic·u·la·tion
ges·ture
ge·sund·heit
get
  got
  got
    or got·ten

  get·ting
get·away
get-to·geth·er
get·up
gew·gaw
gey·ser
Gha·na
Gha·na·ian
  or Gha·nian

ghast·li·ness
ghast·ly
gher·kin

ghet·to
  pl ghet·tos *or*
    ghet·toes

ghet·to·iza·tion
ghet·to·ize
ghost·li·ness
ghost·ly
ghost·write
ghost-writ·er
ghoul·ish
gi·ant
gi·ant·ess
gi·ant·ism
gib
gib·ber
gib·ber·ish
gib·bet
gib·bon
gib·bos·i·ty
gib·bous
gibe
  taunt (see jibe)

gib·er
gib·lets
Gib·son
gid·di·ly
gid·di·ness
gid·dy
gift·ed
gig
  gigged
  gig·ging
gi·gan·tic
gi·gan·ti·cal·ly
gig·gle
gig·gly

gig·o·lo
gild
  overlay with gold
  (*see* guild)

  gild·ed
    or gilt

  gild·ing
gilt
  gold (*see* guilt)

gilt-edged
  or gilt-edge

gim·crack
gim·let
gim·mick
gim·mick·ry
gim·micky
gimpy
gin
  ginned
  gin·ning
gin·ger
gin·ger·bread
gin·ger·ly
gin·ger·snap
ging·ham
gin·gi·vi·tis
gi·raffe
gird
  gird·ed
    or girt

  gird·ing
gird·er
gir·dle
girl·hood
girl·ish

girth
gist
give
  gave
  giv·en
  giv·ing
give-and-take
give·away
giv·en
giz·mo
  or gis·mo

giz·zard
gla·brous
gla·cé
gla·cial
gla·ci·ate
gla·ci·a·tion
gla·cier
gla·ci·ol·o·gist
gla·ci·ol·o·gy
glad·den
glad·i·a·tor
glad·i·a·to·ri·al
glad·i·o·la
glad·i·o·lus
  pl glad·i·o·li *or*
    glad·i·o·lus *or*
    glad·i·o·lus·es

glad·ly
glad·ness
glad·some
glad·stone
glam·or·ize
  also glam·our·ize

glam·or·ous
  also glam·our·ous

glam·our
  or glam·or

glanc·ing
glan·du·lar
glar·ing
glass·ful
glass·i·ly
glass·ine
glass·i·ness
glass·ware
glassy
glau·co·ma
gla·zier
glaz·ing
glean·able
glean·er
glean·ings
glee·ful
glee·ful·ly
Glen·dale
glib·ly
glib·ness
glid·er
glim·mer
glimpse
glis·ten
glit·ter
glit·tery
gloam·ing
gloat
glob·al
glob·al·ly
globe-trot·ter
glob·u·lar
glob·ule

glob·u·lin
glock·en·spiel
gloom·i·ly
gloom·i·ness
gloomy
glo·ri·fi·ca·tion
glo·ri·fy
glo·ri·ous
glo·ry
glos·sa·ry
gloss·i·ly
gloss·i·ness
glossy
glot·tal
glot·tis
  pl glot·tis·es *or*
  glot·ti·des

glow·er
glow·worm
glu·cose
glue
glu·ey
glu·i·ly
glut
  glut·ted
  glut·ting
glu·ta·mate
glu·ten
glu·ten·ous
  containing gluten (see
  glutinous)

glu·ti·nous
  sticky (see glutenous)

glut·ton
glut·ton·ous
glut·tony

glyc·er·in
  or glyc·er·ine

glyc·er·ol
gly·co·gen
G-man
gnarled
gnash
gnat
gnaw
gneiss
gnome
gnom·ish
Gnos·tic
gnos·ti·cism
gnu
go
  went
  gone
  go·ing
goad
go-ahead
goal·ie
goal·keep·er
goal·post
goa·tee
goat·skin
gob·ble
gob·ble·dy·gook
  or gob·ble·de·gook

gob·bler
go-be·tween
gob·let
gob·lin
god·child
god·daugh·ter

god·dess
god·fa·ther
god·less
god·like
god·li·ness
god·ly
god·moth·er
god·par·ent
god·send
god·son
go-get·ter
gog·gle
gog·gles
go-go
go·ings-on
goi·ter
  also goi·tre

gold·brick
gold·en
gold·en·rod
gold·field
gold-filled
gold·finch
gold·fish
gold·smith
golf·er
go·nad
gon·do·la
gon·do·lier
gon·er
gon·fa·lon
gon·or·rhea
gon·or·rhe·al
good
  bet·ter

best
good-bye
  or good-by

good-heart·ed
good-hu·mored
good-look·ing
good·ly
good-na·tured
good·ness
good-tem·pered
good·will
goody-goody
goof·i·ness
goofy
goose
  pl geese

goose·ber·ry
goose·flesh
goose·neck
go·pher
Gor·di·an knot
gorge
gor·geous
Gor·gon·zo·la
go·ril·la
gor·man·dize
gor·man·diz·er
gory
gos·hawk
gos·ling
gos·pel
gos·sa·mer
gos·sip
Goth·ic
gouache
  painting (see gauche)

Gou·da
gouge
gou·lash
gourd
  plant (see gourde)

gourde
  currency (see gourd)

gour·mand
gour·met
gout
gov·ern
gov·er·nance
gov·ern·ess
gov·ern·ment
gov·ern·men·tal
gov·er·nor
gov·er·nor-gen·
  er·al
  pl gov·er·nors-
  gen·er·al *or*
  gov·er·nor-
  gen·er·als

grab
  grabbed
  grab·bing
grace·ful
grace·ful·ly
grace·less
gra·cious
grack·le
gra·da·tion
grad·er
gra·di·ent
grad·u·al
grad·u·al·ism
grad·u·al·ly

grad·u·ate
grad·u·a·tion
graf·fi·to
  pl graf·fi·ti

graft·er
gra·ham
  crack·er
grain·field
grainy
gram
  or gramme

gram·mar
gram·mar·i·an
gram·mat·i·cal
gram·mat·i·cal·ly
gra·na·ry
gran·dam
  or gran·dame

grand·child
grand·daugh·ter
gran·dee
gran·deur
grand·fa·ther
gran·dil·o·quence
gran·dil·o·quent
gran·di·ose
grand·ly
grand·moth·er
grand·par·ent
Grand Rap·ids
grand·son
grand·stand
grange
gran·ite
gran·ite·ware

gran·ny
 or gran·nie

grant·ee

grant-in-aid
 pl grants-in-aid

grant·or
gran·u·lar
gran·u·late
gran·u·la·tion
gran·ule
grape·fruit
grape·shot
grape·vine
graph·ic
graph·i·cal·ly
graph·ics
graph·ite
grap·nel
grap·ple
grap·pling
grapy
grasp·er
grass·hop·per
grass·land
grassy
grate·ful
grate·ful·ly
grat·er
grat·i·fi·ca·tion
grat·i·fy
grat·ing
gra·tis
grat·i·tude
gra·tu·itous
gra·tu·ity

gra·va·men
 pl gra·va·mens or
 gra·vam·i·na

grave
 graved
 grav·en
  or graved

 grav·ing
grav·el
 grav·eled
  or grav·elled

 grav·el·ing
  or grav·el·ling

grav·el·ly
grave·ly
grave·stone
grave·yard
grav·i·tate
grav·i·ta·tion
grav·i·ty
gra·vy
gray·ish
grease·paint
greas·i·ness
greasy
Great Brit·ain
great·coat
great·ly
great·ness
Gre·cian
Greece
greed·i·ly
greed·i·ness
greedy
Greek

green·back
green·belt
green·ery
green·gro·cer
green·horn
green·house
green·ish
green·ness
green·room
Greens·boro
green·sward
greet·er
greet·ing
gre·gar·i·ous
grem·lin
Gre·na·da
gre·nade
gren·a·dier
gren·a·dine
grey·hound
grid·dle
grid·iron
griev·ance
griev·ous
grill
 cooking (see grille)

gril·lage
grille
 or grill
 grating (see grill)

grill·work
gri·mace
grim·i·ness
grim·ly
grimy
grin

grinned
grin·ning
grind
ground
grind·ing
grind·er
grind·stone
grip
hold (see gripe, grippe)

gripped
grip·ping
gripe
complain (see grip, grippe)

grippe
influenza (see grip, gripe)

gris-gris
pl gris-gris

gris·li·ness
gris·ly
grist
gris·tle
gris·tli·ness
gris·tly
grist·mill
grit
grit·ted
grit·ting
grit·ti·ness
grit·ty
griz·zled
griz·zly
gro·cer
gro·cery

grog·gi·ly
grog·gi·ness
grog·gy
gro·gram
groin
grom·met
gro·schen
pl gro·schen

gros·grain
gross·ly
gross·ness
grosz
pl gro·szy

gro·tesque
gro·tesque·ly
gro·tes·que·rie
grot·to
pl grot·toes *also*
grot·tos

grouch·i·ly
grouch·i·ness
grouchy
ground·er
ground·hog
ground·less
ground·wa·ter
ground·work
group·ing
grouse
pl grouse *or*
grous·es

grov·el
grov·eled
or grov·elled

grov·el·ing
or grov·el·ling

grov·el·er
grow
grew
grown
grow·ing
grow·er
growl·er
growl·ing
grown-up
growth
grub
grubbed
grub·bing
grub·bi·ly
grub·bi·ness
grub·by
grub·stake
grudge
grudg·ing·ly
gru·el
gru·el·ing
or gru·el·ling

grue·some
gruff·ly
grum·ble
grum·bler
grump·i·ly
grump·i·ness
grumpy
Gru·yère
G-string
gua·no
gua·ra·ni
pl gua·ra·nis *or*
gua·ra·nies

guar·an·tee

guar·an·tor
guar·an·ty
guard·house
guard·ian
guard·room
guards·man
Gua·te·ma·la
Gua·te·ma·lan
gua·va
gu·ber·na·to·ri·al
guern·sey
guer·ril·la
  or gue·ril·la

guess·ti·mate
guess·work
guest
guf·faw
guid·able
guid·ance
guide·book
guide·line
gui·don
guild
  association (*see* gild)

guil·der
guild·hall
guile
guile·ful
guile·ful·ly
guile·less
guil·lo·tine
guilt
  blame (*see* gilt)

guilt·i·ly
guilt·i·ness

guilt·less
guilty
Guin·ea
Guin·ea-Bis·sau
Guin·ean
guise
gui·tar
gulch
gul·den
  pl gul·dens *or*
    gul·den

gul·let
gull·ibil·i·ty
gull·ible
  or gull·able

gull·ibly
gul·ly
gum
  gummed
  gum·ming
gum·bo
gum·boil
gum·drop
gum·mi·ness
gum·my
gump·tion
gum·shoe
gun
  gunned
  gun·ning
gun·boat
gun·cot·ton
gun·fight
gun·fire
gun·lock
gun·man

gun·met·al
gun·ner
gun·nery
gun·ny
gun·ny·sack
gun·point
gun·pow·der
gun·run·ner
gun·ship
gun·shot
gun-shy
gun·smith
gun·wale
  or gun·nel

gup·py
gur·gle
gu·ru
gush·er
gushy
gus·set
gus·ta·to·ry
gust·i·ly
gust·i·ness
gus·to
  pl gus·toes

gusty
gut
  gut·ted
  gut·ting
gut·less
gutsy
gut·ta-per·cha
gut·ter
gut·ter·snipe
gut·tur·al

gut·tur·al·ly
Guy·ana
Guy·a·nese
guy·ot
guz·zle
gym·na·si·um
  pl gym·na·si·ums *or*
    gym·na·sia
gym·nast
gym·nas·tic
gym·no·sperm
gy·ne·co·log·i·cal
gy·ne·col·o·gist
gy·ne·col·o·gy
gyp
  gypped
  gyp·ping
gyp·sum
gyp·sy
gy·rate
gy·ra·tion
gy·ro·com·pass
gy·ro·scope
gy·ro·sta·bi·liz·er
gy·ro·stat

H

ha·ba·ne·ra
ha·be·as cor·pus
hab·er·dash·er
hab·er·dash·ery
ha·bil·i·ment
hab·it
hab·it·abil·i·ty
hab·it·able

hab·it·ably
ha·bi·tant
hab·i·tat
hab·i·ta·tion
hab·it-form·ing
ha·bit·u·al
ha·bit·u·al·ly
ha·bit·u·ate
ha·bit·u·a·tion
ha·bi·tué
ha·chure
ha·ci·en·da
hack·le
hack·man
hack·ney
hack·neyed
hack·saw
hack·work
had·dock
Ha·des
hag·gard
hag·gis
hag·gle
hag·gler
ha·gi·og·ra·pher
ha·gi·og·ra·phy
hail
  ice, greet (see hale)

hail·stone
hail·storm
hair·breadth
  or hairs·breadth

hair·brush
hair·cloth
hair·cut

hair·do
  pl hair·dos

hair·dress·er
hair·i·ness
hair·less
hair·line
hair·piece
hair·pin
hair-rais·ing
hair·split·ter
hair·split·ting
hair·spring
hair·style
hair-trig·ger
hairy
Hai·ti
Hai·tian
ha·la·la
  also ha·la·lah
  pl ha·la·la *or*
    ha·la·las

ha·la·tion
hal·berd
  or hal·bert

hal·cy·on
hale
  healthy, haul (see
    hail)

ha·ler
half
  pl halves

half·back
half-baked
half-breed
half-caste
half-cocked

half-dol·lar
half·heart·ed
half-length
half-life
half-light
half-mast
half-moon
half-slip
half-staff
half·tone
half-track
half-truth
half·way
half-wit
half-wit·ted
hal·i·but
ha·lide
Hal·i·fax
ha·lite
hal·i·to·sis
hal·le·lu·jah
hal·liard
  var of halyard
hall·mark
hal·low
hal·lowed
Hal·low·een
hal·lu·ci·nate
hal·lu·ci·na·tion
hal·lu·ci·na·to·ry
hal·lu·ci·no·gen
hal·lu·ci·no·gen·
  ic
hall·way
ha·lo
  pl ha·los *or* ha·loes

halo·gen
hal·ter
halt·ing
halve
hal·yard
  or hal·liard

ham
  hammed
  ham·ming
ham·burg·er
  or ham·burg

Ham·il·ton
ham·let
ham·mer
ham·mer·head
ham·mer·lock
ham·mock
Ham·mond
ham·my
ham·per
Hamp·ton
ham·ster
ham·string
hand·bag
hand·ball
hand·bar·row
hand·bill
hand·book
hand·car
hand·clasp
hand·cuff
hand·ful
  pl hand·fuls *also*
  hands·ful
hand·gun
hand·i·cap

hand·i·capped
hand·i·cap·ping
hand·i·cap·per
hand·i·craft
hand·i·crafts·man
hand·i·ly
hand·i·ness
hand·i·work
hand·ker·chief
  pl hand·ker·chiefs
  also
  hand·ker·chieves

han·dle
han·dle·bar
hand·made
hand·maid·en
  or hand·maid

hand-me-down
hand·off
hand·out
hand·pick
hand·rail
hand·saw
hands-down
hand·set
hand·shake
hand·some
  good looking (see
  hansom)

hand·spike
hand·spring
hand-to-hand
hand·wo·ven
hand·writ·ing
hand·writ·ten
handy

handy·man
hang
  hung
    also hanged
  hang·ing
han·gar
  airplanes (*see* hanger)
hang·dog
hang·er
  one that hangs
  (*see* hangar)
hang·er-on
  pl hangers-on
hang·ing
hang·man
hang·nail
hang·out
hang·over
han·ker
han·ky-pan·ky
han·som
  cab (*see* handsome)

Ha·nuk·kah
  or Cha·nu·kah

hao·le
hap·haz·ard
hap·less
hap·pen
hap·pen·ing
hap·pen·stance
hap·pi·ly
hap·pi·ness
hap·py
hap·py-go-lucky
hara-kiri

ha·rangue
ha·rangu·er
ha·rass
ha·rass·ment
har·bin·ger
har·bor
har·bor·age
hard-and-fast
hard·back
hard·ball
hard-bit·ten
hard-boiled
hard·edge
hard·en
hard·ened
hard·head·ed
hard·heart·ed
har·di·hood
har·di·ly
har·di·ness
hard·ly
hard-of-hear·ing
hard·pan
hard-shell
hard·ship
hard·stand
hard-sur·face
hard·tack
hard·top
hard·ware
hard·wood
hard·work·ing
har·dy
hare·brained
hare·lip
hare·lipped

har·em
har·le·quin
har·lot
harm·ful
harm·ful·ly
harm·less
har·mon·ic
har·mon·i·ca
har·mon·i·cal·ly
har·mon·ics
har·mo·ni·ous
har·mo·ni·um
har·mo·ni·za·tion
har·mo·nize
har·mo·ny
har·ness
harp·er
har·poon
harp·si·chord
har·py
har·ri·dan
har·ri·er
Har·ris·burg
har·row
har·ry
harsh·ness
Hart·ford
har·um-scar·um
har·vest
har·vest·er
has-been
hash·ish
has·sle
has·sock
haste
has·ten

hast·i·ly
hast·i·ness
hasty
hat·box
hatch
hatch·ery
hatch·et
hatch·ing
hatch·way
hate·ful
hate·ful·ly
ha·tred
hat·ter
haugh·ti·ly
haugh·ti·ness
haugh·ty
haul·age
haul·er
haunch
haunt
haunt·ing·ly
haute cou·ture
hau·teur
have
  had
  hav·ing
  has
ha·ven
have-not
hav·er·sack
hav·oc
Hawaii
Ha·wai·ian
hawk
hawk·er
hawk·ish

haw·ser
haw·thorn
hay·cock
hay·fork
hay·loft
hay·mow
hay·rack
hay·rick
hay·seed
hay·wire
haz·ard
haz·ard·ous
ha·zel
ha·zel·nut
haz·i·ly
haz·i·ness
hazy
head·ache
head·band
head·board
head·dress
head·ed
head·er
head·first
head·gear
head·hunt·er
head·i·ly
head·i·ness
head·ing
head·land
head·less
head·light
head·line
head·lin·er
head·lock
head·long

head·man
head·mas·ter
head·mis·tress
head·most
head·note
head-on
head·phone
head·piece
head·pin
head·quar·ters
head·rest
head·set
head·ship
heads·man
head·stall
head·stock
head·stone
head·strong
head·wait·er
head·wa·ter
head·way
head·word
head·work
heady
heal
  cure (*see* heel)

heal·er
health·ful
health·i·ly
health·i·ness
healthy
heap
hear
  heard
  hear·ing

hear·er
hear·ken
hear·say
hearse
heart·ache
heart·beat
heart·break
heart·bro·ken
heart·burn
heart·en
heart·felt
hearth
hearth·stone
heart·i·ly
heart·i·ness
heart·land
heart·less
heart·rend·ing
heart·sick
heart·sore
heart·string
heart·throb
heart-to-heart
hearty
heat·ed·ly
heat·er
heath
hea·then
heath·er
heat·stroke
heave
  heaved
  or hove

  heav·ing
heav·en

heav·en·ward
heav·i·ly
heavi·ness
heavy
heavy-du·ty
heavy-hand·ed
heavy·heart·ed
heavy·set
heavy·weight
He·bra·ic
He·brew
heck·le
heck·ler
hect·are
hec·tic
hec·ti·cal·ly
hedge
hedge·hog
hedge·hop
hedge·row
he·do·nism
he·do·nist
he·do·nis·tic
heed·ful
heed·ful·ly
heed·less
heel
  foot (see heal)

hefty
he·gem·o·ny
he·gi·ra
  also he·ji·ra

heif·er
height
height·en

hei·nous
heir
  inheritor (see air)

heir·ess
heir·loom
Hel·e·na
he·li·cal
he·li·coid
  or he·li·coi·dal

he·li·cop·ter
he·lio·cen·tric
he·lio·trope
he·li·port
he·li·um
he·lix
  pl hel·i·ces *also*
  he·lix·es

hell-bent
hell·cat
Hel·len·ic
Hel·le·nist
Hel·le·nis·tic
hel·lion
hell·ish
hel·lo
  pl hel·los

helm
hel·met
helms·man
hel·ot
help·er
help·ful
help·ful·ly
help·less
help·mate

hel·ter-skel·ter
hem
  hemmed
  hem·ming
he·mal
he-man
he·ma·tite
he·ma·tol·o·gist
he·ma·tol·o·gy
hemi·sphere
hemi·spher·i·cal
hem·line
hem·lock
he·mo·glo·bin
  also hae·mo·glo·bin

he·mo·ly·sis
he·mo·lyt·ic
he·mo·phil·ia
he·mo·phil·i·ac
hem·or·rhage
hem·or·rhag·ic
hem·or·rhoid
hem·stitch
hence·forth
hence·for·ward
hench·man
hen·na
hen·peck
he·pat·ic
hep·a·ti·tis
hep·ta·gon
hep·tam·e·ter
her·ald
he·ral·dic
her·ald·ry

her·ba·ceous
her·bar·i·um
her·bi·cid·al
her·bi·cide
her·bi·vore
her·biv·o·rous
her·cu·le·an
herd·er
herds·man
here·abouts
  or here·about

here·af·ter
here·by
he·red·i·tary
he·red·i·ty
here·in
here·of
here·on
her·e·sy
her·e·tic
he·ret·i·cal
here·to
here·to·fore
here·un·der
here·un·to
here·upon
here·with
her·i·ta·ble
her·i·tage
her·met·ic
  also her·met·i·cal

her·met·i·cal·ly
her·mit
her·mit·age
her·nia

her·ni·ate
he·ro
  pl he·roes

he·ro·ic
he·ro·ical·ly
he·ro·ics
her·o·in
  narcotic (see heroine)

her·o·ine
  female hero (see
  heroin)

her·o·ism
her·on
her·pes
her·pe·tol·o·gist
her·pe·tol·o·gy
her·ring
her·ring·bone
her·self
hes·i·tance
hes·i·tan·cy
hes·i·tant
hes·i·tate
hes·i·ta·tion
het·ero·dox
het·ero·doxy
het·er·o·ge·ne·ity
het·er·o·ge·neous
het·ero·sex·u·al
het·ero·sex·u·al·
  i·ty
hew
  cut (see hue)

  hewed
  hewed
    or hewn

hew·ing
hexa·chlo·ro·
phene
hexa·gon
hex·ag·o·nal
hexa·gram
hex·am·e·ter
hey·day
Hi·a·le·ah
hi·a·tus
hi·ba·chi
hi·ber·nate
hi·ber·na·tion
hi·ber·na·tor
hi·bis·cus
hic·cup
    also hic·cough

hic·cuped
    also hic·cupped

hic·cup·ing
    also hic·cup·ping

hick·o·ry
hi·dal·go
    pl hi·dal·gos

hide
    hid
    hid·den
        or hid

    hid·ing
hide·away
hide·bound
hid·eous
hide·out
hie
    hied

hy·ing
    or hie·ing
hi·er·ar·chi·cal
    or hi·er·ar·chic

hi·er·ar·chi·cal·
ly
hi·er·ar·chy
hi·ero·glyph·ic
    or hi·ero·glyph·i·cal

hi-fi
hig·gle·dy-pig·gle·
dy
high·ball
high·born
high·boy
high·bred
high·brow
high·er-up
high·fa·lu·tin
high-flown
high-fly·ing
high-hand·ed
high-hat
high·land
high·land·er
high-lev·el
high·light
high-mind·ed
high·ness
high-oc·tane
high-pres·sure
high-rise
high·road
high-sound·ing
high-spir·it·ed

high-strung
high·tail
high-ten·sion
high-test
high-toned
high-wa·ter
high·way
high·way·man
hi·jack
    or high-jack

hi·jack·er
hik·er
hi·lar·i·ous
hi·lar·i·ty
hill·bil·ly
hill·ock
hill·side
hill·top
hilly
him·self
hin·der
hind·most
hind·quar·ter
hin·drance
hind·sight
Hin·du·ism
hin·ter·land
hip·bone
hip·pie
    or hip·py

Hip·po·crat·ic
hip·po·drome
hip·po·pot·a·mus
    pl hip·po·pot·a·mus·
    es *or* hip·po·pot·
    a·mi

hip·ster
hire·ling
hir·sute
His·pan·ic
his·ta·mine
his·to·gen
his·to·gen·e·sis
his·to·gram
his·tol·o·gist
his·tol·o·gy
his·to·ri·an
his·tor·ic
his·tor·i·cal
his·tor·i·cal·ly
his·to·ric·i·ty
his·to·ri·og·ra·
  pher
his·to·ri·og·ra·
  phy
his·to·ry
his·tri·on·ic
his·tri·on·i·cal·ly
his·tri·on·ics
hit
  hit
  hit·ting
hitch·hike
hitch·hik·er
hith·er·to
hit·ter
hive
  bee house

hives
  pl hives
  allergic disorder

hoard
  accumulate (see
    horde)
hoar·frost
hoar·i·ness
hoarse
  harsh (see horse)
hoarse·ly
hoary
hoax
hob·ble
hob·by
hob·by·horse
hob·gob·lin
hob·nail
hob·nob
  hob·nobbed
  hob·nob·bing
ho·bo
  pl ho·boes *also*
    ho·bos
hob·by·ist
hock·ey
ho·cus-po·cus
hodge·podge
ho·gan
hog·gish
hogs·head
hog-tie
hog·wash
hoi pol·loi
hoist
ho·kum
hold
  held
  hold·ing

hold·out
hold·over
hold·up
hol·i·day
ho·li·ness
Hol·land
  (see Netherlands)

Hol·land·er
hol·low
hol·ly
hol·ly·hock
Hol·ly·wood
ho·lo·caust
ho·lo·gram
ho·lo·graph
ho·log·ra·phy
hol·stein
hol·ster
ho·ly
hom·age
hom·bre
hom·burg
home·body
home·bred
home·com·ing
home·grown
home·land
home·less
home·li·ness
home·ly
home·made
home·mak·er
ho·meo·path·ic
ho·me·op·a·thy
hom·er

home·room
home·sick
home·spun
home·stead
home·stead·er
home·stretch
home·ward
  or home·wards

home·work
hom·ey
  also homy

ho·mi·cid·al
ho·mi·cide
hom·i·let·ic
hom·i·let·ics
hom·i·ly
hom·i·nid
hom·i·noid
hom·i·ny
ho·mo·ge·ne·i·ty
ho·mo·ge·neous
ho·mog·e·ni·za·
  tion
ho·mog·e·nize
ho·mog·e·nous
ho·mo·graph
ho·mol·o·gous
hom·onym
ho·mo·phone
ho·mo sa·pi·ens
ho·mo·sex·u·al
ho·mo·sex·u·al·i·
  ty
Hon·du·ran
Hon·du·ras

hone
hon·est
hon·es·ty
hon·ey
hon·ey·bee
hon·ey·comb
hon·ey·dew
hon·ey·moon
hon·ey·suck·le
hon·ky-tonk
Ho·no·lu·lu
hon·or
hon·or·able
hon·or·ably
hon·o·rar·i·um
  pl hon·o·rar·ia *also*
  hon·o·rar·i·ums

hon·or·ary
hon·or·if·ic
hood·ed
hood·lum
hoo·doo
  pl hoo·doos

hood·wink
hoo·ey
hoof
  pl hooves *or* hoofs

hoo·kah
hook·up
hook·worm
hoo·li·gan
hoop·la
hoo·te·nan·ny
hop
  hopped
  hop·ping

hope·ful
hope·ful·ly
hope·less
hop·per
hop·scotch
horde
  throng (see hoard)

hore·hound
ho·ri·zon
hor·i·zon·tal
hor·i·zon·tal·ly
hor·mon·al
hor·mone
horn·book
hor·net
horn·pipe
horn·swog·gle
horny
hor·o·log·i·cal
ho·rol·o·gist
ho·rol·o·gy
horo·scope
hor·ren·dous
hor·ri·ble
hor·ri·bly
hor·rid
hor·ri·fy
hor·ror
hors d'oeuvre
horse
  animal (see hoarse)

horse·back
horse·flesh
horse·fly
horse·hair

horse·hide
horse·laugh
horse·man
horse·play
horse·pow·er
horse·rad·ish
horse·shoe
horse·whip
horse·wom·an
hors·ey
　or horsy

hor·ta·tive
hor·ta·to·ry
hor·ti·cul·tur·al
hor·ti·cul·ture
hor·ti·cul·tur·ist
ho·san·na
hose
　pl hose *or* hos·es

ho·siery
hos·pice
hos·pi·ta·ble
hos·pi·ta·bly
hos·pi·tal
hos·pi·tal·i·ty
hos·pi·tal·iza·tion
hos·pi·tal·ize
hos·tage
hos·tel
hos·tel·er
hos·tel·ry
host·ess
hos·tile
hos·tile·ly
hos·til·i·ty

hos·tler
hot·bed
hot-blood·ed
hot·box
ho·tel
hot·foot
　pl hot·foots

hot·head·ed
hot·house
hot-rod·der
hot·shot
hour·glass
hour·ly
house
　pl hous·es

house·boat
house·boy
house·break·ing
house·bro·ken
house·clean
house·coat
house·fly
house·ful
house·hold
house·keep·er
house·lights
house·man
house·maid
house·moth·er
house·top
house·warm·ing
house·wife
house·work
hous·ing
Hous·ton

hov·el
hov·er
Hov·er·craft
how·be·it
how·dah
how·ev·er
how·it·zer
howl·er
how·so·ev·er
hoy·den
hua·ra·che
hub·bub
hu·bris
huck·le·ber·ry
huck·ster
hud·dle
hue
　color (see hew)

huff·ish
huffy
hug
　hugged
　hug·ging
huge·ly
Hu·gue·not
hu·la
　also hu·la-hu·la

hulk·ing
hul·la·ba·loo
　pl hul·la·ba·loos

hum
　hummed
　hum·ming
hu·man
hu·mane

hu·mane·ly
hu·man·ism
hu·man·ist
hu·man·is·tic
hu·man·i·tar·i·
an
hu·man·i·ty
hu·man·iza·tion
hu·man·ize
hu·man·kind
hu·man·ly
hum·ble
hum·bler
hum·bly
hum·bug
hum·ding·er
hum·drum
hu·mer·al
hu·mer·us
hu·mid
hu·mid·i·fi·ca·
tion
hu·mid·i·fi·er
hu·mid·i·fy
hu·mid·i·ty
hu·mi·dor
hu·mil·i·ate
hu·mil·i·a·tion
hu·mil·i·ty
hum·ming·bird
hum·mock
hu·mor
hu·mor·ist
hu·mor·ous
hump-back
hu·mus

hunch·back
hun·dred
hun·dredth
hun·dred·weight
Hun·gar·i·an
Hun·ga·ry
hun·ger
hun·gri·ly
hun·gry
hun·ky-do·ry
hunt·er
Hun·ting·ton
Beach
hunt·ress
hunts·man
Hunts·ville
hur·dle
obstacle (see hurtle)

hur·dy-gur·dy
hurl·er
hur·ly-bur·ly
hur·rah
hur·ri·cane
hur·ried·ly
hur·ried·ness
hur·ry
hurt
hurt
hurt·ing
hurt·ful
hur·tle
hurl (see hurdle)

hus·band
hus·band·man
hus·band·ry

hush-hush
husk·er
hus·ki·ly
hus·ki·ness
husk·ing
hus·ky
hus·sar
hus·sy
hus·tings
hus·tle
hus·tler
huz·zah
or huz·za

hy·a·cinth
hy·brid
hy·brid·iza·tion
hy·brid·ize
hy·dran·gea
hy·drant
hy·drate
hy·drau·lic
hy·drau·lics
hy·dride
hy·dro
pl hy·dros

hy·dro·car·bon
hy·dro·chlo·ric
acid
hy·dro·elec·tric
hy·dro·foil
hy·dro·gen
hy·dro·ge·nate
hy·dro·ge·na·tion
hy·drog·e·nous
hy·dro·log·ic

hy·drol·o·gist
hy·drol·o·gy
hy·dro·ly·sis
hy·drom·e·ter
hy·dron·ic
hy·dro·pho·bia
hy·dro·plane
hy·dro·pon·ics
hy·dro·stat·ic
hy·dro·ther·a·py
hy·drous
hy·drox·ide
hy·e·na
hy·giene
hy·gien·ic
hy·gien·i·cal·ly
hy·gien·ist
hy·grom·e·ter
hy·gro·scop·ic
hy·men
hy·me·ne·al
hymn
hym·nal
hym·no·dy
hym·nol·o·gy
hy·per·acid·i·ty
hy·per·ac·tive
hy·per·bar·ic
hy·per·bo·la
   curve

hy·per·bo·le
   exaggeration

hy·per·bol·ic
hy·per·crit·i·cal

hy·per·crit·i·cal·
  ly
hy·per·gly·ce·mia
   excess sugar (see
   hypoglycemia)

hy·per·sen·si·tive
hy·per·sen·si·tiv·
  i·ty
hy·per·son·ic
hy·per·ten·sion
hy·per·tro·phic
hy·per·tro·phy
hy·phen
hy·phen·ate
hy·phen·ation
hyp·no·sis
hyp·not·ic
hyp·not·i·cal·ly
hyp·no·tism
hyp·no·tist
hyp·no·tize
hy·po·chon·dria
hy·po·chon·dri·ac
hy·poc·ri·sy
hyp·o·crite
hyp·o·crit·i·cal
hyp·o·crit·i·cal·ly
hy·po·der·mic
hy·po·gly·ce·mia
   decrease of sugar
   (see hyperglycemia)

hy·pot·e·nuse
hy·poth·e·cate
hy·poth·e·sis
hy·poth·e·size
hy·po·thet·i·cal

hy·po·thet·i⁀cal·
  ly
hys·ter·ec·to·my
hys·te·ria
hys·ter·ic
hys·ter·i·cal
hys·ter·i·cal·ly
hys·ter·ics

I

iam·bic
ibi·dem
ice·berg
ice·boat
ice·bound
ice·box
ice·break·er
ice-cold
ice·house
Ice·land
Ice·land·er
Ice·lan·dic
ice·man
ice-skate
ich·thy·ol·o·gist
ich·thy·ol·o·gy
ici·cle
ic·i·ly
ic·i·ness
ic·ing
icon
   or ikon

icon·o·clasm
icon·o·clast

icy
Ida·ho
idea
ide·al
ide·al·ism
ide·al·ist
ide·al·is·tic
ide·al·is·ti·cal·ly
ide·al·iza·tion
ide·al·ize
ide·al·ly
ide·ate
ide·ation
idem
iden·ti·cal
iden·ti·cal·ly
iden·ti·fi·able
iden·ti·fi·ably
iden·ti·fi·ca·tion
iden·ti·fi·er
iden·ti·fy
iden·ti·ty
ideo·gram
ideo·graph
ideo·log·i·cal
   also ideo·log·ic

ideo·log·i·cal·ly
ide·ol·o·gist
ide·ol·o·gy
id·i·o·cy
id·i·om
id·i·om·at·ic
id·i·om·at·i·cal·
   ly
id·io·syn·cra·sy

id·io·syn·crat·ic
id·io·syn·crat·i·
   cal·ly
id·i·ot
id·i·ot·ic
id·i·ot·i·cal·ly
idle
   inactive (*see* idol,
      idyll)
idle·ness
idler
idly
idol
   object of worship
      (*see* idle, idyll)
idol·a·ter
idol·a·trous
idol·a·try
idol·iza·tion
idol·ize
idyll
   or idyl
   poem (*see* idle, idol)
idyl·lic
if·fy
ig·loo
   pl ig·loos

ig·ne·ous
ig·nit·able
   also ig·nit·ible
ig·nite
ig·ni·tion
ig·no·ble
ig·no·bly
ig·no·min·i·ous
ig·no·mi·ny

ig·no·ra·mus
ig·no·rance
ig·no·rant
ig·nore
igua·na
ikon
   var of icon

il·e·itis
il·e·um
   pl il·ea
   intestine (*see* ilium)

il·i·um
   pl il·ia
   bone (*see* ileum)

ill
   worse
   worst
ill-ad·vised
ill-be·ing
ill-bod·ing
ill-bred
il·le·gal
il·le·gal·i·ty
il·le·gal·ly
il·leg·i·bil·i·ty
il·leg·i·ble
il·leg·i·bly
il·le·git·i·ma·cy
il·le·git·i·mate
il·le·git·i·mate·ly
ill-fat·ed
ill-fa·vored
ill-got·ten
ill-hu·mored
il·lib·er·al

il·lic·it
unlawful (see elicit)

il·lim·it·able

il·lim·it·ably

Il·li·nois

il·lit·er·a·cy

il·lit·er·ate

ill-man·nered

ill-na·tured

ill·ness

il·log·i·cal

il·log·i·cal·ly

ill-sort·ed

ill-starred

ill-tem·pered

ill-treat

il·lu·mi·nate

il·lu·mi·na·tion

il·lu·mi·na·tor

il·lu·mine

ill-us·age

ill-use

il·lu·sion
mistaken idea (see allusion)

il·lu·sion·ist

il·lu·sive
deceptive (see allusive)

il·lu·so·ry

il·lus·trate

il·lus·tra·tion

il·lus·tra·tive

il·lus·tra·tor

il·lus·tri·ous

im·age

im·ag·ery

imag·in·able

imag·in·ably

imag·i·nary

imag·i·na·tion

imag·i·na·tive

imag·ine

im·ag·ism

im·ag·ist

im·bal·ance

im·be·cile

im·be·cil·i·ty

im·bed
var of embed

im·bibe

im·bib·er

im·bri·cate

im·bri·ca·tion

im·bro·glio
pl im·bro·glios

im·brue

im·bue

im·i·ta·ble

im·i·tate

im·i·ta·tion

im·i·ta·tive

im·i·ta·tor

im·mac·u·late

im·ma·nent
inherent (see eminent, imminent)

im·ma·te·ri·al

im·ma·ture

im·ma·tu·ri·ty

im·mea·sur·able

im·mea·sur·ably

im·me·di·a·cy

im·me·di·ate

im·me·di·ate·ly

im·me·mo·ri·al

im·mense

im·mense·ly

im·men·si·ty

im·merse

im·mer·sion

im·mi·grant

im·mi·grate
come into a country (see emigrate)

im·mi·gra·tion

im·mi·nence

im·mi·nent
impending (see eminent, immanent)

im·mis·ci·ble

im·mit·i·ga·ble

im·mo·bile

im·mo·bil·i·ty

im·mo·bi·li·za·tion

im·mo·bi·lize

im·mod·er·a·cy

im·mod·er·ate

im·mod·est

im·mod·es·ty

im·mo·late

im·mo·la·tion

im·mor·al

im·mo·ral·i·ty

im·mor·al·ly

im·mor·tal

im·mor·tal·i·ty
im·mor·tal·ize
im·mor·tal·ly
im·mov·abil·i·ty
im·mov·able
im·mov·ably
im·mune
im·mu·ni·ty
im·mu·ni·za·tion
im·mu·nize
im·mu·nol·o·gist
im·mu·nol·o·gy
im·mure
im·mu·ta·bil·i·ty
im·mu·ta·ble
im·mu·ta·bly
im·pact
im·pact·ed
im·pair
im·pair·ment
im·pa·la
im·pale
im·pal·pa·bil·i·ty
im·pal·pa·ble
im·pal·pa·bly
im·pan·el
im·part
im·part·able
*able to
   communicate
   (see impartible)*
im·par·tial
im·par·tial·i·ty
im·par·tial·ly
im·par·ti·ble
*not partible
   (see impartable)*

im·pass·able
*not passable (see
   impassible)*

im·pass·ably
im·passe
im·pas·si·ble
*unfeeling (see
   impassable)*

im·pas·si·bly
im·pas·sioned
im·pas·sive
im·pas·siv·i·ty
im·pa·tience
im·pa·tient
im·peach
im·peach·ment
im·pec·ca·bil·i·ty
im·pec·ca·ble
im·pec·ca·bly
im·pe·cu·nious
im·ped·ance
im·pede
im·ped·i·ment
im·ped·i·men·ta
im·pel
  im·pelled
  im·pel·ling
im·pend
im·pen·e·tra·bil·i·ty
im·pen·e·tra·ble
im·pen·e·tra·bly
im·pen·i·tent
im·per·a·tive
im·per·ceiv·able

im·per·cep·ti·bil·i·ty
im·per·cep·ti·ble
im·per·cep·ti·bly
im·per·cep·tive
im·per·fect
im·per·fec·tion
im·per·fo·rate
im·pe·ri·al
im·pe·ri·al·ism
im·pe·ri·al·ist
im·pe·ri·al·is·tic
im·pe·ri·al·is·ti·cal·ly
im·pe·ri·al·ly
im·per·il
  im·per·iled
  or im·per·illed

  im·per·il·ing
  or im·per·il·ling

im·pe·ri·ous
im·per·ish·abil·i·ty
im·per·ish·able
im·per·ish·ably
im·per·ma·nence
im·per·ma·nen·cy
im·per·ma·nent
im·per·me·abil·i·ty
im·per·me·able
im·per·me·ably
im·per·mis·si·bil·i·ty
im·per·mis·si·ble

im·per·son·al
im·per·son·al·i·ty
im·per·son·al·ize
im·per·son·al·ly
im·per·son·ate
im·per·son·ation
im·per·son·ator
im·per·ti·nence
im·per·ti·nent
im·per·turb·abil·
　i·ty
im·per·turb·able
im·per·turb·ably
im·per·vi·ous
im·pe·ti·go
im·pet·u·os·i·ty
im·pet·u·ous
im·pe·tus
im·pi·ety
im·pinge
im·pinge·ment
im·pi·ous
imp·ish
im·pla·ca·ble
im·pla·ca·bly
im·plant
im·plan·ta·tion
im·plau·si·bil·i·ty
im·plau·si·ble
im·plau·si·bly
im·ple·ment
im·ple·men·ta·
　tion
im·pli·cate
im·pli·ca·tion
im·plic·it

im·plode
im·plore
im·plo·sion
im·plo·sive
im·ply
im·po·lite
im·pol·i·tic
im·pon·der·abil·
　i·ty
im·pon·der·a·ble
im·pon·der·a·bly
im·port
im·port·able
im·por·tance
im·por·tant
im·por·ta·tion
im·port·er
im·por·tu·nate
im·por·tune
im·por·tu·ni·ty
im·pose
im·pos·ing
im·po·si·tion
im·pos·si·bil·i·ty
im·pos·si·ble
im·pos·si·bly
im·post
im·pos·tor
　or im·pos·ter

im·pos·ture
im·po·tence
im·po·ten·cy
im·po·tent
im·pound
im·pov·er·ish

im·prac·ti·ca·bil·
　i·ty
im·prac·ti·ca·ble
im·prac·ti·ca·bly
im·prac·ti·cal
im·prac·ti·cal·i·
　ty
im·pre·cate
im·pre·ca·tion
im·pre·cise
im·pre·ci·sion
im·preg·na·bil·i·
　ty
im·preg·na·ble
im·preg·na·bly
im·preg·nate
im·preg·na·tion
im·pre·sa·rio
　pl im·pre·sa·ri·os

im·press
im·press·ible
im·pres·sion
im·pres·sion·abil·
　i·ty
im·pres·sion·able
im·pres·sion·ably
im·pres·sion·ism
im·pres·sion·ist
im·pres·sion·is·tic
im·pres·sive
im·pres·sive·ly
im·press·ment
im·pri·ma·tur
im·print
im·pris·on

im·pris·on·ment
im·prob·a·bil·i·ty
im·prob·a·ble
im·prob·a·bly
im·promp·tu
im·prop·er
im·pro·pri·ety
im·prov·abil·i·ty
im·prov·able
im·prove
im·prove·ment
im·prov·i·dence
im·prov·i·dent
im·pro·vi·sa·tion
im·pro·vise
im·pro·vis·er
or im·pro·vi·sor

im·pru·dence
im·pru·dent
im·pu·dence
im·pu·dent
im·pugn
im·pulse
im·pul·sion
im·pul·sive
im·pul·sive·ly
im·pu·ni·ty
im·pu·ri·ty
im·put·abil·i·ty
im·put·able
im·pu·ta·tion
im·pute
in·abil·i·ty
in ab·sen·tia

in·ac·ces·si·bil·i·ty
in·ac·ces·si·ble
in·ac·cu·ra·cy
in·ac·cu·rate
in·ac·tion
in·ac·ti·vate
in·ac·ti·va·tion
in·ac·tive
in·ac·tiv·i·ty
in·ad·e·qua·cy
in·ad·e·quate
in·ad·mis·si·bil·i·ty
in·ad·mis·si·ble
in·ad·ver·tence
in·ad·ver·ten·cy
in·ad·ver·tent
in·ad·vis·abil·i·ty
in·ad·vis·able
in·alien·abil·i·ty
in·alien·able
in·alien·ably
in·al·ter·abil·i·ty
in·al·ter·able
in·al·ter·ably
in·amo·ra·ta
inane
in·an·i·mate
inan·i·ty
in·ap·pli·ca·bil·i·ty
in·ap·pli·ca·ble
in·ap·pli·ca·bly
in·ap·pre·cia·ble
in·ap·pre·cia·bly

in·ap·pro·pri·ate
in·apt
not suitable (see
inept)

in·ap·ti·tude
in·ar·tic·u·late
in·as·much as
in·at·ten·tion
in·at·ten·tive
in·au·di·bil·i·ty
in·au·di·ble
in·au·di·bly
in·au·gu·ral
in·au·gu·rate
in·au·gu·ra·tion
in·aus·pi·cious
in·board
in·born
in·bound
in·bred
in·breed·ing
in·cal·cu·la·bil·i·ty
in·cal·cu·la·ble
in·cal·cu·la·bly
in·can·des·cence
in·can·des·cent
in·can·ta·tion
in·ca·pa·bil·i·ty
in·ca·pa·ble
in·ca·pac·i·tate
in·ca·pac·i·ta·tion
in·ca·pac·i·ty
in·car·cer·ate
in·car·cer·a·tion

in·car·nate
in·car·na·tion
in·cau·tious
in·cen·di·a·rism
in·cen·di·ary
in·cense
in·cen·tive
in·cep·tion
in·cep·tive
in·cer·ti·tude
in·ces·sant
in·cest
in·ces·tu·ous
in·cho·ate
in·ci·dence
in·ci·dent
in·ci·den·tal
in·ci·den·tal·ly
in·cin·er·ate
in·cin·er·a·tion
in·cin·er·a·tor
in·cip·i·en·cy
  also in·cip·i·ence

in·cip·i·ent
in·cise
in·ci·sion
in·ci·sive
in·ci·sive·ly
in·ci·sor
in·ci·ta·tion
in·cite
in·cite·ment
in·ci·vil·i·ty
in·clem·en·cy
in·clem·ent

in·clin·able
in·cli·na·tion
in·cline
in·clin·ing
in·cli·nom·e·ter
in·clud·able
  or in·clud·ible

in·clude
in·clu·sion
in·clu·sive
in·cog·ni·to
in·cog·ni·zant
in·co·her·ence
in·co·her·ent
in·com·bus·ti·ble
in·come
in·com·ing
in·com·men·su·
  ra·ble
in·com·men·su·
  ra·bly
in·com·men·su·
  rate
in·com·mode
in·com·mo·di·ous
in·com·mu·ni·ca·
  bil·i·ty
in·com·mu·ni·ca·
  ble
in·com·mu·ni·ca·
  bly
in·com·mu·ni·ca·
  do
in·com·mu·ni·ca·
  tive

in·com·mut·able
in·com·mut·ably
in·com·pa·ra·bil·
  i·ty
in·com·pa·ra·ble
in·com·pa·ra·bly
in·com·pat·i·bil·
  i·ty
in·com·pat·i·ble
in·com·pe·tence
in·com·pe·ten·cy
in·com·pe·tent
in·com·plete
in·com·pre·hen·
  si·ble
in·com·press·ible
in·con·ceiv·abil·i·
  ty
in·con·ceiv·able
in·con·ceiv·ably
in·con·clu·sive
in·con·gru·ent
in·con·gru·ity
in·con·gru·ous
in·con·se·quen·
  tial
in·con·se·quen·
  tial·ly
in·con·sid·er·able
in·con·sid·er·ate
in·con·sid·er·ate·
  ly
in·con·sis·ten·cy
  also in·con·sis·tence

in·con·sis·tent

in·con·sol·able
in·con·sol·ably
in·con·spic·u·ous
in·con·stan·cy
in·con·stant
in·con·test·abil·i·ty
in·con·test·able
in·con·test·ably
in·con·ti·nence
in·con·ti·nent
in·con·trol·la·ble
in·con·tro·vert·ible
in·con·tro·vert·ibly
in·con·ve·nience
in·con·ve·nient
in·con·vert·ibil·i·ty
in·con·vert·ible
in·con·vert·ibly
in·cor·po·rate
in·cor·po·rat·ed
in·cor·po·ra·tion
in·cor·po·ra·tor
in·cor·po·re·al
in·cor·po·re·al·ly
in·cor·rect
in·cor·ri·gi·bil·i·ty
in·cor·ri·gi·ble
in·cor·ri·gi·bly
in·cor·rupt
in·cor·rupt·ibil·i·ty

in·cor·rupt·ible
in·cor·rupt·ibly
in·creas·able
in·crease
in·creas·ing·ly
in·cred·ibil·i·ty
in·cred·i·ble
in·cred·i·bly
in·cre·du·li·ty
in·cred·u·lous·ly
in·cre·ment
in·cre·men·tal
in·crim·i·nate
in·crim·i·na·tion
in·crim·i·na·to·ry
in·crust
var of encrust
in·crus·ta·tion
in·cu·bate
in·cu·ba·tion
in·cu·ba·tor
in·cu·bus
   pl in·cu·bi *also*
   in·cu·bus·es
in·cul·cate
in·cul·ca·tion
in·cul·pa·ble
in·cul·pate
in·cul·pa·tion
in·cul·pa·to·ry
in·cum·ben·cy
in·cum·bent
in·cu·nab·u·lum
   pl in·cu·nab·u·la
in·cur
in·curred

in·cur·ring
in·cur·abil·i·ty
in·cur·able
in·cur·ably
in·cu·ri·ous
in·cur·sion
in·debt·ed
in·de·cen·cy
in·de·cent
in·de·ci·pher·able
in·de·ci·sion
in·de·ci·sive
in·de·clin·able
in·de·co·rous
in·de·co·rum
in·deed
in·de·fa·ti·ga·bil·i·ty
in·de·fat·i·ga·ble
in·de·fat·i·ga·bly
in·de·fea·si·ble
in·de·fea·si·bly
in·de·fen·si·bil·i·ty
in·de·fen·si·ble
in·de·fen·si·bly
in·de·fin·able
in·def·i·nite
in·del·i·ble
in·del·i·bly
in·del·i·ca·cy
in·del·i·cate
in·dem·ni·fi·ca·tion
in·dem·ni·fy
in·dem·ni·ty

in·dent
in·den·ta·tion
in·den·tion
in·den·ture
in·de·pen·dence
in·de·pen·den·cy
in·de·pen·dent
in·de·scrib·able
in·de·scrib·ably
in·de·struc·ti·bil·
i·ty
in·de·struc·ti·ble
in·de·struc·ti·bly
in·de·ter·min·
able
in·de·ter·min·
ably
in·de·ter·mi·na·
cy
in·de·ter·mi·nate
in·de·ter·mi·
nate·ly
in·de·ter·mi·na·
tion
in·de·ter·min·ism
in·dex
  pl in·dex·es *or*
    in·di·ces

in·dex·er
In·dia
In·di·an
In·di·ana
In·di·a·nap·o·lis
in·di·cate
in·di·ca·tion
in·dic·a·tive

in·di·ca·tor
in·di·cia
in·dict
  charge (see indite)

in·dict·able
in·dict·ment
in·dif·fer·ence
in·dif·fer·ent
in·dif·fer·ent·ism
in·di·gence
in·di·gene
  also in·di·gen

in·dig·e·nous
in·di·gent
in·di·gest·ibil·i·ty
in·di·gest·ible
in·di·ges·tion
in·dig·nant
in·dig·na·tion
in·dig·ni·ty
in·di·go
  pl in·di·gos *or*
    in·di·goes

in·di·rect
in·di·rec·tion
in·dis·cern·ible
in·dis·creet
  imprudent

in·dis·crete
  not separated

in·dis·cre·tion
  imprudence

in·dis·crim·i·nate
in·dis·pens·abil·i·
ty

in·dis·pens·able
in·dis·pens·ably
in·dis·posed
in·dis·po·si·tion
in·dis·put·able
in·dis·put·ably
in·dis·sol·u·ble
in·dis·sol·u·bly
in·dis·tinct
in·dis·tin·guish·
able
in·dis·tin·guish·
ably
in·dite
  compose (see indict)

in·di·vid·u·al
in·di·vid·u·al·ism
in·di·vid·u·al·ist
in·di·vid·u·al·is·
tic
in·di·vid·u·al·is·
ti·cal·ly
in·di·vid·u·al·i·ty
in·di·vid·u·al·
iza·tion
in·di·vid·u·al·ize
in·di·vid·u·al·ly
in·di·vis·i·bil·i·ty
in·di·vis·i·ble
in·di·vis·i·bly
in·doc·tri·nate
in·doc·tri·na·tion
in·doc·tri·na·tor
in·do·lence
in·do·lent

in·dom·i·ta·bil·i·
ty
in·dom·i·ta·ble
in·dom·i·ta·bly
In·do·ne·sia
In·do·ne·sian
in·door
in·doors
in·dorse
    var of endorse

in·du·bi·ta·bil·i·
ty
in·du·bi·ta·ble
in·du·bi·ta·bly
in·duce
in·duce·ment
in·duct
in·duc·tance
in·duct·ee
in·duc·tion
in·duc·tive
in·duc·tor
in·dulge
in·dul·gence
in·dul·gent
in·du·rate
in·du·ra·tion
in·dus·tri·al
in·dus·tri·al·ism
in·dus·tri·al·ist
in·dus·tri·al·iza·
tion
in·dus·tri·al·ize
in·dus·tri·al·ly
in·dus·tri·ous

in·dus·try
ine·bri·ate
ine·bri·a·tion
in·ebri·ety
in·ed·i·ble
in·ed·it·ed
in·ed·u·ca·ble
in·ef·fa·bil·i·ty
in·ef·fa·ble
in·ef·fa·bly
in·ef·face·abil·i·
ty
in·ef·face·able
in·ef·fec·tive
in·ef·fec·tu·al
in·ef·fec·tu·al·ly
in·ef·fi·ca·cious
in·ef·fi·ca·cy
in·ef·fi·cien·cy
in·ef·fi·cient
in·elas·tic
in·elas·tic·i·ty
in·el·e·gance
in·el·e·gant
in·el·i·gi·bil·i·ty
in·el·i·gi·ble
in·el·o·quent
in·eluc·ta·bil·i·ty
in·eluc·ta·ble
in·eluc·ta·bly
in·ept
    unfit (see inapt)

in·ep·ti·tude
in·equal·i·ty
in·eq·ui·ta·ble

in·eq·ui·ty
    injustice (see
    iniquity)

in·erad·i·ca·ble
in·erad·i·ca·bly
in·er·ran·cy
in·er·rant
in·ert
in·er·tia
in·er·tial
in·es·cap·able
in·es·cap·ably
in·es·sen·tial
in·es·ti·ma·ble
in·es·ti·ma·bly
in·ev·i·ta·bil·i·ty
in·ev·i·ta·ble
in·ev·i·ta·bly
in·ex·act
in·ex·cus·able
in·ex·cus·ably
in·ex·haust·ibil·i·
ty
in·ex·haust·ible
in·ex·haust·ibly
in·ex·o·ra·ble
in·ex·o·ra·bly
in·ex·pe·di·en·cy
in·ex·pe·di·ent
in·ex·pen·sive
in·ex·pe·ri·ence
in·ex·pert
in·ex·pi·a·ble
in·ex·pli·ca·bil·i·
ty
in·ex·pli·ca·ble

in·ex·pli·ca·bly
in·ex·press·ibil·i·ty
in·ex·press·ible
in·ex·press·ibly
in·ex·pres·sive
in·ex·pug·na·ble
in·ex·pug·na·bly
in ex·ten·so
in·ex·tin·guish·able
in·ex·tin·guish·ably
in ex·tre·mis
in·ex·tri·ca·bil·i·ty
in·ex·tri·ca·ble
in·ex·tri·ca·bly
in·fal·li·bil·i·ty
in·fal·li·ble
in·fal·li·bly
in·fa·mous
in·fa·my
in·fan·cy
in·fant
in·fan·ti·cide
in·fan·tile
in·fan·til·ism
in·fan·til·i·ty
in·fan·try
in·fan·try·man
in·fat·u·ate
in·fat·u·a·tion
in·fect
in·fec·tion
in·fec·tious

in·fec·tive
in·fec·tor
in·fe·lic·i·tous
in·fe·lic·i·ty
in·fer
  in·ferred
  in·fer·ring
  in·fer·able
  or in·fer·ri·ble
in·fer·ence
in·fer·en·tial
in·fer·en·tial·ly
in·fe·ri·or
in·fe·ri·or·i·ty
in·fer·nal
in·fer·nal·ly
in·fer·no
in·fer·tile
in·fer·til·i·ty
in·fest
in·fes·ta·tion
in·fi·del
in·fi·del·i·ty
in·field
in·field·er
in·fight·ing
in·fil·trate
in·fil·tra·tion
in·fil·tra·tor
in·fi·nite
in·fi·nite·ly
in·fin·i·tes·i·mal
in·fin·i·tes·i·mal·ly
in·fin·i·tive

in·fin·i·tude
in·fin·i·ty
in·firm
in·fir·ma·ry
in·fir·mi·ty
in·flame
in·flam·ma·ble
in·flam·ma·tion
in·flam·ma·to·ry
in·flat·able
in·flate
in·fla·tion
in·fla·tion·ary
in·flect
in·flec·tion
in·flex·i·bil·i·ty
in·flex·i·ble
in·flex·i·bly
in·flict
in·flic·tion
in·flo·res·cence
in·flow
in·flu·ence
in·flu·en·tial
in·flu·en·za
in·flux
in·fold
in·form
in·for·mal
in·for·mal·i·ty
in·for·mal·ly
in·for·mant
in·for·ma·tion
in·for·ma·tive
in·formed
in·form·er

in·fra
in·frac·tion
in·fran·gi·bil·i·ty
in·fran·gi·ble
in·fran·gi·bly
in·fra·red
in·fra·son·ic
in·fre·quent
in·fringe
in·fringe·ment
in·fu·ri·ate
in·fu·ri·a·tion
in·fuse
in·fus·ible
in·fu·sion
in·gath·er·ing
in·ge·nious
clever (see
ingenuous)

in·ge·nue
or in·gé·nue

in·ge·nu·ity
in·gen·u·ous
straightforward (see
ingenious)

in·gest
in·gest·ible
in·ges·tion
in·glo·ri·ous
in·got
in·grain
in·grained
in·grate
in·gra·ti·ate
in·gra·ti·at·ing
in·grat·i·tude

in·gre·di·ent
in·gress
in-group
in·grow·ing
in·grown
in·hab·it
in·hab·it·able
in·hab·it·an·cy
in·hab·it·ant
in·hal·ant
in·ha·la·tion
in·ha·la·tor
in·hale
in·hal·er
in·har·mon·ic
in·har·mo·ni·ous
in·har·mo·ny
in·here
in·her·ence
in·her·ent
in·her·it
in·her·it·able
in·her·i·tance
in·her·i·tor
in·hib·it
in·hi·bi·tion
in·hib·i·tor
or in·hib·it·er

in·hib·i·to·ry
in·hos·pi·ta·ble
in·hos·pi·ta·bly
in-house
in·hu·man
in·hu·mane
in·hu·man·i·ty

in·hu·ma·tion
in·im·i·cal
in·im·i·cal·ly
in·im·i·ta·ble
in·im·i·ta·bly
in·iq·ui·tous
in·iq·ui·ty
wickedness (see
inequity)

ini·tial
ini·tialed
or ini·tialled

ini·tial·ing
or ini·tial·ling

ini·tial·ly
ini·ti·ate
ini·ti·a·tion
ini·tia·tive
ini·ti·a·tor
ini·tia·to·ry
in·ject
in·jec·tion
in·jec·tor
in·ju·di·cious
in·junc·tion
in·jure
in·ju·ri·ous
in·ju·ry
in·jus·tice
ink·blot
in·kling
ink·stand
ink·well
inky
in·laid
in·land

in-law
in·lay
in·let
in·mate
in me·di·as res
in me·mo·ri·am
in·most
in·nards
in·nate
in·nate·ly
in·ner
in·ner-di·rect·ed
in·ner·most
in·ner·sole
in·ning
inn·keep·er
in·no·cence
in·no·cent
in·noc·u·ous
in·no·vate
in·no·va·tion
in·no·va·tive
in·no·va·tor
in·nu·en·do
  pl in·nu·en·dos *or*
    in·nu·en·does

in·nu·mer·a·ble
in·nu·mer·a·bly
in·oc·u·late
in·oc·u·la·tion
in·of·fen·sive
in·op·er·a·ble
in·op·er·a·tive
in·op·por·tune
in·or·di·nate
in·or·gan·ic

in·pa·tient
in·put
in·quest
in·qui·etude
in·quire
in·quir·er
in·quir·ing·ly
in·qui·ry
in·qui·si·tion
in·quis·i·tive
in·quis·i·tor
in re
in rem
in·road
in·rush
in·sa·lu·bri·ous
in·sane
in·san·i·tary
in·san·i·ty
in·sa·tia·bil·i·ty
in·sa·tia·ble
in·sa·tia·bly
in·sa·tiate
in·scribe
in·scrip·tion
in·scru·ta·bil·i·ty
in·scru·ta·ble
in·scru·ta·bly
in·seam
in·sect
in·sec·ti·cide
in·se·cure
in·se·cu·ri·ty
in·sem·i·na·tion
in·sem·i·nate
in·sen·sate

in·sen·si·bil·i·ty
in·sen·si·ble
in·sen·si·bly
in·sen·si·tive
in·sen·si·tiv·i·ty
in·sen·tience
in·sen·tient
in·sep·a·ra·bil·i·
  ty
in·sep·a·ra·ble
in·sep·a·ra·bly
in·sert
in·ser·tion
in·set
  in·set
    or in·set·ted

  in·set·ting
in·shore
in·side
in·sid·er
in·sid·i·ous
in·sight
in·sig·nia
  or in·sig·ne
  pl in·sig·nia *or*
    in·sig·ni·as

in·sig·nif·i·cance
in·sig·nif·i·cant
in·sin·cere
in·sin·cere·ly
in·sin·cer·i·ty
in·sin·u·ate
in·sin·u·at·ing
in·sin·u·a·tion
in·sip·id
in·si·pid·i·ty

in·sist
in·sis·tence
in·sis·tent
in si·tu
in·so·far
in·sole
in·so·lence
in·so·lent
in·sol·u·bil·i·ty
in·sol·u·ble
in·sol·u·bly
in·solv·able
in·solv·ably
in·sol·ven·cy
in·sol·vent
in·som·nia
in·so·much
in·sou·ci·ance
in·sou·ci·ant
in·spect
in·spec·tion
in·spec·tor
in·spi·ra·tion
in·spire
in·spir·er
in·spir·it
in·sta·bil·i·ty
in·stall
  or in·stal

  in·stalled
  in·stall·ing
in·stal·la·tion
in·stall·ment
  or in·stal·ment

in·stance

in·stant
in·stan·ta·neous
in·stan·ter
in·state
in sta·tu quo
in·stead
in·step
in·sti·gate
in·sti·ga·tion
in·sti·ga·tor
in·still
  also in·stil

  in·stilled
  in·still·ing
in·stinct
in·stinc·tive
in·stinc·tu·al
in·sti·tute
in·sti·tu·tion
in·sti·tu·tion·al·
  ize
in·sti·tu·tion·al·
  ly
in·struct
in·struc·tion
in·struc·tive
in·struc·tor
in·stru·ment
in·stru·men·tal
in·stru·men·tal·
  ist
in·stru·men·tal·i·
  ty
in·stru·men·tal·ly
in·stru·men·ta·
  tion

in·sub·or·di·nate
in·sub·or·di·na·
  tion
in·sub·stan·tial
in·sub·stan·ti·al·
  i·ty
in·suf·fer·able
in·suf·fer·ably
in·suf·fi·cien·cy
in·suf·fi·cient
in·su·lant
in·su·lar
in·su·lar·i·ty
in·su·late
in·su·la·tion
in·su·la·tor
in·su·lin
in·sult
in·su·per·a·ble
in·su·per·a·bly
in·sup·port·able
in·sup·port·ably
in·sup·press·ible
in·sup·press·ibly
in·sur·abil·i·ty
in·sur·able
in·sur·ance
in·sure
in·sured
in·sur·er
in·sur·gence
in·sur·gen·cy
in·sur·gent
in·sur·mount·able
in·sur·mount·ably
in·sur·rec·tion

in·sur·rec·tion·
  ary
in·sur·rec·tion·ist
in·sus·cep·ti·bil·
  i·ty
in·sus·cep·ti·ble
in·sus·cep·ti·bly
in·tact
in·ta·glio
in·take
in·tan·gi·bil·i·ty
in·tan·gi·ble
in·tan·gi·bly
in·te·ger
in·te·gral
in·te·grate
in·te·gra·tion
in·teg·ri·ty
in·teg·u·ment
in·tel·lect
in·tel·lec·tu·al
in·tel·lec·tu·al·
  ize
in·tel·lec·tu·al·ly
in·tel·li·gence
in·tel·li·gent
in·tel·li·gen·tsia
in·tel·li·gi·bil·i·
  ty
in·tel·li·gi·ble
in·tel·li·gi·bly
in·tem·per·ance
in·tem·per·ate
in·tend
in·ten·dant
in·tend·ed

in·tense
in·tense·ly
in·ten·si·fi·ca·
  tion
in·ten·si·fy
in·ten·si·ty
in·ten·sive
in·tent
in·ten·tion
in·ten·tion·al
in·ten·tion·al·ly
in·ter
  in·terred
  in·ter·ring
in·ter·act
in·ter·ac·tion
in·ter alia
in·ter·breed
in·ter·ca·late
in·ter·ca·la·tion
in·ter·cede
in·ter·cept
in·ter·cep·tion
in·ter·cep·tor
in·ter·ces·sion
in·ter·ces·sor
in·ter·ces·so·ry
in·ter·change
in·ter·change·able
in·ter·col·le·giate
in·ter·com
in·ter·com·mu·
  ni·ca·tion
in·ter·con·ti·nen·
  tal
in·ter·cos·tal

in·ter·course
in·ter·cul·tur·al
in·ter·de·nom·i·
  na·tion·al
in·ter·de·part·
  men·tal
in·ter·de·pen·
  dence
in·ter·de·pen·
  den·cy
in·ter·de·pen·
  dent
in·ter·dict
in·ter·dic·tion
in·ter·dis·ci·plin·
  ary
in·ter·est
in·ter·est·ing
in·ter·face
in·ter·faith
in·ter·fere
in·ter·fer·ence
in·ter·fer·on
in·ter·fuse
in·ter·im
in·te·ri·or
in·ter·ject
in·ter·jec·tion
in·ter·jec·tion·al·
  ly
in·ter·lace
in·ter·lard
in·ter·lay·er
in·ter·leaf
in·ter·leave
in·ter·line

in·ter·lin·ear
in·ter·lin·ing
in·ter·link
in·ter·lock
in·ter·lo·cu·tion
in·ter·loc·u·tor
in·ter·loc·u·to·ry
in·ter·lop·er
in·ter·lude
in·ter·lu·nar
in·ter·mar·riage
in·ter·mar·ry
in·ter·me·di·ary
in·ter·me·di·ate
in·ter·ment
in·ter·mez·zo
  pl in·ter·mez·zi *or*
  in·ter·mez·zos

in·ter·mi·na·ble
in·ter·mi·na·bly
in·ter·min·gle
in·ter·mis·sion
in·ter·mit·tent
in·ter·mix
in·tern
  confine

in·tern
  or in·terne
  doctor

in·ter·nal
in·ter·nal·iza·tion
in·ter·nal·ize
in·ter·na·tion·al
in·ter·na·tion·al·
  iza·tion

in·ter·na·tion·al·
  ize
in·ter·na·tion·al·
  ly
in·ter·ne·cine
in·tern·ee
in·ter·nist
in·tern·ment
in·tern·ship
in·ter·nun·cio
in·ter·of·fice
in·ter·pen·e·trate
in·ter·pen·e·tra·
  tion
in·ter·per·son·al
in·ter·per·son·al·
  ly
in·ter·plan·e·tary
in·ter·play
in·ter·po·late
in·ter·po·la·tion
in·ter·pose
in·ter·po·si·tion
in·ter·pret
in·ter·pre·ta·tion
in·ter·pret·er
in·ter·pre·tive
in·ter·ra·cial
in·ter·reg·num
  pl in·ter·reg·nums *or*
  in·ter·reg·na
in·ter·re·late
in·ter·re·la·tion
in·ter·ro·gate
in·ter·ro·ga·tion
in·ter·rog·a·tive

in·ter·ro·ga·tor
in·ter·rog·a·to·ry
in·ter·rupt
in·ter·rup·tion
in·ter·scho·las·tic
in·ter·sect
in·ter·sec·tion
in·ter·sperse
in·ter·sper·sion
in·ter·state
in·ter·stel·lar
in·ter·stice
in·ter·sti·tial
in·ter·tid·al
in·ter·twine
in·ter·twist
in·ter·ur·ban
in·ter·val
in·ter·vene
in·ter·ven·tion
in·ter·ven·tion·
  ism
in·ter·ven·tion·ist
in·ter·view
in·ter·view·er
in·ter·weave
in·ter·wove
  also in·ter·weaved

in·ter·wo·ven
  also in·ter·weaved

in·ter·weav·ing
in·tes·tate
in·tes·ti·nal
in·tes·tine
in·ti·ma·cy

involuntary

in·ti·mate
in·ti·ma·tion
in·tim·i·date
in·tim·i·da·tion
in·to
in·tol·er·a·ble
in·tol·er·a·bly
in·tol·er·ance
in·tol·er·ant
in·to·na·tion
in·tone
in to·to
in·tox·i·cant
in·tox·i·cate
in·tox·i·ca·tion
in·trac·ta·bil·i·ty
in·trac·ta·ble
in·trac·ta·bly
in·tra·mu·ral
in·tra·mus·cu·lar
in·tran·si·gence
in·tran·si·gent
in·tran·si·tive
in·tra·state
in·tra·uter·ine
in·tra·ve·nous
in·trep·id
in·tre·pid·i·ty
in·tri·ca·cy
in·tri·cate
in·trigue
in·trin·sic
in·trin·si·cal·ly
in·tro·duce
in·tro·duc·tion
in·tro·duc·to·ry

in·tro·spec·tion
in·tro·spec·tive
in·tro·ver·sion
in·tro·vert
in·trude
in·trud·er
in·tru·sion
in·tru·sive
in·tu·ition
in·tu·itive
in·tu·mes·cence
in·tu·mes·cent
in·un·date
in·un·da·tion
in·ure
in·vac·uo
in·vade
in·vad·er
in·val·id
    not valid

in·va·lid
    sickly

in·val·i·date
in·val·i·da·tion
in·valu·able
in·valu·ably
in·vari·able
in·vari·ably
in·va·sion
in·vec·tive
in·veigh
in·vei·gle
in·vent
in·ven·tion
in·ven·tive

in·ven·tor
in·ven·to·ry
in·ver·ness
in·verse
in·ver·sion
in·vert
in·ver·te·brate
in·vest
in·ves·ti·gate
in·ves·ti·ga·tion
in·ves·ti·ga·tor
in·ves·ti·ture
in·vest·ment
in·ves·tor
in·vet·er·ate
in·vid·i·ous
in·vig·o·rate
in·vig·o·ra·tion
in·vin·ci·bil·i·ty
in·vin·ci·ble
in·vin·ci·bly
in·vi·o·la·bil·i·ty
in·vi·o·la·ble
in·vi·o·la·bly
in·vi·o·late
in·vis·i·bil·i·ty
in·vis·i·ble
in·vis·i·bly
in·vi·ta·tion
in·vite
in·vit·ing
in·vo·ca·tion
in·voice
in·voke
in·vol·un·tari·ly
in·vol·un·tary

in·vo·lute
in·vo·lu·tion
in·volve
in·vul·ner·a·bil·
  i·ty
in·vul·ner·a·ble
in·vul·ner·a·bly
in·ward
  or in·wards

in·ward·ly
in-wrought
io·dide
io·dine
io·dize
ion
ion·ic
ion·iza·tion
ion·ize
iono·sphere
io·ta
Io·wa
ip·so fac·to
Iran
Ira·ni·an
Iraq
Iraqi
iras·ci·bil·i·ty
iras·ci·ble
iras·ci·bly
irate
ire·ful
Ire·land
ir·i·des·cence
ir·i·des·cent
iris
  pl iris·es *or* iri·des

Irish
Irish·man
irk·some
iron·bound
iron·clad
iron·ic
  or iron·i·cal

iron·i·cal·ly
iron·ware
iron·work
iro·ny
ir·ra·di·ate
ir·ra·di·a·tion
ir·ra·tio·nal
ir·ra·tio·nal·i·ty
ir·ra·tio·nal·ly
ir·re·claim·able
ir·rec·on·cil·abil·
  i·ty
ir·rec·on·cil·able
ir·rec·on·cil·ably
ir·re·cov·er·able
ir·re·cov·er·ably
ir·re·deem·able
ir·re·deem·ably
ir·re·den·tism
ir·re·den·tist
ir·re·duc·ible
ir·re·fut·able
ir·re·fut·ably
ir·reg·u·lar
ir·reg·u·lar·i·ty
ir·rel·e·vance
ir·rel·e·van·cy
ir·rel·e·vant

ir·re·li·gious
ir·re·me·di·a·ble
ir·re·me·di·a·bly
ir·re·mov·able
ir·re·mov·ably
ir·rep·a·ra·ble
ir·rep·a·ra·bly
ir·re·place·able
ir·re·press·ible
ir·re·press·ibly
ir·re·proach·able
ir·re·proach·ably
ir·re·sist·ible
ir·re·sist·ibly
ir·res·o·lute
ir·res·o·lu·tion
ir·re·solv·able
ir·re·spec·tive of
ir·re·spon·si·bil·
  i·ty
ir·re·spon·si·ble
ir·re·spon·si·bly
ir·re·triev·able
ir·re·triev·ably
ir·rev·er·ence
ir·rev·er·ent
ir·re·vers·ible
ir·re·vers·ibly
ir·rev·o·ca·ble
ir·re·vo·ca·bly
ir·ri·gate
ir·ri·ga·tion
ir·ri·ta·bil·i·ty
ir·ri·ta·ble
ir·ri·ta·bly
ir·ri·tant

ir·ri·tate
ir·ri·ta·tion
ir·rupt
   to rush in (see erupt)
ir·rup·tion
isin·glass
Is·lam
Is·lam·ic
is·land
isle
   island (see aisle)

is·let
   small island (see eyelet)

iso·bar
iso·late
iso·la·tion
iso·la·tion·ism
iso·la·tion·ist
iso·mer
iso·met·ric
iso·met·ri·cal·ly
iso·met·rics
isos·ce·les
iso·therm
iso·ther·mal
iso·tope
iso·to·pic
Is·ra·el
Is·rae·li
is·su·ance
is·sue
isth·mi·an
isth·mus
Ital·ian

ital·ic
ital·i·cize
It·a·ly
itch
itch·i·ness
itchy
item·iza·tion
item·ize
it·er·ate
it·er·a·tion
itin·er·ant
itin·er·ary
it·self
ivied
ivo·ry
Ivo·ry Coast
ivy

J

jab
   jabbed
   jab·bing
jab·ber
jab·ber·wocky
ja·bot
ja·cinth
jack·al
jack·a·napes
jack·ass
jack·boot
jack·daw
jack·et
jack·ham·mer

jack-in-the-box
   pl jack-in-the-box·es
      or jacks-in-the-box

jack-in-the-pul·pit
   pl jack-in-the-
      pul·pits *or* jacks-
      in-the-pul·pit

jack·knife
jack-of-all-trades
   pl jacks-of-all-
      trades

jack-o'-lan·tern
jack·pot
jack·rab·bit
jack·screw
Jack·son
Jack·son·ville
jack·straw
jac·o·net
jac·quard
jac·que·rie
jad·ed
jade·ite
jag
   jagged
   jag·ging
jag·ged
jag·uar
jai alai
jail·bird
jail·break
jail·er
   or jail·or
ja·lopy
jal·ou·sie
   window blind (see jealousy)

jam
  jammed
  jam·ming
Ja·mai·ca
Ja·mai·can
jam·ba·laya
jam·bo·ree
jan·gle
jan·i·tor
Jan·u·ary
Ja·pan
Jap·a·nese
jar
  jarred
  jar·ring
jar·di·niere
jar·gon
jas·mine
jas·per
ja·to unit
jaun·dice
jaun·diced
jaun·ti·ly
jaun·ti·ness
jaun·ty
jav·e·lin
jaw·bone
jaw·break·er
Jay·cee
jay·vee
jay·walk
jay·walk·er
jazz·i·ly
jazz·i·ness
jazzy
jeal·ous

jeal·ou·sy
  *suspicion (see
  jalousie)*

jeans
Jef·fer·son City
je·hu
je·june
Jell-O
jel·ly
jel·ly·fish
jen·ny
jeop·ar·dize
jeop·ar·dy
jer·boa
jer·e·mi·ad
jerk·i·ly
jer·kin
jerk·i·ness
jerk·wa·ter
jerky
  in fits and starts

jer·ky
  meat

jer·o·bo·am
jer·ry-built
jer·sey
jes·sa·mine
jest·er
Je·su·it
je·su·it·ic
  or je·su·it·i·cal

je·su·it·i·cal·ly
jet
  jet·ted
  jet·ting

je·té
jet·port
jet-pro·pelled
jet·sam
jet·ti·son
jet·ty
jeu d'es·prit
  pl jeux d'es·prit

jew·el
jew·el·er
  or jew·el·ler

jew·el·ry
Jew·ish
Jew·ry
jibe
  agree (see gibe)

jif·fy
jig
  jigged
  jig·ging
jig·ger
jig·gle
jig·saw
jim-dan·dy
jim·my
jim·son·weed
jin·gle
jin·go·ism
jin·go·is·tic
jin·go·is·ti·cal·ly
jin·rik·i·sha
jinx
jit·ney
jit·ter·bug
jit·ter

jit·tery
jiu·jit·su
   or jiu·jut·su
   var of jujitsu

job
   jobbed
   job·bing
job·ber
job·hold·er
job·less·ness
jock·ey
jock·strap
jo·cose
jo·cos·i·ty
joc·u·lar
joc·u·lar·i·ty
jo·cund
jo·cun·di·ty
jodh·pur
jog
   jogged
   jog·ging
jog·ger
jog·gle
john·ny
joie de vi·vre
join·er
joint·ly
jok·er
jol·li·ty
jol·ly
jon·quil
Jor·dan
Jor·da·ni·an
jos·tle
jot

jot·ted
jot·ting
jour·nal
jour·nal·ese
jour·nal·ism
jour·nal·ist
jour·nal·is·tic
jour·ney
jour·ney·man
jo·vial
jo·vi·al·i·ty
jo·vial·ly
jowl
joy·ful
joy·ful·ly
joy·ous
joy·ride
joy·rid·er
ju·bi·lant
ju·bi·la·tion
ju·bi·lee
Ju·da·ic
Ju·da·ism
judg·ment
   or judge·ment

ju·di·ca·ture
ju·di·cial
ju·di·cial·ly
ju·di·cia·ry
ju·di·cious
ju·do
jug·ger·naut
jug·gle
jug·gler
jug·u·lar

juic·er
juic·i·ly
juic·i·ness
juicy
ju·jit·su
   or ju·jut·su *or*
   jiu·jit·su *or*
   jiu·jut·su

ju·jube
juke·box
ju·lep
ju·li·enne
Ju·ly
jum·ble
jum·bo
   pl jum·bos

jump·er
jump·i·ness
jumpy
jun
jun·co
   pl jun·cos *or*
   jun·coes

junc·tion
junc·ture
June
Ju·neau
jun·gle
ju·nior
ju·ni·per
jun·ker
jun·ket
junk·ie
   or junky

junk·yard
jun·ta

Ju·pi·ter
ju·rid·i·cal
  or ju·rid·ic

ju·rid·i·cal·ly
ju·ris·dic·tion
ju·ris·dic·tion·al
ju·ris·pru·dence
ju·ris·pru·den·
  tial·ly
ju·rist
ju·ris·tic
ju·ror
ju·ry
jus·tice
jus·ti·cia·ble
jus·ti·fi·able
jus·ti·fi·ably
jus·ti·fi·ca·tion
jus·ti·fy
just·ly
jut
  jut·ted
  jut·ting
jute
ju·ve·nile
ju·ve·nil·ia
jux·ta·pose
jux·ta·po·si·tion

K

ka·bob
  or ke·bab *or*
  ke·bob

Ka·bu·ki
kaf·fee·klatsch

kai·ser
ka·lei·do·scope
ka·lei·do·scop·ic
ka·ma·ai·na
ka·mi·ka·ze
kan·ga·roo
Kan·sas
ka·olin
  also ka·oline

ka·pok
ka·put
  also ka·putt

kar·a·kul
kar·at
  or car·at
  gold measure (see
  carat,
  caret, carrot)

ka·ra·te
kar·ma
ka·ty·did
kat·zen·jam·mer
kay·ak
kayo
  kay·oed
  kayo·ing
ka·zoo
  pl ka·zoos

ke·bab
  or ke·bob
  var of kabob

kedge
keel·boat
keel·haul
keel·son
keen·ly

keep
  kept
  keep·ing
keep·er
keep·sake
keg·ler
kel·vin
ken·nel
ke·no
Ken·tucky
Ke·nya
Ke·nyan
ke·pi
ker·a·tin
ker·chief
ker·nel
  seed, core (see
  colonel)

ker·o·sene
  or ker·o·sine

ker·sey
ker·sey·mere
ketch·up
  var of cat·sup

ke·tene
ke·tone
ket·tle
ket·tle·drum
key
  lock (see quay)

key·board
key·hole
key·note
key·not·er
key·stone

key·way
kha·ki
khe·dive
Khmer
kib·butz
  pl kib·but·zim
kib·itz·er
ki·bosh
kick·back
kick·off
kid
  kid·ded
  kid·ding
kid·nap
  kid·napped
    or kid·naped
  kid·nap·ping
    or kid·nap·ing
kid·nap·per
  or kid·nap·er
kid·ney
kid·skin
kill·er
kill·ing
kill·joy
kiln
ki·lo
  pl ki·los
kilo·cy·cle
ki·lo·gram
kilo·li·ter
ki·lo·me·ter
ki·lo·volt
kilo·watt
kilo·watt-hour

kil·ter
ki·mo·no
  pl ki·mo·nos

kin·der·gar·ten
kind·heart·ed
kin·dle
kind·li·ness
kin·dling
kind·ly
kin·dred
ki·ne·mat·ic
  or ki·ne·mat·i·cal

ki·ne·mat·ics
kin·e·scope
ki·ne·si·ol·o·gy
ki·net·ic
ki·net·ics
kin·folk
  or kin·folks

king·bolt
king·dom
king·fish
king·fish·er
king·ly
king·mak·er
king·pin
king-size
  or king-sized

kinky
kins·folk
kin·ship
kins·man
kins·wom·an
ki·osk

kip
  pl kip *or* kips

kip·per
kir·tle
kis·met
kitch·en
kitch·en·ette
kitch·en·ware
kitsch
kit·ten
kit·ten·ish
kit·ty
kit·ty-cor·ner
  or kit·ty-cor·nered
  var of catercorner
klep·to·ma·nia
klep·to·ma·ni·ac
knap·sack
knave
  rogue (see nave)

knav·ery
knav·ish
knead
  massage (see need)

knee·cap
knee-deep
knee-high
knee·hole
kneel
  knelt
    or kneeled

  kneel·ing
knick·ers
knick·knack
knife
  pl knives

knife-edge
knight
   rank (see night)

knight-er·rant
knight·hood
knit
  knit
   or knit·ted

  knit·ting
knit·ter
knit·wear
knob·by
knock·about
knock·down
knock·er
knock-kneed
knock·out
knoll
knot
  knot·ted
  knot·ting
knot·hole
knot·ty
know
  knew
  known
  know·ing
know·able
know-how
know-it-all
knowl·edge
knowl·edge·able
knowl·edge·ably
Knox·ville
knuck·le

knuck·le·bone
knurl
ko·ala
ko·bo
kohl·ra·bi
kooky
  also kook·ie

ko·peck
  also ko·pek

Ko·ran
Ko·rea
Ko·re·an
ko·ru·na
  pl ko·ru·ny *or*
  ko·ru·nas

ko·sher
kow·tow
kro·na
  pl kro·nur
  Icelandic currency

kro·na
  pl kro·nor
  Swedish currency

kro·ne
  pl kro·ner
  Danish and
  Norwegian
  currency

kryp·ton
ku·do
  pl ku·dos

ku·lak
kum·quat
ku·rus
  pl ku·rus

Ku·wait
  or Ku·weit *or*
  Ko·wait *or*
  Al Ku·wait

Ku·waiti
kwa·cha
  pl kwa·cha

kwash·i·or·kor
kyat

L

la·bel
  la·beled
   or la·belled

  la·bel·ing
   or la·bel·ling

la·bi·al
la·bile
la·bor
lab·o·ra·to·ry
la·bored
la·bor·er
la·bo·ri·ous
la·bor·sav·ing
la·bur·num
lab·y·rinth
lab·y·rin·thine
lac·er·ate
lac·er·a·tion
la·ches
  pl la·ches

lach·ry·mal
  or lach·ri·mal

lach·ry·mose

lac·ing
lack·a·dai·si·cal
lack·a·dai·si·cal·
  ly
lack·ey
lack·lus·ter
la·con·ic
la·con·i·cal·ly
lac·quer
la·crosse
lac·tate
lac·ta·tion
lac·te·al
lac·tic
lac·tose
la·cu·na
  pl la·cu·nae *or*
  la·cu·nas

la·cus·trine
lacy
lad·der
lad·der-back
lad·en
lad·ing
la·dle
la·dy
la·dy·bug
la·dy·fin·ger
la·dy-in-wait·ing
  pl la·dies-in-wait·ing

la·dy·like
la·dy·love
la·dy·ship
lag
  lagged
  lag·ging

la·ger
lag·gard
la·gniappe
la·goon
lair
  den *(see layer)*

lais·sez-faire
la·ity
lak·er
la·ma
  monk *(see llama)*

lam·baste
  or lam·bast

lam·bent
lam·bre·quin
lamb·skin
lame
  disabled

la·mé
  brocade

la·ment
la·men·ta·ble
la·men·ta·bly
lam·en·ta·tion
lam·i·na
  pl lam·i·nae
  or lam·i·nas

lam·i·nat·ed
lam·i·na·tion
lamp·black
lamp·light·er
lam·poon
lam·prey
la·nai
lanc·er

lan·cet
lan·dau
land·ed
land·fall
land·fill
land·form
land·hold·er
land·ing
land·la·dy
land·locked
land·lord
land·lub·ber
land·mark
land·mass
land·own·er
land·scape
land·slide
lands·man
land·ward
  also land·wards

lan·guage
lan·guid
lan·guish
lan·guor
lan·guor·ous
lank·i·ness
lanky
lan·o·lin
Lan·sing
lan·tern
lan·yard
Laos
Lao·tian
lap
  lapped

lap·ping
lap·board
lap·dog
la·pel
lap·i·dary
lap·in
la·pis la·zu·li
lap·pet
lapse
lar·ce·nous
lar·ce·ny
lar·der
large·ly
large-scale
lar·gess
  or lar·gesse
lar·go
  pl lar·gos
lar·i·at
lark·spur
lar·va
  pl lar·vae *also*
  lar·vas
lar·val
la·ryn·geal
lar·yn·gi·tis
lar·ynx
  pl la·ryn·ges *or*
  lar·ynx·es
las·car
las·civ·i·ous
la·ser
lash·ing
las·si·tude
las·so
  pl las·sos *or* las·soes

Las·tex
last·ing
Las Ve·gas
lat·a·kia
latch
latch·key
latch·string
late·com·er
la·teen
  also la·teen·er

late·ly
la·ten·cy
la·tent
lat·er·al
lat·er·al·ly
la·tex
  pl la·ti·ces *or*
  la·tex·es
lath
  strip of wood
lathe
  machine
lath·er
Lat·in
lat·i·tude
lat·i·tu·di·nar·i·
  an
la·trine
lat·ter
lat·ter-day
lat·tice
lat·tice·work
Lat·via
Lat·vi·an
laud·able

laud·ably
lau·da·num
lau·da·to·ry
laugh·able
laugh·ing·stock
laugh·ter
launch·er
laun·der
laun·der·er
laun·dress
Laun·dro·mat
laun·dry
laun·dry·man
laun·dry·wom·an
lau·re·ate
lau·rel
la·va
la·va·bo
la·va·liere
  or la·val·liere

lav·a·to·ry
lav·en·der
lav·ish
law-abid·ing
law·break·er
law·ful
law·ful·ly
law·giv·er
law·less
law·mak·er
law·suit
law·yer
lax·a·tive
lax·ity
lax·ness

lay
  laid
  lay·ing
lay·er
  level (see lair)

lay·ette
lay·man
lay·off
lay·out
la·zi·ly
la·zi·ness
la·zy
la·zy·bones
leach
  filter (see leech)

lead
  led
  lead·ing
lead·en
lead·er
lead·er·ship
lead-in
lead·ing
lead·off
lead-up
leaf
  pl leaves

leaf·age
leaf·let
leafy
league
lea·guer
  camp, siege

leagu·er
  league member

leak
  escape (see leek)

leak·age
leaky
lean
  incline (see lien)

lean·ness
lean-to
leap
  leaped
    or leapt

leap·ing
leap·frog
learned
learn·er
learn·ing
lease·hold
least
least·wise
leath·er
leath·ery
leave
  left
  leav·ing
leav·en
leav·en·ing
leave-tak·ing
leav·ings
Leb·a·nese
Leb·a·non
lech·er
lech·er·ous
lech·ery
lec·tern
lec·tor

lec·ture
lec·tur·er
le·der·ho·sen
ledge
led·ger
leech
  or leach
  worm (see leach)

leek
  plant (see leak)

leery
lee·ward
lee·way
left-hand·ed
left·ist
left·over
leg
  legged
  leg·ging
leg·a·cy
le·gal
le·gal·ism
le·gal·is·tic
le·gal·i·ty
le·gal·iza·tion
le·gal·ize
le·gal·ly
leg·ate
leg·a·tee
le·ga·tion
le·ga·to
le·ga·tor
leg·end
leg·end·ary
leg·er·de·main

leg·ging
  or leg·gin

leg·gy
leg·horn
leg·i·bil·i·ty
leg·i·ble
leg·i·bly
le·gion
le·gion·ary
le·gion·naire
leg·is·late
leg·is·la·tion
leg·is·la·tive
leg·is·la·tor
leg·is·la·ture
le·gist
le·git·i·ma·cy
le·git·i·mate
le·git·i·mate·ly
le·git·i·mize
leg·man
le·gume
le·gu·mi·nous
lei
lei·sure
lei·sure·li·ness
lei·sure·ly
leit·mo·tiv
  or leit·mo·tif

lek
lem·ming
lem·on
lem·on·ade
lem·pi·ra
le·mur

lend
  lent
  lend·ing
lend·er
lend-lease
length
length·en
length·wise
lengthy
le·nien·cy
le·nient
len·i·tive
len·i·ty
lens
  also lense

Lent·en
len·til
le·one
le·o·nine
leop·ard
le·o·tard
lep·er
lep·re·chaun
lep·ro·sy
lep·rous
lep·ton
  pl lep·ta

les·bi·an
le·sion
Le·so·tho
les·see
less·en
  *make less (see
  lesson)*

less·er
  smaller (see lessor)

les·son
  *instruction (see
  lessen)*

les·sor
  *one who leases out
  (see lesser)*

let
  let
  let·ting
let·down
le·thal
le·thal·ly
le·thar·gic
leth·ar·gy
let·ter
let·ter·er
let·ter·head
let·ter-per·fect
let·ter·press
let·tuce
let·up
leu
  pl lei

leu·ke·mia
leu·ko·cyte
  also leu·co·cyte

lev
  pl le·va

lev·ee
  *embankment (see
  levy)*

lev·el
  lev·eled
    or lev·elled

  lev·el·ing
    or lev·el·ling

lev·el·er
or lev·el·ler

lev·el·head·ed
lev·el·ly
lev·er
le·ver·age
le·vi·a·than
lev·i·tate
lev·i·ta·tion
lev·i·ty
levy
impose (see levee)

lewd
lewd·ness
lex·i·cog·ra·pher
lex·i·co·graph·ic
lex·i·cog·ra·phy
lex·i·con
Lex·ing·ton
li·a·bil·i·ty
li·a·ble
responsible (see libel)

li·ai·son
li·ar
one who lies (see lyre)

li·ba·tion
li·bel
malign (see liable)

li·beled
or li·belled

li·bel·ing
or li·bel·ling

li·bel·er
or li·bel·ler

li·bel·ous
or li·bel·lous

lib·er·al
lib·er·al·ism
lib·er·al·i·ty
lib·er·al·iza·tion
lib·er·al·ize
lib·er·al·ly
lib·er·ate
lib·er·a·tion
lib·er·a·tor
Li·be·ria
Li·be·ri·an
lib·er·tar·i·an
lib·er·tine
lib·er·ty
li·bid·i·nal
li·bid·i·nous
li·bi·do
li·brar·i·an
li·brary
li·bret·tist
li·bret·to
pl li·bret·tos *or*
li·bret·ti

Lib·ya
Lib·y·an
li·cense
also li·cence

li·cens·ee
li·cen·ti·ate
li·cen·tious
li·chen
lic·it
lick·e·ty-split
lick·spit·tle

lic·o·rice
li·do
lie
rest, recline

lay
lain
ly·ing
lie
tell an untruth

lied
ly·ing
lie
untruth (see lye)

Liech·ten·stein
Liech·ten·stein·er
lied
pl lie·der
song

lien
claim (see lean)

lieu
lieu·ten·an·cy
lieu·ten·ant
life
pl lives

life·blood
life·boat
life·guard
life·less
life·like
life·line
life·long
life·sav·er
life·sav·ing

life-size
or life-sized

life·time
life·work
lift·off
lig·a·ment
lig·a·ture
light
light·ed
or lit

light·ing
light·en
ligh·ter
barge

light·er
one that lights

light·face
light-fin·gered
light-foot·ed
light-hand·ed
light-head·ed
light·heart·ed
light·house
light·ing
light·ly
light·ning
light·proof
light·ship
lights-out
light·weight
light-year
lig·ne·ous
lig·nite
lik·able
also like·able

like·li·hood
like·ly
like-mind·ed
lik·en
like·ness
like·wise
lik·ing
li·ku·ta
pl ma·ku·ta

li·lac
lil·li·pu·tian
lily
lily-white
limb
appendage (see limn)

lim·ber
lim·bo
pl lim·bos

lime·ade
lime·light
lim·er·ick
lime·stone
lim·it
lim·i·ta·tion
lim·it·ed
limn
draw (see limb)

lim·ou·sine
lim·pet
lim·pid
limp·ly
lin·age
lines (see lineage)

linch·pin

Lin·coln
lin·den
lin·eage
ancestry (see linage)

lin·eal
lin·ea·ment
outline (see liniment)

lin·ear
line·man
lin·en
lin·er
lines·man
line·up
lin·ger
lin·ger·ie
lin·go
pl lin·goes

lin·gua fran·ca
pl lin·gua fran·cas
or lin·guae
fran·cae

lin·gual
lin·guist
lin·guis·tic
lin·guis·tics
lin·i·ment
balm (see lineament)

lin·ing
link·age
link·up
li·no·leum
Li·no·type
lin·seed
lin·sey-wool·sey

lin·tel
li·on
li·on·ess
li·on·heart·ed
li·on·iza·tion
li·on·ize
lip·id
　　also lip·ide

lip·read·ing
lip·stick
liq·ue·fac·tion
liq·ue·fi·able
liq·ue·fi·er
liq·ue·fy
　　also liq·ui·fy

li·ques·cent
li·queur
liq·uid
liq·ui·date
liq·ui·da·tion
liq·ui·da·tor
li·quid·i·ty
li·quor
li·ra
　　pl li·re *also* li·ras

lisle
lis·some
　　also lis·som

lis·ten
lis·ten·er
list·ing
list·less
lit·a·ny
li·ter
　　or li·tre

lit·er·a·cy
lit·er·al
　　verbatim (see littoral)

lit·er·al·ly
lit·er·ary
lit·er·ate
li·te·ra·ti
lit·er·a·ture
lithe
lithe·some
litho·graph
li·tho·gra·pher
li·thog·ra·phy
Lith·u·a·nia
Lith·u·a·nian
lit·i·ga·ble
lit·i·gant
lit·i·gate
lit·i·ga·tion
li·ti·gious
lit·mus
li·tre
　　var of liter

lit·ter
lit·ter·a·teur
lit·ter·bug
lit·tle
Lit·tle Rock
lit·to·ral
　　shore (see literal)

li·tur·gi·cal
li·tur·gi·cal·ly
lit·ur·gist
lit·ur·gy

liv·able
　　also live·able

live·li·hood
live·li·ness
live·long
live·ly
liv·en
liv·er
liv·er·ied
liv·er·wort
liv·er·wurst
liv·ery
liv·ery·man
live·stock
liv·id
liv·ing
Li·vo·nia
liz·ard
lla·ma
　　animal (see lama)

lla·no
　　pl lla·nos

load
　　pack (see lode)

load·ed
load·stone
loaf
　　pl loaves

loaf·er
loamy
loan
　　lend (see lone)

loan·word

loath
also loathe
adj (see loathe)

loathe
verb (see loath)

loath·ing

loath·some

lob
lobbed
lob·bing

lo·bar

lob·by

lob·by·ist

lob·ster

lo·cal

lo·cale

lo·cal·i·ty

lo·cal·iza·tion

lo·cal·ize

lo·cal·ly

lo·cate

lo·ca·tion

lock·er

lock·et

lock·jaw

lock·out

lock·smith

lock·step

lock·up

lo·co·mo·tion

lo·co·mo·tive

lo·co·mo·tor

lo·cus
pl lo·ci

lo·cust

lo·cu·tion

lode
ore deposit (see
load)

lode·star

lode·stone

lodge
contain (see loge)

lodg·er

lodg·ing

lodg·ment
or lodge·ment

loess

loft·i·ly

loft·i·ness

lofty

log
logged
log·ging

log·a·rithm

loge
theater section (see
lodge)

log·ger

log·ger·head

log·gia

log·ic

log·i·cal

log·i·cal·ly

lo·gi·cian

lo·gis·tics

log·jam

logo·gram

logo·graph

logo·type

log·roll·ing

lo·gy
also log·gy

loin·cloth

loi·ter

loi·ter·er

lol·li·pop
or lol·ly·pop

Lon·don

lone
solitary (see loan)

lone·li·ness

lone·ly

lone·some

Long Beach

long·bow

long-dis·tance

lon·gev·i·ty

long·hair

long-haired

long·hand

long·ing

lon·gi·tude

lon·gi·tu·di·nal

lon·gi·tu·di·nal·
ly

long-lived

long-play·ing

long-range

long·shore·man

long-suf·fer·ing

long-term

long-wind·ed

look·er-on
pl look·ers-on

look·out

loo·ny
  or loo·ney

loop·hole
loose-joint·ed
loose·ly
loos·en
loose·ness
loot·er
lop
  lopped
  lop·ping
lop-eared
lop·sid·ed
lo·qua·cious
lo·quac·i·ty
lord·ly
lor·do·sis
lord·ship
lor·gnette
lor·ry
Los An·ge·les
lose
  lost
  los·ing
los·er
lo·tion
lot·tery
lo·tus
  also lo·tos

loud·mouthed
loud·speak·er
Lou·i·si·ana
Lou·is·ville
louse
  pl lice

lousy
lout·ish
lou·ver
  or lou·vre

lov·able
  also love·able

love·li·ness
love·ly
lov·er
love·sick
lov·ing
low·born
low·boy
low·bred
low·brow
low·down
low·er
low·er·case
low·er·most
low-key
  also low-keyed

low·land
low-lev·el
low·li·ness
low·ly
low-pres·sure
low-rise
low-spir·it·ed
low-ten·sion
lox
  pl lox *or* lox·es

loy·al
loy·al·ist
loy·al·ly
loy·al·ty

loz·enge
lu·au
lub·ber
Lub·bock
lu·bri·cant
lu·bri·cate
lu·bri·ca·tion
lu·bri·ca·tor
lu·bri·cious
  or lu·bri·cous

lu·cent
lu·cid
lu·cid·i·ty
Lu·cite
luck·i·ly
lucky
lu·cra·tive
lu·cre
lu·cu·bra·tion
lu·di·crous
lug
  lugged
  lug·ging
lug·gage
lug·ger
lu·gu·bri·ous
lug·worm
luke·warm
lul·la·by
lum·ba·go
lum·ber
lum·ber·jack
lum·ber·yard
lu·men
  pl lu·mi·na *or* lu·mens

lu·mi·nary
lu·mi·nos·i·ty
lu·mi·nous
lum·mox
lump·i·ly
lump·i·ness
lump·ish
lumpy
lu·na·cy
lu·nar
lu·na·tic
lun·cheon
lun·cheon·ette
lunch·room
lung·fish
lung·wort
lunk·head
lu·pine
lu·rid
lus·cious
lush·ness
lus·ter
    or lus·tre

lus·ter·ware
lust·i·ly
lust·i·ness
lus·trous
lusty
Lu·ther·an
Lu·ther·an·ism
Lux·em·bourg
    or Lux·em·burg

Lux·em·bourg·er
    or Lux·em·burg·er

lux·u·ri·ance

lux·u·ri·ant
lux·u·ri·ate
lux·u·ri·ous
lux·u·ry
ly·ce·um
lye
    corrosive (see lie)

ly·ing
ly·ing-in
    pl ly·ings-in *or* ly·ing-ins

lymph
lym·phat·ic
lym·pho·cyte
lynch
lynx
    pl lynx *or* lynx·es

lyre
    harp (see liar)

lyr·ic
lyr·i·cal
lyr·i·cal·ly
lyr·i·cism
lyr·i·cist

M

ma·ca·bre
mac·ad·am
mac·ad·am·ize
ma·caque
mac·a·ro·ni
    pl mac·a·ro·nis *or* mac·a·ro·nies

mac·a·roon
ma·caw

Mc·Coy
mac·er·ate
mac·er·a·tion
ma·chete
mach·i·nate
mach·i·na·tion
ma·chine
ma·chine·like
ma·chin·ery
ma·chin·ist
mack·er·el
mack·i·naw
mack·in·tosh
    also mac·in·tosh

Ma·con
mac·ra·me
mac·ro
    pl mac·ros

mac·ro·cosm
ma·cron
mac·ro·scop·ic
mac·ule
Mad·a·gas·can
Mad·a·gas·car
mad·am
    pl mes·dames *or* mad·ams
    form of address

ma·dame
    pl mes·dames *or* ma·dames
    title

mad·cap
mad·den
mad·der
Ma·dei·ra

ma·de·moi·selle
   pl ma·de·moi·selles
   or mes·de·moi·
   selles

made-up
mad·house
Mad·i·son
mad·ly
mad·man
mad·ness
ma·dras
mad·ri·gal
mad·wom·an
mael·strom
mae·stro
   pl mae·stros *or*
   mae·stri

Ma·fia
mag·a·zine
ma·gen·ta
mag·got
mag·goty
ma·gi
mag·ic
mag·i·cal
mag·i·cal·ly
ma·gi·cian
mag·is·te·ri·al
mag·is·tra·cy
mag·is·tral
mag·is·trate
mag·ma
mag·na·nim·i·ty
mag·nan·i·mous
mag·nate
   important person
   (*see* magnet)

mag·ne·sia
mag·ne·sium
mag·net
   one that attracts (*see*
   magnate)

mag·net·ic
mag·ne·tism
mag·ne·ti·za·tion
mag·ne·tize
mag·ne·to
mag·ne·tom·e·ter
mag·ne·to·sphere
mag·ni·fi·ca·tion
mag·nif·i·cence
mag·nif·i·cent
mag·ni·fi·er
mag·ni·fy
mag·nil·o·quence
mag·nil·o·quent
mag·ni·tude
mag·no·lia
mag·num
mag·pie
ma·ha·ra·ja
   or ma·ha·ra·jah

ma·ha·ra·ni
   or ma·ha·ra·nee

ma·hat·ma
ma·hog·a·ny
maid·en
maid·en·hair
maid·en·hood
maid·en·ly
maid-in-wait·ing
   pl maids-in-wait·ing

maid·ser·vant
mail·bag
mail·box
mail·er
mail·ing
mail·man
maim
Maine
main·land
main·ly
main·mast
main·sail
main·sheet
main·spring
main·stay
main·stream
main·tain
main·tain·able
main·te·nance
mai·son·ette
maî·tre d'hô·tel
   pl maî·tres d'hô·tel

maize
   grain (*see* maze)

ma·jes·tic
ma·jes·ti·cal·ly
maj·es·ty
ma·jol·i·ca
   also ma·iol·i·ca

ma·jor
ma·jor·do·mo
ma·jor·i·ty
ma·jus·cule
mak·able
   or make·able

make
  made
  mak·ing
make-be·lieve
make-do
mak·er
make·shift
make·up
ma·ku·ta
  pl of likuta

mal·ad·ap·ta·tion
mal·adapt·ed
mal·ad·just·ed
mal·ad·min·is·ter
mal·ad·min·is·
  tra·tion
mal·adroit
mal·a·dy
mal·aise
mal·a·prop·ism
mal·ap·ro·pos
ma·lar·ia
ma·lar·i·al
Ma·la·wi
Ma·la·wi·an
Ma·lay·sia
Ma·lay·sian
mal·con·tent
mal de mer
Mal·dive
Mal·div·i·an
male·dic·tion
male·fac·tion
male·fac·tor
ma·lef·ic

ma·lef·i·cence
ma·lef·i·cent
male·ness
ma·lev·o·lence
ma·lev·o·lent
mal·fea·sance
mal·for·ma·tion
mal·formed
mal·func·tion
mal·ice
ma·li·cious
ma·lign
ma·lig·nan·cy
ma·lig·nant
ma·lig·ni·ty
ma·lin·ger
ma·lin·ger·er
Ma·li
Ma·li·an
mall
  promenade (*see* maul)

mal·lard
mal·le·a·bil·i·ty
mal·lea·ble
mal·let
mal·low
malm·sey
mal·nour·ished
mal·nu·tri·tion
mal·oc·clu·sion
mal·odor·ous
mal·prac·tice
Mal·ta
Mal·tese
malt·ose

mal·treat
mam·bo
ma·ma
  or mam·ma

mam·mal
mam·ma·li·an
mam·ma·ry
mam·mon
mam·moth
man
  pl men

man
  manned
  man·ning
man-about-town
  pl men-about-town

man·a·cle
man·age
man·age·abil·i·ty
man·age·able
man·age·ably
man·age·ment
man·ag·er
man·a·ge·ri·al
ma·ña·na
man-at-arms
  pl men-at-arms

man·da·mus
man·da·rin
man·date
man·da·to·ry
man·di·ble
man·do·lin
  also man·do·line

man·drake

man·drel
also man·dril
metal bar

man·drill
baboon

ma·nege
also ma·nège
horsemanship (see ménage)

ma·neu·ver
ma·neu·ver·abil·
i·ty
ma·neu·ver·able
man·ful
man·ful·ly
man·ga·nese
mange
man·gel-wur·zel
man·ger
man·gle
man·gler
man·go
pl man·goes *or* man·gos

man·grove
mangy
man·han·dle
man·hat·tan
man·hole
man·hood
man-hour
man·hunt
ma·nia
ma·ni·ac
ma·ni·a·cal
ma·ni·a·cal·ly

man·ic
man·ic-de·pres·
sive
man·i·cure
man·i·cur·ist
man·i·fest
man·i·fes·ta·tion
man·i·fes·to
pl man·i·fes·tos *or*
man·i·fes·toes

man·i·fold
man·i·kin
or man·ni·kin

Ma·nila
ma·nip·u·late
ma·nip·u·la·tion
ma·nip·u·la·tive
ma·nip·u·la·tor
Man·i·to·ba
man·kind
man·li·ness
man·ly
man-made
man·na
manned
man·ne·quin
man·ner
mode (see manor)

man·nered
man·ner·ism
man·ner·ly
man·nish
man-of-war
pl men-of-war

man·or
estate (see manner)

ma·no·ri·al
man pow·er
or man·pow·er

man·qué
man·sard
man·ser·vant
pl men·ser·vants

man·sion
man-size
or man-sized

man·slaugh·ter
man·ta
man·teau
man·tel
fireplace shelf (see
mantle)

man·telet
man·tel·piece
man·til·la
man·tis
pl man·tis·es *or*
man·tes

man·tle
garment (see
mantel)

man·u·al
man·u·al·ly
man·u·fac·to·ry
man·u·fac·ture
man·u·fac·tur·er
man·u·mis·sion
man·u·mit
man·u·mit·ted
man·u·mit·ting
ma·nure
manu·script

many
  more
  most
many·fold
many-sid·ed
map
  mapped
  map·ping
ma·ple
mar
  marred
  mar·ring
mar·a·bou
  or mar·a·bout

ma·ra·ca
mar·a·schi·no
ma·ras·mus
mar·a·thon
ma·raud
ma·raud·er
mar·ble
mar·ble·ize
mar·bling
mar·cel
  mar·celled
  mar·cel·ling
March
march·er
mar·chio·ness
march-past
Mar·di Gras
mar·ga·rine
mar·ga·ri·ta
mar·gay
mar·gin

mar·gin·al
mar·gin·al·ly
mar·gi·na·lia
mar·grave
ma·ri·a·chi
mar·i·gold
mar·i·jua·na
  or mar·i·hua·na

ma·rim·ba
ma·ri·na
mar·i·nade
  noun
mar·i·nate
  or mar·i·nade
  verb
ma·rine
mar·i·ner
mar·i·o·nette
mar·i·tal
mar·i·time
mar·jo·ram
mark·down
marked
mark·ed·ly
mark·er
mar·ket
mar·ket·abil·i·ty
mar·ket·able
mar·ket·ing
mar·ket·place
mark·ing
mark·ka
  pl mark·kaa *or*
  mark·kas

marks·man
marks·man·ship

mark·up
mar·lin
  fish

mar·line
  also mar·lin
  rope

mar·line·spike
  also mar·lin·spike

mar·ma·lade
mar·mo·re·al
mar·mo·set
mar·mot
ma·roon
mar·quee
mar·quess
  or marquis

mar·que·try
mar·quise
mar·qui·sette
mar·riage
mar·riage·able
mar·ried
mar·row
mar·row·bone
mar·ry
Mars
mar·shal
  lead (see martial)

  mar·shaled
  or mar·shalled

  mar·shal·ing
  or mar·shal·ling

marsh·mal·low
marshy
mar·su·pi·al

mar·ten
   mammal (see
     martin)

mar·tial
   warlike (see
     marshal)

mar·tian

mar·tin
   bird (see marten)

mar·ti·net
mar·tin·gale
mar·ti·ni
mar·tyr
mar·tyr·dom
mar·vel
   mar·veled
     or mar·velled

   mar·vel·ing
     or mar·vel·ling

   mar·vel·ous
     or mar·vel·lous

Marx·ism
Marx·ist
Mary·land
mar·zi·pan
mas·cara
mas·con
mas·cot
mas·cu·line
mas·cu·lin·i·ty
ma·ser
mask
   conceal (see
     masque)

mas·och·ism
mas·och·ist

mas·och·is·tic
ma·son
Ma·son·ic
ma·son·ry
masque
   also mask
   play (see mask)

mas·quer·ade
Mas·sa·chu·setts
mas·sa·cre
mas·sage
mas·seur
mas·seuse
mas·sif
   mountain

mas·sive
   huge

mass-pro·duce
mas·ter
master-at-arms
   pl masters-at-arms

mas·ter·ful
mas·ter·ful·ly
mas·ter·ly
mas·ter·mind
mas·ter·piece
mas·ter·stroke
mas·ter·work
mas·tery
mast·head
mas·ti·cate
mas·ti·ca·tion
mas·tiff
mast·odon
mas·toid

mas·tur·bate
mas·tur·ba·tion
mat
   mat·ted
   mat·ting

mat·a·dor
match·book
match·less
match·lock
match·mak·er
match·wood
ma·te·ri·al
   of matter (see
     matériel)

ma·te·ri·al·ism
ma·te·ri·al·ist
ma·te·ri·al·is·tic
ma·te·ri·al·is·ti·
   cal·ly
ma·te·ri·al·iza·
   tion
ma·te·ri·al·ize
ma·te·ri·al·ly
ma·te·ria med·i·
   ca
ma·té·ri·el
   or ma·te·ri·el
   equipment (see
     material)

ma·ter·nal
ma·ter·nal·ly
ma·ter·ni·ty
math·e·mat·i·cal
   also math·e·matic

math·e·mat·i·cal·
   ly

math·e·ma·ti·
  cian
math·e·mat·ics
mat·i·nee
  or mat·i·née

mat·ins
ma·tri·arch
ma·tri·ar·chal
ma·tri·ar·chy
ma·tri·cid·al
ma·tri·cide
ma·tric·u·lant
ma·tric·u·late
ma·tric·u·la·tion
ma·tri·lin·eal
ma·tri·lin·eal·ly
mat·ri·mo·nial
mat·ri·mo·nial·ly
mat·ri·mo·ny
ma·trix
  pl ma·tri·ces *or*
    ma·trix·es

ma·tron
ma·tron·ly
mat·ro·nym·ic
mat·ter
mat·ter-of-fact
mat·ting
mat·tins
mat·tock
mat·tress
mat·u·rate
mat·u·ra·tion
ma·ture
ma·tu·ri·ty

mat·zo
  pl mat·zoth *or*
    mat·zos

maud·lin
maul
  mangle (see mall)

maun·der
Mau·ri·ta·nia
Mau·ri·ta·nian
Mau·ri·tian
Mau·ri·ti·us
mau·so·le·um
  pl mau·so·le·ums *or*
    mau·so·lea

mauve
mav·er·ick
ma·vis
mawk·ish
max·il·la
  pl max·il·lae *or*
    max·il·las

max·im
max·i·mal
max·i·mal·ly
max·i·mum
  pl max·i·ma *or*
    max·i·mums

May
may·ap·ple
may·be
may·flow·er
may·hem
may·on·naise
may·or
may·or·al·ty
may·pole

maze
  intricate network
  (*see* maize)

ma·zur·ka
  also ma·zour·ka

mead·ow
mead·ow·lark
mea·ger
  or mea·gre

mea·ger·ly
meal·time
mealy
mealy·mouthed
mean
  intend (see mien)

meant
mean·ing
me·an·der
mean·ing
mean·ing·ful
mean·ing·less
mean·ly
mean·ness
mean·time
mean·while
mea·sles
mea·sly
mea·sur·abil·i·ty
mea·sur·able
mea·sur·ably
mea·sure
mea·sure·less
mea·sure·ment
mea·sur·er
meat
  food (see meet, mete)

meat·ball
meat·i·ness
me·atus
　pl me·atus·es *or*
　me·atus

meaty
mec·ca
me·chan·ic
me·chan·i·cal
me·chan·i·cal·ly
me·chan·ics
mech·a·nism
mech·a·nis·tic
mech·a·nis·ti·cal·
　ly
mech·a·ni·za·tion
mech·a·nize
med·al
　award (*see* meddle)

med·al·ist
　or med·al·list

me·dal·lion
med·dle
　interfere (*see*
　medal)

med·dler
med·dle·some
me·dia
me·di·al
me·di·an
me·di·ate
me·di·a·tion
me·di·a·tor
med·ic
med·i·ca·ble
med·ic·aid

med·i·cal
med·i·cal·ly
medi·care
med·i·cate
med·i·ca·tion
me·dic·i·nal
me·dic·i·nal·ly
med·i·cine
med·i·co
　pl med·i·cos

me·di·eval
　or me·di·ae·val

me·di·eval·ist
me·di·o·cre
me·di·oc·ri·ty
med·i·tate
med·i·ta·tion
med·i·ta·tive
Med·i·ter·ra·nean
me·di·um
　pl me·di·ums *or*
　me·dia

med·ley
me·dul·la
　pl me·dul·las *or*
　me·dul·lae

me·dul·la
　ob·lon·ga·ta
meek·ly
meek·ness
meer·schaum
meet
　come upon (*see*
　meat, mete)

met
meet·ing

meet·ing·house
mega·cy·cle
mega·death
mega·lith
meg·a·lo·ma·nia
meg·a·lo·ma·ni·
　ac
meg·a·lo·ma·ni·
　a·cal
mega·lop·o·lis
mega·phone
mega·ton
mei·o·sis
mel·a·mine
mel·an·cho·lia
mel·an·chol·ic
mel·an·choly
mé·lange
mel·a·nin
mel·ba toast
me·lee
me·lio·rate
me·lio·ra·tion
me·lio·ra·tive
mel·lif·lu·ous
mel·low
me·lo·de·on
me·lod·ic
me·lod·i·cal·ly
me·lo·di·ous
melo·dra·ma
melo·dra·mat·ic
melo·dra·mat·i·
　cal·ly
mel·o·dy
mel·on

melt
  melt·ed
  melt·ed
   also mol·ten

  melt·ing
mel·ton
melt·wa·ter
mem·ber
mem·ber·ship
mem·brane
mem·bra·nous
me·men·to
  pl me·men·tos *or*
  me·men·toes

me·men·to mo·ri
memo
  pl mem·os

mem·oir
mem·o·ra·bil·ia
mem·o·ra·ble
mem·o·ra·bly
mem·o·ran·dum
  pl mem·o·ran·dums
  or mem·o·ran·da

me·mo·ri·al
me·mo·ri·al·ize
mem·o·ri·za·tion
mem·o·rize
mem·o·ry
Mem·phis
men·ace
men·ac·ing·ly
mé·nage
  household (see
  manege)

me·nag·er·ie

men·da·cious
men·dac·i·ty
Men·de·lian
men·di·cant
men·folk
  or men·folks

men·ha·den
me·nial
me·nial·ly
men·in·gi·tis
me·nis·cus
  pl me·nis·ci *also*
  me·nis·cus·es

meno·paus·al
meno·pause
me·no·rah
men·ses
men·stru·al
men·stru·ate
men·stru·a·tion
men·su·ra·bil·i·ty

men·su·ra·ble
men·su·ra·tion
men·tal
men·tal·i·ty
men·tal·ly
men·thol
men·tho·lat·ed
men·tion
men·tion·able
men·tor
menu
me·phit·ic
mer·can·tile
mer·can·til·ism

mer·ce·nary
mer·cer·ize
mer·chan·dise
mer·chan·dis·er
mer·chant
mer·ci·ful
mer·ci·ful·ly
mer·ci·less
mer·cu·ri·al
mer·cu·ri·al·ly
mer·cu·ric
mer·cu·ry
mer·cy
mere·ly
mer·e·tri·cious
mer·gan·ser
merg·er
me·rid·i·an
me·ringue
me·ri·no
  pl me·ri·nos

mer·it
mer·i·to·ri·ous
mer·maid
mer·ri·ly
mer·ri·ment
mer·ry
mer·ry-an·drew
mer·ry-go-round
mer·ry·mak·er
mer·ry·mak·ing
Mer·thi·o·late
me·sa
més·al·liance
mes·cal

mes·ca·line
mes·dames
  pl of madam,
    madame

mes·de·moi·selles
  pl of mademoiselle

mesh·work
mes·mer·ism
mes·mer·ize
me·son
mes·quite
mes·sage
mes·sen·ger
mes·si·ah
mes·si·an·ic
mes·sieurs
  pl of monsieur

mess·i·ly
mess·i·ness
mess·mate
messy
mes·ti·zo
  pl mes·ti·zos

met·a·bol·ic
me·tab·o·lism
me·tab·o·lize
met·al
  chemical element
    (see mettle)

met·aled
  or met·alled

met·al·ing
  or met·al·ling

me·tal·lic
met·al·lur·gi·cal

met·al·lur·gist
met·al·lur·gy
met·al·ware
met·al·work
meta·mor·phic
meta·mor·phism
meta·mor·phose
meta·mor·pho·sis
met·a·phor
met·a·phor·i·cal
met·a·phor·i·cal·
  ly
meta·phys·ic
meta·phys·i·cal
meta·phys·i·cal·
  ly
meta·phys·ics
me·tas·ta·sis
  pl me·tas·ta·ses

meta·tar·sal
meta·tar·sus
mete
  allot (see meat, meet)

me·tem·psy·cho·
  sis
me·te·or
me·te·or·ic
me·te·or·i·cal·ly
me·te·or·ite
me·te·or·oid
me·te·o·ro·log·ic
  or me·te·o·ro·log·i·
    cal

me·te·o·ro·log·i·
  cal·ly

me·te·o·rol·o·gist
me·te·o·rol·o·gy
me·ter
meth·a·done
  or meth·a·don

meth·ane
meth·a·nol
meth·od
me·thod·i·cal
  or me·thod·ic

me·thod·i·cal·ly
Meth·od·ist
meth·od·ize
meth·od·olog·i·
  cal
meth·od·olog·i·
  cal·ly
meth·od·ol·o·gy
me·tic·u·lous
mé·tier
me-too
met·ric
met·ri·cal
met·ri·cal·ly
met·ro
  pl met·ros

met·ro·nome
me·trop·o·lis
met·ro·pol·i·tan
met·tle
  spirit (see metal)

met·tle·some
Mex·i·can
Mex·i·co
mez·za·nine

mez·zo·so·pra·no
Mi·ami
mi·as·ma
  pl mi·as·mas *or*
    mi·as·ma·ta

mi·ca
Mich·i·gan
mi·crobe
mi·cro·bi·al
mi·cro·cir·cuit
mi·cro·copy
mi·cro·cosm
mi·cro·fiche
mi·cro·film
mi·cro·form
mi·cro·groove
mi·crom·e·ter
mi·cron
mi·cro·or·gan·ism
mi·cro·phone
mi·cro·print
mi·cro·probe
mi·cro·read·er
mi·cro·scope
mi·cro·scop·ic
mi·cro·scop·i·cal·
  ly
mi·cros·co·py
mi·cro·wave
mid·day
mid·den
mid·dle
mid·dle-aged
mid·dle-brow
mid·dle·man
middle-of-the-road

middle-of-the-road·
  er
mid·dle·weight
mid·dling
mid·dy
  midshipman, blouse
    (see midi)

midg·et
midi
  skirt (see middy)

mid·land
mid·most
mid·night
mid·point
mid·riff
mid·sec·tion
mid·ship·man
mid·ships
midst
mid·stream
mid·sum·mer
mid·way
mid·week
mid·wife
mid·wife·ry
mid·win·ter
mid·year
mien
  appearance (see mean)

might
  strength (see mite)

might·i·ly
might·i·ness
mighty
mi·gnon·ette

mi·graine
mi·grant
mi·grate
mi·gra·tion
mi·gra·to·ry
mi·ka·do
  pl mi·ka·dos

mil
  thousandth, coin (see
    mill)

mil·dew
mild·ly
mild·ness
mile·age
mile·post
mil·er
mi·le·si·mo
mile·stone
mill
  building (see mil)

mi·lieu
mil·i·tan·cy
mil·i·tant
mil·i·tari·ly
mil·i·ta·rism
mil·i·ta·ris·tic
mil·i·ta·ri·za·tion
mil·i·ta·rize
mil·i·tary
mil·i·tate
mi·li·tia
mi·li·tia·man
milk·er
milk·i·ness
milk·maid
milk·man

milk·sop
milk·weed
milk·wort
milky
mill·dam
mil·len·ni·al
mil·len·ni·um
　pl mil·len·nia *or*
　mil·len·ni·ums

mill·er
mil·let
mil·li·ard
mil·li·bar
mil·lieme
mil·li·gram
mil·lime
mil·li·me·ter
mil·li·ner
mil·li·nery
mill·ing
mil·lion
mil·lion·aire
mil·lionth
mill·pond
mill·race
mill·stone
mill·stream
mill·wright
Mil·wau·kee
mim·eo·graph
mim·er
mi·me·sis
mi·met·ic
mim·ic
　mim·icked
　mim·ick·ing

mim·ic·ry
mi·mo·sa
min·a·ret
mi·na·to·ry
mince·meat
minc·ing
mind·ed
mind-ex·pand·ing
mind·ful
mind·ful·ly
mind·less
mine·lay·er
min·er
　one that mines (see
　minor)

min·er·al
min·er·al·iza·tion
min·er·al·ize
min·er·al·og·i·cal
min·er·al·o·gist
min·er·al·o·gy
min·e·stro·ne
mine·sweep·er
min·gle
min·ia·ture
min·ia·tur·ist
min·ia·tur·iza·
　tion
min·ia·tur·ize
mini·bus
min·ié ball
min·im
min·i·mal
min·i·mal·ly
min·i·mi·za·tion
min·i·mize

min·i·mum
　pl min·i·ma *or*
　min·i·mums

min·ing
min·ion
min·is·cule
mini·skirt
mini·state
min·is·ter
min·is·te·ri·al
min·is·trant
min·is·tra·tion
min·is·try
mini·track
min·i·ver
mink
　pl mink *or* minks

Min·ne·ap·o·lis
min·ne·sing·er
Min·ne·so·ta
min·now
mi·nor
　lesser (see miner)

mi·nor·i·ty
min·strel
min·strel·sy
mint·age
mint·er
minty
min·u·end
min·u·et
mi·nus
mi·nus·cule
min·ute
　noun

mi·nute
adj

mi·nute·ly
min·ute·man
mi·nu·tia
pl mi·nu·ti·ae

minx
mir·a·cle
mi·rac·u·lous
mir·a·dor
mi·rage
mir·ror
mirth·ful
mirth·ful·ly
miry
mis·ad·ven·ture
mis·al·li·ance
mis·al·lo·ca·tion
mis·an·thrope
mis·an·throp·ic
mis·an·throp·i·
  cal·ly
mis·an·thro·py
mis·ap·pli·ca·tion
mis·ap·ply
mis·ap·pre·hend
mis·ap·pre·hen·
  sion
mis·ap·pro·pri·
  ate
mis·ap·pro·pri·a·
  tion
mis·be·got·ten
mis·be·have
mis·be·hav·ior

mis·be·lief
mis·be·liev·er
mis·brand
mis·cal·cu·late
mis·cal·cu·la·tion
mis·call
mis·car·riage
mis·car·ry
mis·cast
mis·ce·ge·na·tion
mis·cel·la·nea
mis·cel·la·ne·ous
mis·cel·la·ny
mis·chance
mis·chief
mis·chie·vous
mis·ci·bil·i·ty
mis·ci·ble
mis·con·ceive
mis·con·cep·tion
mis·con·duct
mis·con·struc·tion
mis·con·strue
mis·count
mis·cre·ant
mis·cue
mis·deal
mis·deed
mis·de·mean·ant
mis·de·mean·or
mis·di·rect
mis·di·rec·tion
mis·do·er
mis·do·ing
mise-en-scène
mi·ser

mis·er·a·ble
mis·er·a·bly
mi·ser·li·ness
mi·ser·ly
mis·ery
mis·es·ti·mate
mis·es·ti·ma·tion
mis·fea·sance
mis·file
mis·fire
mis·fit
mis·for·tune
mis·giv·ing
mis·gov·ern
mis·gov·ern·ment
mis·guid·ance
mis·guide
mis·han·dle
mis·hap
mish·mash
mis·in·form
mis·in·for·ma·
  tion
mis·in·ter·pret
mis·in·ter·pre·ta·
  tion
mis·judge
mis·judg·ment
mis·lay
mis·lead
mis·man·age
mis·man·age·
  ment
mis·match
mis·mate
mis·name

mis·no·mer
mi·sog·a·mist
mi·sog·a·my
mi·sog·y·nist
mi·sog·y·ny
mis·place
mis·play
mis·print
mis·pri·sion
mis·pro·nounce
mis·pro·nun·ci·a·
  tion
mis·quo·ta·tion
mis·quote
mis·read
mis·rep·re·sent
mis·rep·re·sen·
  ta·tion
mis·rule
mis·sal
  book (see missile)

mis·send
  mis·sent
  mis·send·ing
mis·shape
mis·shap·en
mis·sile
  weapon (see missal)

mis·sile·ry
  also mis·sil·ry

miss·ing
mis·sion
mis·sion·ary
mis·sion·er
Mis·sis·sip·pi

mis·sive
Mis·sou·ri
mis·spell
mis·spend
mis·state
mis·state·ment
mis·step
mis·tak·able
mis·take
  mis·took
  mis·tak·en
  mis·tak·ing
mis·ter
mist·i·ly
mis·time
mist·i·ness
mis·tle·toe
mis·tral
mis·treat
mis·treat·ment
mis·tress
mis·tri·al
mis·trust
misty
mis·un·der·stand
mis·us·age
mis·use
mis·val·ue
mis·ven·ture
mite
  small thing (see
  might)

mi·ter
  or mi·tre

  mi·tered
  or mi·tred

mi·ter·ing
  or mi·tring

mit·i·gate
mit·i·ga·tion
mit·i·ga·tive
mit·i·ga·tor
mi·to·sis
  pl mi·to·ses

mitt
mit·ten
mix·able
mix·er
mix·ture
mix-up
miz·zen
  or miz·en

miz·zen·mast
mne·mon·ic
mne·mon·ics
moat
  trench (see mote)

mob
  mobbed
  mob·bing
Mo·bile
mo·bile
mo·bil·i·ty
mo·bi·li·za·tion
mo·bi·lize
mob·oc·ra·cy
mob·ster
moc·ca·sin
mo·cha
mock·er
mock·ery

mock·he·ro·ic
mock·ing·bird
mock-up
mod·al
mod·el
  mod·eled
    or mod·elled
  mod·el·ing
    or mod·el·ling
mod·er·ate
mod·er·ate·ly
mod·er·a·tion
mod·er·a·to
mod·er·a·tor
mod·ern
mod·ern·ism
mod·ern·is·tic
mo·der·ni·ty
mod·ern·iza·tion
mod·ern·ize
mod·ern·iz·er
mod·est
mod·es·ty
mod·i·cum
mod·i·fi·ca·tion
mod·i·fi·er
mod·i·fy
mod·ish
mo·diste
mod·u·lar
mod·u·late
mod·u·la·tion
mod·u·la·tor
mod·ule
mo·dus ope·ran·di
  pl mo·di ope·ran·di

mo·dus vi·ven·di
  pl mo·di vi·ven·di

mo·gul
  or Mo·ghul

mo·hair
moi·ety
moi·ré
  or moire

moist·en
moist·ly
moist·ness
mois·ture
mo·lar
mo·las·ses
mold·board
mold·er
mold·i·ness
mold·ing
moldy
mo·lec·u·lar
mol·e·cule
mole·hill
mole·skin
mo·lest
mo·les·ta·tion
mo·lest·er
mol·li·fi·ca·tion
mol·li·fy
mol·lusk
  or mol·lusc

mol·ly·cod·dle
molt
mol·ten
mol·to
mo·lyb·de·num

mo·ment
mo·men·tari·ly
mo·men·tary
mo·men·tous
mo·men·tum
  pl mo·men·ta *or*
  mo·men·tums

Mo·na·can
Mo·na·co
mo·nad
mon·arch
mo·nar·chi·cal
  or mo·nar·chic

mon·ar·chism
mon·ar·chist
mon·ar·chy
mon·as·te·ri·al
mon·as·tery
mo·nas·tic
mo·nas·ti·cal·ly
mo·nas·ti·cism
mon·au·ral
Mon·day
Mon·e·gasque
mon·e·tari·ly
mon·e·tary
mon·e·ti·za·tion
mon·e·tize
mon·ey
  pl mon·eys *or*
  mon·ies

mon·ey·bags
mon·eyed
  also mon·ied

mon·ey·lend·er
mon·ey-mak·er

mon·ey·wort
mon·ger
Mon·go·lia
Mon·go·lian
mon·gol·ism
Mon·gol·oid
mon·goose
   pl mon·goos·es
   also mon·geese

mon·grel
mo·nism
mo·nist
mon·i·tor
mon·i·to·ry
mon·key
mon·key·shine
monk·ish
monks·hood
mono·chro·mat·ic
mono·chro·mat·i·
   cal·ly
mono·chrome
mon·o·cle
mon·oc·u·lar
mon·o·dy
mo·nog·a·mist
mo·nog·a·mous
mo·nog·a·my
mono·gram
mono·graph
mo·nog·y·ny
mono·lith
mono·logue
   also mono·log

mono·logu·ist
   or mo·no·lo·gist

mono·ma·nia
mono·ma·ni·ac
mono·nu·cle·o·sis
mono·pho·nic
mono·plane
mo·nop·o·list
mo·nop·o·lis·tic
mo·nop·o·lis·ti·
   cal·ly
mo·nop·o·li·za·
   tion
mo·nop·o·lize
mo·nop·o·ly
mono·rail
mono·syl·lab·ic
mono·syl·lab·i·
   cal·ly
mono·syl·la·ble
mono·the·ism
mono·the·ist
mono·tone
mo·not·o·nous
mo·not·o·ny
mono·type
mon·ox·ide
mon·sei·gneur
   pl mes·sei·gneurs

mon·sieur
   pl mes·sieurs

mon·si·gnor
   pl mon·si·gnors *or*
   mon·si·gno·ri

mon·soon
mon·ster
mon·strance
mon·stros·i·ty

mon·strous
mon·tage
mon·ta·gnard
Mon·tana
mon·tane
Mon·tes·so·ri·an
Mont·gom·ery
month·ly
Mont·pe·lier
Mon·tre·al
mon·u·ment
mon·u·men·tal
mon·u·men·tal·ly
mood·i·ly
mood·i·ness
moody
moon·beam
moon-eyed
moon·light
moon·light·er
moon·lit
moon·scape
moon·shine
moon·stone
moon·struck
moor·age
moor·ing
moor·land
moose
   pl moose
   animal (*see* mousse)

mop
   mopped
   mop·ping
mop·board
mop·pet

mop-up
mo·raine
mor·al
mo·rale
mor·al·ist
mor·al·is·tic
mor·al·is·ti·cal·ly
mo·ral·i·ty
mor·al·iza·tion
mor·al·ize
mor·al·iz·er
mor·al·ly
mo·rass
mor·a·to·ri·um
   pl mor·a·to·ri·ums
    or
    mor·a·to·ria

mor·bid
mor·bid·i·ty
mor·dant
   caustic (see mordent)

mor·dent
   music (see mordant)

more·over
mo·res
mor·ga·nat·ic
mor·ga·nat·i·cal·
  ly
morgue
mor·i·bund
mor·i·bun·di·ty
Mor·mon
Mor·mon·ism
morn·ing
   day (see mourning)

Mo·roc·can

Mo·roc·co
mo·ron
mo·ron·ic
mo·ron·i·cal·ly
mo·rose
mor·pheme
mor·phe·mic
mor·phia
mor·phine
mor·pho·log·i·cal
mor·pho·log·i·
  cal·ly
mor·phol·o·gist
mor·phol·o·gy
mor·ris
mor·row
mor·sel
mor·tal
mor·tal·i·ty
mor·tal·ly
mor·tar
mor·tar·board
mort·gage
mort·gag·ee
mort·gag·or
mor·ti·cian
mor·ti·fi·ca·tion
mor·ti·fy
mor·tise
   also mor·tice

mort·main
mor·tu·ary
mo·sa·ic
mo·sey
mosque

mos·qui·to
   pl mos·qui·toes
    also mos·qui·tos

moss·back
moss-grown
mossy
most·ly
mote
   particle (see moat)

mo·tel
mo·tet
moth·ball
moth-eat·en
moth·er
moth·er·hood
moth·er·house
moth·er-in-law
   pl moth·ers-in-law

moth·er·land
moth·er·less
moth·er·li·ness
moth·er·ly
moth·er-of-pearl
mo·tif
mo·tile
mo·til·i·ty
mo·tion
mo·ti·vate
mo·ti·va·tion
mo·tive
mo·tiv·i·ty
mot·ley
mo·tor
mo·tor·boat
mo·tor·cade
mo·tor·car

mo·tor·cy·cle
mo·tor·cy·clist
mo·tor·drome
mo·tor·ist
mo·tor·iza·tion
mo·tor·ize
mo·tor·man
mo·tor·truck
mot·tle
mot·to
  pl mot·toes *also*
  mot·tos

mou·lage
mound
mount·able
moun·tain
moun·tain·eer
moun·tain·ous
moun·tain·side
moun·tain·top
moun·te·bank
Mount·ie
mount·ing
mourn·er
mourn·ful
mourn·ful·ly
mourn·ing
  grief (see morning)

mouse
  pl mice
  rodent (see mousse)

mous·er
mousse
  dessert (see moose,
  mouse)

mous·se·line

mous·se·line de
  soie
  pl mous·se·lines de
  soie

mousy
  or mous·ey

mouth·ful
mouth·part
mouth·piece
mouth·wash
mou·ton
  sheepskin (see mutton)

mov·abil·i·ty
mov·able
  or move·able

mov·ably
move·ment
mov·er
mov·ie
mov·ing
mow
  mowed
  mowed
   or mown

mow·ing
mow·er
Mo·zam·bique
much
  more
  most
mu·ci·lage
mu·ci·lag·i·nous
muck·rak·er
mu·cous
  adj

mu·cus
  noun

mud·di·ly
mud·di·ness
mud·dle
mud·dle·head·ed
mud·dler
mud·dy
mud·guard
mud·sling·er
mu·ez·zin
muf·fin
muf·fle
muf·fler
muf·ti
mug
  mugged
  mug·ging

mug·ger
mug·gi·ness
mug·gy
mug·wump
muk·luk
mu·lat·to
  pl mu·lat·toes *or*
  mu·lat·tos

mul·ber·ry
mulch
mulct
mul·ish
mul·lah
mul·let
mul·li·gan stew
mul·li·ga·taw·ny
mul·lion
mul·ti·col·ored

mul·ti·far·i·ous
mul·ti·form
mul·ti·lane
mul·ti·lat·er·al
mul·ti·lat·er·al·ly
mul·ti·lev·el
mul·ti·me·dia
mul·ti·mil·lion·aire
mul·ti·na·tion·al
mul·ti·par·tite
mul·ti·par·ty
mul·ti·ple
mul·ti·ple-choice
mul·ti·pli·cand
mul·ti·pli·ca·tion
mul·ti·plic·i·ty
mul·ti·pli·er
mul·ti·ply
mul·ti·tude
mul·ti·tu·di·nous
mul·ti·ver·si·ty
mul·ti·vi·ta·min
mum·ble
mum·bler
mum·ble·ty-peg
or mum·ble-the-peg

mum·bo jum·bo
mum·mer
mum·mery
mum·mi·fi·ca·tion
mum·mi·fy
mum·my

mun·dane
mung bean
mu·nic·i·pal
mu·nic·i·pal·i·ty
mu·nic·i·pal·ly
mu·nif·i·cence
mu·nif·i·cent
mu·ni·tion
mu·ral
mu·ral·ist
mur·der
mur·der·er
mur·der·ess
mur·der·ous
murk·i·ly
murk·i·ness
murky
mur·mur
mur·mur·er
mur·rain
mus·ca·dine
mus·ca·tel
mus·cle
body tissue (see mussel)

mus·cle-bound
mus·cu·lar
mus·cu·lar·i·ty
mus·cu·la·ture
mu·sette
mu·se·um
mush·i·ly
mush·i·ness
mush·room
mushy
mu·sic

mu·si·cal
of music (see musicale)

mu·si·cale
concert (see musical)

mu·si·cal·ly
mu·si·cian
mu·si·col·o·gist
mu·si·col·o·gy
mus·keg
mus·kel·lunge
mus·ket
mus·ke·teer
mus·ket·ry
musk·i·ness
musk·mel·on
musk·rat
musky
Mus·lim
mus·lin
mus·sel
shell fish (see muscle)

muss·i·ly
muss·i·ness
mussy
mus·tache
mus·tang
mus·tard
mus·ter
must·i·ly
must·i·ness
musty
mu·ta·bil·i·ty
mu·ta·ble
mu·ta·bly
mu·tant

mu·tate
mu·ta·tion
mu·ta·tis
　mu·tan·dis
mute·ly
mu·ti·late
mu·ti·la·tion
mu·ti·la·tor
mu·ti·neer
mu·ti·nous
mu·ti·ny
mut·ter
mut·ton
　meat (see mouton)

mut·ton·chops
mu·tu·al
mu·tu·al·i·ty
mu·tu·al·ly
muu·muu
muz·zle
my·col·o·gist
my·col·o·gy
my·co·sis
my·elin
my·eli·tis
my·ia·sis
my·na
　or my·nah

myo·gen·ic
my·o·pia
my·o·pic
my·o·pi·cal·ly
myr·i·ad
myr·mi·don
myrrh

myr·tle
my·self
mys·te·ri·ous
mys·tery
mys·tic
mys·ti·cal
mys·ti·cal·ly
mys·ti·cism
mys·ti·fi·ca·tion
mys·ti·fy
mys·tique
myth
myth·i·cal
myth·i·cal·ly
myth·o·log·i·cal
myth·o·log·i·cal·
　ly
my·thol·o·gist
my·thol·o·gy

N

nab
　nabbed
　nab·bing
na·bob
na·celle
na·cre
na·dir
nag
　nagged
　nag·ging
na·iad
　pl na·iads or na·ia·
　des

nain·sook

na·ive
　or na·ïve

na·ive·ly
na·ive·té
　or na·ïve·té
　or na·ive·te

na·ive·ty
　also na·ïve·ty

na·ked
nam·by-pam·by
name·able
　also nam·able

name·less
name·ly
name·plate
name·sake
nan·keen
nan·ny
nap
　napped
　nap·ping
na·palm
na·pery
naph·tha
naph·tha·lene
nap·kin
na·po·leon
nap·per
nap·py
nar·cis·sism
nar·cis·sist
nar·cis·sis·tic
nar·cis·sus
　pl nar·cis·sus or nar·
　cis·sus·es or nar·
　cis·si

nar·co·lep·sy
nar·co·sis
   pl nar·co·ses

nar·cot·ic
nar·co·tize
na·ris
   pl na·res

nar·rate
nar·ra·tion
nar·ra·tive
nar·ra·tor
nar·row
nar·row-mind·ed
nar·whal
   also nar·wal *or*
     nar·whale

na·sal
na·sal·i·ty
na·sal·iza·tion
na·sal·ize
na·sal·ly
na·scence
na·scent
Nash·ville
na·so·phar·ynx
nas·ti·ly
nas·ti·ness
nas·tur·tium
nas·ty
na·tal
na·tal·i·ty
na·tant
na·ta·to·ri·al
   or na·ta·to·ry

na·ta·to·ri·um

na·tion
na·tion·al
na·tion·al·ism
na·tion·al·ist
na·tion·al·is·tic
na·tion·al·is·ti·
   cal·ly
na·tion·al·i·ty
na·tion·al·iza·
   tion
na·tion·al·ize
na·tion·al·ly
na·tion·hood
na·tion-state
na·tion·wide
na·tive
na·tiv·ism
na·tiv·ist
na·tiv·i·ty
nat·ti·ly
nat·ti·ness
nat·ty
nat·u·ral
nat·u·ral·ism
nat·u·ral·ist
nat·u·ral·is·tic
nat·u·ral·is·ti·
   cal·ly
nat·u·ral·iza·tion
nat·u·ral·ize
nat·u·ral·ly
na·ture
naught
naugh·ti·ly
naugh·ti·ness
naughty

Na·u·ru
nau·sea
nau·se·ate
nau·seous
nau·ti·cal
nau·ti·cal·ly
nau·ti·lus
   pl nau·ti·lus·es *or*
     nau·ti·li

na·val
   of a navy (see navel)

nave
   center of a church
   (*see* knave)

na·vel
   abdominal depression
   (*see* naval)

nav·i·ga·bil·i·ty
nav·i·ga·ble
nav·i·gate
nav·i·ga·tion
nav·i·ga·tor
na·vy
nay
   no (see née, neigh)

na·ya pai·sa
   pl na·ye pai·se

na·zi
Na·zism
   or Na·zi·ism

Ne·an·der·thal
near·by
near·ly
near·ness
near·sight·ed
neat·ly

neat·ness
Ne·bras·ka
neb·u·la
　　pl neb·u·las *or* neb·
　　u·lae

neb·u·lar
neb·u·lize
neb·u·los·i·ty
neb·u·lous
nec·es·sar·i·ly
nec·es·sary
ne·ces·si·tate
ne·ces·si·tous
ne·ces·si·ty
neck·er·chief
　　pl neck·er·chiefs
　　　also
　　neck·er·chieves

neck·lace
neck·line
neck·tie
ne·crol·o·gist
ne·crol·o·gy
nec·ro·man·cer
nec·ro·man·cy
ne·crop·o·lis
　　pl ne·crop·o·lis·es *or*
　　ne·crop·o·les *or*
　　ne·crop·o·leis *or*
　　ne·crop·o·li

nec·rop·sy
ne·cro·sis
　　pl ne·cro·ses

nec·tar
nec·tar·ine
née
　　or nee
　　born (see nay, neigh)

need
　　require (see knead)

need·ful
need·ful·ly
need·i·ness
nee·dle
nee·dle·like
nee·dle·point
nee·dler
need·less
nee·dle·work
nee·dling
needy
ne'er-do-well
ne·far·i·ous
ne·gate
ne·ga·tion
neg·a·tive
neg·a·tive·ly
neg·a·tiv·ism
neg·a·tiv·i·ty
ne·glect
ne·glect·ful
neg·li·gee
　　also neg·li·gé

neg·li·gence
neg·li·gent
neg·li·gi·bil·i·ty
neg·li·gi·ble
neg·li·gi·bly
ne·go·tia·bil·i·ty
ne·go·tia·ble
ne·go·tiant
ne·go·ti·ate
ne·go·ti·a·tion

ne·go·ti·a·tor
ne·gri·tude
Ne·gro
　　pl Ne·groes

Ne·groid
ne·gus
neigh
　　horse cry (see nay,
　　née)

neigh·bor
neigh·bor·hood
neigh·bor·li·ness
neigh·bor·ly
nei·ther
nel·son
nem·a·tode
Nem·bu·tal
nem·e·sis
　　pl nem·e·ses

ne·moph·i·la
neo·clas·sic
neo·clas·si·cal
neo·clas·si·cism
neo·co·lo·nial
neo·co·lo·nial·ism
neo·lith·ic
ne·ol·o·gism
ne·ol·o·gy
neo·my·cin
ne·on
neo·phyte
neo·plasm
neo·prene
Ne·pal
Nep·a·lese
Ne·pali

ne·pen·the
neph·ew
ne·phri·tis
ne plus ul·tra
nep·o·tism
Nep·tune
nerve·less
nerve-rack·ing
   or nerve-wrack·ing

ner·vous
nervy
nes·tle
nest·ling
net
   net·ted
   net·ting
neth·er
Neth·er·land·er
Neth·er·lands
   or Hol·land

neth·er·most
neth·er·world
net·ting
net·tle
net·tle·some
net·work
neu·ral
neu·ral·gia
neu·ral·gic
neur·as·the·nia
neur·as·then·ic
neu·rit·ic
neu·ri·tis
neu·ro·log·i·cal
neu·rol·o·gist

neu·rol·o·gy
neu·ro·mus·cu·
   lar
neu·ron
   also neu·rone

neu·ro·sis
   pl neu·ro·ses

neu·rot·ic
neu·rot·i·cal·ly
neu·ter
neu·tral
neu·tral·ism
neu·tral·i·ty
neu·tral·iza·tion
neu·tral·ize
neu·tral·iz·er
neu·tri·no
neu·tron
Ne·va·da
nev·er
nev·er·more
nev·er-nev·er land
nev·er·the·less
ne·vus
   pl ne·vi

New·ark
New Bed·ford
new·born
New Bruns·wick
new·com·er
new·el
new·fan·gled
new-fash·ioned
new·found
New·found·land

New Hamp·shire
New Ha·ven
new·ish
New Jer·sey
new·ly
new·ly·wed
New Mex·i·co
new·ness
New Or·leans
New·port News
news·boy
news·break
news·cast
news·cast·er
news·let·ter
news·man
news·mon·ger
news·pa·per
news·pa·per·man
news·print
news·reel
news·stand
news·wor·thy
New York
New Zea·land
New Zea·land·er
nex·us
   pl nex·ux·es *or* nex·
   us

ngwee
   pl ngwee

ni·a·cin
Ni·ag·a·ra
nib·ble
Nic·a·ra·gua
Nic·a·ra·guan

nice·ly
nice·ness
nice·ty
niche
nick
nick·el
nick·el·ode·on
nick·name
nic·o·tine
nic·o·tin·ic
niece
nif·ty
Ni·ger
Ni·ge·ria
Ni·ge·ri·an
nig·gard·li·ness
nig·gard·ly
nig·gling
night
   dark (*see* knight)

night·cap
night·clothes
night·club
night·dress
night·fall
night·gown
night·hawk
night·in·gale
night·long
night·ly
night·mare
night·shade
night·shirt
night·stick
night·time

night·walk·er
ni·hil·ism
ni·hil·ist
ni·hil·is·tic
Ni·ke
nim·ble
nim·bly
nim·bus
   pl nim·bi *or* nim·bus·
   es
Nim·rod
nin·com·poop
nine·pins
nine·teen
nine·teenth
nine·ti·eth
nine·ty
nin·ny
ni·non
ninth
nip
   nipped
   nip·ping
nip·per
nip·ple
nip·py
nip-up
nir·va·na
ni·sei
   pl ni·sei *also* ni·seis
ni·ter
   also ni·tre
nit-pick·ing
ni·trate
ni·tra·tion
ni·tric

ni·tro
   pl ni·tros

ni·tro·gen
ni·trog·e·nous
ni·tro·glyc·er·in
   or ni·tro·glyc·er·ine

nit·ty-grit·ty
nit·wit
no·bil·i·ty
no·ble
no·ble·man
no·blesse oblige
no·bly
no·body
noc·tur·nal
noc·tur·nal·ly
noc·turne
noc·u·ous
nod
   nod·ded
   nod·ding
nod·al
node
nod·u·lar
nod·ule
no·el
nog·gin
no-good
noise·less
noise·mak·er
nois·i·ly
nois·i·ness
noi·some
noisy

no·lo con·ten·de·
re
no·mad
no·mad·ic
no-man's-land
nom de guerre
   pl noms de guerre

nom de plume
   pl noms de plume

no·men·cla·ture
nom·i·nal
nom·i·nal·ly
nom·i·nate
nom·i·na·tion
nom·i·na·tive
nom·i·na·tor
nom·i·nee
non·age
no·na·ge·nar·i·an
non·aligned
non·align·ment
non·book
non·can·di·date
nonce
non·cha·lance
non·cha·lant
non·com
non·com·ba·tant
non·com·mis·
sioned
non·com·mit·tal
non com·pos men·
tis
non·con·duc·tor
non·con·form·ist

non·con·for·mi·ty
non·co·op·er·a·
tion
non·de·script
non·en·ti·ty
none·such
none·the·less
non·fic·tion
non·in·ter·ven·
tion
non·met·al
non·me·tal·lic
non·pa·reil
non·par·ti·san
non·plus
  non·plussed
   also non·plused

  non·plus·sing
   also non·plus·ing

non·prof·it
non·res·i·dent
non·re·sis·tance
non·re·stric·tive
non·sched·uled
non·sense
non·sen·si·cal
non·sen·si·cal·ly
non se·qui·tur
non·sked
non·skid
non·stop
non·sup·port
non trop·po
non·union
non·vi·o·lence

noo·dle
noon·day
noon·time
no-par
  or no-par-val·ue

Nor·folk
nor·mal
nor·mal·cy
nor·mal·i·ty
nor·mal·iza·tion
nor·mal·ize
nor·mal·ly
nor·ma·tive
Norse
north·bound
North Car·o·li·na
North Da·ko·ta
north·east
north·east·er·ly
north·east·ern
north·er·ly
north·ern
north·ern·most
north·ward
north·wards
north·west
north·west·er·ly
north·west·ern
Nor·way
Nor·we·gian
nose·band
nose·bleed
nose·gay
nose·piece
no-show

nos·i·ly
nos·i·ness
nos·tal·gia
nos·tal·gic
nos·tal·gi·cal·ly
nos·tril
nos·trum
nosy
  or nos·ey

no·ta be·ne
no·ta·bil·i·ty
no·ta·ble
no·ta·bly
no·tar·i·al
no·ta·ri·za·tion
no·ta·rize
no·ta·ry pub·lic
  pl no·ta·ries pub·lic
  or no·ta·ry pub·
  lics

no·tate
no·ta·tion
no·ta·tion·al
notch
notch·back
note·book
note·case
not·ed
note·wor·thi·ly
note·wor·thi·ness
note·wor·thy
noth·ing
noth·ing·ness
no·tice
no·tice·able
no·tice·ably

no·ti·fi·ca·tion
no·ti·fi·er
no·ti·fy
no·tion
no·tion·al
no·to·ri·ety
no·to·ri·ous
no-trump
not·with·stand·
  ing
nou·gat
nought
nour·ish
nour·ish·ing
nour·ish·ment
nou·veau riche
  pl nou·veaux riches

no·va
  pl no·vas *or* no·vae

No·va Sco·tia
nov·el
nov·el·ette
nov·el·ist
nov·el·iza·tion
nov·el·ize
no·vel·la
  pl no·vel·las *or* no·
  vel·le

nov·el·ty
No·vem·ber
no·ve·na
nov·ice
no·vi·tiate
now·a·days
no·way
  or no·ways

no·where
no·wise
nox·ious
noz·zle
nth
nu·ance
nub·ble
nub·bly
nu·bile
nu·cle·ar
nu·cle·ate
nu·cle·ic acid
nu·cle·on
nu·cle·on·ics
nu·cle·us
  pl nu·clei *also*
  nu·cle·us·es

nu·clide
nude
nudge
nud·ism
nud·ist
nu·di·ty
nu·ga·to·ry
nug·get
nui·sance
nul·li·fi·ca·tion
nul·li·fi·er
nul·li·fy
nul·li·ty
numb
num·ber
num·ber·less
numb·ly
numb·ness
nu·mer·a·ble

nu·mer·al
nu·mer·ate
nu·mer·a·tion
nu·mer·a·tor
nu·mer·ic
nu·mer·i·cal
nu·mer·i·cal·ly
nu·mer·ol·o·gy
nu·mer·ous
nu·mis·mat·ic
nu·mis·mat·ics
nu·mis·ma·tist
num·skull
nun·ci·a·ture
nun·cio
   pl nun·ci·os

nun·nery
nup·tial
nurse·maid
nurs·ery
nurs·ery·man
nur·ture
nut·crack·er
nut·hatch
nut·meg
nut·pick
nu·tria
nu·tri·ent
nu·tri·ment
nu·tri·tion
nu·tri·tious
nu·tri·tive
nut·shell
nut·ty
nuz·zle

ny·lon
nym·pho·ma·nia
nym·pho·ma·ni·
  ac

O

oaf·ish
oak·en
Oak·land
oa·kum
oar
  long pole (see ore*)*

oar·lock
oars·man
oa·sis
  pl oa·ses

oat·cake
oat·en
oath
oat·meal
ob·bli·ga·to
  pl ob·bli·ga·tos *also*
  ob·bli·ga·ti

ob·du·ra·cy
ob·du·rate
obe·di·ence
obe·di·ent
obei·sance
obei·sant
obe·lisk
obese
obe·si·ty
obey
ob·fus·cate

ob·fus·ca·tion
ob·fus·ca·to·ry
obi
obit
obi·ter dic·tum
  pl obi·ter dic·ta

obit·u·ary
ob·ject
ob·jec·ti·fy
ob·jec·tion
ob·jec·tion·able
ob·jec·tion·ably
ob·jec·tive
ob·jec·tive·ly
ob·jec·tiv·i·ty
ob·jec·tor
ob·jet d'art
  pl ob·jets d'art

ob·jur·gate
ob·jur·ga·tion
ob·late
ob·la·tion
ob·li·gate
ob·li·ga·tion
oblig·a·to·ry
oblige
oblig·ing
oblique
oblique·ly
obliq·ui·ty
oblit·er·ate
oblit·er·a·tion
obliv·i·on
obliv·i·ous
ob·long

ob·lo·quy
ob·nox·ious
oboe
obo·ist
ob·scene
ob·scene·ly
ob·scen·i·ty
ob·scu·ran·tism
ob·scu·ran·tist
ob·scure
ob·scure·ly
ob·scu·ri·ty
ob·se·qui·ous
ob·se·quy
ob·serv·able
ob·serv·ably
ob·ser·vance
ob·ser·vant
ob·ser·va·tion
ob·ser·va·to·ry
ob·serve
ob·serv·er
ob·sess
ob·ses·sion
ob·ses·sive
ob·sid·i·an
ob·so·lesce
ob·so·les·cence
ob·so·les·cent
ob·so·lete
ob·sta·cle
ob·stet·ric
  or ob·stet·ri·cal

ob·ste·tri·cian
ob·stet·rics

ob·sti·na·cy
ob·sti·nate
ob·sti·nate·ly
ob·strep·er·ous
ob·struct
ob·struc·tion
ob·struc·tion·ism
ob·struc·tion·ist
ob·struc·tive
ob·struc·tor
ob·tain
ob·tain·able
ob·trude
ob·tru·sion
ob·tru·sive
ob·tuse
ob·verse
ob·vert
ob·vi·ate
ob·vi·a·tion
ob·vi·ous
oc·a·ri·na
oc·ca·sion
oc·ca·sion·al
oc·ca·sion·al·ly
oc·ci·den·tal
oc·clude
oc·clu·sion
oc·clu·sive
oc·cult
oc·cul·ta·tion
oc·cult·ism
oc·cu·pan·cy
oc·cu·pant
oc·cu·pa·tion
oc·cu·pa·tion·al

oc·cu·pa·tion·al·
  ly
oc·cu·pi·er
oc·cu·py
oc·cur
oc·cur·rence
ocean
ocean·go·ing
oce·an·ic
ocean·og·ra·pher
ocean·o·graph·ic
ocean·og·ra·phy
ocean·ol·o·gy
oce·lot
ocher
  or ochre

o'·clock
oc·ta·gon
oc·tag·o·nal
oc·tag·o·nal·ly
oc·tane
oc·tave
oc·ta·vo
  pl oc·ta·vos

oc·tet
Oc·to·ber
oc·to·ge·nar·i·an
oc·to·pod
oc·to·pus
oc·to·roon
oc·u·lar
oc·u·list
odd·ball
odd·i·ty
odd·ly

odd·ment
odds-on
odi·ous
odi·um
odom·e·ter
odor
odor·ant
odor·ous
od·ys·sey
oe·di·pal
Oe·di·pus
of·fal
waste (see awful)

off·beat
off-col·or
or off-col·ored

of·fend
of·fend·er
of·fense
or of·fence

of·fen·sive
of·fer
of·fer·ing
of·fer·to·ry
off·hand
off·hand·ed
of·fice
of·fice·hold·er
of·fi·cer
of·fi·cial
of·fi·cial·dom
of·fi·cial·ly
of·fi·ci·ant
of·fi·ci·ate
of·fi·ci·a·tion

of·fi·cious
off·ing
off·ish
off·print
off·set
off·shoot
off·shore
off·spring
pl off·spring *also* off·springs

off·stage
off-the-rec·ord
off-white
of·ten
of·ten·times
or oft·times

ogle
ogre
ogre·ish
Ohio
ohm
ohm·me·ter
oil·cloth
oil·er
oil·i·ly
oil·i·ness
oil·seed
oil·skin
oil·stone
oily
oint·ment
OK
or okay

OK'd
or okayed

OK'·ing
or okay·ing

Okla·ho·ma
okra
old·en
old-fash·ioned
old·ish
old-line
old·ster
old-tim·er
old-world
ole·ag·i·nous
ole·an·der
oleo
pl ole·os

oleo·mar·ga·rine
ol·fac·tion
ol·fac·to·ry
oli·garch
oli·gar·chic
or oli·gar·chi·cal

oli·gar·chy
oli·gop·o·ly
ol·ive
Olym·pia
olym·pi·ad
Olym·pic
Oma·ha
Oman
om·buds·man
pl om·buds·men

ome·ga
om·elet
or om·elette

omen

om·i·nous
omis·si·ble
omis·sion
omit
  omit·ted
  omit·ting
om·ni·bus
om·ni·di·rec·tion·
  al
om·nip·o·tence
om·nip·o·tent
om·ni·pres·ence
om·ni·pres·ent
om·ni·range
om·ni·science
om·ni·scient
om·niv·o·rous
once-over
on·com·ing
one·ness
oner·ous
one·self
one-shot
one-sid·ed
one·time
one-to-one
one-track
one-up·man·ship
one-way
on·go·ing
on·ion
on·ion·skin
on-line
on·look·er
on·ly
on·o·mato·poe·ia

on·o·mato·poe·ic
  or on·o·mato·po·et·
  ic
on·o·mato·poe·i·
  cal·ly
  or on·o·mato·po·et·
  i·cal·ly
on·rush
on·set
on·shore
on·slaught
On·tar·io
on·to
onus
on·ward
  also on·wards
on·yx
oo·dles
oozy
opac·i·ty
opal
opal·es·cence
opal·es·cent
opaque
opaque·ly
open-air
open-and-shut
open-end
open·er
open-eyed
open·hand·ed
open·heart·ed
open-hearth
open·ing
open·mind·ed
open·mouthed

open·ness
open·work
op·era
op·er·a·ble
op·er·a·bly
op·er·ate
op·er·at·ic
op·er·at·i·cal·ly
op·er·a·tion
op·er·a·tion·al
op·er·a·tive
op·er·a·tor
op·er·et·ta
oph·thal·mic
oph·thal·mol·o·
  gist
oph·thal·mol·o·gy
opi·ate
opin·ion
opin·ion·at·ed
opi·um
opos·sum
  pl opos·sums *also*
  opos·sum
op·po·nent
op·por·tune
op·por·tune·ly
op·por·tun·ism
op·por·tun·ist
op·por·tu·nis·tic
op·por·tu·ni·ty
op·pose
op·po·site
op·po·si·tion
op·press
op·pres·sion

op·pres·sive
op·pres·sive·ly
op·pres·sor
op·pro·bri·ous
op·pro·bri·um
op·tic
op·ti·cal
op·ti·cal·ly
op·ti·cian
op·tics
op·ti·mal
op·ti·mal·ly
op·ti·mism
op·ti·mist
op·ti·mis·tic
op·ti·mis·ti·cal·ly
op·ti·mize
op·ti·mum
  pl op·ti·ma *also* op·
  ti·mums

op·tion
op·tion·al
op·tion·al·ly
op·to·met·ric
op·tom·e·trist
op·tom·e·try
op·u·lence
op·u·lent
opus
  pl opera *also* opus·es

or·a·cle
  prophesier (see
  auricle)

orac·u·lar
oral
  spoken (see aural)

oral·ly
or·ange
or·ange·ade
orang·utan
  or orang·ou·tan

orate
ora·tion
or·a·tor
or·a·tor·i·cal
or·a·tor·i·cal·ly
or·a·to·rio
  pl or·a·to·ri·os

or·a·to·ry
or·bic·u·lar
or·bit
or·bit·al
or·chard
or·ches·tra
or·ches·tral
or·ches·trate
or·ches·tra·tion
or·chid
or·dain
or·deal
or·der
or·dered
or·der·li·ness
or·der·ly
or·di·nal
or·di·nance
  law (see ordnance)

or·di·nari·ly
or·di·nary
or·di·nate
or·di·na·tion

ord·nance
  military supplies (see
  ordinance)

or·dure
ore
  mineral (see oar)

öre
  pl öre

oreg·a·no
Or·e·gon
or·gan
or·gan·dy
  also or·gan·die

or·gan·ic
or·gan·i·cal·ly
or·gan·ism
or·gan·ist
or·gan·iz·able
or·ga·ni·za·tion
or·ga·ni·za·tion·
  al
or·ga·nize
or·ga·niz·er
or·gan·za
or·gasm
or·gi·as·tic
or·gi·as·ti·cal·ly
or·gu·lous
or·gy
ori·el
ori·ent
Ori·en·tal
ori·en·tate
ori·en·ta·tion
or·i·fice

ori·flamme
ori·ga·mi
or·i·gin
orig·i·nal
orig·i·nal·i·ty
orig·i·nal·ly
orig·i·nate
orig·i·na·tion
orig·i·na·tor
ori·ole
or·i·son
Or·lon
or·mo·lu
or·na·ment
or·na·men·tal
or·na·men·ta·tion
or·nate
or·nate·ly
or·nery
or·ni·thol·o·gist
or·ni·thol·o·gy
orog·e·ny
oro·tund
or·phan
or·phan·age
or·ris
orth·odon·tics
orth·odon·tist
or·tho·dox
or·tho·doxy
or·tho·graph·ic
or·thog·ra·phy
or·tho·pe·dic
   also or·tho·pae·dic

or·tho·pe·dics
   also or·tho·pae·dics

or·tho·pe·dist
os·cil·late
os·cil·la·tion
os·cil·la·tor
os·cil·la·to·ry
os·cil·lo·scope
os·cu·late
os·cu·la·tion
osier
os·mo·sis
os·mot·ic
os·prey
os·si·fi·ca·tion
os·si·fy
os·su·ary
os·ten·si·ble
os·ten·si·bly
os·ten·ta·tion
os·ten·ta·tious
os·teo·path
os·teo·path·ic
os·te·op·a·thy
os·tra·cism
os·tra·cize
os·trich
oth·er
oth·er·wise
oth·er·world
oti·ose
Ot·ta·wa
ot·ter
ot·to·man
our·selves
oust·er
out·age
out-and-out

out·bal·ance
out·bid
out·board
out·bound
out·break
out·build·ing
out·burst
out·cast
out·class
out·come
out·crop
out·cry
out·dat·ed
out·dis·tance
out·do
out·door
   also out·doors
   adj

out·doors
   adverb, noun

out·draw
out·er
out·er·most
out·face
out·field
out·field·er
out·fight
out·fit
   out·fit·ted
   out·fit·ting
out·fit·ter
out·flank
out·flow
out·fox
out·gen·er·al
out·go

out·go·ing
out·grow
out·growth
out·guess
out·house
out·ing
out·land·ish
out·last
out·law
out·law·ry
out·lay
out·let
out·li·er
out·line
out·live
out·look
out·ly·ing
out·ma·neu·ver
out·match
out·mod·ed
out·most
out·num·ber
out-of-bounds
out-of-date
out-of-door
   or out-of-doors

out-of-the-way
out·pa·tient
out·play
out·point
out·post
out·pour
out·put
out·rage
out·ra·geous

out·rank
ou·tré
out·reach
out·ride
out·rid·er
out·rig·ger
out·right
out·run
out·sell
out·set
out·shine
out·side
out·sid·er
out·sit
out·size
out·skirt
out·smart
out·spo·ken
out·spread
out·stand·ing
out·sta·tion
out·stay
out·stretch
out·strip
out·ward
out·ward·ly
out·wear
out·weigh
out·wit
out·work
out·worn
oval
oval·ly
ovar·i·an
ova·ry
ova·tion

ov·en
oven·bird
over·abun·dance
over·abun·dant
over·act
over·ac·tive
over·age
over·all
over·arm
over·awe
over·bal·ance
over·bear·ing
over·bid
over·blown
over·board
over·build
over·bur·den
over·call
over·cap·i·tal·ize
over·cast
over·charge
over·cloud
over·coat
over·come
over·con·fi·dence
over·crowd
over·do
over·dose
over·draft
over·draw
over·dress
over·drive
over·due
over·em·pha·size
over·es·ti·mate
over·ex·pose

over·ex·po·sure
over·ex·tend
over·flight
over·flow
over·grow
over·hand
over·hang
over·haul
over·head
over·hear
over·heat
over·in·dulge
over·in·dul·gence
over·joy
over·kill
over·land
over·lap
over·lay
over·leap
over·lie
over·load
over·long
over·look
over·lord
over·ly
over·match
over·much
over·night
over·pass
over·play
over·pow·er
over·price
over·print
over·pro·tect
over·rate
over·reach

over·ride
  over·rode
  over·rid·den
  over·rid·ing
over·ripe
over·rule
over·run
  over·ran
  over·run·ning
over·seas
over·see
  over·saw
  over·seen
  over·see·ing
over·seer
over·sell
  over·sold
  over·sell·ing
over·sen·si·tive
over·set
over·sexed
over·shad·ow
over·shoe
over·shoot
  over·shot
  over·shoot·ing
over·sight
over·sim·pli·fi·ca·
  tion
over·sim·pli·fy
over·size
  or over·sized

over·sleep
over·spend
  over·spent

over·spend·ing
over·spread
over·state
over·state·ment
over·stay
over·step
over·strung
over·stuff
over·sub·scribe
over·sup·ply
overt
over·take
  over·took
  over·tak·en
  over·tak·ing
over·tax
over-the-count·er
over·throw
  over·threw
  over·thrown
  over·throw·ing
over·time
over·tone
over·train
over·trick
over·trump
over·ture
over·turn
over·use
over·ween·ing
over·weigh
over·weight
over·whelm
over·wind
  over·wound
  also over·wind·ed

over·wind·ing
over·work
over·write
 over·wrote
 over·writ·ten
 over·writ·ing
over·wrought
ovip·a·rous
ovoid
 or ovoi·dal

ovu·late
ovu·la·tion
ovu·la·to·ry
ovule
ovum
 pl ova

owe
owl·ish
own·er
ox
 pl ox·en

ox·blood
ox·bow
ox·ford
ox·i·da·tion
ox·ide
ox·i·dize
oxy·acet·y·lene
ox·y·gen
ox·y·gen·ate
ox·y·gen·ation
oxy·mo·ron
 pl oxy·mo·ra

oys·ter
ozone

P

pa·'an·ga
pab·u·lum
pace·mak·er
pac·er
pachy·derm
pach·ys·an·dra
pa·cif·ic
pac·i·fi·ca·tion
pac·i·fi·er
pac·i·fism
pac·i·fist
pac·i·fy
pack·age
pack·ag·er
pack·er
pack·et
pack·ing
pack·ing·house
pack·sack
pack·sad·dle
pack·thread
pact
pad
 pad·ded
 pad·ding
pad·dle
pad·dle·ball
pad·dock
pad·dy
pad·lock
pa·dre
pae·an
 song (see peon*)*

pa·gan

pag·eant
pag·eant·ry
page boy
 or page·boy

pag·i·nate
pag·i·na·tion
pa·go·da
pail
 bucket (see pale*)*

pail·ful
pain
 hurt (see pane*)*

pain·ful
pain·ful·ly
pain·less
pains·tak·ing
paint·brush
paint·er
paint·ing
pair
 two (see pare, pear*)*

pai·sa
 pl pai·se *or* pai·sa
 or pai·sas

pais·ley
pa·ja·mas
Pa·ki·stan
Pa·ki·stani
pal·ace
pal·a·din
pa·lan·quin
pal·at·able
pal·at·ably
pal·a·tal
pal·a·tal·iza·tion

pal·ate
roof of the mouth (see palette, pallet)

pa·la·tial

pal·a·tine

pa·la·ver

pale
light (see pail)

pale·face

pa·le·og·ra·pher

pa·le·og·ra·phy

Pa·leo·lith·ic

pa·le·on·to·lo·gist

pa·le·on·tol·o·gy

pal·ette
painter's tablet (see palate, pallet)

pa·limp·sest

pal·in·drome

pal·ing

pal·i·sade

pal·la·di·um

pall·bear·er

pal·let
bed (see palate, palette)

pal·li·ate

pal·lia·tive

pal·lid

pal·lor

pal·mate
also pal·mat·ed

pal·met·to
pl pal·met·tos *or* pal·met·toes

palm·ist·ry

pal·o·mi·no

pal·pa·ble

pal·pa·bly

pal·pate

pal·pi·tate

pal·pi·ta·tion

pal·sied

pal·sy

pal·tri·ness

pal·try

pam·pa
pl pam·pas

pam·per

pam·phlet

pam·phle·teer

pan
panned
pan·ning

pan·a·cea

pa·nache

Pan·a·ma

Pan·a·ma·ni·an

Pan-Amer·i·can

pan·a·tela

pan·cake

pan·chro·mat·ic

pan·cre·as

pan·cre·at·ic

pan·da

pan·dem·ic

pan·de·mo·ni·um

pan·der

pan·der·er

pan·dow·dy

pane
glass (see pain)

pan·e·gy·ric

pan·e·gy·rist

pan·el

pan·eled
or pan·elled

pan·el·ing
or pan·el·ling

pan·el·ing
noun

pan·el·ist

pan·fish

pan·han·dle

pan·han·dler

pan·ic
pan·icked
pan·ick·ing

pan·icky

pan·i·cle

pan·ic-strick·en

pan·jan·drum

pan·nier
or pan·ier

pan·o·plied

pan·o·ply

pan·ora·ma

pan·oram·ic

pan·sy

pan·ta·loons

pan·the·ism

pan·the·ist

pan·the·is·tic

pan·the·on

pan·ther

pant·ie
or panty

pan·to·mime
pan·to·mim·ic
pan·try
pant·suit
panty hose
pa·pa·cy
pa·pal
pa·paw
pa·pa·ya
pa·per
pa·per·back
pa·per·hang·er
pa·per·weight
pa·pery
pa·pier-mâ·ché
pa·pil·la
  pl pa·pil·lae

pap·il·lary
pap·il·lo·ma
  pl pap·il·lo·mas *or*
  pap·il·lo·ma·ta
pa·pil·lote
pa·poose
pa·pri·ka
Pa·pua New
  Guin·ea
pap·ule
pa·py·rus
  pl pa·py·rus·es
  or pa·py·ri

pa·ra
  pl pa·ras *or* pa·ra

par·a·ble
pa·rab·o·la
pa·ra·bol·ic
para·chute

para·chut·ist
pa·rade
par·a·digm
par·a·dise
par·a·di·si·a·cal
par·a·di·si·a·cal·
  ly
par·a·dox
par·a·dox·i·cal
par·a·dox·i·cal·ly
par·af·fin
par·a·gon
para·graph
Par·a·guay
Par·a·guay·an
par·a·keet
  or par·ra·keet

par·al·lax
par·al·lel
par·al·lel·ism
par·al·lel·o·gram
pa·ral·y·sis
  pl pa·ral·y·ses

par·a·lyt·ic
par·a·ly·za·tion
par·a·lyze
par·a·me·cium
  pl par·a·me·cia *also*
  par·a·me·ciums

pa·ram·e·ter
  factor (*see* perimeter)

par·a·mount
par·a·mount·cy
par·amour
para·noia

para·noi·ac
para·noid
par·a·pet
par·a·pher·na·lia
para·phrase
para·ple·gia
para·ple·gic
para·psy·chol·o·
  gy
par·a·site
par·a·sit·ic
  also par·a·sit·i·cal

par·a·sit·i·cal·ly
par·a·sit·ism
par·a·si·tol·o·gist
par·a·si·tol·o·gy
para·sol
para·thy·roid
para·troop·er
para·troops
para·ty·phoid
par·boil
par·buck·le
par·cel
  par·celed
   or par·celled

  par·cel·ing
   or par·cel·ling

parch·ment
par·don
par·don·able
par·don·ably
pare
  trim (*see* pair, pear)

par·e·gor·ic

par·ent
par·ent·age
pa·ren·tal
pa·ren·the·sis
  pl pa·ren·the·ses

pa·ren·the·size
par·en·thet·ic
  or par·en·thet·i·cal

par·en·thet·i·cal·
  ly
par·ent·hood
pa·re·sis
  pl pa·re·ses

par ex·cel·lence
par·fait
pa·ri·ah
pa·ri·etal
pari-mu·tu·el
par·ing
pa·ri pas·su
par·ish
pa·rish·io·ner
par·i·ty
par·ka
park·way
par·lance
par·lay
  bets

par·ley
  discussion

par·lia·ment
par·lia·men·tar·
  i·an
par·lia·men·ta·ry
par·lor

Par·ma
Par·me·san
pa·ro·chi·al
pa·ro·chi·al·ly
par·o·dist
par·o·dy
pa·role
pa·rol·ee
par·ox·ysm
par·ox·ys·mal
par·quet
par·que·try
par·ra·keet
  var of parakeet

par·ri·cide
par·rot
par·ry
parse
par·sec
par·si·mo·ni·ous
par·si·mo·ny
pars·ley
pars·nip
par·son
par·son·age
par·take
  par·took
  par·tak·en
  par·tak·ing
par·tak·er
par·terre
par·the·no·gen·e·
  sis
par·tial
par·tial·i·ty

par·tial·ly
par·ti·ble
par·tic·i·pant
par·tic·i·pate
par·tic·i·pa·tion
par·tic·i·pa·tor
par·tic·i·pa·to·ry
par·ti·cip·i·al
par·ti·cip·i·al·ly
par·ti·ci·ple
par·ti·cle
par·ti-col·ored
par·tic·u·lar
par·tic·u·lar·i·ty
par·tic·u·lar·iza·
  tion
par·tic·u·lar·ize
par·tic·u·lar·ly
par·tic·u·late
part·ing
par·ti·san
  or par·ti·zan

par·ti·san·ship
par·tite
par·ti·tion
par·ti·tive
part·ly
part·ner
part·ner·ship
par·tridge
part-song
part-time
par·tu·ri·ent
par·tu·ri·tion
par·ty

par·ve·nu
Pas·a·de·na
pa·sha
pass
  go by (see past)

  passed
  pass·ing
pass·able
pass·ably
pas·sage
pas·sage·way
pass·book
pas·se
pas·sel
pas·sen·ger
passe-par·tout
pass·er
pas·ser·by
  pl pas·sers·by

pas·ser·ine
pas·si·ble
pas·sim
pass·ing
pas·sion
pas·sion·ate
pas·sion·ate·ly
pas·sive
pas·sive·ly
pas·siv·i·ty
pass·key
Pass·over
pass·port
pass·word
past
  ago, beyond (see pass)

pas·ta
paste
paste·board
pas·tel
pas·tern
pas·teur·iza·tion
pas·teur·ize
pas·teur·iz·er
pas·tiche
pas·tille
  also pas·til

pas·time
past·i·ness
pas·tor
pas·to·ral
pas·tor·ate
pas·tra·mi
  also pas·tro·mi

past·ry
pas·tur·age
pas·ture
pasty
pat
  pat·ted
  pat·ting
patch
patch·board
patch·work
pa·tel·la
  pl pa·tel·lae *or* pa·
  tel·las

pat·en
  plate (see patten)

pa·tent
pat·ent·able

pat·en·tee
pa·ter·fa·mil·i·as
  pl pa·tres·fa·mil·i·as

pa·ter·nal
pa·ter·nal·ism
pa·ter·nal·is·tic
pa·ter·nal·ly
pa·ter·ni·ty
Pat·er·son
pa·thet·ic
pa·thet·i·cal·ly
path·find·er
patho·gen
patho·gen·ic
patho·ge·nic·i·ty
patho·log·i·cal
  or patho·log·ic

patho·log·i·cal·ly
pa·thol·o·gist
pa·thol·o·gy
pa·thos
path·way
pa·tience
pa·tient
pa·ti·na
  pl pa·ti·nas *or*
  pa·ti·nae

pa·tio
  pl pa·ti·os

pa·tois
  pl pa·tois

pa·tri·arch
pa·tri·ar·chal
pa·tri·arch·ate
pa·tri·ar·chy

pa·tri·cian
pat·ri·cide
pat·ri·lin·eal
pat·ri·mo·ny
pa·tri·ot
pa·tri·ot·ic
pa·tri·ot·i·cal·ly
pa·tri·o·tism
pa·tris·tic
pa·trol
  pa·trolled
  pa·trol·ling
pa·trol·man
pa·tron
pat·ron·age
pa·tron·ess
pa·tron·ize
pat·ro·nym·ic
pa·troon
pat·sy
pat·ten
  shoe (see paten)

pat·ter
pat·tern
pat·ty
  also pat·tie

pau·ci·ty
paunch·i·ness
paunchy
pau·per
pau·per·ize
pa·vane
  also pa·van

pave·ment
pa·vil·ion

pav·ing
pawn·bro·ker
pawn·shop
pay
  paid
    also payed

  pay·ing
pay·able
pay·check
pay·ee
pay·er
  also pay·or

pay·load
pay·mas·ter
pay·ment
pay·off
pay·roll
pea
  pl peas *also* pease

peace
  tranquillity (see piece)

peace·able
peace·ably
peace·ful
peace·ful·ly
peace·mak·er
peace·time
peach
pea·cock
pea·fowl
pea·hen
peak
  mountain (see peek, pique)

peal
  resound (see peel)

pea·nut
pear
  fruit (see pair, pare)

pearl
  gem (see purl)

pearly
pear-shaped
peas·ant
peas·ant·ry
pea·shoot·er
peb·ble
peb·bly
pe·can
pec·ca·dil·lo
  pl pec·ca·dil·loes *or*
  pec·ca·dil·los

pec·ca·ry
pec·tate
pec·tin
pec·to·ral
pec·u·late
pec·u·la·tion
pe·cu·liar
pe·cu·liar·i·ty
pe·cu·liar·ly
pe·cu·ni·ary
ped·a·gog·ic
ped·a·gog·i·cal·ly
ped·a·gogue
  also ped·a·gog

ped·a·go·gy
ped·al
  ped·aled
    also ped·alled

  ped·al·ing
    also ped·al·ling

ped·ant
pe·dan·tic
pe·dan·ti·cal·ly
ped·dle
ped·dler
  or ped·lar

ped·er·ast
ped·er·as·ty
ped·es·tal
pe·des·tri·an
pe·di·at·ric
pe·di·a·tri·cian
  or pe·di·a·trist

pe·di·at·rics
pedi·cab
ped·i·cure
ped·i·gree
ped·i·greed
ped·i·ment
pe·dol·o·gist
pe·dol·o·gy
pe·dom·e·ter
pe·dun·cle
peek
  look (see peak, pique)

peel
  skin (see peal)

peel·ing
peen
  or pein

peep·hole
peer
  equal, look (see pier)

peer·age

peer·less
peeve
pee·vish
pee·wee
peg
  pegged
  peg·ging
pei·gnoir
pe·jo·ra·tive
Pe·king·ese
  or Pe·kin·ese

pe·koe
pel·age
pe·lag·ic
pel·i·can
pel·la·gra
pel·let
pell-mell
pel·lu·cid
pel·vic
pel·vis
  pl pel·vis·es *or* pel·ves

pem·mi·can
  also pem·i·can

pen
  penned
  pen·ning
pe·nal
pe·nal·iza·tion
pe·nal·ize
pen·al·ty
pen·ance
pen·chant
pen·cil

pen·ciled
  or pen·cilled

pen·cil·ing
  or pen·cil·ling

pen·dant
  also pen·dent
  noun

pen·dent
  or pen·dant
  adj

pend·ing
pen·du·lous
pen·du·lum
pe·ne·plain
  also pe·ne·plane

pen·e·tra·bil·i·ty
pen·e·tra·ble
pen·e·tra·bly
pen·e·trate
pen·e·trat·ing
pen·e·tra·tion
pen·e·tra·tive
pen·guin
pen·hold·er
pen·i·cil·lin
pen·in·su·la
pen·in·su·lar
pe·nis
  pl pe·nes *or* pe·nis·es

pen·i·tence
pen·i·tent
pen·i·ten·tial
pen·i·ten·tial·ly
pen·i·ten·tia·ry
pen·knife

pen·man·ship
pen·nant
pen·ni
　pl pen·nia *or* pen·nis
pen·ni·less
pen·non
Penn·syl·va·nia
pen·ny
　pl pen·nies *or* pence
pen·ny-pinch
pen·ny·weight
pen·ny·wise
pen·ny·wort
pe·no·log·i·cal
pe·nol·o·gist
pe·nol·o·gy
pen·sion
pen·sion·er
pen·sive
pen·sive·ly
pen·ta·cle
pen·ta·gon
pen·tag·o·nal
pen·tam·e·ter
pen·ta·ton·ic
　scale
Pen·te·cost
Pen·te·cos·tal
pent·house
pen·tom·ic
pe·nu·che
pen·ul·ti·mate
pen·um·bra
　pl pen·um·brae *or*
　pen·um·bras
pe·nu·ri·ous

pen·u·ry
pe·on
　laborer (*see* paean)
pe·on·age
pe·o·ny
peo·ple
　pl peo·ple
Pe·o·ria
pep
　pepped
　pep·ping
pep·lum
pep·per
pep·per·box
pep·per·corn
pep·per·mint
pep·pery
pep·pi·ness
pep·py
pep·sin
pep·tic
pep·tone
per·am·bu·late
per·am·bu·la·tion
per·am·bu·la·tor
per an·num
per·cale
per cap·i·ta
per·ceiv·able
per·ceiv·ably
per·ceive
per·cent
　pl per·cent *or* per·
　cents
per·cent·age
per·cen·tile

per·cept
per·cep·ti·bil·i·ty
per·cep·ti·ble
per·cep·ti·bly
per·cep·tion
per·cep·tive
per·cep·tu·al
per·cep·tu·al·ly
per·chance
Per·che·ron
per·cip·i·ence
per·cip·i·ent
per·co·late
per·co·la·tion
per·co·la·tor
per·cus·sion
per·cus·sive
per di·em
per·di·tion
per·du·ra·bil·i·ty
per·du·ra·ble
per·du·ra·bly
per·e·gri·na·tion
pe·remp·to·ri·ly
pe·remp·to·ri·
　ness
pe·remp·to·ry
pe·ren·ni·al
pe·ren·ni·al·ly
per·fect
per·fect·ibil·i·ty
per·fect·ible
per·fec·tion
per·fec·tion·ist
per·fec·to
per·fid·i·ous

per·fi·dy
per·fo·rate
per·fo·ra·tion
per·fo·ra·tor
per·force
per·form
per·form·able
per·for·mance
per·fume
per·fum·ery
per·func·to·ri·ly
per·func·to·ri·
  ness
per·func·to·ry
per·go·la
per·haps
peri·cyn·thi·on
per·i·gee
peri·he·lion
per·il
  per·iled
    also per·illed
  per·il·ing
    also per·il·ling
per·il·ous
peri·lune
pe·rim·e·ter
  boundary (see
    parameter)
pe·ri·od
pe·ri·od·ic
pe·ri·od·i·cal
pe·ri·od·i·cal·ly
pe·ri·od·ic·i·ty
peri·odon·tal
peri·pa·tet·ic

pe·riph·er·al
pe·riph·er·al·ly
pe·riph·ery
pe·riph·ra·sis
  pl pe·riph·ra·ses
peri·phras·tic
pe·rique
peri·scope
peri·scop·ic
per·ish
per·ish·abil·i·ty
per·ish·able
peri·stal·sis
peri·stal·tic
peri·style
peri·to·ni·tis
peri·wig
per·i·win·kle
per·jure
per·jur·er
per·ju·ri·ous
per·ju·ry
perk·i·ly
perk·i·ness
perky
per·ma·frost
per·ma·nence
per·ma·nen·cy
per·ma·nent
per·man·ga·nate
per·me·abil·i·ty
per·me·able
per·me·ably
per·me·ance
per·me·ate
per·me·ation

per·mis·si·bil·i·ty
per·mis·si·ble
per·mis·si·bly
per·mis·sion
per·mis·sive
per·mit
  per·mit·ted
  per·mit·ting
per·mu·ta·tion
per·mute
per·ni·cious
per·orate
per·ora·tion
per·ox·ide
per·pen·dic·u·lar
per·pe·trate
per·pe·tra·tion
per·pe·tra·tor
per·pet·u·al
per·pet·u·al·ly
per·pet·u·ate
per·pet·u·a·tion
per·pet·u·a·tor
per·pe·tu·ity
per·plex
per·plexed
per·plexed·ly
per·plex·i·ty
per·qui·site
  privilege (see
    prerequisite)

per se
per·se·cute
per·se·cu·tion
per·se·cu·tor
per·se·ver·ance

per·se·vere
Per·sian
per·si·flage
per·sim·mon
per·sist
per·sis·tence
per·sis·ten·cy
per·sis·tent
per·snick·e·ty
per·son
per·son·able
per·son·age
per·son·al
private (see personnel)
per·son·al·i·ty
character (see
personalty)
per·son·al·ize
per·son·al·ly
per·son·al·ty
property (see
personality)
per·so·na non
gra·ta
per·so·nate
adj
per·son·ate
verb
per·son·i·fi·ca·
tion
per·son·i·fi·er
per·son·i·fy
per·son·nel
employees (see
personal)
per·spec·tive

per·spi·ca·cious
per·spi·cac·i·ty
per·spi·cu·i·ty
per·spic·u·ous
per·spi·ra·tion
per·spi·ra·to·ry
per·spire
per·suad·able
per·suade
per·sua·si·ble
per·sua·sion
per·sua·sive
per·tain
per·ti·na·cious
per·ti·nac·i·ty
per·ti·nence
per·ti·nen·cy
per·ti·nent
pert·ly
pert·ness
per·turb
per·tur·ba·tion
Pe·ru
pe·rus·al
pe·ruse
Pe·ru·vi·an
per·vade
per·va·sive
per·verse
per·verse·ly
per·ver·sion
per·ver·si·ty
per·ver·sive
per·vert
per·vi·ous
pe·se·ta

pe·se·wa
pes·ky
pe·so
pl pe·sos
pes·si·mism
pes·si·mist
pes·si·mis·tic
pes·si·mis·ti·cal·
ly
pes·ter
pest·hole
pes·ti·cide
pes·tif·er·ous
pes·ti·lence
pes·ti·lent
pes·ti·len·tial
pes·tle
pet
pet·ted
pet·ting
pet·al
pe·tard
pe·ter
pet·i·ole
pet·it
pe·tite
pe·tit four
pl petits fours *or* petit
fours
pe·ti·tion
pe·ti·tion·er
pet·rel
pet·ri·fac·tion
pet·ri·fy
pet·ro·chem·i·cal
pe·trog·ra·phy

pet·rol
pet·ro·la·tum
pe·tro·leum
pet·ro·log·ic
pe·trol·o·gist
pe·trol·o·gy
pet·ti·coat
pet·ti·fog
  pet·ti·fogged
  pet·ti·fog·ging
pet·ti·fog·ger
pet·ti·ly
pet·ti·ness
pet·tish
pet·ty
pet·u·lance
pet·u·lant
pe·tu·nia
pew·ter
pey·o·te
  or pey·otl

pfen·nig
pha·eton
phago·cyte
pha·lanx
  pl pha·lanx·es *or*
  pha·lan·ges

phal·a·rope
phal·lic
phal·lus
  pl phal·li *or* phal·lus·
  es

phan·tasm
phan·tas·ma·go·
  ria

phan·tas·ma·go·
  ric
phan·tom
pha·raoh
phar·i·sa·ic
phar·i·sa·ical
phar·i·sa·ical·ly
phar·i·see
phar·ma·ceu·ti·
  cal
  also phar·ma·ceu·tic
phar·ma·ceu·tics
phar·ma·cist
phar·ma·cog·no·
  sy
phar·ma·co·log·i·
  cal
phar·ma·co·log·i·
  cal·ly
phar·ma·col·o·
  gist
phar·ma·col·o·gy
phar·ma·co·poe·
  ia
phar·ma·cy
phar·os
pha·ryn·geal
phar·ynx
  pl pha·ryn·ges *also*
  phar·ynx·es

phase
  aspect (see faze)

phase·out
pheas·ant
phe·no·bar·bi·tal
phe·nol

phe·no·lic
phe·nom·e·nal
phe·nom·e·non
  pl phe·nom·e·na *or*
  phe·nom·e·nons

phi·al
Phil·a·del·phia
phi·lan·der
phi·lan·der·er
phil·an·throp·ic
phil·an·thro·pist
phi·lan·thro·py
phil·a·tel·ic
phi·lat·e·list
phi·lat·e·ly
phil·har·mon·ic
phi·lip·pic
Phil·ip·pine
Phil·ip·pines
phi·lis·tine
phil·o·den·dron
  pl phil·o·den·drons
  or
  phil·o·den·dra

phil·o·log·i·cal
phi·lol·o·gist
phi·lol·o·gy
phi·los·o·pher
philo·soph·ic
philo·soph·i·cal·
  ly
phi·los·o·phize
phi·los·o·phy
phil·ter
  or phil·tre
  potion (see filter)

phle·bi·tis

phlegm
phleg·mat·ic
phleg·mat·i·cal·ly
phlox
   pl phlox *or* phlox·es

pho·bia
pho·bic
phoe·be
Phoe·nix
pho·neme
pho·ne·mic
pho·ne·mi·cal·ly
pho·ne·mics
pho·net·ic
pho·net·i·cal·ly
pho·ne·ti·cian
pho·net·ics
phon·ic
pho·ni·cal·ly
phon·ics
pho·ni·ly
pho·ni·ness
pho·no·graph
pho·no·graph·ic
pho·no·log·i·cal
pho·no·log·i·cal·ly
pho·nol·o·gist
pho·nol·o·gy
pho·ny
   or pho·ney

phos·phate
phos·phat·ic
phos·pho·res·cence

phos·pho·res·cent
phos·phor·ic
phos·pho·rus
pho·to
   pl pho·tos

pho·to·cell
pho·to·chro·mic
pho·to·com·po·si·tion
pho·to·copy
pho·to·elec·tric
pho·to·elec·tron
pho·to·emis·sive
pho·to·en·grave
pho·to·en·grav·ing
pho·to·flash
pho·to·flood
pho·to·ge·nic
pho·tog·ra·pher
pho·to·graph·ic
pho·to·graph·i·cal·ly
pho·tog·ra·phy
pho·to·gra·vure
pho·to·litho·graph
pho·to·li·thog·ra·phy
pho·to·map
pho·tom·e·ter
pho·to·met·ric
pho·tom·e·try
pho·to·mi·cro·graph

pho·to·mu·ral
pho·ton
pho·to-off·set
pho·to·sen·si·tive
pho·to·sen·si·ti·za·tion
pho·to·stat
pho·to·syn·the·sis
phra·se·ol·o·gy
phras·ing
phre·net·ic
phre·nol·o·gy
phy·lac·tery
phy·log·e·ny
phy·lum
   pl phy·la

phys·ic
phys·i·cal
phys·i·cal·ly
phy·si·cian
phys·i·cist
phys·ics
phys·i·og·no·my
phys·io·graph·ic
phys·i·og·ra·phy
phys·i·o·log·i·cal
   or phys·i·o·log·ic

phys·i·o·log·i·cal·ly
phys·i·ol·o·gist
phys·i·ol·o·gy
phys·io·ther·a·py
phy·sique
phy·to·gen·ic
pi
   mathematics (*see* pie)

pi
also pie
jumble type (see pie)

pied
pi·ing
pi·a·nis·si·mo
pi·an·ist
pi·ano
also pi·ano·forte

pi·as·ter
or pi·as·tre

pi·az·za
pi·ca
pi·ca·resque
pic·a·yune
pic·ca·lil·li
pic·co·lo
pl pic·co·los

pice
pl pice

pick·ax
pick·er·el
pick·et
pick·ings
pick·le
pick·pock·et
pick·up
picky
pic·nic
pic·nicked
pic·nick·ing
pic·nick·er
pi·cot
pic·to·graph
pic·to·ri·al

pic·to·ri·al·ly
pic·ture
pic·tur·esque
pid·dle
pid·dling
pid·gin
language (see pigeon)

pie
pastry (see pi)

pie·bald
piece
fragment (see peace)

pièce de ré·sis·
tance
piece-dye
piece·meal
piece·work
piece·work·er
pied-à-terre
pied·mont
pier
landing (see peer)

pierce
Pierre
pi·etism
pi·ety
pi·geon
bird (see pidgin)

pi·geon·hole
pi·geon-toed
pig·gish
pig·gy·back
pig·head·ed
pig·ment
pig·men·ta·tion

pig·pen
pig·skin
pig·sty
pig·tail
pik·er
pi·las·ter
pil·chard
pil·fer
pil·fer·age
pil·fer·er
pil·grim
pil·grim·age
pil·ing
pil·lage
pil·lar
pill·box
pil·lion
pil·lo·ry
pil·low
pil·low·case
pi·lot
pi·lot·age
pi·lot·house
pil·sner
also pil·sen·er

pi·ma
pi·men·to
pim·per·nel
pim·ple
pim·pled
pim·ply
pin
pinned
pin·ning
pin·afore

pi·ña·ta
  or pi·na·ta

pin·ball

pince-nez

pin·cer
  instrument (see
    pincher)

pinch·cock

pinch·er
  one that pinches (see
    pincer)

pinch-hit

pin·cush·ion

pine·ap·ple

pine·wood

pin·feath·er

pin·fish

Ping-Pong

pin·head

pin·hole

pin·ion

pink·eye

pin·kie
  or pin·ky

pin·nace

pin·na·cle

pin·nate

pi·noch·le

pi·ñon
  or pin·yon
  pl pi·ñons *or* pin·
    yons
  or pi·ño·nes

pin·point

pin·prick

pin·set·ter

pin·stripe

pin-striped

pin·to
  pl pin·tos *also* pin·
    toes

pint-size
  or pint-sized

pin·up

pin·wale

pin·wheel

pin·work

pin·worm

pi·o·neer

pi·ous

pipe·ful

pipe·line

pip·er

pi·pette
  or pi·pet

pip·ing

pip·pin

pip-squeak

pi·quan·cy

pi·quant

pique
  resentment (see peak,
    peek)

pi·qué
  or pi·que
  fabric

pi·ra·cy

pi·rate

pi·rat·i·cal

pi·rat·i·cal·ly

pir·ou·ette

pis·ca·to·ri·al

pis·mire

pis·tach·io

pis·til
  flower part (see pistol)

pis·til·late

pis·tol
  handgun (see pistil)

pis·tol-whip

pis·ton

pit
  pit·ted
  pit·ting

pit-a-pat

pitch

pitch-black

pitch·blende

pitch-dark

pitch·er

pitch·fork

pitch·man

pitch·out

pit·e·ous

pit·fall

pit·head

pith·ec·an·thro·
  pus

pith·i·ly

pith·i·ness

pithy

piti·able

piti·ably

piti·ful

piti·ful·ly

piti·less

pi·ton

pit·tance

pit·ted
pit·ter-pat·ter
Pitts·burg
  Calif., Kans.

Pitts·burgh
  Penna.

pi·tu·itary
pity
pity·ing
piv·ot
piv·ot·al
pix·ie
  or pixy

pix·ie·ish
piz·za
piz·ze·ri·a
piz·zi·ca·to
pla·ca·bil·i·ty
pla·ca·ble
pla·ca·bly
plac·ard
pla·cate
pla·ce·bo
  pl pla·ce·bos

place·ment
pla·cen·ta
  pl pla·cen·tas *or*
  pla·cen·tae

pla·cen·tal
plac·er
plac·id
pla·cid·i·ty
plack·et
pla·gia·rism
pla·gia·rist

pla·gia·rize
plague
plain
  clear (see plane)

plain·clothes·man
plain·ly
plain·ness
plain·spo·ken
plaint
plain·tiff
plain·tive
plain·tive·ly
plait
  pleat (see plate)

plan
  planned
  plan·ning
plane
  level (see plain)

plan·et
plan·e·tar·i·um
plan·e·tary
plan·e·tes·i·mal
plan·e·toid
plan·e·tol·o·gy
plan·gen·cy
plan·gent
plank·ing
plank·ton
plan·tain
plan·ta·tion
plant·er
plaque
plas·ma
plas·ter

plas·ter·board
plas·ter·er
plas·tic
plas·ti·cal·ly
plas·tic·i·ty
plas·ti·cize
plat
  plat·ted
  plat·ting
plate
  dish (see plait)

pla·teau
  pl pla·teaus *or* pla·
  teaux

plate·ful
plat·en
plat·form
plat·ing
plat·i·num
plat·i·tude
plat·i·tu·di·nous
pla·ton·ic
pla·ton·i·cal·ly
pla·toon
plat·ter
platy·pus
  pl platy·pus·es *also*
  platy·pi

plau·dit
plau·si·bil·i·ty
plau·si·ble
plau·si·bly
pla·ya
play·able
play·act
play·back

play·bill
play·book
play·boy
play-by-play
play·er
play·ful
play·ful·ly
play·ful·ness
play·go·er
play·ground
play·house
play·land
play·mate
play-off
play·pen
play·room
play·suit
play·thing
play·wear
play·wright
pla·za
plea
plead
   plead·ed
    or pled
   plead·ing
plead·er
pleas·ant
pleas·ant·ry
please
pleas·ing
plea·sur·able
plea·sur·ably
plea·sure
ple·be·ian
pleb·i·scite

plec·trum
   pl plec·tra
pledge
ple·na·ry
pleni·po·ten·tia·
ry
plen·i·tude
plen·te·ous
plen·ti·ful
plen·ti·ful·ly
plent·i·tude
plen·ty
ple·num
   pl ple·nums *or* ple·na
pleth·o·ra
pleu·ri·sy
plex·us
pli·abil·i·ty
pli·able
pli·ably
pli·an·cy
pli·ant
pli·ers
plight
plis·sé
   or plis·se
plod
   plod·ded
   plod·ding
plod·der
plop
   plopped
   plop·ping
plot
   plot·ted

plot·ting
plot·ter
plov·er
   pl plov·er *or* plov·ers
plow
   or plough
plow·boy
plow·share
pluck·i·ly
pluck·i·ness
plucky
plug
   plugged
   plug·ging
plum
   fruit (*see* plumb)
plum·age
plumb
   weight (*see* plum)
plumb·er
plumb·ing
plum·met
plump·ish
plump·ness
plun·der
plun·der·er
plunge
plung·er
plu·per·fect
plu·ral
plu·ral·ism
plu·ral·is·tic
plu·ral·i·ty
plu·ral·iza·tion
plu·ral·ize

plus
　pl plus·es *also* plus·
　　ses

plush·ly

plushy

plu·toc·ra·cy

plu·to·crat

plu·to·crat·ic

plu·to·crat·i·cal·
　ly

plu·to·ni·um

plu·vi·al

ply
　plied
　ply·ing

ply·wood

pneu·mat·ic

pneu·mo·nia

poach·er

po·chard

pock·et

pock·et·book

pock·et·ful

pock·et·knife

pock·et-size
　or pock·et-sized

pock·mark

po·co·sin

po·di·a·trist

po·di·a·try

po·di·um
　pl po·di·ums *or* po·
　　dia

po·em

po·esy

po·et

po·et·ess

po·et·ic
　or po·et·i·cal

po·et·i·cal·ly

po·et·ry

po·grom

poi·gnan·cy

poi·gnant

poin·ci·ana

poin·set·tia

point-blank

point·ed

point·ed·ly

point·er

poin·til·lism

poin·til·list
　also poin·til·liste

point·less

poi·son

poi·son·ous

pok·er

poky
　or pok·ey

Po·land

po·lar

Po·lar·is

po·lar·i·ty

po·lar·iza·tion

po·lar·ize

Po·lar·oid

pol·der

pole
　staff (see poll)

pole·ax

pole·cat

po·lem·ic
　or po·lem·i·cal

po·lem·i·cal·ly

po·lem·i·cist

pole·star

po·lice

po·lice·man

po·lice·wom·an

pol·i·cy

pol·i·cy·hold·er

po·lio

po·lio·my·eli·tis

Pol·ish

pol·ish

po·lite

po·lite·ly

po·lite·ness

po·li·tésse

pol·i·tic

po·lit·i·cal

po·lit·i·cal·ly

pol·i·ti·cian

pol·i·tick

po·lit·i·co
　pl po·lit·i·cos *also*
　　po·lit·i·coes

pol·i·tics

pol·i·ty

pol·ka

poll
　survey (see pole)

pol·lack
　or pol·lock

pol·len

pol·li·nate

pol·li·na·tion
pol·li·na·tor
pol·li·nize
pol·li·wog
  or pol·ly·wog

poll·ster
pol·lut·ant
pol·lute
pol·lut·er
pol·lu·tion
po·lo
po·lo·naise
pol·ter·geist
pol·troon
poly·an·drous
poly·an·dry
poly·clin·ic
poly·es·ter
poly·eth·yl·ene
po·lyg·a·mous
po·lyg·a·my
poly·glot
poly·gon
po·lyg·o·nal
poly·graph
poly·mer
poly·mer·ic
po·ly·mer·iza·tion
Poly·ne·sian
poly·no·mi·al
pol·yp
poly·phon·ic
  or poly·phon·ous

po·lyph·o·ny
poly·sty·rene

poly·syl·lab·ic
poly·syl·la·ble
poly·tech·nic
poly·the·ism
poly·the·is·tic
poly·un·sat·u·
  rat·ed
po·made
pome·gran·ate
pom·mel
  pom·meled
    or pom·melled

  pom·mel·ing
    or pom·mel·ling

pom·pa·dour
pom·pa·no
  pl pom·pa·no *or*
  pom·pa·nos

pom-pom
pom·pon
pom·pos·i·ty
pomp·ous
Pon·ce
pon·cho
  pl pon·chos

pon·der
pon·der·a·ble
pon·der·ous
pon·gee
pon·iard
pon·tiff
pon·tif·i·cal
pon·tif·i·cal·ly
pon·tif·i·cate
pon·toon

po·ny
po·ny·tail
poo·dle
pooh-pooh
  also pooh

pool·room
poor·house
poor·ly
pop
  popped
  pop·ping
pop·corn
pop-eyed
pop·gun
pop·in·jay
pop·lar
pop·lin
pop-off
pop·over
pop·py
pop·py·cock
pop·u·lace
  masses (see populous)

pop·u·lar
pop·u·lar·i·ty
pop·u·lar·i·za·
  tion
pop·u·lar·ize
pop·u·lar·iz·er
pop·u·lar·ly
pop·u·late
pop·u·la·tion
pop·u·lous
  crowded (see
  populace)

pop-up

por·ce·lain
por·ce·lain·ize
por·cine
por·cu·pine
pore
   ponder (see pour)
pork·er
por·nog·ra·pher
por·no·graph·ic
por·nog·ra·phy
po·ros·i·ty
po·rous
por·phy·ry
por·poise
por·ridge
por·rin·ger
por·ta·bil·i·ty
por·ta·ble
por·ta·bly
por·tage
por·tal
por·tal-to-por·tal
port·cul·lis
porte co·chere
por·tend
por·tent
por·ten·tous
por·ter
por·ter·house
port·fo·lio
   pl port·fo·lios
port·hole
por·ti·co
   pl por·ti·coes *or*
   por·ti·cos
por·tiere

por·tion
Port·land
port·li·ness
port·ly
port·man·teau
   pl port·man·teaus *or*
   port·man·teaux
por·trait
por·trait·ist
por·trai·ture
por·tray
por·tray·al
Ports·mouth
Por·tu·gal
Por·tu·guese
   pl Por·tu·guese

pos·er
   one who poses

po·seur
   affected person

pos·it
po·si·tion
pos·i·tive
pos·i·tive·ly
pos·i·tiv·ism
pos·i·tron
pos·se
pos·sess
pos·sessed
pos·ses·sion
pos·ses·sive
pos·sess·or
pos·si·bil·i·ty
pos·si·ble
pos·si·bly

pos·sum
post·age
post·al
post·box
post·card
post·clas·si·cal
post·con·so·nan·
   tal
post·date
post·di·lu·vi·an
post·doc·tor·al
post·er
pos·te·ri·or
pos·ter·i·ty
post·grad·u·ate
post·haste
post·hole
post·hu·mous
post·hyp·not·ic
pos·til·ion
   or pos·til·lion

post·lude
post·man
post·mark
post·mas·ter
post me·ri·di·em
post·mis·tress
post·mor·tem
post·na·sal
post·na·tal
post·op·er·a·tive
post·paid
post·par·tum
post·pone
post·pone·ment

post·script
pos·tu·lant
pos·tu·late
pos·tu·la·tion
pos·tu·la·tor
pos·ture
post·war
po·sy
pot
  pot·ted
  pot·ting
po·ta·ble
po·tage
pot·ash
po·ta·tion
po·ta·to
  pl po·ta·toes

pot·bel·lied
pot·bel·ly
pot·boil·er
po·ten·cy
po·tent
po·ten·tate
po·ten·tial
po·ten·ti·al·i·ty
po·ten·tial·ly
pot·ful
poth·er
pot·herb
pot·hole
pot·hook
po·tion
pot·latch
pot·luck
pot·pie

pot·pour·ri
pot·sherd
pot·shot
pot·tage
pot·ter
pot·tery
pouchy
poul·tice
poul·try
poul·try·man
pounce
pound-fool·ish
pour
  flow (see pore)

pour·par·ler
pout
pov·er·ty
pov·er·ty-strick·
  en
pow·der
pow·dery
pow·er
pow·er·ful
pow·er·ful·ly
pow·er·house
pow·er·less
pow·wow
pox
prac·ti·ca·bil·i·ty
prac·ti·ca·ble
prac·ti·ca·bly
prac·ti·cal
prac·ti·cal·i·ty
prac·ti·cal·ly
prac·tice
  or prac·tise

prac·ticed
  or prac·tised

prac·tic·er
prac·ti·tio·ner
prae·to·ri·an
prag·mat·ic
  also prag·mat·i·cal

prag·mat·i·cal·ly
prag·ma·tism
prag·ma·tist
prai·rie
praise·wor·thy
pra·line
prance
pranc·er
prank·ster
prat·fall
pra·tique
prat·tle
pray
  entreat (see prey)

prayer
  request

pray·er
  one that prays

prayer·ful
prayer·ful·ly
preach·er
preach·ment
pre·ad·o·les·cence
pre·ad·o·les·cent
pre·am·ble
pre·ar·range
pre·ar·range·
  ment

pre·as·signed
pre·can·cel
pre·can·cel·la·
    tion
pre·car·i·ous
pre·cau·tion
pre·cau·tion·ary
pre·cede
pre·ce·dence
pre·ce·dent
    prior

prec·e·dent
    example

pre·ced·ing
pre·cept
pre·cep·tor
pre·cinct
pre·ci·os·i·ty
pre·cious
prec·i·pice
pre·cip·i·tan·cy
pre·cip·i·tate
pre·cip·i·tate·ly
pre·cip·i·ta·tion
pre·cip·i·tous
pré·cis
    pl pré·cis
    summary

pre·cise
    exact

pre·cise·ly
pre·ci·sion
pre·clude
pre·clu·sive
pre·co·cious

pre·coc·i·ty
pre·con·ceive
pre·con·cep·tion
pre·con·di·tion
pre·cook
pre·cur·sor
pre·da·ceous
    or pre·da·cious

pre·dac·i·ty
pre·date
pred·a·tor
pred·a·to·ri·ly
pred·a·to·ry
pre·de·cease
pre·de·ces·sor
pre·des·ig·nate
pre·des·ig·na·tion
pre·des·ti·na·tion
pre·des·tine
pre·de·ter·mine
pred·i·ca·ble
pre·dic·a·ment
pred·i·cate
pred·i·ca·tion
pre·dict
pre·dict·abil·i·ty
pre·dict·able
pre·dict·ably
pre·dic·tion
pre·di·gest
pre·di·ges·tion
pre·di·lec·tion
pre·dis·pose
pre·dis·po·si·tion
pre·dom·i·nance

pre·dom·i·nant
pre·dom·i·nate
pre·em·i·nence
pre·em·i·nent
pre·empt
pre·emp·tion
pre·emp·tive
pre·emp·tor
pre·ex·ist
pre·ex·is·tence
pre·ex·is·tent
pre·fab
pre·fab·ri·cate
pre·fab·ri·ca·tion
pref·ace
pref·a·to·ry
pre·fect
pre·fec·ture
pre·fer
    pre·ferred
    pre·fer·ring
pref·er·a·bil·i·ty
pref·er·a·ble
pref·er·a·bly
pref·er·ence
pref·er·en·tial
pre·fer·ment
pre·fig·u·ra·tion
pre·fig·u·ra·tive
pre·fig·ure
pre·fix
pre·flight
pre·form
preg·nan·cy
preg·nant
pre·heat

pre·hen·sile
pre·his·tor·ic
pre·judge
prej·u·dice
prej·u·di·cial
prel·a·cy
prel·ate
pre·lim·i·nary
pre·lude
pre·ma·ture
pre·ma·ture·ly
pre·med
pre·med·i·cal
pre·med·i·tate
pre·med·i·ta·tion
pre·mier
   chief

pre·miere
   first performance

prem·ise
pre·mi·um
pre·mix
pre·mo·ni·tion
pre·mon·i·to·ry
pre·na·tal
pre·oc·cu·pan·cy
pre·oc·cu·pa·tion
pre·oc·cu·pied
pre·oc·cu·py
pre·op·er·a·tive
pre·or·dain
prep·a·ra·tion
pre·pa·ra·to·ry
pre·pare
pre·pared·ness

pre·pay
pre·pon·der·ance
pre·pon·der·ant
pre·pon·der·ate
prep·o·si·tion
prep·o·si·tion·al
pre·pos·sess
pre·pos·sess·ing
pre·pos·ses·sion
pre·pos·ter·ous
pre·puce
pre·re·cord
pre·req·ui·site
   required beforehand
   (*see* perquisite)

pre·rog·a·tive
pres·age
   noun

pre·sage
   verb

pres·by·ter
Pres·by·te·ri·an
pres·by·tery
pre·school
pre·science
pre·scient
pre·scribe
   direct (*see* proscribe)

pre·scrip·tion
pre·scrip·tive
pre·sell
pres·ence
pres·ent
   noun

pre·sent
   verb

pre·sent·abil·i·ty
pre·sent·able
pre·sent·ably
pre·sen·ta·tion
pres·ent-day
pre·sen·ti·ment
   premonition (*see*
   presentment)

pres·ent·ly
pre·sent·ment
   presentation (*see*
   presentiment)

pre·serv·able
pres·er·va·tion
pre·ser·va·tive
pre·serve
pre·serv·er
pre·set
pre·shrunk
pre·side
pres·i·den·cy
pres·i·dent
pres·i·den·tial
pre·si·dio
   pl pre·si·di·os

pre·sid·i·um
   pl pre·sid·ia *or* pre·
   sid·i·ums

pre·sig·ni·fy
pre·soak
press·board
press·er
press·ing
press·man
press·room
press·run

pres·sure
pres·sur·iza·tion
pres·sur·ize
press·work
pres·ti·dig·i·ta·
    tion
pres·ti·dig·i·ta·
    tor
pres·tige
pres·ti·gious
pres·tis·si·mo
pres·to
    pl pres·tos

pre·stress
pre·sum·able
pre·sum·ably
pre·sume
pre·sump·tion
pre·sump·tive
pre·sump·tu·ous
pre·sup·pose
pre·sup·po·si·tion
pre·teen
pre·tend
pre·tend·er
pre·tense
    or pre·tence

pre·ten·sion
pre·ten·tious
pre·ten·tious·ness
pret·er·it
    or pret·er·ite

pre·ter·nat·u·ral
pre·ter·nat·u·ral·
    ly

pre·test
pre·text
pret·ti·fy
pret·ti·ly
pret·ti·ness
pret·ty
pret·zel
pre·vail
pre·vail·ing
prev·a·lence
prev·a·lent
pre·var·i·cate
pre·var·i·ca·tion
pre·var·i·ca·tor
pre·vent
pre·vent·abil·i·ty
pre·vent·able
pre·ven·ta·tive
pre·ven·tion
pre·ven·tive
pre·view
pre·vi·ous
pre·vi·sion
pre·war
prey
    victim (see pray)

price-cut·ter
price·less
prick·le
prick·li·ness
prick·ly
pride·ful
pride·ful·ly
prie-dieu
    pl prie-dieux

priest·ess
priest·hood
priest·ly
prig·gish
pri·ma·cy
pri·ma don·na
pri·ma fa·cie
pri·mal
pri·mar·i·ly
pri·ma·ry
pri·mate
prim·er
pri·me·val
prim·i·tive
pri·mo·gen·i·tor
pri·mo·gen·i·ture
pri·mor·di·al
prim·rose
Prince Ed·ward
    Is·land
prince·ly
prin·cess
    noun

prin·cess
    or prin·cesse
    adj

prin·ci·pal
    chief (see principle)

prin·ci·pal·i·ty
prin·ci·pal·ly
prin·ci·ple
    fundamental law (see
    principal)

prin·ci·pled
print·able
print·er

print·ing
print·out
pri·or
pri·or·ess
pri·or·i·ty
pri·o·ry
prism
pris·mat·ic
pris·on
pris·on·er
pris·si·ness
pris·sy
pris·tine
pri·va·cy
pri·vate
pri·va·teer
pri·vate·ly
pri·va·tion
priv·et
priv·i·lege
priv·i·leged
privy
prize·fight
prize·win·ner
prob·a·bil·i·ty
prob·a·ble
prob·a·bly
pro·bate
pro·ba·tion
pro·ba·tion·ary
pro·ba·tion·er
pro·ba·tive
pro·ba·to·ry
pro·bi·ty
prob·lem

prob·lem·at·ic
  or prob·lem·at·i·cal
prob·lem·at·i·cal·
  ly
pro·bos·cis
  pl pro·bos·cises *also*
  pro·bos·ci·des
pro·ca·the·dral
pro·ce·dur·al
pro·ce·dur·al·ly
pro·ce·dure
pro·ceed
pro·ceed·ing
pro·ceeds
pro·cess
pro·ces·sion
pro·ces·sion·al
pro·cès-ver·bal
  pl pro·cès-ver·baux
pro·claim
proc·la·ma·tion
pro·cliv·i·ty
pro·con·sul
pro·cras·ti·nate
pro·cras·ti·na·
  tion
pro·cras·ti·na·tor
pro·cre·ant
pro·cre·ate
pro·cre·ation
pro·cre·ative
pro·cre·ator
pro·crus·te·an
proc·tol·o·gist
proc·tol·o·gy
proc·tor

proc·to·ri·al
pro·cur·able
proc·u·ra·tor
pro·cure
pro·cure·ment
pro·cur·er
prod
  prod·ded
  prod·ding
prod·i·gal
prod·i·gal·i·ty
prod·i·gal·ly
pro·di·gious
prod·i·gy
pro·duce
pro·duc·er
prod·uct
pro·duc·tion
pro·duc·tive
pro·duc·tiv·i·ty
pro·fa·na·tion
pro·fa·na·to·ry
pro·fane
pro·fane·ly
pro·fan·i·ty
pro·fess
pro·fessed
pro·fessed·ly
pro·fes·sion
pro·fes·sion·al
pro·fes·sion·al·
  ism
pro·fes·sion·al·ize
pro·fes·sion·al·ly
pro·fes·sor
pro·fes·so·ri·al

pro·fes·sor·ship
prof·fer
pro·fi·cien·cy
pro·fi·cient
pro·file
prof·it
  gain (see prophet)

prof·it·abil·i·ty
prof·it·able
prof·it·ably
prof·i·teer
prof·li·ga·cy
prof·li·gate
pro for·ma
pro·found
pro·fun·di·ty
pro·fuse
pro·fuse·ly
pro·fu·sion
pro·gen·i·tor
prog·e·ny
prog·na·thous
prog·no·sis
  pl prog·no·ses

prog·nos·tic
prog·nos·ti·cate
prog·nos·ti·ca·
  tion
prog·nos·ti·ca·tor
pro·gram
  also pro·gramme

  pro·grammed
  or pro·gramed

  pro·gram·ming
  or pro·gram·ing

pro·gram·ma·ble
pro·gram·mat·ic
pro·grammed
  or pro·gramed

pro·gram·mer
  also pro·gram·er

pro·gram·ming
  or pro·gram·ing

prog·ress
  noun

pro·gress
  verb

pro·gres·sion
pro·gres·sive
pro·gres·sive·ly
pro·hib·it
pro·hi·bi·tion
pro·hi·bi·tion·ist
pro·hib·i·tive
pro·hib·i·to·ry
proj·ect
  noun

pro·ject
  verb

pro·ject·able
pro·jec·tile
pro·jec·tion
pro·jec·tion·ist
pro·jec·tive
pro·jec·tor
pro·le·gom·e·non
  pl pro·le·gom·e·na

pro·le·tar·i·an
pro·le·tar·i·an·
  iza·tion

pro·le·tar·i·an·
  ize
pro·le·tar·i·at
pro·lif·er·ate
pro·lif·er·a·tion
pro·lif·ic
pro·lif·i·cal·ly
pro·lix
pro·lix·i·ty
pro·loc·u·tor
pro·logue
pro·long
pro·lon·gate
pro·lon·ga·tion
prom·e·nade
prom·i·nence
prom·i·nent
pro·mis·cu·ity
pro·mis·cu·ous
prom·ise
prom·is·ing
prom·is·so·ry
prom·on·to·ry
pro·mote
pro·mot·er
pro·mo·tion
pro·mo·tion·al
prompt·book
prompt·er
promp·ti·tude
prompt·ly
pro·mul·gate
pro·mul·ga·tion
prone·ness
pro·noun
pro·nounce

pro·nounce·able
pro·nounced
pro·nounce·ment
pron·to
pro·nun·ci·a·
   men·to
   pl pro·nun·ci·a·men·
   tos *or* pro·nun·ci·
   a·men·toes

pro·nun·ci·a·tion
proof·read
proof·read·er
prop
   propped
   prop·ping
pro·pa·gan·da
pro·pa·gan·dist
pro·pa·gan·dize
prop·a·gate
prop·a·ga·tion
pro·pane
pro·pel
   pro·pelled
   pro·pel·ling
pro·pel·lant
   or pro·pel·lent

pro·pel·ler
pro·pen·si·ty
prop·er
prop·er·tied
prop·er·ty
proph·e·cy
   noun, prediction (see prophesy*)*

proph·e·si·er

proph·e·sy
   verb, to predict

proph·et
   predictor (see profit*)*

proph·et·ess
pro·phet·ic
   or pro·phet·i·cal

pro·phet·i·cal·ly
pro·phy·lac·tic
pro·phy·lax·is
   pl pro·phy·lax·es

pro·pin·qui·ty
pro·pi·ti·able
pro·pi·ti·ate
pro·pi·ti·a·tion
pro·pi·tia·to·ry
pro·pi·tious
prop·jet en·gine
prop·man
pro·po·nent
pro·por·tion
pro·por·tion·able
pro·por·tion·ably
pro·por·tion·al
pro·por·tion·al·ly
pro·por·tion·ate
pro·por·tion·ate·
   ly
pro·pos·al
pro·pose
pro·pos·er
prop·o·si·tion
pro·pound
pro·pri·etary
pro·pri·etor

pro·pri·etress
pro·pri·ety
pro·pul·sion
pro·pul·sive
pro ra·ta
pro·rate
pro·ro·ga·tion
pro·rogue
pro·sa·ic
pro·sa·i·cal·ly
pro·sce·ni·um
pro·scribe
   prohibit (see prescribe*)*

pro·scrib·er
pro·scrip·tion
pro·scrip·tive
pros·e·cut·able
pros·e·cute
pros·e·cu·tion
pros·e·cu·tor
pros·e·lyte
pros·e·ly·tism
pros·e·ly·tize
pro·sem·i·nar
pros·o·dy
pros·pect
pro·spec·tive
pro·spec·tive·ly
pros·pec·tor
pro·spec·tus
pros·per
pros·per·i·ty
pros·per·ous
pros·tate
   gland (see prostrate*)*

pros·the·sis
  pl pros·the·ses

pros·thet·ic
pros·ti·tute
pros·ti·tu·tion
pros·trate
  helpless (see prostate)

pros·tra·tion
prosy
pro·tag·o·nist
pro·te·an
pro·tect
pro·tec·tion
pro·tec·tion·ism
pro·tec·tion·ist
pro·tec·tive
pro·tec·tor
pro·tec·tor·ate
pro·tec·tress
pro·té·gé
  masc.

pro·té·gée
  fem.

pro·tein
pro tem
pro tem·po·re
pro·test
prot·es·tant
Prot·es·tant·ism
pro·tes·ta·tion
pro·tho·no·tar·i·al
pro·tho·no·ta·ry
  or pro·to·no·ta·ry
pro·tho·rax

pro·to·col
pro·to·his·to·ry
pro·ton
pro·to·plasm
pro·to·type
pro·to·zo·an
pro·tract
pro·trac·tion
pro·trac·tor
pro·trude
pro·tru·sion
pro·tu·ber·ance
pro·tu·ber·ant
proud·ly
prov·able
prov·ably
prove
  proved
  proved
    or prov·en

  prov·ing
prov·e·nance
prov·en·der
pro·ve·nience
prov·erb
pro·ver·bi·al
pro·ver·bi·al·ly
pro·vide
pro·vid·ed
Prov·i·dence
prov·i·dence
prov·i·dent
prov·i·den·tial
prov·i·den·tial·ly
pro·vid·er

pro·vid·ing
prov·ince
pro·vin·cial
pro·vin·cial·ism
pro·vin·cial·ly
pro·vi·sion
pro·vi·sion·al
pro·vi·sion·al·ly
pro·vi·so
  pl pro·vi·sos *or* pro·vi·soes

pro·vi·so·ry
prov·o·ca·tion
pro·voc·a·tive
pro·voke
pro·vok·ing
pro·vost
pro·vost mar·shal
prow·ess
prowl
prowl·er
prox·i·mal
prox·i·mal·ly
prox·i·mate
prox·im·i·ty
prox·i·mo
proxy
pru·dence
pru·dent
pru·den·tial
pru·dent·ly
prud·ery
prud·ish
pru·nel·la
  also pru·nelle

pru·ri·ence

pru·ri·ent
pry
   pried
   pry·ing
psalm
psalm·book
psalm·ist
psalm·o·dy
Psal·ter
psal·tery
   also psal·try

pseu·do
pseud·onym
pseud·on·y·mous
pseu·do·sci·en·
   tif·ic
psit·ta·co·sis
pso·ri·a·sis
psy·che
psy·che·del·ic
psy·che·del·i·cal·
   ly
psy·chi·at·ric
psy·chi·at·ri·cal·
   ly
psy·chi·a·trist
psy·chi·a·try
psy·chic
   also psy·chi·cal

psy·chi·cal·ly
psy·cho
psy·cho·anal·y·sis
psy·cho·an·a·lyst
psy·cho·an·a·lyt·
   ic

psy·cho·an·a·lyt·
   i·cal·ly
psy·cho·an·a·lyze
psy·cho·bi·o·log·
   i·cal
psy·cho·bi·ol·o·gy
psy·cho·chem·i·
   cal
psy·cho·dra·ma
psy·cho·dy·nam·
   ic
psy·cho·dy·nam·
   i·cal·ly
psy·cho·dy·nam·
   ics
psy·cho·gen·e·sis
psy·cho·ge·net·ic
psy·cho·log·i·cal
   also psy·cho·log·ic

psy·cho·log·i·cal·
   ly
psy·chol·o·gist
psy·chol·o·gize
psy·chol·o·gy
psy·cho·met·ric
psy·cho·met·ri·
   cal·ly
psy·cho·met·rics
psy·cho·mo·tor
psy·cho·neu·ro·
   sis
psy·cho·neu·rot·
   ic
psy·cho·path
psy·cho·path·ic

psy·cho·path·i·
   cal·ly
psy·cho·patho·
   log·i·cal
psy·cho·phar·ma·
   ceu·ti·cal
psy·cho·sis
psy·cho·so·mat·ic
psy·cho·so·mat·i·
   cal·ly
psy·cho·ther·a·
   pist
psy·chot·ic
psy·chot·i·cal·ly
pto·maine
pu·ber·ty
pu·bes
pu·bic
pub·lic
pub·li·ca·tion
pub·li·cist
pub·lic·i·ty
pub·li·cize
pub·lic·ly
pub·lic-spir·it·ed
pub·lish
pub·lish·er
puck·er
puck·ish
pud·ding
pud·dle
pud·dling
pudg·i·ness
pudgy
pueb·lo
pu·er·ile

pu·er·il·i·ty
pu·er·per·al
Puer·to Ri·can
Puer·to Ri·co
puff·ball
puff·ery
puffy
pu·gi·lism
pu·gi·list
pu·gi·lis·tic
pug·na·cious
pug·nac·i·ty
puk·ka
pul
  pl puls *or* pu·li

pul·chri·tude
pul·chri·tu·di·
  nous
pull·back
pul·let
pul·ley
Pull·man
pull·out
pull·over
pul·mo·nary
pul·mo·tor
pulp·i·ness
pul·pit
pulp·wood
pulpy
pul·sar
pul·sate
pul·sa·tion
pul·sa·tor
pulse

pul·ver·i·za·tion
pul·ver·ize
pu·ma
pum·ice
pum·mel
  pum·meled
  or pum·melled

pum·mel·ing
  or pum·mel·ling

pum·per·nick·el
pump·kin
pun
  punned
  pun·ning
punch·board
punch-drunk
pun·cheon
punch·er
punc·til·io
punc·til·i·ous
punc·tu·al
punc·tu·al·i·ty
punc·tu·al·ly
punc·tu·ate
punc·tu·a·tion
punc·tu·a·tor
punc·ture
pun·dit
pun·gen·cy
pun·gent
pu·ni·ly
pu·ni·ness
pun·ish
pun·ish·able
pun·ish·ment

pu·ni·tive
pun·ster
punt·er
pu·ny
pu·pa
  pl pu·pae *or* pu·pas

pu·pil
pup·pet
pup·pe·teer
pup·pet·ry
pup·py
pur·blind
pur·chas·able
pur·chase
pur·chas·er
pur·dah
pure·bred
pu·ree
pure·ly
pur·ga·tion
pur·ga·tive
pur·ga·to·ry
purge
pu·ri·fi·ca·tion
pu·ri·fi·ca·to·ry
pu·ri·fi·er
pu·ri·fy
pur·ism
pur·ist
pu·ri·tan
pu·ri·tan·i·cal
pu·ri·tan·i·cal·ly
pu·ri·ty
purl
  knit (*see* pearl)

pur·lieu
pur·loin
pur·ple
pur·plish
pur·port
pur·pose
pur·pose·ful
pur·pose·ful·ly
pur·pose·less
pur·pose·ly
purs·er
purs·lane
pur·su·ance
pur·su·ant
pur·sue
pur·su·er
pur·suit
pu·ru·lence
pu·ru·lent
pur·vey
pur·vey·ance
pur·vey·or
pur·view
push-but·ton
push·cart
push·er
push·over
push·pin
pushy
pu·sil·la·nim·i·ty
pu·sil·lan·i·mous
pussy·foot
pus·tu·lant
pus·tule
put
   place (see putt)

put
put·ting
pu·ta·tive
put-on
put·out
pu·tre·fac·tion
pu·tre·fy
pu·tres·cence
pu·tres·cent
pu·trid
putsch
putt
   golf stroke (see put)

put·tee
put·ter
   one that puts

putt·er
   golf club

put·ty
puz·zle
puz·zle·ment
puz·zler
pya
pyg·my
py·lon
py·or·rhea
pyr·a·mid
py·ra·mi·dal
pyre
Py·rex
py·rol·y·sis
py·ro·ma·nia
py·ro·ma·ni·ac
py·rom·e·ter

py·ro·tech·nics
py·rox·y·lin
pyr·rhic
py·thon

Q

Qa·tar
   or Ka·tar

qin·tar
quack·ery
quack·ish
quad·ran·gle
qua·dran·gu·lar
quad·rant
qua·drat·ic
qua·drat·ics
qua·dren·ni·al
qua·dren·ni·al·ly
qua·dren·ni·um
   pl qua·dren·ni·ums
   or qua·dren·nia

quad·ri·lat·er·al
qua·drille
qua·dril·lion
quad·ri·par·tite
qua·droon
quad·ru·ped
qua·dru·ple
qua·dru·plet
qua·dru·pli·cate
quaff
quag·mire
qua·hog
   also qua·haug

quail

quaint·ly

Quak·er

qual·i·fi·ca·tion

qual·i·fied

qual·i·fi·er

qual·i·fy

qual·i·ta·tive

qual·i·ty

qualm

quan·da·ry

quan·ti·fi·able

quan·ti·fi·ca·tion

quan·ti·fi·er

quan·ti·fy

quan·ti·ta·tive

quan·ti·ty

quan·tum
  pl quan·ta

quar·an·tin·able

quar·an·tine

quark

quar·rel
  quar·reled
    or quar·relled

  quar·rel·ing
    or quar·rel·ling

quar·rel·some

quar·ry

quart

quar·ter

quar·ter·back

quar·ter·deck

quar·ter·fi·nal

quar·ter·ly

quar·ter·mas·ter

quar·ter·sawed
  also quar·ter·sawn

quar·tet
  also quar·tette

quar·to
  pl quar·tos

quartz

qua·sar

quash

qua·si

qua·si-ju·di·cial

qua·si-pub·lic

qua·ter·na·ry

qua·train

qua·ver

quay
  wharf (see key)

queas·i·ly

queas·i·ness

quea·sy
  also quea·zy

Que·bec

que·bra·cho

queer·ly

quell

quench·able

quer·u·lous

que·ry

quest

ques·tion

ques·tion·able

ques·tion·ably

ques·tion·naire

quet·zal
  pl quet·zals *or* quet·za·les

queue
  line (see cue)

quib·ble

quick·en

quick-freeze

quick·ie

quick·ly

quick·sand

quick·sil·ver

quick·step

quick-tem·pered

quick-wit·ted

quid pro quo

qui·es·cence

qui·es·cent

qui·et·ly

qui·etude

qui·etus

quince

qui·nine

quin·quen·ni·al

quin·quen·ni·al·ly

quin·sy

quin·tal

quin·tes·sence

quint·es·sen·tial

quin·tet
  also quin·tette

quin·til·lion

quin·tu·ple

quin·tup·let

quin·tu·pli·cate

quip
  quipped
  quip·ping
quire
  paper (see choir)

quirk
quis·ling
quit
  quit
    also quit·ted

  quit·ting
quit·claim
quit·tance
quit·ter
quiv·er
quix·ot·ic
quix·ot·i·cal·ly
quiz
  pl quiz·zes

quiz
  quizzed
  quiz·zing
quiz·zi·cal
quoit
quon·dam
Quon·set
quo·rum
quo·ta
quot·able
quo·ta·tion
quote
quo·tid·i·an
quo·tient
qursh

R

rab·bet
  groove (see rabbit)

rab·bi
rab·bin·ate
rab·bin·ic
  or rab·bin·i·cal

rab·bit
  animal (see rabbet)

rab·ble
rab·ble-rous·er
ra·bid
ra·bies
rac·coon
race·course
race·horse
ra·ceme
rac·er
race·track
race·way
ra·cial
ra·cial·ism
ra·cial·ly
rac·i·ly
rac·i·ness
rac·ing
rac·ism
rac·ist
rack·et
rack·e·teer
ra·con·teur
racy
ra·dar
ra·dar·scope

ra·di·al
ra·di·al·ly
ra·di·ance
ra·di·an·cy
ra·di·ant
ra·di·ate
ra·di·a·tion
ra·di·a·tor
rad·i·cal
rad·i·cal·ism
rad·i·cal·ly
ra·dio
  pl ra·di·os

ra·dio·ac·tive
ra·dio·ac·tiv·i·ty
ra·dio·car·bon
ra·dio·gen·ic
ra·dio·gram
ra·dio·graph
ra·di·og·ra·phy
ra·dio·iso·tope
ra·di·ol·o·gist
ra·di·ol·o·gy
ra·di·om·e·ter
ra·dio·pho·to
ra·di·os·co·py
ra·dio·sonde
ra·dio·tel·e·graph
ra·dio·te·leg·ra·
  phy
ra·dio·tele·phone
ra·dio·ther·a·pist
ra·dio·ther·a·py
rad·ish
ra·di·um

ra·di·us
  pl ra·dii *also* ra·di·
     us·es

ra·dix
  pl ra·di·ces *or* ra·
     dix·es

ra·don
raf·fia
raff·ish
raf·fle
raf·ter
rag·a·muf·fin
rag·ged
rag·ing
rag·lan
ra·gout
rag·pick·er
rag·time
rag·weed
rail·ing
rail·lery
rail·road
rail·way
rai·ment
rain
  shower (see reign,
     rein)

rain·bow
rain·coat
rain·drop
rain·fall
rain·mak·ing
rain·proof
rain·storm
rain·wa·ter
rain·wear

rainy
raise
  lift (see raze)

rai·sin
rai·son d'être
ra·ja
  or ra·jah

rake-off
rak·ish
Ra·leigh
ral·ly
ram
  rammed
  ram·ming
ram·ble
ram·bler
ram·bunc·tious
ra·mie
ram·i·fi·ca·tion
ram·i·fy
ram·jet en·gine
ram·page
ram·pa·geous
ram·pan·cy
ram·pant
ram·part
ram·rod
ram·shack·le
ranch·er
ran·cid
ran·cid·i·ty
ran·cor
ran·cor·ous
rand
ran·dom

ran·dom·iza·tion
ran·dom·ize
rang·er
rang·i·ness
rangy
ra·ni
  or ra·nee

rank·ing
ran·kle
ran·sack
ran·som
rant·er
rap
  knock (see wrap)

  rapped
  rap·ping
ra·pa·cious
ra·pac·i·ty
rape
rape·seed
rap·id
rap·id-fire
ra·pid·i·ty
rap·id·ly
ra·pi·er
rap·ine
rap·ist
rap·pen
  pl rap·pen

rap·port
rap·proche·ment
rap·scal·lion
rapt
rapt·ly
rap·ture

rap·tur·ous
ra·ra avis
rare·bit
rar·efac·tion
rar·efy
   also rar·i·fy

rare·ly
rar·i·ty
ras·cal
ras·cal·i·ty
ras·cal·ly
rash·er
rash·ly
rash·ness
rasp·ber·ry
rat
   rat·ted
   rat·ting
ratch·et
rath·er
rat·i·fi·ca·tion
rat·i·fy
ra·ti·né
   or ra·tine

rat·ing
ra·tio
   pl ra·tios

ra·ti·o·ci·nate
ra·ti·o·ci·na·tion
ra·tion
ra·tio·nal
ra·tio·nale
ra·tio·nal·ism
ra·tio·nal·ist
   or ra·tio·nal·is·tic

ra·tio·nal·i·ty
ra·tio·nal·iza·tion
ra·tio·nal·ize
ra·tio·nal·ly
rat·line
rat·tan
rat·teen
rat·tle
rat·tle·brain
rat·tler
rat·tle·snake
rat·tle·trap
rat·tling
rat·trap
rat·ty
rau·cous
raun·chy
rav·age
rav·ag·er
rav·el
   rav·eled
     or rav·elled
   ra·vel·ing
     or rav·el·ling
ra·ven
rav·en·ous
ra·vine
rav·i·o·li
rav·ish
raw·boned
raw·hide
ray·on
raze
   demolish (*see* raise)

ra·zor

ra·zor-backed
   or ra·zor·back

ra·zor·bill
raz·zle-daz·zle
razz·ma·tazz
reach·able
re·act
re·ac·tion
re·ac·tion·ary
re·ac·ti·vate
re·ac·ti·va·tion
re·ac·tive
re·ac·tiv·i·ty
re·ac·tor
read·abil·i·ty
read·able
read·ably
read·er
readi·ly
readi·ness
read·ing
read·out
ready
ready-made
ready-to-wear
re·agent
re·al
   actual (*see* reel)

re·al·ism
re·al·ist
re·al·is·tic
re·al·is·ti·cal·ly
re·al·i·ty
   real (*see* realty)

re·al·iz·able

re·al·iza·tion
re·al·ize
re·al·ly
realm
Re·al·tor
re·al·ty
  real estate (see reality)
ream·er
reap·er
re·arm
re·ar·ma·ment
rear·most
rear·ward
rea·son
rea·son·abil·i·ty
rea·son·able
rea·son·ably
rea·son·ing
re·as·sur·ance
re·as·sure
re·bate
reb·el
  noun

re·bel
  verb

  re·belled
  re·bel·ling
re·bel·lion
re·bel·lious
re·birth
re·born
re·bound
re·broad·cast
re·buff
re·build

re·buke
re·bus
re·but
  re·but·ted
  re·but·ting
re·but·tal
re·cal·ci·trance
re·cal·ci·trant
re·cal·cu·late
re·cal·cu·la·tion
re·call
re·call·able
re·cant
re·can·ta·tion
re·cap
  re·capped
  re·cap·ping
re·ca·pit·u·late
re·ca·pit·u·la·tion
re·cap·pa·ble
re·cap·ture
re·cast
re·cede
re·ceipt
re·ceiv·able
re·ceive
re·ceiv·er
re·ceiv·er·ship
re·cen·cy
re·cen·sion
re·cent
re·cep·ta·cle
re·cep·tion
re·cep·tion·ist
re·cep·tive

re·cep·tiv·i·ty
re·cep·tor
re·cess
re·ces·sion
re·ces·sion·al
re·ces·sive
re·cher·ché
re·cid·i·vism
re·cid·i·vist
rec·i·pe
re·cip·i·ent
re·cip·ro·cal
re·cip·ro·cal·ly
re·cip·ro·cate
re·cip·ro·ca·tion
rec·i·proc·i·ty
re·ci·sion
re·cit·al
rec·i·ta·tion
rec·i·ta·tive
re·cite
reck·less
reck·on
reck·on·ing
re·claim
re·claim·able
rec·la·ma·tion
re·cline
re·cluse
rec·og·ni·tion
rec·og·niz·abil·i·ty
rec·og·niz·able
rec·og·niz·ably
re·cog·ni·zance
rec·og·nize

re·coil
re·coil·less
rec·ol·lect
rec·ol·lec·tion
re·com·bi·na·tion
rec·om·mend
rec·om·mend·able
rec·om·men·da·
   tion
re·com·mit
re·com·mit·tal
rec·om·pense
rec·on·cil·abil·i·
   ty
rec·on·cil·able
rec·on·cile
rec·on·cil·er
rec·on·cil·i·a·tion
re·con·dite
re·con·di·tion
re·con·firm
re·con·fir·ma·tion
re·con·nais·sance
re·con·noi·ter
re·con·sid·er
re·con·sid·er·a·
   tion
re·con·sti·tute
re·con·struct
re·con·struc·tion
re·con·ver·sion
re·con·vert
re·cord
   verb

rec·ord
   noun

re·cord·er
re·cord·ist
re·count
re·coup
re·course
re·cov·er
   regain

re-cov·er
   cover again

re·cov·er·able
re·cov·ery
rec·re·ant
rec·re·ate
   refresh

re·cre·ate
   create again

rec·re·ation
   play

re·cre·ation
   renewal

rec·re·ation·al
rec·re·ative
   refreshing

re·cre·ative
   *able to create
   again*

re·crim·i·nate
re·crim·i·na·tion
re·crim·i·na·to·ry
re·cruit
rec·tal
rect·an·gle
rect·an·gu·lar
rec·ti·fi·able
rec·ti·fi·ca·tion

rec·ti·fi·er
rec·ti·fy
rec·ti·lin·ear
rec·ti·tude
rec·to
   pl rec·tos

rec·tor
rec·to·ry
rec·tum
   pl rec·tums *or* rec·ta

re·cum·ben·cy
re·cum·bent
re·cu·per·ate
re·cu·per·a·tion
re·cu·per·a·tive
re·cur
   re·curred
   re·cur·ring
re·cur·rence
re·cur·rent
re·cy·cle
re·dact
re·dac·tion
re·dac·tor
red-blood·ed
red·cap
red-car·pet
red·coat
red·den
red·dish
re·dec·o·rate
re·dec·o·ra·tion
re·deem
re·deem·able
re·deem·er

re·demp·tion
re·demp·tive
re·demp·to·ry
re·de·sign
re·de·vel·op·ment
red-hand·ed
red·head
red-hot
re·di·rect
re·di·rec·tion
re·dis·trib·ute
re·dis·tri·bu·tion
re·dis·trict
red-let·ter
red·o·lence
red·o·lent
re·dou·ble
re·doubt
re·doubt·able
re·doubt·ably
re·dound
red-pen·cil
re·dress
red·skin
red·top
re·duce
re·duc·ible
re·duc·tion
re·dun·dan·cy
re·dun·dant
re·du·pli·cate
re·du·pli·ca·tion
red·wood
re·echo
re·ed·u·cate
re·ed·u·ca·tion

reedy
reek
  smell (see wreak)
reel
  spool (see real)
re·elect
re·em·ploy
re·en·act
re·en·try
re·fash·ion
re·fec·tion
re·fec·to·ry
re·fer
  re·ferred
  re·fer·ring
re·fer·able
ref·er·ee
ref·er·ence
ref·er·en·dum
  pl ref·er·en·da *or*
    ref·er·en·dums
ref·er·ent
ref·er·en·tial
re·fer·ral
re·fill
re·fill·able
re·fi·nance
re·fine
re·fined
re·fine·ment
re·fin·er
re·fin·ery
re·fin·ish
re·fit
re·flect
re·flec·tion

re·flec·tive
re·flec·tor
re·flex
re·flex·ive
re·for·est
re·for·es·ta·tion
re·form
  improve
reform
  form again
ref·or·ma·tion
re·for·ma·to·ry
re·form·er
re·fract
re·frac·tion
re·frac·tive
re·frac·tor
re·frac·to·ry
re·frain
re·fran·gi·ble
re·fresh
re·fresh·ment
re·frig·er·ant
re·frig·er·ate
re·frig·er·a·tion
re·frig·er·a·tor
ref·uge
ref·u·gee
re·ful·gence
re·ful·gent
re·fund
re·fund·able
re·fur·bish
re·fus·al
re·fuse
  verb

ref·use
   noun

re·fut·able
re·fut·ably
ref·u·ta·tion
re·fute
re·gain
re·gal
   royal

re·gale
   entertain

re·ga·lia
re·gal·ly
re·gard
re·gard·ing
re·gard·less
re·gat·ta
re·gen·cy
re·gen·er·a·cy
re·gen·er·ate
re·gen·er·a·tion
re·gen·er·a·tive
re·gen·er·a·tor
re·gent
reg·i·cide
re·gime
   also ré·gime

reg·i·men
reg·i·ment
reg·i·men·tal
reg·i·men·ta·tion
Re·gi·na
re·gion
re·gion·al
re·gion·al·ly

reg·is·ter
reg·is·trant
reg·is·trar
reg·is·tra·tion
reg·is·try
re·gress
re·gres·sion
re·gres·sive
re·gret
  re·gret·ted
  re·gret·ting
re·gret·ful
re·gret·ful·ly
re·gret·ta·ble
re·gret·ta·bly
re·group
reg·u·lar
reg·u·lar·i·ty
reg·u·lar·ize
reg·u·lar·ly
reg·u·late
reg·u·la·tion
reg·u·la·tive
reg·u·la·tor
reg·u·la·to·ry
re·gur·gi·tate
re·gur·gi·ta·tion
re·ha·bil·i·tate
re·ha·bil·i·ta·tion
re·ha·bil·i·ta·tive
re·hash
re·hear·ing
re·hears·al
re·hearse
reign
   rule (see rain, rein)

re·im·burs·able
re·im·burse
re·im·burse·ment
rein
   restrain (see rain, reign)

re·in·car·nate
re·in·car·na·tion
rein·deer
re·in·fec·tion
re·in·force
re·in·force·ment
re·in·state
re·in·state·ment
re·in·sur·ance
re·in·sure
re·in·ter·pret
re·in·ter·pre·ta·
   tion
re·is·sue
re·it·er·ate
re·it·er·a·tion
re·ject
re·jec·tion
re·joice
re·join
re·join·der
re·ju·ve·nate
re·ju·ve·na·tion
re·lapse
re·lat·able
re·late
re·lat·ed
re·la·tion
re·la·tion·ship
rel·a·tive

rel·a·tive·ly
rel·a·tiv·is·tic
rel·a·tiv·i·ty
re·la·tor
re·lax
re·lax·ant
re·lax·ation
re·lay
re·lease
rel·e·gate
rel·e·ga·tion
re·lent
re·lent·less
rel·e·vance
rel·e·van·cy
rel·e·vant
re·lia·bil·i·ty
re·li·able
re·li·ably
re·li·ance
re·li·ant
rel·ic
re·lief
re·liev·able
re·lieve
re·liev·er
re·li·gion
re·li·gi·os·i·ty
re·li·gious
re·line
re·lin·quish
rel·i·quary
rel·ish
re·luc·tance
re·luc·tant
re·ly

re·main
re·main·der
re·mains
re·make
re·mand
re·mark
re·mark·able
re·mark·ably
re·me·di·a·ble
re·me·di·al
re·me·di·al·ly
rem·e·dy
re·mem·ber
re·mem·brance
re·mind
rem·i·nisce
rem·i·nis·cence
rem·i·nis·cent
re·miss
re·mis·si·ble
re·mis·sion
re·mit
  re·mit·ted
  re·mit·ting
re·mit·tal
re·mit·tance
rem·nant
re·mod·el
re·mon·strance
re·mon·strant
re·mon·strate
re·mon·stra·tion
re·mon·stra·tive
re·mon·stra·tor
re·morse
re·morse·ful

re·mote
re·mote·ly
re·mote·ness
re·mount
re·mov·able
re·mov·al
re·move
re·mu·ner·ate
re·mu·ner·a·tion
re·mu·ner·a·tive
re·mu·ner·a·tor
re·nais·sance
re·nal
re·nas·cence
rend
  rent
  rend·ing
ren·der
ren·dez·vous
  ren·dez·voused
  ren·dez·vous·
    ing
  ren·dez·vouses
ren·di·tion
ren·e·gade
re·nege
re·new
re·new·able
re·new·al
ren·net
ren·nin
re·nom·i·nate
re·nounce
ren·o·vate
ren·o·va·tion
ren·o·va·tor

re·nown
re·nowned
rent·al
re·num·ber
re·nun·ci·a·tion
re·open
re·or·der
re·or·ga·ni·za·
  tion
re·or·ga·nize
re·pack·age
re·pair
re·pair·able
re·pair·man
rep·a·ra·ble
rep·a·ra·tion
re·par·a·tive
rep·ar·tee
re·past
re·pa·tri·ate
re·pa·tri·a·tion
re·pay
re·pay·able
re·pay·ment
re·peal
re·peat
re·peat·ed
re·pel
  re·pelled
  re·pel·ling
re·pel·lent
  also re·pel·lant

re·pent
re·pen·tance
re·pen·tant

re·per·cus·sion
rep·er·toire
rep·er·tory
rep·e·ti·tion
rep·e·ti·tious
re·pet·i·tive
re·pet·i·tive·ly
re·place
re·place·able
re·place·ment
re·plen·ish
re·plete
re·plete·ness
re·ple·tion
rep·li·ca
rep·li·cate
rep·li·ca·tion
re·ply
  re·plied
  re·ply·ing
re·port
re·port·able
re·port·age
re·port·ed·ly
re·port·er
rep·or·to·ri·al
re·pose
re·pos·i·to·ry
re·pos·sess
re·pos·ses·sion
re·pous·sé
rep·re·hend
rep·re·hen·si·ble
rep·re·hen·si·bly
rep·re·hen·sion
rep·re·sent

rep·re·sen·ta·tion
rep·re·sen·ta·tive
re·press
re·pres·sion
re·pres·sive
re·prieve
rep·ri·mand
re·print
re·pri·sal
re·prise
re·pro
  pl re·pros

re·proach
re·proach·able
re·proach·ful
re·proach·ful·ly
rep·ro·bate
rep·ro·ba·tion
re·pro·duce
re·pro·duc·ible
re·pro·duc·tion
re·pro·duc·tive
re·proof
re·prove
re·prov·ing·ly
rep·tile
rep·til·i·an
re·pub·lic
re·pub·li·can
re·pub·li·ca·tion
re·pub·lish
re·pu·di·ate
re·pu·di·a·tion
re·pug·nance
re·pug·nant

re·pulse
re·pul·sion
re·pul·sive
re·pul·sive·ly
rep·u·ta·bil·i·ty
rep·u·ta·ble
rep·u·ta·bly
rep·u·ta·tion
re·pute
re·put·ed
re·quest
re·qui·em
re·quire
re·quire·ment
req·ui·site
req·ui·si·tion
re·quit·al
re·quite
rer·e·dos
re·run
  re·ran
  re·run
  re·run·ning
re·sal·able
re·sale
re·scale
re·scind
re·scis·sion
re·script
res·cue
res·cu·er
re·search
re·sec·tion
re·sem·blance
re·sem·ble
re·sent

re·sent·ful
re·sent·ful·ly
re·sent·ment
re·ser·pine
res·er·va·tion
re·serve
re·served
re·serv·ist
res·er·voir
res ges·tae
re·shape
re·ship
re·shuf·fle
re·side
res·i·dence
res·i·den·cy
res·i·dent
res·i·den·tial
res·i·den·tial·ly
re·sid·u·al
re·sid·u·al·ly
re·sid·u·ary
res·i·due
re·sid·u·um
  pl re·sid·ua

re·sign
res·ig·na·tion
re·sign·ed·ly
re·sil·ience
re·sil·ien·cy
re·sil·ient
res·in
res·in·ate
res·in·ous
re·sist

re·sis·tance
re·sis·tant
re·sist·er
  one who resists (see
  resistor)
re·sist·ible
  or re·sist·able
re·sis·tor
  electrical device (see
  resister)
res·o·lute
res·o·lute·ly
res·o·lu·tion
re·solv·able
re·solve
res·o·nance
res·o·nant
res·o·nate
res·o·na·tor
re·sorb
re·sorp·tion
re·sort
re·sound
re·sound·ing
re·source
re·source·ful
re·spect
re·spect·abil·i·ty
re·spect·able
re·spect·ably
re·spect·ful
re·spect·ful·ly
re·spect·ing
re·spec·tive
re·spec·tive·ly
res·pi·ra·tion

res·pi·ra·tor
re·spi·ra·to·ry
re·spire
re·spite
re·splen·dence
re·splen·dent
re·spond
re·spon·dent
re·sponse
re·spon·si·bil·i·ty
re·spon·si·ble
re·spon·si·bly
re·spon·sive
re·start
re·state
res·tau·rant
res·tau·ra·teur
rest·ful
rest·ful·ly
res·ti·tu·tion
res·tive
res·tive·ly
rest·less
re·stor·able
res·to·ra·tion
re·stor·ative
re·store
re·strain
re·strain·able
re·strained
re·straint
re·strict
re·stric·tion
re·stric·tive
re·sult
re·sul·tant

re·sume
re·su·mé
   or re·su·me *or*
   re·su·mé
re·sump·tion
re·su·pi·nate
re·sur·gence
re·sur·gent
res·ur·rect
res·ur·rec·tion
re·sus·ci·tate
re·sus·ci·ta·tion
re·sus·ci·ta·tor
ret
   ret·ted
   ret·ting
re·tail
re·tail·er
re·tain
re·tain·er
re·take
   re·took
   re·tak·en
   re·tak·ing
re·tal·i·ate
re·tal·i·a·tion
re·tal·ia·to·ry
re·tard
re·tar·da·tion
re·tard·ed
retch
   vomit (see wretch)
re·tell
   re·told
   re·tell·ing
re·ten·tion

re·ten·tive
re·ten·tiv·i·ty
re·test
ret·i·cence
ret·i·cent
ret·i·cle
re·tic·u·lar
re·tic·u·late
ret·i·na
   pl ret·i·nas *or* ret·i·
   nae
ret·i·nue
re·tire
re·tire·ment
re·tir·ing
re·tool
re·tort
re·touch
re·trace
re·tract
re·tract·able
re·trac·tile
re·trac·tion
re·trac·tor
re·tread
re·treat
re·trench
re·trench·ment
re·tri·al
re·tri·bu·tion
re·trib·u·tive
re·trib·u·to·ry
re·triev·able
re·triev·al
re·trieve
re·triev·er

ret·ro·ac·tive
ret·ro·cede
ret·ro·ces·sion
ret·ro·fire
ret·ro·grade
ret·ro·gress
ret·ro·gres·sion
ret·ro-rock·et
ret·ro·spect
ret·ro·spec·tion
ret·ro·spec·tive
re·turn
re·turn·able
re·turn·ee
re·uni·fi·ca·tion
re·uni·fy
re·union
re·unite
re·us·able
re·use
rev
  revved
  rev·ving
re·val·u·ate
re·val·u·a·tion
re·val·ue
re·vamp
re·vanche
re·vanch·ist
re·veal
rev·eil·le
rev·el
  rev·eled
    or rev·elled

  rev·el·ing
    or rev·el·ling

rev·e·la·tion
rev·el·er
  or rev·el·ler

rev·el·ry
re·venge
re·venge·ful
re·veng·er
rev·e·nue
rev·e·nu·er
re·ver·ber·ate
re·ver·ber·a·tion
re·vere
rev·er·ence
rev·er·end
rev·er·ent
rev·er·en·tial
rev·er·ie
  or rev·ery

re·vers
  lapel (see reverse)

re·ver·sal
re·verse
  opposite (see revers)

re·vers·ibil·i·ty
re·vers·ible
re·vers·ibly
re·ver·sion
re·ver·sion·ary
re·vert
re·vert·ible
re·view
re·view·er
re·vile
re·vil·er
re·vis·able

re·vise
re·vis·er
  or re·vi·sor

re·vi·sion
re·vi·sion·ism
re·vi·so·ry
re·vi·tal·iza·tion
re·vi·tal·ize
re·viv·al
re·viv·al·ist
re·vive
re·viv·i·fy
re·vo·ca·ble
re·vo·ca·tion
re·voke
re·vok·er
re·volt
re·volt·ing
rev·o·lu·tion
rev·o·lu·tion·ary
rev·o·lu·tion·ist
rev·o·lu·tion·ize
re·volv·able
re·volve
re·volv·er
re·volv·ing
re·vue
re·vul·sion
re·wake
re·wak·en
re·ward
re·wind
  re·wound
  re·wind·ing
re·work

re·write
  re·wrote
  re·writ·ten
  re·writ·ing
re·zone
rhap·sod·ic
rhap·sod·i·cal·ly
rhap·so·dize
rhap·so·dy
rheo·stat
rhe·sus mon·key
rhet·o·ric
rhe·tor·i·cal
rhe·tor·i·cal·ly
rhet·o·ri·cian
rheu·mat·ic
rheu·mat·i·cal·ly
rheu·ma·tism
rheu·ma·toid
rheumy
Rh factor
rhine·stone
rhi·noc·er·os
rhi·zome
Rhode Is·land
rho·di·um
rho·do·den·dron
rhom·boid
  or rhom·boi·dal
rhom·bus
rhu·barb
rhyme
rhy·o·lite
rhythm
rhyth·mic
  or rhyth·mi·cal

rhyth·mi·cal·ly
ri·al
ri·al·to
rib
  ribbed
  rib·bing
rib·ald
rib·ald·ry
rib·bon
ri·bo·fla·vin
rich·es
rich·ly
Rich·mond
rich·ness
rick·ets
rick·ett·sia
  pl rick·ett·si·as or
     rick·ett·si·ae
rick·ety
rick·ey
rick·sha
  or rick·shaw
ric·o·chet
  ric·o·cheted
    or ric·o·chet·ted
  ric·o·chet·ing
    or ric·o·chet·ting
ric·tus
rid
  rid
    also rid·ded
  rid·ding
rid·able
  or ride·able
rid·dance

rid·dle
ride
  rode
  rid·den
  rid·ing
rid·er
ridge
ridge·pole
rid·i·cule
ri·dic·u·lous
ri·ding
ri·el
rif·fle
riff·raff
ri·fle
ri·fling
rig
  rigged
  rig·ging
rig·ger
  one that rigs (see
    rigor)
right
  correct (see rite)
right-an·gled
  or right-an·gle
righ·teous
right·ful
right·ful·ly
right-hand
right-hand·ed
right·ist
right·ly
right-of-way
right-wing·er
rig·id

ri·gid·i·ty
rig·ma·role
rig·or
   severity (see rigger)

rig·or·ous
rim
  rimmed
  rim·ming
rin·der·pest
ring
  encircle

  ringed
  ring·ing
ring
  sound

  rang
  rung
  ring·ing
ring·er
ring·lead·er
ring·let
ring·mas·ter
ring·side
ring·worm
rink
rins·ing
ri·ot
ri·ot·er
ri·ot·ous
rip
  ripped
  rip·ping
ri·par·i·an
ripe·ly
rip·en

ripe·ness
ri·poste
rip·per
rip·ple
rip·saw
rip·tide
rise
  rose
  ris·en
  ris·ing
ris·er
ris·i·bil·i·ty
ris·i·ble
risk·i·ness
risky
ris·qué
rite
  ceremony (see right)

rit·u·al
rit·u·al·ism
rit·u·al·is·tic
rit·u·al·is·ti·cal·
  ly
rit·u·al·ly
ri·val
  ri·valed
    or ri·valled

  ri·val·ing
    or ri·val·ling
ri·val·ry
rive
  rived
  riv·en
    also rived

  riv·ing

riv·er
riv·er·bed
ri·ver·boat
riv·er·side
riv·et
riv·et·er
riv·u·let
ri·yal
roach
road·abil·i·ty
road·bed
road·block
road·house
road·run·ner
road·side
road·ster
road·way
road·work
roam·er
roan
roar·ing
roast·er
rob
  robbed
  rob·bing
rob·ber
rob·bery
rob·in
ro·bot
ro·bust
Roch·es·ter
rock·bound
rock·er
rock·et
rock·et·ry
rock·fish

Rock·ford
rock-ribbed
rocky
ro·co·co
ro·dent
ro·deo
   pl ro·de·os

roe
   deer, fish eggs (see
   row)

roe·buck
roent·gen
ro·ga·tion
rog·er
rogue
rogu·ery
rogu·ish
roil
   rile (see royal)

rois·ter
rois·ter·er
role
   also rôle
   part (see roll)

roll
   list, bread, move (see
   role)

roll·back
roll·er
roll·er-skate
   verb

rol·lick
ro·ly-po·ly
ro·maine
ro·man à clef
   pl ro·mans à clef

ro·mance
ro·man·tic
ro·man·ti·cal·ly
ro·man·ti·cism
ro·man·ti·cist
ro·man·ti·ci·za·
   tion
ro·man·ti·cize
romp·er
ron·do
   pl ron·dos

roof·ing
roof·top
rook·ery
rook·ie
room·er
   lodger (see rumor)

room·ette
room·ful
room·i·ness
room·mate
roomy
roost·er
root
   plant part (see route)

root·er
root·less
root·let
root·stock
rop·er
rope·way
ro·sa·ry
ro·sé
ro·se·ate
rose-col·ored

rose·mary
ro·se·o·la
ro·sette
rose·wood
Rosh Ha·sha·nah
ros·i·ly
ros·in
ros·i·ness
ros·in·ous
ros·ter
ros·trum
   pl ros·trums *or* ros·
   tra

rosy
rot
   rot·ted
   rot·ting
Ro·tar·i·an
ro·ta·ry
ro·tat·able
ro·tate
ro·ta·tion
ro·ta·tor
ro·ti·fer
ro·tis·ser·ie
ro·to·gra·vure
ro·tor
rot·ten
rot·ten·ness
ro·tund
ro·tun·da
ro·tun·di·ty
roué
rouge
rough
   uneven (see ruff)

rough·age
rough-and-ready
rough-and-tum·ble
rough·cast
rough-dry
rough·en
rough-hew
rough·house
rough·ish
rough·neck
rough·shod
rou·lade
rou·lette
round·about
round·ed
roun·de·lay
round·er
round·house
round·ish
round·ly
round-shoul·dered
round-up
round·worm
rous·ing
roust·about
rout
mob, rummage, defeat
(see route)

route
way (see root, rout)

route·man
rou·tine
row
propel, quarrel, line
(see roe)

row·boat

row·di·ly
row·di·ness
row·dy
row·dy·ish
row·dy·ism
row·el
roy·al
kingly (see roil)

roy·al·ist
roy·al·ly
roy·al·ty
rub
rubbed
rub·bing
rub·ber
rub·ber·ize
rub·ber-stamp
verb

rub·bery
rub·bing
rub·bish
rub·ble
waste (see ruble)

rub·down
ru·bel·la
ru·be·o·la
ru·ble
currency (see rubble)

ru·bric
ru·by
ruck·sack
ruck·us
rud·der
rud·di·ness
rud·dy

rude·ly
rude·ness
ru·di·ment
ru·di·men·ta·ry
rue
rue·ful
rue·ful·ly
ruff
collar (see rough)

ruf·fi·an
ruf·fle
rug·ged
ru·in
ru·in·ation
ru·in·ous
rul·er
rul·ing
Ru·ma·nia
or Ro·ma·nia
or Rou·ma·nia

rum·ba
rum·ble
ru·mi·nant
ru·mi·nate
ru·mi·na·tion
rum·mage
rum·my
ru·mor
hearsay (see roomer)

ru·mor·mon·ger
rum·ple
rum·pus
run
ran
run
run·ning

run·about
run·around
run·away
run·down
   summary

run-down
   dilapidated

rung
   crosspiece (see wrung*)*

run-in
run·ner
run·ner-up
   pl run·ners-up *also*
   run·ner-ups

run·ning
run·ny
run·off
run-on
run·way
ru·pee
ru·pi·ah
   pl ru·pi·ah *or*
   ru·pi·ahs

rup·ture
ru·ral
rush·er
rus·set
Rus·sia
Rus·sian
rus·tic
rus·ti·cal·ly
rus·ti·cate
rus·ti·ca·tion
rust·i·ly
rust·i·ness
rus·tle

rus·tler
rust·proof
rusty
rut
   rut·ted
   rut·ting
ru·ta·ba·ga
ruth·less
Rwan·da
Rwan·dan
rye
   grain (see wry*)*

S

Sab·bath
sab·bat·i·cal
sa·ber
   or sa·bre

sa·ble
sa·ble·fish
sa·bot
sab·o·tage
sab·o·teur
sac
   pouch of animal
   or plant (see sack*)*

sac·cha·rin
   noun

sac·cha·rine
   adj

sac·er·do·tal
sac·er·do·tal·ly
sa·chem
sa·chet
   small bag (see sashay*)*

sack
   bag, fire (see sac*)*

sack·cloth
sack·ful
   pl sack·fuls *or*
   sacks·ful

sack·ing
sac·ra·ment
sac·ra·men·tal
sac·ra·men·tal·ly
Sac·ra·men·to
sa·cred
sac·ri·fice
sac·ri·fi·cial
sac·ri·fi·cial·ly
sac·ri·lege
sac·ri·le·gious
sac·ris·tan
sac·ris·ty
sa·cro·il·i·ac
sac·ro·sanct
sa·crum
   pl sa·cra

sad·den
sad·dle
sad·dle·bag
sad·dle·bow
sad·dle·cloth
sad·iron
sa·dism
sa·dist
sa·dis·tic
sa·dis·ti·cal·ly
sa·fa·ri
safe-con·duct
safe-de·pos·it

safe·guard
safe·keep·ing
safe·light
safe·ty
saf·flow·er
saf·fron
sag
  sagged
  sag·ging
sa·ga
sa·ga·cious
sa·gac·i·ty
sage·brush
sage·ly
sa·go
sail·boat
sail·cloth
sail·er
  ship (see sailor)

sail·fish
sail·ing
sail·or
  one who sails (see
  sailer)

saint·hood
saint·li·ness
Saint Lou·is
saint·ly
Saint Paul
Saint Pe·ters·burg
sake
  purpose

sa·ke
  or sa·ki
  rice wine

sa·laam

sal·abil·i·ty
sal·able
  or sale·able

sa·la·cious
sal·ad
sal·a·man·der
sa·la·mi
sal·a·ried
sal·a·ry
Sa·lem
sal·era·tus
sales·clerk
sales·girl
sales·la·dy
sales·man
sales·man·ship
sales·peo·ple
sales·room
sales·wom·an
sa·lience
sa·lient
sa·line
sa·lin·i·ty
sa·li·va
sal·i·vary
sal·i·vate
sal·i·va·tion
sal·low
sal·ly
salm·on
  pl salm·on *also*
  salm·ons

sal·mo·nel·la
  pl sal·mo·nel·lae *or*
  sal·mo·nel·las *or*
  sal·mo·nel·la

sa·lon
sa·loon
salt·box
salt·cel·lar
salt·er
sal·tine
salt·i·ness
Salt Lake City
salt·pe·ter
salt·shak·er
salt·wa·ter
salt·wort
salty
sa·lu·bri·ous
sal·u·tary
sal·u·ta·tion
sa·lu·ta·to·ri·an
sa·lu·ta·to·ry
sa·lute
salv·able
Sal·va·dor
Sal·va·do·ran
sal·vage
sal·vage·able
sal·va·tion
sal·ver
sal·vo
  pl sal·vos *or* sal·voes

sa·ma·ra
Sa·mar·i·tan
sam·ba
same·ness
sam·o·var
sam·pan
sam·ple

sam·pler
sam·pling
San An·to·nio
san·a·tar·i·um
  pl san·a·tar·i·ums *or*
  san·a·tar·ia

san·a·to·ri·um
  pl san·a·to·ri·ums *or*
  san·a·to·ria

San Ber·nar·di·no
sanc·ti·fi·ca·tion
sanc·ti·fy
sanc·ti·mo·nious
sanc·ti·mo·ny
sanc·tion
sanc·ti·ty
sanc·tu·ary
sanc·tum
  pl sanc·tums *also*
  sanc·ta

san·dal
san·dal·wood
sand·bag
sand·bank
sand·bar
sand·blast
sand·box
sand·er
San Di·ego
sand·hog
sand·i·ness
sand·lot
sand·man
sand·pa·per
sand·pip·er
sand·soap

sand·stone
sand·storm
sand·wich
sandy
sane·ly
San Fran·cis·co
sang·froid
san·gría
san·gui·nary
san·guine
san·i·tar·i·ly
san·i·tar·i·um
san·i·tary
san·i·ta·tion
san·i·tize
san·i·ty
San Jo·se
San Juan
San Ma·ri·no
San·ta Ana
San·ta Fe
São To·mé and
  Prín·ci·pe
sap
  sapped
  sap·ping
sa·pi·ence
sa·pi·ent
sap·ling
sap·phire
sap·py
sap·suck·er
sap·wood
sa·ran
sa·ra·pe
  var of serape

sar·casm
sar·cas·tic
sar·cas·ti·cal·ly
sar·co·ma
  pl sar·co·mas *or* sar·
  co·ma·ta

sar·coph·a·gus
  pl sar·coph·a·gi *also*
  sar·coph·a·gus·es

sar·dine
sar·don·ic
sar·don·i·cal·ly
sa·ri
  or sa·ree
  garment (*see* sorry)

sa·rong
sar·sa·pa·ril·la
sar·to·ri·al
Sas·katch·e·wan
sa·shay
  walk (*see* sachet)

Sas·ka·toon
sas·sa·fras
sassy
sa·tang
sa·tan·ic
sa·tan·i·cal·ly
satch·el
sa·teen
sat·el·lite
sa·tia·ble
sa·tiate
  adj

sa·ti·ate
  verb

sa·ti·ety

sat·in

sat·in·wood

sat·iny

sat·ire

sa·tir·ic
  or sa·tir·i·cal

sa·tir·i·cal·ly

sat·i·rist

sat·i·rize

sat·is·fac·tion

sat·is·fac·to·ri·ly

sat·is·fac·to·ry

sat·is·fi·able

sat·is·fy

sa·trap

sat·u·rant

sat·u·rate

sat·u·ra·tion

Sat·ur·day

sat·ur·nine

sa·tyr

sa·ty·ri·a·sis

sauce·pan

sau·cer

sauc·i·ly

sauc·i·ness

saucy

Sau·di

Sau·di Ara·bia

Sau·di Ara·bi·an

sau·er·kraut

sau·na

saun·ter

sau·sage

sau·té

sau·téed
  or sau·téd

sau·té·ing

sau·terne

sav·age

sav·age·ly

sav·age·ry

Sa·van·nah

sa·vant

sav·able
  or save·able

sav·er
  *one that saves (see
  savor)*

sav·ing

sav·ior
  or sav·iour

sa·voir faire

sa·vor
  also sa·vour
  flavor (see saver)

sa·vor·i·ly

sa·vor·i·ness

sa·vory
  appetizing

sa·vo·ry
  also sa·voury
  herb

saw

  sawed

  sawed
    or sawn

  saw·ing

saw·dust

sawed-off

saw·horse

saw·mill

saw-toothed

sax·o·phone

sax·o·phon·ist

say,

  said

  say·ing

say·able

say·ing

say-so

scab

  scabbed

  scab·bing

scab·bard

scab·by

sca·bies

scab·rous

scaf·fold

scaf·fold·ing

scal·able

scal·age

scal·a·wag

scald·ing

scaled

scale-down

scale·less

scale-up

scal·i·ness

scal·lion

scal·lop

scal·pel

scalp·er

scaly

scam·per

scam·pi

scan

scanned
scan·ning
scan·dal
scan·dal·ize
scan·dal·mon·ger
scan·dal·ous
scan·ner
scant·i·ly
scant·i·ness
scant·ling
scanty
scape·goat
scape·grace
scap·u·la
  pl scap·u·lae *or*
    scap·u·las

scap·u·lar
scar
  scarred
  scar·ring
scar·ab
scarce·ly
scar·ci·ty
scare·crow
scarf
  pl scarves *or* scarfs

scar·i·fi·ca·tion
scar·i·fy
scar·let
scary
  also scar·ey

scat
  scat·ted
  scat·ting
scath·ing
scat·o·log·i·cal

scat·ter
scat·ter·brained
scat·ter·ing
scav·enge
scav·en·ger
sce·nar·io
sce·nar·ist
scene
  stage setting (see see*)*

sce·nery
sce·nic
sce·ni·cal·ly
scent
  smell (see sent*)*

scep·ter
sched·ule
sche·ma
  pl sche·ma·ta

sche·mat·ic
sche·mat·i·cal·ly
scheme
schem·er
schem·ing
scher·zo
  pl scher·zos *or*
    scher·zi

schil·ling
schism
schis·mat·ic
schis·to·so·mi·a·sis
schiz·oid
schizo·phre·nia
schizo·phren·ic
schol·ar

schol·ar·ly
schol·ar·ship
scho·las·tic
scho·las·ti·cal·ly
scho·las·ti·cism
school·bag
school·boy
school·child
  pl school·chil·dren

school·girl
school·house
school·ing
school·marm
school·mate
school·room
school·teach·er
school·work
schoo·ner
sci·at·i·ca
sci·ence
sci·en·tif·ic
sci·en·tif·i·cal·ly
sci·en·tist
scim·i·tar
scin·til·la
scin·til·late
scin·til·la·tion
sci·on
scis·sors
scle·ro·sis
scoff·er
scoff·law
scold·ing
scone
scoop·ful

scoot·er

scorch·er

scorch·ing

score
    pl scores or score

scor·er

score·board

score·card

score·keep·er

score·less

scorn·er

scorn·ful

scorn·ful·ly

scor·pi·on

scot-free

scoun·drel

scour

scourge

scout·ing

scout·mas·ter

scowl

scrab·ble

scrag·gly

scrag·gy

scram·ble

Scran·ton

scrap
    scrapped
    scrap·ping

scrap·book

scrap·er

scrap·per

scrap·ple

scrap·py

scratch

scratch·i·ness

scratchy

scrawl

scraw·ni·ness

scraw·ny

scream·er

screech

screen·able

screen·ing

screen·play

screen·writ·er

screw·ball

screw·driv·er

screw·worm

scrib·ble

scrib·bler

scrim·mage

scrim·mag·er

scrimpy

scrim·shaw

scrip
    certificate (see script)

script
    writing (see scrip)

scrip·tur·al

scrip·tur·al·ly

scrip·ture

script·writ·er

scriv·en·er

scroll·work

scro·tum
    pl scro·ta or
    scro·tums

scroung·er

scroung·ing

scrub

scrubbed

scrub·bing

scrub·by

scruffy

scrump·tious

scru·ple

scru·pu·lous

scru·ta·ble

scru·ti·nize

scru·ti·ny

scu·ba

scuf·fle

scull
    boat (see skull)

scul·lery

scul·lion

scul·pin
    pl scul·pins also
    scul·pin

sculp·tor

sculp·tur·al

sculp·tur·al·ly

sculp·ture

scum·my

scup·per

scup·per·nong

scur·ril·i·ty

scur·ri·lous

scur·ry

scur·vy

scutch·eon

scut·tle

scut·tle·butt

sea·bag

sea·bed

sea·bird

sea·board
sea·borne
sea·coast
sea·far·er
sea·far·ing
sea·food
sea·go·ing
sea-lane
seal·ant
seal·skin
sea·man
sea·man·ship
seam·i·ness
seam·less
sea·mount
seam·stress
seamy
sé·ance
sea·plane
sea·port
sear
  burn (*see* seer)

search·er
search·light
sea·scape
sea·shell
sea·shore
sea·sick
sea·side
sea·son
sea·son·able
sea·son·ably
sea·son·al
sea·son·ing
seat·ing

Se·at·tle
sea·wall
sea·ward
  also sea·wards

sea·wa·ter
sea·way
sea·weed
sea·wor·thy
se·ba·ceous
se·cant
se·cede
se·ces·sion
se·ces·sion·ist
se·clude
se·clu·sion
sec·ond
sec·ond·ari·ly
sec·ond·ary
sec·ond-best
sec·ond-class
sec·ond-guess
sec·ond·hand
sec·ond·ly
sec·ond-rate
se·cre·cy
se·cret
sec·re·tari·al
sec·re·tar·i·at
sec·re·tary
se·crete
se·cre·tion
se·cre·tive
se·cre·to·ry
sect
sec·tar·i·an

sec·tion
sec·tion·al
sec·tion·al·ly
sec·tion·al·ism
sec·tor
sec·u·lar
sec·u·lar·ism
sec·u·lar·iza·tion
sec·u·lar·ize
se·cure
se·cure·ly
se·cu·ri·ty
se·dan
se·date
se·date·ly
se·da·tion
sed·a·tive
sed·en·tary
sed·i·ment
sed·i·men·ta·ry
sed·i·men·ta·tion
se·di·tion
se·di·tious
se·duce
se·duc·er
se·duc·tion
se·duc·tive
se·duc·tress
se·du·li·ty
sed·u·lous
see
  perceive (*see* scene)
  saw
  seen
  see·ing
see·able

seed
  pl seed *or* seeds

seed·er
seed·i·ly
seed·i·ness
seed·ling
seed·time
seek
  sought
  seek·ing
seek·er
seem·ing
seem·li·ness
seem·ly
seep·age
seer
  prophet (see sear*)*

seer·suck·er
see·saw
seethe
seeth·ing
seg·ment
seg·men·tal
seg·men·tal·ly
seg·men·tary
seg·men·ta·tion
seg·re·gate
seg·re·gat·ed
seg·re·ga·tion
seg·re·ga·tion·ist
seis·mic
seis·mo·graph
seis·mog·ra·pher
seis·mo·graph·ic
seis·mog·ra·phy

seis·mol·o·gist
seis·mol·o·gy
seize
sei·zure
sel·dom
se·lect
se·lect·ee
se·lec·tion
se·lec·tive
se·lec·tiv·i·ty
se·lect·man
se·lec·tor
self
  pl selves

self-ab·ne·ga·tion
self-ac·cu·sa·tion
self-act·ing
self-ad·dressed
self-ad·just·ing
self-anal·y·sis
self-ap·point·ed
self-as·sert·ing
self-as·ser·tion
self-as·sur·ance
self-as·sured
self-cen·tered
self-com·mand
self-con·fi·dence
self-con·scious
self-con·tained
self-con·trol
self-con·trolled
self-crit·i·cism
self-de·feat·ing
self-de·fense

self-de·ter·mi·na·tion
self-dis·ci·pline
self-ed·u·cat·ed
self-ef·fac·ing
self-em·ployed
self-ev·i·dent
self-ex·plan·a·to·ry
self-ex·pres·sion
self-gov·erned
self-gov·ern·ing
self-im·age
self-im·por·tance
self-im·posed
self-im·prove·ment
self-in·crim·i·na·tion
self-in·dul·gence
self-in·flict·ed
self-in·ter·est
self·ish
self·less
self-liq·ui·dat·ing
self-load·ing
self-lock·ing
self-made
self-mail·ing
self-op·er·at·ing
self-per·pet·u·at·ing
self-per·pet·u·a·tion
self-pity
self-pity·ing

self-por·trait
self-pos·sessed
self-pres·er·va·
  tion
self-pro·claimed
self-pro·pelled
self-pro·tec·tion
self-reg·u·lat·ing
self-re·li·ance
self-re·spect
self-righ·teous
self-ris·ing
self-rule
self-sac·ri·fice
self-same
self-sat·is·fac·tion
self-sat·is·fied
self-seal·ing
self-seek·ing
self-ser·vice
self-start·ing
self-styled
self-suf·fi·cien·cy
self-suf·fi·cient
self-sus·tain·ing
self-taught
self-wind·ing
sell
  sold
  sell·ing
sell·er
sel·vage
  or sel·vedge

selves
se·man·tic
  also se·man·ti·cal

se·man·tics
sem·a·phore
sem·blance
se·men
se·mes·ter
semi·an·nu·al
semi·an·nu·al·ly
semi·ar·id
semi·au·to·mat·ic
semi·cir·cle
semi·cir·cu·lar
semi·co·lon
semi·con·duc·tor
semi·con·scious
semi·fi·nal
semi·flu·id
semi·for·mal
semi·lu·nar
semi·month·ly
sem·i·nal
sem·i·nar
sem·i·nar·i·an
sem·i·nary
semi·of·fi·cial
se·mi·ot·ic
  or se·mi·ot·ics

semi·per·me·able
semi·pre·cious
semi·pri·vate
semi·pro·fes·sion·
  al
semi·pub·lic
semi·rig·id
semi·skilled
semi·soft

semi·sol·id
semi·sweet
Sem·ite
Se·mit·ic
semi·trail·er
semi·trop·i·cal
  also semi·trop·ic

semi·week·ly
semi·works
semi·year·ly
sen
  pl sen

sen·ate
sen·a·tor
sen·a·to·ri·al
send
  sent
  send·ing
se·ne
Sen·e·gal
Sen·e·ga·lese
se·nes·cence
sen·gi
  pl sen·gi

se·nile
se·nil·i·ty
se·nior
se·nior·i·ty
sen·i·ti
  pl sen·i·ti

sen·na
sen·sa·tion
sen·sa·tion·al
sen·sa·tion·al·ly
sense·less

sen·si·bil·i·ty
sen·si·ble
sen·si·bly
sen·si·tive
sen·si·tiv·i·ty
sen·si·ti·za·tion
sen·si·tize
sen·so·ry
sen·su·al
sen·su·al·i·ty
sen·su·al·ly
sen·su·ous
sen·tence
sen·ten·tious
sen·ti
   pl sen·ti

sen·tient
sen·ti·ment
sen·ti·men·tal
sen·ti·men·tal·i·
   ty
sen·ti·men·tal·ize
sen·ti·men·tal·ly
sen·ti·mo
sen·ti·nel
sen·try
se·pal
sep·a·ra·ble
sep·a·rate
sep·a·rate·ly
sep·a·ra·tion
sep·a·rat·ist
sep·a·ra·tive
sep·a·ra·tor
se·pia

sep·sis
   pl sep·ses

Sep·tem·ber
sep·tic
sep·ti·ce·mia
sep·tu·a·ge·nar·
   i·an
sep·ul·cher
   or sep·ul·chre

se·pul·chral
se·quel
se·quence
se·quen·tial
se·ques·ter
se·ques·trate
se·ques·tra·tion
se·quin
se·quoia
se·ra·glio
ser·a·pe
   or sa·ra·pe

ser·aph
   also ser·a·phim
   pl ser·a·phim *or*
   ser·aphs

se·raph·ic
ser·e·nade
ser·en·dip·i·ty
se·rene
se·rene·ly
se·ren·i·ty
serf
   peasant (see surf*)*

serf·dom
serge
   cloth (see surge*)*

ser·geant
se·ri·al
   of a series (see cereal*)*

se·ri·al·iza·tion
se·ri·al·ize
se·ri·al·ly
se·ries
   pl se·ries

seri·graph
se·ri·ous
ser·mon
se·rous
ser·pent
ser·pen·tine
ser·rate
se·rum
   pl se·rums *or* se·ra

ser·vant
ser·vice
ser·vice·abil·i·ty
ser·vice·able
ser·vice·man
ser·vile
ser·vil·i·ty
serv·ing
ser·vi·tor
ser·vi·tude
ser·vo·mech·a·
   nism
ses·a·me
ses·qui·cen·ten·
   ni·al
ses·sion
   meeting (see cession*)*

set

set
set·ting
set·back
set·screw
set·tee
set·ter
set·ting
set·tle
set·tle·ment
set·tler
set-to
   pl set·tos

set-up
sev·en
sev·en·teen
sev·en·ti·eth
sev·en·ty
sev·er
sev·er·al
sev·er·al·ly
sev·er·ance
se·vere
se·vere·ly
se·ver·i·ty
sew
   stitch (*see* sow)

sewed
sewn
   or sewed

sew·ing
sew·age
sew·er
sew·er·age
sex·a·ge·nar·i·an
sex·i·ness

sex·less
sex-linked
sex·tant
sex·tet
sex·ton
sex·u·al
sex·u·al·i·ty
sex·u·al·ly
Sey·chelles
shab·bi·ly
shab·bi·ness
shab·by
shack·le
shad·i·ly
shad·i·ness
shad·ing
shad·ow
shad·ow·box
shad·owy
shady
shag
   shagged
   shag·ging
shag·gi·ly
shag·gi·ness
shag·gy
shak·able
   or shake·able

shake
   shook
   shak·en
   shak·ing
shake·down
shak·er
shake-up

shak·i·ly
shak·i·ness
sha·ko
   pl sha·kos *or*
   sha·koes

shaky
shal·lop
shal·low
sham
   shammed
   sham·ming
sha·man
sham·ble
sham·bles
shame·faced
shame·faced·ly
shame·ful
shame·ful·ly
shame·less
sham·mer
sham·my
   var of chamois

sham·poo
sham·rock
shang·hai
shan·tung
shan·ty
shan·ty·town
shap·able
   or shape·able

shape·less
shape·li·ness
shape·ly
share·crop·per
share·hold·er
shar·er

shark·skin

sharp·en

sharp-eyed

sharp·shoot·er

sharp-tongued

shat·ter

shave
  shaved
  shaved
    or shav·en

  shav·ing

shawl

sheaf
  pl sheaves

shear
  clip (see sheer)

  sheared
  sheared
    or shorn

  shear·ing

shears

sheath
  noun

sheathe
  verb
  also sheath

sheathed

sheath·ing

she·bang

shed
  shed
  shed·ding

sheen

sheep·fold

sheep·ish

sheep·skin

sheer
  thin, swerve (see
    shear)

sheet·ing

Sheet·rock

sheikh
  or sheik

shelf
  pl shelves

shel·lac
  shel·lacked
  shel·lack·ing

shell·fish

shell·proof

shell·work

shel·ter

shel·ter·belt

shelv·ing

she·nan·i·gan

shep·herd

shep·herd·ess

sher·bet
  or sher·bert

sher·iff

sher·ry

shib·bo·leth

shield

shift·i·ly

shift·i·ness

shift·less

shifty

shi·lingi
  pl shi·lingi

shil·le·lagh
  also shil·la·lah

shil·ling

shilly-shally

shim·mer

shim·mery

shim·my

shin
  shinned
  shin·ning

shin·bone

shin·dig

shine
  shone
    or shined

  shin·ing

shin·er

shin·gle

shin·gles

shin·i·ness

shiny

ship
  shipped
  ship·ping

ship·board

ship·build·ing

ship·mate

ship·ment

ship·per

ship·ping

ship·shape

ship·worm

ship·wreck

ship·wright

ship·yard

shirk·er

shirr

shirr·ing

shirt·ing
shirt·tail
shirt·waist
shiv·er
shoal
shock·er
shock·ing
shod·di·ly
shod·di·ness
shod·dy
shoe
　shod
　　also shoed

　shoe·ing
shoe·horn
shoe·lace
shoe·mak·er
shoe·string
shoo·fly
shoo-in
shoot
　let fly (see chute)

　shot
　shoot·ing
shoot·er
shop
　shopped
　shop·ping
shop·keep·er
shop·lift·er
shop·per
shop·talk
shop·worn
sho·ran
shore·bird

shor·ing
short·age
short·bread
short·cake
short·change
short-cir·cuit
short·com·ing
short·cut
short·en
short·en·ing
short·hand
short·hand·ed
short·horn
short-lived
short·ly
short·sight·ed
short·stop
short-tem·pered
short-term
short·wave
short-wind·ed
shot·gun
should
shoul·der
shov·el
　shov·eled
　　or shov·elled

　shov·el·ing
　　or shov·el·ling

shov·el·ful
　pl shov·el·fuls
　　also shov·els·ful

show
　showed
　shown
　　or showed

show·ing
show·boat
show·case
show·down
show·er
show·ery
show·i·ly
show·i·ness
show·man
show·piece
show·place
show·room
showy
shrap·nel
shred
　shred·ded
　shred·ding
Shreve·port
shrew
shrewd
shrew·ish
shriek
shrift
shrike
shrill·ness
shril·ly
shrine
shrink
　shrank
　　also shrunk

　shrunk
　　or shrunk·en

shrink·able
shrink·age
shrive

shrived
  or shrove

shriv·en
  or shrived

shriv·ing
shriv·el
shriv·eled
  or shriv·elled

shriv·el·ing
  or shriv·el·ling

shrub·bery
shrug
  shrugged
  shrug·ging
shuck
shud·der
shuf·fle
shuf·fle·board
shun
  shunned
  shun·ning
shunt
shut
  shut
  shut·ting
shut·down
shut-in
shut·off
shut·out
shut·ter
shut·tle
shut·tle·cock
shy
  shied
  shy·ing

shy
  shi·er
    or shy·er

  shi·est
    or shy·est

shy·ly
shy·ness
shy·ster
Si·a·mese
  pl Si·a·mese

sib·i·lant
sib·ling
sib·yl
sib·yl·line
sick·bed
sick·en
sick·le
sick·li·ness
sick·ly
sick·ness
sick·room
side·arm
side·board
side·burns
side·car
side-glance
side·kick
side·light
side·line
side·long
side·man
side·piece
si·de·re·al
side·sad·dle
side·show

side·slip
side·spin
side·split·ting
side·step
side·stroke
side·swipe
side·track
side·walk
side·ways
sid·ing
si·dle
siege
si·er·ra
Si·er·ra Le·one
si·es·ta
sieve
sift·er
sigh
sight
  view (see cite, site*)*

sight·ed
sight·less
sight·ly
sight-read
sight-see·ing
sight·seer
sign
  mark (see sine*)*

sig·nal
  sig·naled
    or sig·nalled

  sig·nal·ing
    or sig·nal·ling

sig·nal·ize
sig·nal·ly

sig·na·to·ry
sig·na·ture
sign·board
sign·er
sig·net
sig·nif·i·cance
sig·nif·i·cant
sig·ni·fi·ca·tion
sig·ni·fy
sign·post
si·lage
si·lence
si·lenc·er
si·lent
sil·hou·ette
sil·i·ca
sil·i·cate
si·li·ceous
  or si·li·cious

sil·i·cone
sil·i·co·sis
silk·en
silk·i·ly
silk·i·ness
silk-screen
silk·weed
silk·worm
silky
sil·li·ness
sil·ly
si·lo
  pl si·los

sil·ver
sil·ver·fish
sil·ver·smith

sil·ver-tongued
sil·ver·ware
sil·very
sil·vi·cul·ture
sim·i·an
sim·i·lar
sim·i·lar·i·ty
sim·i·lar·ly
sim·i·le
si·mil·i·tude
sim·mer
si·mo·nize
si·mo·ny
sim·per
sim·ple
sim·ple·mind·ed
sim·ple·ton
sim·plic·i·ty
sim·pli·fi·ca·tion
sim·pli·fi·er
sim·pli·fy
sim·ply
sim·u·late
sim·u·la·tion
sim·u·la·tor
si·mul·ta·ne·ous
sin
  sinned
  sin·ning
sin·cere
sin·cere·ly
sin·cer·i·ty
sine
  math (see sign)

si·ne·cure

si·ne die
si·ne qua non
sin·ew
sin·ewy
sin·ful
sin·ful·ly
sing
  sang
    or sung

  sung
  sing·ing
Sin·ga·pore
singe
  singed
  singe·ing
sing·er
sin·gle
sin·gle-breast·ed
sin·gle-hand·ed
sin·gle-mind·ed
sin·gle-space
sin·gle·ton
sin·gle-track
sin·gly
sing·song
sin·gu·lar
sin·gu·lar·i·ty
sin·is·ter
sink
  sank
    or sunk

  sunk
  sink·ing
sink·able
sink·age

sink·er
sink·hole
sin·ner
sin·u·os·i·ty
sin·u·ous
si·nus
si·nus·itis
sip
  sipped
  sip·ping
si·phon
si·ren
sir·loin
si·roc·co
  pl si·roc·cos
si·sal
sis·ter
sis·ter·hood
sis·ter-in-law
  pl sis·ters-in-law
sis·ter·ly
sit
  sat
  sit·ting
si·tar
sit-down
site
  location (see cite,
    sight)
sit-in
sit·ter
sit·ting
sit·u·ate
sit·u·at·ed
sit·u·a·tion
six-pack

six·pence
six·pen·ny
six·teen
six·ti·eth
six·ty
siz·able
  or size·able

siz·ably
siz·ing
siz·zle
skate·board
skat·er
skein
skel·e·tal
skel·e·ton
skep·tic
skep·ti·cal
skep·ti·cal·ly
skep·ti·cism
sketch·book
sketch·i·ly
sketch·i·ness
sketchy
skew·er
ski
  pl skis

skid
  skid·ded
  skid·ding
ski·er
skiff
ski·ing
skil·let
skill·ful
  or skil·ful

skill·ful·ly
skim
  skimmed
  skim·ming
skim·mer
skimp·i·ly
skimp·i·ness
skimpy
skin
  skinned
  skin·ning
skin-deep
skin·flint
skin·ful
skin·ni·ness
skin·ny
skin·tight
skip
  skipped
  skip·ping
skip·jack
skip·per
skir·mish
skit·ter
skit·tish
ski·wear
skul·dug·ger·y
  or skull·dug·ger·y

skulk·er
skull
  skeleton of the head
  (*see* scull)

skull·cap
sky·borne
sky·diving
sky-high

slipcover

sky·jack·er
sky·lark
sky·light
sky·line
sky·lounge
sky·rock·et
sky·scrap·er
sky·ward
sky·way
sky·writ·ing
slack·en
slack·er
slack·ly
sla·lom
slam
  slammed
  slam·ming
slam-bang
slan·der
slan·der·ous
slang·i·ness
slangy
slant·ways
slant·wise
slap
  slapped
  slap·ping
slap·dash
slap·hap·py
slap·stick
slash·ing
slat
  slat·ted
  slat·ting
slat·tern
slat·tern·li·ness

slaugh·ter
slaugh·ter·house
sla·ver
  drool

slav·er
  slave ship

slav·ery
slav·ish
slay
  kill (see sleigh)

  slew
  slain
  slay·ing
slay·er
slea·zi·ly
slea·zi·ness
slea·zy
sled
  sled·ded
  sled·ding
sledge·ham·mer
sleek·ly
sleep
  slept
  sleep·ing
sleep·er
sleep·i·ly
sleep·i·ness
sleep·less
sleep·walk
sleepy
sleeve·less
sleigh
  snow vehicle (see slay)

sleight
  dexterity (see slight)

slen·der
slen·der·ize
sleuth
slic·er
slick·er
slick·ly
slide
  slid
  slid·ing
slid·er
slight
  frail (see sleight)

slim
  slimmed
  slim·ming
slim·i·ly
slim·i·ness
slim·ness
slimy
sling
  slung
  sling·ing
sling·shot
slink
  slunk
  also slinked

  slink·ing
slinky
slip
  slipped
  slip·ping
slip·case
slip·cov·er

slip·knot
slip-on
slip·over
slip·page
slip·per
slip·peri·ness
slip·pery
slip·shod
slip·stick
slip·stream
slip·up
slit
  slit
  slit·ting
slith·er
slith·ery
sliv·er
slob·ber
sloe
  fruit (see slow*)*

sloe-eyed
slog
  slogged
  slog·ging
slo·gan
sloop
slop
  slopped
  slop·ping
slop·pi·ly
slop·pi·ness
slop·py
slop·work
slosh
slot

slot·ted
slot·ting
sloth·ful
sloth·ful·ly
slouch·er
slouchy
slough
  or sluff

slov·en·li·ness
slov·en·ly
slow
  sluggish (see sloe*)*

slow·down
slow·poke
slow-wit·ted
sludge
sludgy
slug
  slugged
  slug·ging
slug·gard
slug·gish
sluice
sluice·way
slum
  slummed
  slum·ming
slum·ber
slum·ber·ous
  or slum·brous

slum·lord
slump
slur
  slurred
  slur·ring

slush·i·ness
slushy
slut·tish
sly
  sli·er
    also sly·er

  sli·est
    also sly·est

sly·ly
small·ish
small·pox
small-scale
small-time
smart·ly
smash·ing
smash·up
smat·ter
smat·ter·ing
smeary
smell
  smelled
    or smelt

  smell·ing
smelly
smelt
  pl smelts *or* smelt

smelt·er
smid·gen
  or smid·geon *or*
  smid·gin

smi·lax
smil·ing·ly
smirch
smirk
smite

smote
smit·ten
  or smote

smit·ing
smith·er·eens
smithy
smock·ing
smog·gy
smok·able
  or smoke·able

smoke-filled
smoke·less
smoke·stack
smok·i·ly
smok·i·ness
smoky
  also smok·ey

smol·der
  or smoul·der

smooth·bore
smooth·en
smooth·ly
smooth-tongued
smor·gas·bord
smoth·er
smudge
smudg·i·ly
smudg·i·ness
smudgy
smug·gle
smug·gler
smug·ly
smut·ti·ly
smut·ti·ness
smut·ty

snaf·fle
sna·fu
snag
  snagged
  snag·ging
snail-paced
snake·bite
snake·like
snake·skin
snak·i·ly
snaky
snap
  snapped
  snap·ping
snap·back
snap-brim
snap·drag·on
snap·per
snap·pish
snap·py
snap·shot
snar·er
snarly
snatch
snaz·zy
sneak·er
sneak·i·ly
sneak·i·ness
sneak·ing
sneaky
sneer·er
snick·er
snif·fle
snif·ter
snig·ger
snip

snipped
snip·ping
snip·er·scope
snip·pet
snip·py
sniv·el
  sniv·eled
  or sniv·elled

sniv·el·ing
  or sniv·el·ling

snob·bery
snob·bish
snoop·er
snoop·er·scope
snoopy
snor·kel
snout
snow·ball
snow-blind
  or snow-blind·ed

snow·bound
snow·cap
snow·drift
snow·drop
snow·fall
snow·flake
snow·man
snow·mo·bile
snow·mo·bil·ing
snow·plow
snow·shoe
snow·storm
snow·suit
snowy
snub

snubbed
snub·bing
snub-nosed
snuff·er
snuf·fle
snug·gle
snug·ly
soak·age
so-and-so
　pl so-and-sos
　　also so-and-so's

soap·box
soap·stone
soap·suds
soapy
soar
　fly (see sore)

sob
　sobbed
　sob·bing
so·ber
so·bri·ety
so·bri·quet
so-called
soc·cer
so·cia·bil·i·ty
so·cia·ble
so·cia·bly
so·cial
so·cial·ism
so·cial·is·tic
so·cial·ite
so·cial·iza·tion
so·cial·ize
so·cial·ly
so·ci·etal

so·ci·etal·ly
so·ci·ety
so·cio·eco·nom·ic
so·cio·log·i·cal
so·cio·log·i·cal·ly
so·ci·ol·o·gist
so·ci·ol·o·gy
so·ci·om·e·try
so·cio·po·lit·i·cal
so·cio·re·li·gious
sock·et
sock·eye
sod
　sod·ded
　sod·ding
so·da
so·dal·i·ty
sod·den
so·di·um
sod·omy
so·ev·er
so·fa
soft·ball
soft-boiled
soft·bound
soft·en
soft·heart·ed
soft-ped·al
soft-shell
　or soft-shelled

soft-soap
soft-spo·ken
soft·ware
soft·wood
sog·gi·ly

sog·gi·ness
sog·gy
soi·gné
　or soi·gnée

soil·borne
soi·ree
　or soi·rée

so·journ
sol
　also so
　musical note

sol
　pl so·les
　coin

so·lace
so·lar
so·lar·i·um
　pl so·lar·ia *also*
　　so·lar·i·ums

so·lar plex·us
sol·der
sol·dier
sole
　undersurface, fish,
　only (see soul)

so·le·cism
sole·ly
sol·emn
so·lem·ni·fy
so·lem·ni·ty
sol·em·ni·za·tion
sol·em·nize
so·le·noid
so·le·noi·dal
sole·print
sol-fa

sol·fège
so·lic·it
so·lic·i·ta·tion
so·lic·i·tor
so·lic·i·tous
so·lic·i·tude
sol·id
sol·i·dar·i·ty
so·lid·i·fi·ca·tion
so·lid·i·fy
so·lid·i·ty
sol·id-state
so·lil·o·quize
so·lil·o·quy
so·lip·sism
sol·i·taire
sol·i·tary
sol·i·tude
so·lo
  pl so·los

so·lo·ist
so·lon
sol·stice
sol·u·bil·i·ty
sol·u·ble
sol·u·bly
so·lu·tion
solv·abil·i·ty
solv·able
solve
sol·ven·cy
sol·vent
so·ma
So·ma·li
  pl So·ma·li *or*
  So·ma·lis

So·ma·lia
So·ma·lian
so·mat·ic
so·ma·tol·o·gy
som·ber
  or som·bre

som·bre·ro
some·body
some·day
some·how
some·one
some·place
som·er·sault
some·thing
some·time
some·times
some·what
some·where
som·me·lier
som·nam·bu·late
som·nam·bu·lism
som·nam·bu·list
som·no·lence
som·no·lent
so·nar
so·na·ta
son·a·ti·na
sonde
song·bird
song·book
song·ster
song·stress
song·writ·er
son·ic
son-in-law
  pl sons-in-law

son·net
so·nor·i·ty
so·no·rous
soon·er
soothe
sooth·er
sooth·ing·ly
sooth·say·er
soot·i·ly
soot·i·ness
sooty
sop
  sopped
  sop·ping
soph·ism
soph·ist
so·phis·tic
  or so·phis·ti·cal

so·phis·ti·cat·ed
so·phis·ti·ca·tion
soph·ist·ry
soph·o·more
soph·o·mor·ic
so·po·rif·er·ous
sop·o·rif·ic
so·prano
  pl so·pra·nos

sor·bic acid
sor·cer·er
sor·cer·ess
  female wizard

sor·cer·ous
  magical

sor·cery
sor·did

sore
painful (see soar)

sore·ly
sor·ghum
So·rop·ti·mist
so·ror·i·ty
sor·rel
sor·ri·ly
sor·ri·ness
sor·row
sor·row·ful
sor·row·ful·ly
sor·ry
sad (see sari)

sor·tie
so-so
sot·to vo·ce
sou·brette
souf·flé
soul
spirit (see sole)

soul·ful
soul·ful·ly
soul-search·ing
sound·board
sound·ing
sound·ly
sound·proof
soup·con
soupy
sour·dough
sour·ish
sou·sa·phone
sou·tane
South Af·ri·ca

South Af·ri·can
South Bend
south·bound
South Car·o·li·na
South Da·ko·ta
south·east
south·east·er·ly
south·east·ern
south·east·ward
south·er·ly
south·ern
south·ern·most
south·ward
south·west
south·west·er·ly
south·west·ern
south·west·ward
sou·ve·nir
sov·er·eign
also sov·ran

sov·er·eign·ty
also sov·ran·ty

so·vi·et
sow
plant, scatter (see sew)

sowed
sown
or sowed

sow·ing
sow·er
soy·bean
space·craft
space·flight
space·man
space·port

space·ship
space-time
spac·ing
spa·cious
spack·le
spade·ful
spade·work
spa·ghet·ti
Spain
span
spanned
span·ning
span·drel
or span·dril

span·gle
Span·iard
span·iel
Span·ish
spank·ing
span·ner
spar
sparred
spar·ring
spare·ribs
spar·ing·ly
spar·kle
spark·ler
spar·row
sparse·ly
Spar·tan
spasm
spas·mod·ic
spas·mod·i·cal·ly
spas·tic
spat

spat·ted
spat·ting
spa·tial
spa·tial·ly
spat·ter
spat·u·la
spav·in
spav·ined
speak
  spoke
  spo·ken
  speak·ing
speak·easy
speak·er
spear·fish
spear·head
spear·mint
spear·wort
spe·cial
spe·cial·ist
spe·cial·iza·tion
spe·cial·ize
spe·cial·ly
spe·cial·ty
spe·cie
  money
spe·cies
  pl spe·cies
  kind

spec·i·fi·able
spe·cif·ic
spe·cif·i·cal·ly
spec·i·fi·ca·tion
spec·i·fi·er
spec·i·fy
spec·i·men

spe·cious
speck·le
spec·ta·cle
spec·ta·cled
spec·tac·u·lar
spec·ta·tor
spec·ter
  or spec·tre
spec·tral
spec·trom·e·ter
spec·tro·scope
spec·tro·scop·ic
spec·tro·scop·i·
  cal·ly
spec·tros·co·pist
spec·tros·co·py
spec·trum
  pl spec·tra *or*
  spec·trums
spec·u·late
spec·u·la·tion
spec·u·la·tive
spec·u·la·tive·ly
spec·u·la·tor
speech·less
speed
  sped
  or speed·ed
  speed·ing
speed·boat
speed·i·ly
speed·i·ness
speed·om·e·ter
speed·up
speed·way
speed·well

speedy
spe·le·ol·o·gist
spe·le·ol·o·gy
spell·bind·er
spell·bound
spell·er
spe·lunk·er
spend
  spent
  spend·ing
spend·able
spend·thrift
sperm
  pl sperm *or* sperms

sper·ma·ce·ti
sper·ma·to·zo·on
  pl sper·ma·to·zoa

spew
sphere
spher·i·cal
spher·i·cal·ly
spher·oid
sphinc·ter
sphinx
  pl sphinx·es *or*
  sphin·ges

spic·i·ly
spic·i·ness
spick-and-span
  or spic-and-span

spicy
spi·der
spi·dery
spig·ot
spill

spilled
also spilt

spill·ing
spill·age
spill·way
spin
spun
spin·ning
spin·ach
spi·nal
spi·nal·ly
spin·dle
spin·dling
spin·dly
spin·drift
spine·less
spin·et
spin·ner
spin-off
spin·ster
spiny
spi·ral
spi·raled
or spi·ralled

spi·ral·ing
or spi·ral·ling

spi·ral·ly
spir·it
spir·it·ed
spir·it·less
spir·i·tu·al
spir·i·tu·al·ism
spir·i·tu·al·i·ty
spir·i·tu·al·ly
spir·i·tu·ous

spi·ro·chete
or spi·ro·chaete

spit
impale

spit·ted
spit·ting
spit
eject saliva

spit
or spat

spit·ting
spite·ful
spite·ful·ly
spit·fire
spit·tle
spit·toon
splash·board
splash·down
splat·ter
splay·foot
spleen·ful
splen·did
splen·dor
sple·net·ic
splen·ic
splic·er
splin·ter
split
split
split·ting
split-lev·el
splotch
splurge
splut·ter
spoil

spoiled
or spoilt

spoil·ing
spoil·able
spoil·age
spoil·er
spoil·sport
Spo·kane
spo·ken
spoke·shave
spokes·man
spokes·wom·an
spo·li·a·tion
sponge
spong·er
spong·i·ness
spongy
spon·sor
spon·ta·ne·ity
spon·ta·ne·ous
spoo·ner·ism
spoon-feed
spoon-fed
spoon-feed·ing
spoon·ful
pl spoon·fuls *or*
spoons·ful

spo·rad·ic
spo·rad·i·cal·ly
sport·i·ly
sport·i·ness
sport·ing
sport·ive
sports·cast
sports·man
sports·wear

sports·writ·er
sporty
spot
  spot·ted
  spot·ting
spot-check
spot·less
spot·light
spot·ter
spot·ti·ly
spot·ti·ness
spot·ty
sprach·ge·fuhl
sprawl
spray·er
spread
  spread
  spread·ing
spread-ea·gle
spread·er
spright·li·ness
spright·ly
spring
  sprang
    or sprung
  sprung
  spring·ing
spring·board
spring-clean·ing
Spring·field
spring·house
spring·i·ly
spring·i·ness
spring·time
springy
sprin·kle

sprin·kler
sprin·kling
sprint·er
sprock·et
spruce·ly
spry
  spri·er
    or spry·er
  spri·est
    or spry·est
spunk·i·ly
spunk·i·ness
spunky
spur
  spurred
  spur·ring
spu·ri·ous
sput·nik
sput·ter
spu·tum
  pl spu·ta
spy
  spied
  spy·ing
spy·glass
squab·ble
squad·ron
squal·id
squall
squa·lor
squan·der
square·ly
square-rigged
square-shoul·dered
squash·i·ly

squash·i·ness
squashy
squat
  squat·ted
  squat·ting
squat·ter
squawk
squeak·er
squeaky
squeal·er
squea·mish
squee·gee
squeez·er
squelch
squig·gle
squinty
squirmy
squir·rel
squishy
Sri Lan·ka
stab
  stabbed
  stab·bing
sta·bile
sta·bil·i·ty
sta·bi·li·za·tion
sta·bi·lize
sta·bi·liz·er
sta·ble
stac·ca·to
sta·di·um
  pl sta·dia *or*
  sta·di·ums
staff
  pl staffs *or* staves
stage·coach

stage·craft
stage·hand
stage-man·age
stage·struck
stag·ger
stag·i·ly
stag·i·ness
stag·ing
stag·nan·cy
stag·nant
stag·nate
stag·na·tion
stagy
or stag·ey

staid
stain·able
stain·less
stair·case
stair·way
stair·well
stake
post, bet (see steak)

stake·hold·er
sta·lac·tite
sta·lag·mite
stale·ly
stale·mate
stale·ness
stalk·ing-horse
stal·lion
stal·wart
sta·men
plant part (see
stamina)
pl sta·mens *or*
sta·mi·na

Stam·ford
stam·i·na
endurance (see
stamen)

stam·mer
stam·pede
stamp·er
stance
stanch
stan·chion
stand
stood
stand·ing
stan·dard
stan·dard-bear·er
stan·dard·iza·tion
stan·dard·ize
stand·by
stand·ee
stand-in
stand·ing
stand·off
stand·out
stand·pat
stand·pipe
stand·point
stand·still
stand-up
stan·za
staph·y·lo·coc·cus
pl staph·y·lo·coc·ci

sta·ple
sta·pler
star
starred
star·ring

star·board
star-cham·ber
starch·i·ness
starchy
star-crossed
star·dom
star·dust
sta·re de·ci·sis
star·fish
star·gaze
stark·ly
star·less
star·light
star·like
star·ling
star·lit
star·ry
star·ry-eyed
star-span·gled
start·er
star·tle
star·tling
star·va·tion
starve·ling
stat·able
or state·able

state·craft
state·hood
state·house
state·less
state·li·ness
state·ly
state·ment
state·room
state·side

states·man
stat·ic
stat·i·cal·ly
sta·tion
sta·tion·ary
  fixed (see stationery)

sta·tio·ner
sta·tio·nery
  writing materials
  (see stationary)

sta·tion·mas·ter
stat·ism
sta·tis·tic
sta·tis·ti·cal
sta·tis·ti·cal·ly
stat·is·ti·cian
sta·tis·tics
stat·u·ary
stat·ue
stat·u·esque
stat·u·ette
stat·ure
sta·tus
sta·tus quo
stat·ute
stat·u·to·ry
staunch
stave
  staved
    or stove

  stav·ing
stay
  stayed
    or staid

  stay·ing

stay-at-home
stead·fast
stead·i·ly
stead·i·ness
steady
steak
  meat (see stake)

steal
  take (see steel)

  stole
  sto·len
  steal·ing
stealth·i·ly
stealth·i·ness
stealthy
steam·boat
steam·er
steam·i·ly
steam·i·ness
steam·roll·er
steam·ship
steamy
steel
  metal (see steal)

steel·i·ness
steel·work
steely
steel·yard
stee·ple
stee·ple·chase
stee·ple·jack
steep·ly
steer·able
steer·age
steer·er

steers·man
stein
stel·lar
stem
  stemmed
  stem·ming
stem·less
stem·ware
sten·cil
  sten·ciled
    or sten·cilled

  sten·cil·ing
    or sten·cil·ling

ste·nog·ra·pher
steno·graph·ic
steno·graph·i·cal·
  ly
ste·nog·ra·phy
steno·type
steno·typ·ist
sten·to·ri·an
step
  walk (see steppe)

  stepped
  step·ping
step·broth·er
step-by-step
step·child
step·daugh·ter
step-down
step·fa·ther
step-in
step·lad·der
step·moth·er
step·par·ent

steppe
plain (see step)

step·ping-stone

step·sis·ter

step·son

step-up

ster·eo
pl ste·re·os

ste·reo·phon·ic

ste·reo·scope

ste·reo·scop·ic

ste·re·os·co·py

ste·reo·type

ste·reo·typed

ster·ile

ste·ril·i·ty

ster·il·iza·tion

ster·il·ize

ster·il·iz·er

ster·ling

stern·ly

ster·num
pl ster·nums *or*
ster·na

stet
stet·ted
stet·ting

stetho·scope

ste·ve·dore

stew·ard

stew·ard·ess

stick
stuck
stick·ing

stick·er

stick·i·ly

stick·i·ness

stick-in-the-mud

stick·ler

stick-to-it·ive·ness

sticky

stiff·en

stiff-necked

sti·fle

stig·ma
pl stig·ma·ta *or*
stig·mas

stig·mat·ic

stig·ma·tism

stig·ma·tize

stile
steps (see style)

sti·let·to
pl sti·let·tos *or*
sti·let·toes

still·birth

still·born

stilt·ed

Stil·ton

stim·u·lant

stim·u·late

stim·u·la·tion

stim·u·la·tive

stim·u·la·tor

stim·u·lus
pl stim·u·li

sting
stung
sting·ing

sting·er

stin·gi·ly

stin·gi·ness

sting·ray

stin·gy

stink
stank
or stunk

stunk
stink·ing

sti·pend

stip·ple

stip·u·late

stip·u·la·tion

stip·u·la·tor

stir
stirred
stir·ring

stir·ring

stir·rup

stitch

sto·chas·tic

stock·ade

stock·bro·ker

stock·hold·er

stock·i·nette
or stock·i·net

stock·ing

stock-in-trade

stock·man

stock·pile

stock·room

Stock·ton

stocky

stock·yard

stodg·i·ly

stodg·i·ness

stodgy

sto·gie
  or sto·gy

sto·ic
  or sto·i·cal

sto·ical·ly
sto·icism
stoke·hole
stok·er
stol·id
sto·lid·i·ty
stom·ach
stom·ach·ache
stone-blind
stone-broke
stone·cut·ter
stone-deaf
stone·ma·son
stone·ware
stone·work
ston·i·ly
ston·i·ness
stony
stop
  stopped
  stop·ping
stop·cock
stop·gap
stop·light
stop·over
stop·page
stop·per
stop·watch
stor·able
stor·age
store·house

store·keep·er
store·room
store·wide
sto·ried
  or sto·reyed

storm·bound
storm·i·ly
storm·i·ness
stormy
sto·ry
sto·ry·book
sto·ry·tell·er
sto·tin·ka
  pl sto·tin·ki

stout·heart·ed
stout·ly
stove·pipe
stow·age
stow·away
stra·bis·mus
strad·dle
strafe
strag·gle
strag·gler
strag·gly
straight
  not crooked (see strait)

straight-arm
straight·away
straight·edge
straight·en
  make straight (see straiten)

straight-faced

straight·for·ward
  also straight·for·wards

strain·er
strait
  channel (see straight)

strait·en
  confine (see straighten)

strait·jack·et
  or straight·jack·et

strait·laced
  or straight·laced

strange·ly
strang·er
stran·gle
stran·gle·hold
stran·gler
stran·gu·late
stran·gu·la·tion
strap
  strapped
  strap·ping
strap·hang·er
strap·less
strap·ping
strat·a·gem
stra·te·gic
stra·te·gi·cal·ly
strat·e·gist
strat·e·gy
strat·i·fi·ca·tion
strat·i·fy
stra·tig·ra·phy
stra·to·cu·mu·lus
strato·sphere

stra·tum
  pl stra·ta

stra·tus
  pl stra·ti

straw·ber·ry
straw·flow·er
straw·worm
streak·i·ness
streaky
stream·er
stream·line
stream·lined
street·car
strength·en
stren·u·ous
strep·to·coc·cus
  pl strep·to·coc·ci

strep·to·my·cin
stretch·abil·i·ty
stretch·able
stretch·er
stretch·er-bear·er
strew
  strewed
  strewed
    or strewn

  strew·ing
stri·at·ed
stri·a·tion
strick·en
strict·ly
stric·ture
stride
  strode
  strid·den

strid·ing
stri·den·cy
stri·dent
strife
strike
  struck
  struck
    also strick·en

  strik·ing
strike·bound
strike·break·er
strike·out
strike·over
strik·er
strik·ing
string
  strung
  string·ing
strin·gen·cy
strin·gent
string·er
string·i·ness
string·ing
stringy
strip
  stripped
    also stript

  strip·ping
strip-crop·ping
strip·ling
strip·per
strip·tease
strive
  strove
    also strived

striv·en
  or strived

striv·ing
stro·bo·scope
stro·bo·scop·ic
stroll·er
strong-arm
strong·box
strong·hold
strong-mind·ed
stron·tium
strop
  stropped
  strop·ping
stro·phe
stro·phic
struc·tur·al
struc·tur·al·ly
struc·ture
strug·gle
strum
  strummed
  strum·ming
strum·pet
strut
  strut·ted
  strut·ting
strych·nine
Stu·art
stub
  stubbed
  stub·bing
stub·ble
stub·bly
stub·born
stub·born·ness

stub·by
stuc·co
    pl stuc·cos *or*
        stuc·coes

stud
    stud·ded
    stud·ding
stud·book
stud·ding
stu·dent
stud·horse
stud·ied
stu·dio
    pl stu·dios

stu·di·ous
stuff·i·ly
stuff·i·ness
stuff·ing
stuffy
stul·ti·fi·ca·tion
stul·ti·fy
stum·ble
stun
    stunned
    stun·ning
stu·pe·fac·tion
stu·pe·fy
stu·pen·dous
stu·pid
stu·pid·i·ty
stu·por
stur·di·ly
stur·dy
stur·geon
stut·ter

sty
    pl sties *or* styes
    pig pen

sty
    or stye
    pl sties *or* styes
    eyelid swelling

style
    fashion (*see* stile)

style·book
styl·ish
styl·ist
sty·lis·ti·cal·ly
sty·lis·tics
styl·i·za·tion
styl·ize
sty·lus
    pl sty·li *also*
        sty·lus·es

sty·mie
    sty·mied
    sty·mie·ing
styp·tic
sty·rene
su·able
sua·sion
sua·sive
suave·ly
sua·vi·ty
sub
    subbed
    sub·bing
sub·agen·cy
sub·ar·ea
sub·as·sem·bly
sub·atom·ic

sub·av·er·age
sub·base·ment
sub·bing
sub·class
sub·com·mit·tee
sub·con·scious
sub·con·ti·nent
sub·con·tract
sub·con·trac·tor
sub·cul·ture
sub·cu·ta·ne·ous
sub·dis·ci·pline
sub·di·vide
sub·di·vi·sion
sub·due
sub·en·try
sub·fam·i·ly
sub·freez·ing
sub·group
sub·hu·man
sub·ject
sub·jec·tion
sub·jec·tive
sub·jec·tiv·i·ty
sub·join
sub ju·di·ce
sub·ju·gate
sub·ju·ga·tion
sub·junc·tive
sub·lease
sub·let
sub·li·mate
sub·li·ma·tion
sub·lime
sub·lim·i·nal
sub·lim·i·nal·ly

sub·lim·i·ty
sub·lu·na·ry
   also sub·lu·nar

sub·mar·gin·al
sub·mar·gin·al·ly
sub·ma·rine
sub·merge
sub·mer·gence
sub·mers·ible
sub·mer·sion
sub·mis·sion
sub·mis·sive
sub·mit
   sub·mit·ted
   sub·mit·ting
sub·nor·mal
sub·nor·mal·i·ty
sub·or·bit·al
sub·or·der
sub·or·di·nate
sub·or·di·na·tion
sub·orn
sub·or·na·tion
sub·plot
sub·poe·na
sub·re·gion
sub ro·sa
sub·scribe
sub·scrib·er
sub·scrip·tion
sub·se·quent
sub·ser·vi·ence
sub·ser·vi·ent
sub·side
sub·si·dence

sub·sid·iary
sub·si·di·za·tion
sub·si·dize
sub·si·dy
sub·sist
sub·sis·tence
sub·soil
sub·son·ic
sub·spe·cies
sub·stance
sub·stan·dard
sub·stan·tial
sub·stan·tial·ly
sub·stan·ti·ate
sub·stan·ti·a·tion
sub·stan·tive
sub·sta·tion
sub·sti·tut·able
sub·sti·tute
sub·sti·tu·tion
sub·stra·tum
   pl sub·stra·ta

sub·struc·ture
sub·sume
sub·sur·face
sub·ter·fuge
sub·ter·ra·nean
sub·ti·tle
sub·tle
sub·tle·ty
sub·tly
sub·tract
sub·trac·tion
sub·tra·hend
sub·trop·i·cal

sub·urb
sub·ur·ban
sub·ur·ban·ite
sub·ur·bia
sub·ven·tion
sub·ver·sion
sub·ver·sive
sub·vert
sub·way
suc·ceed
suc·cess
suc·cess·ful
suc·cess·ful·ly
suc·ces·sion
suc·ces·sive
suc·ces·sive·ly
suc·ces·sor
suc·cinct
suc·cor
   help (see sucker*)*

suc·co·tash
suc·cu·lence
suc·cu·lent
suc·cumb
such·like
suck·er
   one that sucks (see succor*)*

suck·le
suck·ling
su·cre
su·crose
suc·tion
Su·dan
Su·da·nese
sud·den

sud·den·ness
su·do·rif·ic
sudsy
suede
  or suède

su·et
suf·fer
suf·fer·able
suf·fer·ably
suf·fer·ance
suf·fer·ing
suf·fice
suf·fi·cien·cy
suf·fi·cient
suf·fix
suf·fo·cate
suf·fo·ca·tion
suf·fra·gan
suf·frage
suf·frag·ette
suf·frag·ist
suf·fuse
suf·fu·sion
sug·ar
sug·ar·cane
sug·ar·coat
sug·ar·plum
sug·ary
sug·gest
sug·gest·ibil·i·ty
sug·gest·ible
sug·ges·tion
sug·ges·tive
sui·cid·al
sui·cide

sui ge·ner·is
sui ju·ris
suit
  legal action, clothes,
  cards, befit (see
  suite)

suit·abil·i·ty
suit·able
suit·ably
suit·case
suite
  apartment, music
  (see suit, sweet)

suit·ing
suit·or
sul·fa
sul·fa·nil·amide
sul·fate
  or sul·phate

sul·fide
  or sul·phide

sul·fur
  or sul·phur

sul·fu·ric
sul·fu·rous
sulk·i·ly
sulk·i·ness
sulky
sul·len
sul·len·ness
sul·ly
sul·tan
sul·ta·na
sul·tan·ate
sul·tri·ness
sul·try

sum
  summed
  sum·ming
su·mac
  or su·mach

sum·mari·ly
sum·ma·ri·za·tion
sum·ma·rize
sum·ma·ry
  concise (see
  summery)

sum·ma·tion
sum·mer
sum·mer·house
sum·mer·time
sum·mery
  like summer (see
  summary)

sum·mit
sum·mon
sum·mons
  pl sum·mons·es

sump·tu·ous
sun
  sunned
  sun·ning
sun·baked
sun·bathe
sun·beam
sun·bon·net
sun·burn
  sun·burned
    or sun·burnt

  sun·burn·ing
sun·burst
sun·dae

Sun·day
sun·der
sun·di·al
sun·down
sun·dries
sun·dry
sun·fish
sun·flow·er
sun·glass·es
sunk·en
sun·lamp
sun·light
sun·lit
sun·ny
sun·rise
sun·set
sun·shade
sun·shine
sun·spot
sun·stroke
sun·suit
sun·tan
sun·up
sup
  supped
  sup·ping
su·per
su·per·abun·
  dance
su·per·abun·dant
su·per·an·nu·ate
su·per·an·nu·at·
  ed
su·perb
su·per·car·go
su·per·cil·ious

su·per·con·duc·
  tiv·i·ty
su·per·con·duc·
  tor
su·per·ego
su·per·fi·cial
su·per·fi·ci·al·i·
  ty
su·per·fi·cial·ly
su·per·flu·ity
su·per·flu·ous
su·per·high·way
su·per·hu·man
su·per·im·pose
su·per·in·duce
su·per·in·duc·tion
su·per·in·tend
su·per·in·ten·
  dence
su·per·in·ten·
  den·cy
su·per·in·ten·
  dent
su·pe·ri·or
su·pe·ri·or·i·ty
su·per·la·tive
su·per·lin·er
su·per·man
su·per·mar·ket
su·per·nal
su·per·nat·u·ral
su·per·nat·u·ral·
  ly
su·per·nu·mer·
  ary
su·per·pow·er

su·per·scribe
su·per·script
su·per·scrip·tion
su·per·sede
su·per·se·dure
su·per·sen·si·tive
su·per·son·ic
su·per·son·i·cal·
  ly
su·per·sti·tion
su·per·sti·tious
su·per·struc·ture
su·per·tank·er
su·per·vene
su·per·ven·tion
su·per·vise
su·per·vi·sion
su·per·vi·sor
su·per·vi·so·ry
su·pine
sup·per
sup·plant
sup·ple
sup·ple·ment
sup·ple·men·tal
sup·ple·men·ta·ry
sup·pli·ant
sup·pli·cant
sup·pli·cate
sup·pli·ca·tion
sup·pli·er
sup·ply
sup·port
sup·port·able
sup·port·ive
sup·pose

sup·posed
sup·pos·ing
sup·pos·ed·ly
sup·po·si·tion
sup·pos·i·to·ry
sup·press
sup·pres·sant
sup·press·ible
sup·pres·sion
sup·pres·sor
sup·pu·rate
sup·pu·ra·tion
su·pra
su·prem·a·cist
su·prem·a·cy
su·preme
sur·cease
sur·charge
sur·cin·gle
sure·fire
sure·foot·ed
sure·ly
sure·ty
surf
   sea swell (see serf)

sur·face
surf·board
surf·boat
sur·feit
surf·er
surf·ing
surge
   sweep (see serge)

sur·geon
sur·gery

sur·gi·cal
sur·gi·cal·ly
Su·ri·nam
   or Su·ri·na·me

sur·li·ness
sur·ly
sur·mise
sur·mount
sur·name
sur·pass
sur·plice
   vestment

sur·plus
   excess

sur·prise
   also sur·prize

sur·pris·ing
sur·re·al·ism
sur·re·al·ist
sur·re·al·is·ti·
   cal·ly
sur·ren·der
sur·rep·ti·tious
sur·rey
sur·ro·gate
sur·round
sur·round·ings
sur·tax
sur·veil·lance
sur·vey
sur·vey·ing
sur·vey·or
sur·viv·al
sur·vive
sur·vi·vor

sus·cep·ti·bil·i·ty
sus·cep·ti·ble
sus·cep·ti·bly
sus·pect
sus·pend
sus·pend·er
sus·pense
sus·pen·sion
sus·pen·so·ry
sus·pi·cion
sus·pi·cious
sus·tain
sus·tain·able
sus·te·nance
su·ture
su·zer·ain
su·zer·ain·ty
svelte
swab
   swabbed
   swab·bing
swad·dle
swad·dling
swag·ger
swal·low
swal·low·tail
swal·low-tailed
swampy
swank
   or swanky

swans·down
swap
   swapped
   swap·ping
swarth·i·ness

swar·thy
swash·buck·ler
swas·ti·ka
swat
  swat·ted
  swat·ting
swatch
swath
  or swathe
  sweep of a scythe
swathe
  to wrap
swathe
  or swath
  swathing band
sway·back
Swa·zi
  pl Swa·zi *or* Swa·zis

Swa·zi·land
swear
  swore
  sworn
  swear·ing
sweat
  sweat
  or sweat·ed

  sweat·ing
sweat·band
sweat·box
sweat·er
sweat·i·ly
sweat·i·ness
sweat·shop
sweaty
Swe·den
Swed·ish

sweep
  swept
  sweep·ing
sweep·back
sweep·er
sweep-sec·ond
sweep·stakes
  also sweep·stake

sweet
  pleasing, candy (see suite)
sweet·bread
sweet·bri·er
sweet·en
sweet·heart
sweet·meat
sweet-talk
swell
  swelled
  swelled
  or swol·len

  swell·ing
swel·ter
swept-back
swerve
swift·ly
swig
  swigged
  swig·ging
swill
swim
  swam
  swum
  swim·ming
swim·mer
swim·suit

swin·dle
swin·dler
swine
  pl swine

swing
  swung
  swing·ing
swin·ish
Swiss
  pl Swiss

switch
switch·back
switch·board
switch-hit·ter
switch·man
switch·yard
Swit·zer·land
swiv·el
  swiv·eled
  or swiv·elled

  swiv·el·ing
  or swiv·el·ling

sword·fish
sword·play
swords·man
sword·tail
Syb·a·rite
Syb·a·rit·ic
syc·a·more
syc·o·phant
syc·o·phan·tic
syl·lab·ic
syl·lab·i·ca·tion
syl·lab·i·fi·ca·tion
syl·lab·i·fy

syl·la·ble
syl·la·bus
  pl syl·la·bi *or*
    syl·la·bus·es

syl·lo·gism
syl·lo·gis·tic
sylph
syl·van
sym·bi·o·sis
  pl sym·bi·o·ses

sym·bi·ot·ic
sym·bol
  sign (see cymbal)

sym·bol·ic
  or sym·bol·i·cal

sym·bol·i·cal·ly
sym·bol·ism
sym·bol·iza·tion
sym·bol·ize
sym·met·ri·cal
  or sym·met·ric

sym·met·ri·cal·ly
sym·me·try
sym·pa·thet·ic
sym·pa·thet·i·
  cal·ly
sym·pa·thize
sym·pa·thiz·er
sym·pa·thy
sym·phon·ic
sym·pho·ny
sym·po·sium
  pl sym·po·sia *or*
    sym·po·siums

symp·tom
symp·tom·at·ic

syn·a·gogue
  or syn·a·gog

syn·apse
syn·chro·mesh
syn·chron·ic
syn·chro·nism
syn·chro·ni·za·
  tion
syn·chro·nize
syn·chro·nous
syn·chro·tron
syn·co·pate
syn·co·pa·tion
syn·co·pe
syn·cret·ic
syn·cre·tism
syn·di·cal·ism
syn·di·cate
syn·di·ca·tion
syn·drome
syn·ec·do·che
syn·ecol·o·gy
syn·er·gism
syn·er·gist
syn·er·gis·ti·cal·
  ly
syn·od
syn·od·i·cal
  or syn·od·ic

syn·onym
syn·on·y·mous
syn·on·y·my
syn·op·sis
  pl syn·op·ses

syn·op·size

syn·op·tic
  also syn·op·ti·cal

syn·tac·tic
  or syn·tac·ti·cal

syn·tac·ti·cal·ly
syn·tax
syn·the·sis
  pl syn·the·ses

syn·the·size
syn·thet·ic
  also syn·thet·i·cal

syn·thet·i·cal·ly
syph·i·lis
syph·i·lit·ic
Syr·a·cuse
Syr·ia
Syr·i·an
sy·ringe
syr·up
syr·upy
sys·tem
sys·tem·at·ic
  also sys·tem·at·i·cal

sys·tem·at·i·cal·
  ly
sys·tem·ati·za·
  tion
sys·tem·atize
sys·tem·ic
sys·tem·iza·tion
sys·tem·ize

T

tab

tabbed
tab·bing
Ta·bas·co
tab·by
tab·er·na·cle
ta·ble
tab·leau
  pl tab·leaux *also*
  tab·leaus

ta·ble·cloth
ta·ble d'hôte
ta·ble-hop
ta·ble·land
ta·ble·spoon
ta·ble·spoon·ful
  pl ta·ble·spoon·fuls
  or
  ta·ble·spoons·ful

tab·let
ta·ble·top
ta·ble·ware
tab·loid
ta·boo
  also ta·bu

ta·bor
  also ta·bour

tab·o·ret
  or tab·ou·ret

tab·u·lar
tab·u·late
tab·u·la·tion
tab·u·la·tor
ta·chom·e·ter
tac·it
tac·i·turn
tac·i·tur·ni·ty

tacki·ness
tack·le
tacky
ta·co
  pl ta·cos

Ta·co·ma
tact·ful
tact·ful·ly
tac·tic
tac·ti·cal
tac·ti·cian
tac·tics
tac·tile
tact·less
tad·pole
taf·fe·ta
taff·rail
taf·fy
tag
  tagged
  tag·ging
tai·ga
tail·board
tail·coat
tail·gate
tail·light
tai·lor
tai·lor-made
tail·piece
tail·spin
ta·ka
take
  took
  tak·en
  tak·ing

take·off
take·out
take-over
tak·er
tak·ing
ta·la
talc
tal·cum pow·der
tal·ent
tales·man
  juror

tal·is·man
  charm
  pl tal·is·mans

talk·ative
talk·er
talk·ing-to
talky
Tal·la·has·see
tal·low
tal·ly
tal·ly·ho
  pl tal·ly·hos

Tal·mud
tal·mu·dic
tal·on
tam·able
  or tame·able

ta·ma·le
tam·a·rack
tam·a·rind
tam·ba·la
tam·bour
tam·bou·rine
tame·ly

tam·er
tam-o'-shan·ter
Tam·pa
tam·per
tam·pon
tan
  tanned
  tan·ning
tan·a·ger
tan·bark
tan·dem
tan·ge·lo
tan·gent
tan·gen·tial
tan·ger·ine
tan·gi·bil·i·ty
tan·gi·ble
tan·gi·bly
tan·gle
tan·go
  pl tan·gos

tangy
tank·age
tan·kard
tank·er
tan·ner
tan·nery
tan·nic
tan·nin
tan·ta·lize
tan·ta·mount
tan·trum
Tan·za·nia
Tan·za·ni·an
tap

tapped
tap·ping
ta·per
  candle, diminish
    (see tapir)

tape-re·cord
tap·es·tried
tap·es·try
tape·worm
tap·hole
tap·i·o·ca
ta·pir
  animal (see taper)

tap·pet
tap·room
tap·root
tar
  tarred
  tar·ring
tar·an·tel·la
ta·ran·tu·la
tar·di·ly
tar·di·ness
tar·dy
tare
  weed, weight
    allowance (see
    tear)

tar·get
tar·iff
tar·nish
ta·ro
  pl ta·ros

tar·pau·lin
tar·pon
tar·ra·gon

tar·ry
tar·tan
tar·tar
tar·tar·ic acid
tart·ly
task·mas·ter
tas·sel
  tas·seled
  or tas·selled

  tas·sel·ing
  or tas·sel·ling

taste·ful
taste·ful·ly
taste·less
tast·er
tast·i·ly
tast·i·ness
tasty
tat
  tat·ted
  tat·ting
tat·ter
tat·ter·de·ma·lion
tat·tered
tat·ter·sall
tat·ting
tat·tle
tat·tle·tale
tat·too
  pl tat·toos

taught
  past of teach (see
    taut)

taunt·er
taupe

taut
tense (see taught)

tau·to·log·i·cal
tau·to·log·i·cal·ly
tau·tol·o·gy
tav·ern
taw·dri·ly
taw·dri·ness
taw·dry
taw·ny
tax·abil·i·ty
tax·able
tax·a·tion
tax-ex·empt
taxi
pl tax·is *also* tax·ies

taxi
tax·ied
taxi·ing
or taxy·ing

taxi·cab
taxi·der·mist
taxi·der·my
taxi·me·ter
tax·ing
tax·o·nom·ic
tax·on·o·my
tax·pay·er
T-bar lift
T-bone
tea
beverage (see tee)

teach
taught
teach·ing

teach·abil·i·ty
teach·able
teach·er
teach-in
tea·cup
tea·cup·ful
pl tea·cup·fuls *or*
tea·cups·ful

tea·house
tea·ket·tle
teak·wood
team
group (see teem)

team·mate
team·ster
team·work
tea·pot
tear
rip (see tare)

tore
torn
tear·ing
tear
cry (see tier)

tear·drop
tear·ful
tear·ful·ly
tea·room
tear·stained
tea·sel
teas·er
tea·spoon
tea·spoon·ful
pl tea·spoon·fuls *also*
tea·spoons·ful

teat

tea·time
tech·nic
tech·ni·cal
tech·ni·cal·i·ty
tech·ni·cal·ly
tech·ni·cian
tech·nique
tech·noc·ra·cy
tech·no·crat
tech·no·log·i·cal
or tech·no·log·ic

tech·no·log·i·cal·
ly
tech·nol·o·gist
tech·nol·o·gy
tec·ton·ic
tec·ton·ics
te·dious
te·di·um
tee
golf (see tea)

teed
tee·ing
teem
abound (see team)

teen·age
or teen·aged

teen·ag·er
tee·ter
tee·to·tal·er
or tee·to·tal·ler

tee·to·tal·ism
tele·cast
tele·cast
also tele·cast·ed

tele·cast·ing
tele·cast·er
tele·com·mu·ni·
  ca·tion
tele·course
tele·film
tele·ge·nic
tele·gram
tele·graph
te·leg·ra·pher
tele·graph·ic
tele·graph·i·cal·ly
te·leg·ra·phy
tele·ki·ne·sis
tele·me·ter
te·lem·e·try
te·le·o·log·i·cal
  also te·le·o·log·ic

te·le·ol·o·gy
tele·path·ic
tele·path·i·cal·ly
te·lep·a·thy
tele·phone
tele·phon·ic
tele·phon·i·cal·ly
te·le·pho·ny
tele·pho·to
tele·pho·tog·ra·
  phy
tele·play
tele·print·er
Tele·Promp·Ter
tele·ran
tele·scope
tele·scop·ic

tele·thon
Tele·type
tele·type·writ·er
tele·view·er
tele·vise
tele·vi·sion
tel·ex
tell
  told
  tell·ing
tell·er
tell·tale
tel·pher
tem·blor
te·mer·i·ty
tem·per
tem·pera
tem·per·a·ment
tem·per·a·men·
  tal
tem·per·a·men·
  tal·ly
tem·per·ance
tem·per·ate
tem·per·a·ture
tem·pest
tem·pes·tu·ous
tem·plate
  or tem·plet

tem·ple
tem·po
  pl tem·pi *or* tem·pos

tem·po·ral
tem·po·rar·i·ly
tem·po·rary

tem·po·ri·za·tion
tem·po·rize
temp·ta·tion
tempt·er
tempt·ress
ten·a·bil·i·ty
ten·a·ble
te·na·cious
te·nac·i·ty
ten·an·cy
ten·ant
ten·ant·ry
ten·den·cy
ten·den·tious
  also ten·den·cious

ten·der
  soft, offer

tend·er
  one that tends

ten·der·foot
  pl ten·der·feet *also*
  ten·der·foots

ten·der·heart·ed
ten·der·ize
ten·der·loin
ten·der·ly
ten·der·ness
ten·don
ten·dril
te·neb·ri·ous
ten·e·brous
ten·e·ment
ten·et
ten·fold
Ten·nes·see

ten·nis
ten·on
ten·or
ten·pin
tense·ly
tense·ness
ten·sile
ten·sion
ten·si·ty
ten·sor
ten·ta·cle
ten·ta·tive
ten·ta·tive·ly
ten·ter
ten·ter·hook
tenth
tenth-rate
te·nu·i·ty
ten·u·ous
ten·ure
ten·ured
te·pee
tep·id
te·qui·la
ter·cen·te·na·ry
ter·gi·ver·sate
ter·i·ya·ki
ter·ma·gant
ter·mi·na·ble
ter·mi·na·bly
ter·mi·nal
ter·mi·nal·ly
ter·mi·nate
ter·mi·na·tion
ter·mi·na·tor
ter·mi·nol·o·gy

ter·mi·nus
  pl ter·mi·ni *or*
    ter·mi·nus·es
ter·mite
ter·na·ry
terp·sich·o·re·an
ter·race
ter·ra·cot·ta
ter·ra fir·ma
ter·rain
Ter·ra·my·cin
ter·ra·pin
ter·rar·i·um
  pl ter·rar·ia *or*
    ter·rar·i·ums
ter·raz·zo
ter·res·tri·al
ter·ri·ble
ter·ri·bly
ter·ri·er
ter·rif·ic
ter·rif·i·cal·ly
ter·ri·fy
ter·ri·fy·ing
ter·ri·to·ri·al
ter·ri·to·ri·al·i·ty
ter·ri·to·ry
ter·ror
ter·ror·ism
ter·ror·ist
ter·ror·iza·tion
ter·ror·ize
ter·ry
terse·ly
ter·tia·ry
tes·sel·late

tes·sel·lat·ed
tes·sel·la·tion
tes·ta·ment
tes·ta·men·ta·ry
tes·tate
tes·ta·tor
tes·ta·trix
tes·ti·cle
tes·ti·fi·er
tes·ti·fy
tes·ti·ly
tes·ti·mo·ni·al
tes·ti·mo·ny
tes·ti·ness
tes·tos·ter·one
tes·ty
tet·a·nus
tête-à-tête
teth·er
tet·ra·cy·cline
tet·ra·eth·yl
te·tral·o·gy
te·tram·e·ter
Tex·as
text·book
tex·tile
tex·tu·al
tex·tu·al·ly
tex·tur·al
tex·ture
Thai
Thai·land
tha·lid·o·mide
thank·ful
thank·ful·ly
thank·less

thanks·giv·ing
that
   pl those

thatch
thaw
the·ater
   or the·atre

the·ater·go·er
the·at·ri·cal
the·at·rics
theft
the·ism
the·ist
the·is·tic
the·mat·ic
the·mat·i·cal·ly
theme
them·selves
thence·forth
thence·for·ward
   also
     thence·for·wards

the·oc·ra·cy
theo·crat·ic
   also theo·crat·i·cal

the·od·o·lite
theo·lo·gian
theo·log·i·cal
   also theo·log·ic

the·ol·o·gy
the·o·rem
the·o·ret·i·cal
   also the·o·ret·ic

the·o·ret·i·cal·ly
the·o·re·ti·cian

the·o·rize
the·o·ry
the·os·o·phist
the·os·o·phy
ther·a·peu·tic
ther·a·peu·ti·cal·
   ly
ther·a·peu·tics
ther·a·pist
ther·a·py
there·abouts
   or there·about

there·af·ter
there·at
there·by
there·for
   in return for

there·fore
   for that reason

there·from
there·in
there·of
there·on
there·to
there·upon
there·with
ther·mal
therm·ion
ther·mo·dy·nam·
   i·cal·ly
ther·mo·dy·nam·
   ics
ther·mo·form
ther·mom·e·ter

ther·mo·nu·cle·ar
ther·mo·plas·tic
ther·mos
ther·mo·set·ting
ther·mo·sphere
ther·mo·stat
ther·mo·stat·i·
   cal·ly
the·sau·rus
   pl the·sau·ri *or*
     the·sau·rus·es

the·sis
   pl the·ses

thes·pi·an
thi·a·mine
   also thi·a·min

thick·en
thick·et
thick·head·ed
thick·ly
thick·ness
thick·set
thick-skinned
thief
   pl thieves

thieve
thiev·ery
thigh·bone
thim·ble
thim·ble·ful
thin
   thinned
   thin·ning
think
   thought

think·ing
think·able
think·er
thin·ly
thin·ner
thin·ness
thin-skinned
third-class
third-rate
thirst·i·ly
thirst·i·ness
thirsty
thir·teen
thir·teenth
thir·ti·eth
thir·ty
this
pl these

this·tle
this·tle·down
thith·er
thith·er·ward
thole
thong
tho·rac·ic
tho·rax
pl tho·rax·es *or*
tho·ra·ces

thorny
thor·ough
thor·ough·bred
thor·ough·fare
thor·ough·go·ing
thor·ough·ness
though
thought

thought·ful
thought·ful·ly
thought·less
thou·sand
pl thou·sands *or*
thou·sand

thou·sandth
thrall·dom
or thral·dom

thrash·er
thread·bare
thread·i·ness
thready
threat·en
3-D
three-deck·er
three-di·men·
sion·al
three·fold
three-hand·ed
three-legged
three-piece
three-quar·ter
three·score
three·some
thren·o·dy
thresh·er
thresh·old
thrice
thrift·i·ly
thrift·less
thrifty
thril·ler
thrive
throve
or thrived

thriv·en
also thrived

thriv·ing
throat·i·ly
throat·i·ness
throaty
throb
throbbed
throb·bing
throe
pang (see throw)

throm·bo·sis
pl throm·bo·ses

throne
throng
throt·tle
through
*by way of, finished
(see throw)*

through·out
through·way
or thruway

throw
*hurl (see throe,
through)*

threw
thrown
throw·ing
throw·away
throw·back
thrum
thrummed
thrum·ming
thrust
thrust
thrust·ing

thrust·er
  also thrust·or

thru·way
  var of throughway

thud
  thud·ded
  thud·ding
thumb·hole
thumb·nail
thumb·print
thumb·screw
thumb·tack
thump
thun·der
thun·der·bird
thun·der·bolt
thun·der·clap
thun·der·cloud
thun·der·head
thun·der·ous
thun·der·show·er
thun·der·storm
thun·der·struck
Thurs·day
thwack
thwart
thyme
  herb (see time)

thy·mus
thy·roid
  or thy·roi·dal

ti·ara
tib·ia
  pl tib·i·ae *also*
  tib·i·as

tic
  twitch (see tick)

tick
  beat, insect (see tic)

tick·er
tick·et
tick·ing
tick·le
tick·ler
tick·lish
tick·tack·toe
  also tic-tac-toe

tid·al
tid·bit
tid·dle·dy·winks
  or tid·dly·winks

tide·land
tide·mark
tide·wa·ter
tide·way
ti·di·ly
ti·di·ness
tid·ing
ti·dy
tie
  tied
  ty·ing
    or tie·ing

tie·back
tie-in
tie·pin
tier
  row (see tear)

tie-up
tif·fa·ny

ti·ger
ti·ger·eye
  or ti·ger's-eye

ti·ger·ish
tight·en
tight·fist·ed
tight-lipped
tight-mouthed
tight·ness
tight·rope
tights
tight·wad
ti·glon
ti·gress
til·ing
till·able
till·age
till·er
  one that tills

til·ler
  steering lever, sprout

tim·bal
  drum

tim·bale
  food

tim·ber
  wood (see timbre)

tim·ber·land
tim·ber·line
tim·bre
  also tim·ber
  sound (see timber)

tim·brel
time
  period (see thyme)

time-con·sum·ing
time-hon·ored
time·keep·er
time-lapse
time·less
time·li·ness
time·ly
time-out
time·piece
tim·er
time-sav·er
time·sav·ing
time·serv·er
time-shar·ing
time·ta·ble
time·worn
tim·id
ti·mid·i·ty
tim·id·ly
tim·ing
tim·o·rous
tim·o·thy
tim·pa·ni
tim·pa·nist
tin
  tinned
  tin·ning
tinc·ture
tin·der
tin·der·box
tin·foil
tinge
  tinged
  tinge·ing
    or ting·ing

tin·gle
tin·horn
ti·ni·ly
ti·ni·ness
tin·ker
tin·ker·er
tin·kle
tin·kly
tin·ni·ly
tin·ni·ness
tin·ny
tin·plate
tin·sel
  tin·seled
    or tin·selled

  tin·sel·ing
    or tin·sel·ling

tin·smith
tint·ing
tin·tin·nab·u·la·
  tion
tin·type
tin·ware
tin·work
ti·ny
tip
  tipped
  tip·ping
tip-off
tip·pet
tip·ple
tip·pler
tip·si·ly
tip·si·ness
tip·ster

tip·sy
tip·toe
tip-top
ti·rade
tired
tire·less
tire·some
tis·sue
ti·tan
ti·tan·ic
tithe
tith·ing
ti·tian
tit·il·late
tit·il·la·tion
ti·tle
ti·tled
ti·tle-hold·er
tit·mouse
  pl tit·mice

ti·tra·tion
tit·ter
tit·tle-tat·tle
tit·u·lar
tiz·zy
toad·stool
toady
to-and-fro
toast·er
toast·mas·ter
to·bac·co
to·bac·co·nist
to·bog·gan
toc·ca·ta
toc·sin
  alarm (*see* toxin)

to·day
tod·dle
tod·dler
tod·dy
to-do
   pl to-dos

toe
  toed
  toe·ing
toe-dance
toe·hold
toe-in
toe·less
toe·nail
toe·piece
tof·fee
  or tof·fy

tog
  togged
  tog·ging
to·ga
to·geth·er
tog·gle
To·go
  or To·go·land

To·go·lese
toi·let
toi·let·ry
toil·some
toil·worn
to·ken
to·ken·ism
tole
  metal (see toll*)*

To·le·do

tol·er·a·ble
tol·er·a·bly
tol·er·ance
tol·er·ant
tol·er·ate
tol·er·a·tion
toll
  tax, sound (see tole*)*

toll·booth
toll·gate
toll·house
toll·man
tom·a·hawk
to·ma·to
  pl to·ma·toes

tom·boy
tomb·stone
tom·cat
tom·fool·ery
to·mor·row
tom-tom
ton
  pl tons *also* ton
  weight (see tun*)*

ton·al
to·nal·i·ty
tone-deaf
tone·less
Ton·ga
tongs
tongue
  tongued
  tongu·ing
tongue-lash·ing
tongue-tied
ton·ic

to·night
ton·nage
ton·neau
ton·sil
ton·sil·lec·to·my
ton·sil·li·tis
ton·so·ri·al
ton·sure
ton·tine
tool·box
tool·head
tool·hold·er
tool·mak·er
tool·room
tooth
  pl teeth

tooth·ache
tooth·brush
tooth·less
tooth·paste
tooth·pick
tooth·some
tooth·wort
toothy
top
  topped
  top·ping
to·paz
top·coat
to·pee
  or to·pi

To·pe·ka
top·er
top-flight
top-heavy

top·ic
top·i·cal
top·i·cal·i·ty
top·i·cal·ly
top·knot
top·less
top·mast
top·most
top-notch
to·pog·ra·pher
top·o·graph·ic
top·o·graph·i·cal
top·o·graph·i·cal·ly
to·pog·ra·phy
to·po·log·i·cal
to·po·log·i·cal·ly
to·pol·o·gist
to·pol·o·gy
to·pos
  pl to·poi

top·ping
top·ple
top·sail
top·side
top·soil
top·stitch
top·sy-tur·vy
toque
To·rah
torch·bear·er
torch·light
to·re·ador
tor·ment
tor·men·tor
  also tor·ment·er

tor·na·do
  pl tor·na·does *or*
    tor·na·dos
To·ron·to
tor·pe·do
  pl tor·pe·does
tor·pid
tor·pid·i·ty
tor·por
torque
Tor·rance
tor·rent
tor·ren·tial
tor·ren·tial·ly
tor·rid
tor·sion
tor·so
  pl tor·sos *or* tor·si
tort
  wrongful act
torte
  pl tor·ten *or* tortes
  cake
tor·til·la
tor·toise
tor·toise-shell
tor·tu·ous
  winding (see
    torturous)
tor·ture
tor·tur·er
tor·tur·ous
  painful (see
    tortuous)
toss-up
tot

tot·ted
tot·ting
to·tal
to·taled
  or to·talled
to·tal·ing
  or to·tal·ling
to·tal·i·tar·i·an
to·tal·i·ty
to·tal·iza·tor
  or to·tal·isa·tor
to·tal·ly
to·tem
tot·ter
tou·can
touch·able
touch·back
touch·down
tou·ché
touch·i·ly
touch·i·ness
touch·ing
touch·mark
touch·stone
touch-type
touchy
tough·en
tough-mind·ed
tough·ness
tou·pee
tour de force
  pl tours de force
tour·ism
tour·ist
tour·ma·line

tour·na·ment
tour·ney
tour·ni·quet
tou·sle
tow·age
to·ward
  or to·wards

tow·boat
tow·el
  tow·eled
    or tow·elled

  tow·el·ing
    or tow·el·ling

tow·er
tow·er·ing
tow·head
tow·head·ed
tow·line
towns·folk
town·ship
towns·man
towns·peo·ple
tow·path
tow·rope
tox·e·mia
tox·ic
tox·i·cant
tox·ic·i·ty
tox·i·co·log·ic
tox·i·co·log·i·cal·
  ly
tox·i·col·o·gist
tox·i·col·o·gy
tox·in
  poison (see tocsin*)*

tox·in-an·ti·tox·in
trace·able
trac·er
trac·ery
tra·chea
  pl tra·che·ae

tra·cho·ma
trac·ing
track
  route, follow (see
    tract*)*

track·age
track-and-field
track·less
track·walk·er
tract
  pamphlet, land (see
    track*)*

trac·ta·bil·i·ty
trac·ta·ble
trac·ta·bly
trac·tion
trac·tor
trade-in
trade-last
trade·mark
trad·er
trades·man
trades·peo·ple
tra·di·tion
tra·di·tion·al
tra·di·tion·al·ly
tra·duce
tra·duc·er
traf·fic
  traf·ficked

traf·fick·ing
traf·fick·er
tra·ge·di·an
tra·ge·di·enne
trag·e·dy
trag·ic
  also trag·i·cal

trag·i·cal·ly
tragi·com·e·dy
tragi·com·ic
  also tragi·com·i·cal

trail·blaz·er
trail·er
train·able
train·ee
train·er
train·ing
train·load
train·man
trait
trai·tor
trai·tor·ous
trai·tress
  or trai·tor·ess

tra·jec·to·ry
tram·mel
  tram·meled
    or tram·melled

  tram·mel·ing
    or tram·mel·ling

tram·ple
tram·po·line
tran·quil
tran·quil·ize
  or tran·quil·lize

tran·quil·iz·er
  also tran·quil·liz·er

tran·quil·li·ty
  or tran·quil·i·ty

tran·quil·ly
trans·act
trans·ac·tion
trans·ac·tion·al
trans·ac·tor
trans·at·lan·tic
trans·ceiv·er
tran·scend
tran·scen·dence
tran·scen·dent
tran·scen·den·tal
tran·scen·den·tal·ism
trans·con·ti·nen·tal
tran·scribe
tran·script
tran·scrip·tion
trans·duce
trans·duc·er
tran·sect
tran·sec·tion
tran·sept
trans·fer
  trans·ferred
  trans·fer·ring
trans·fer·able
trans·fer·al
trans·fer·ence
trans·fig·u·ra·tion

trans·fig·ure
trans·fix
trans·fix·ion
trans·form
trans·form·able
trans·for·ma·tion
trans·form·er
trans·fuse
trans·fus·ible
  or trans·fus·able

trans·fu·sion
trans·gress
trans·gres·sion
trans·gres·sor
tran·sience
tran·sient
tran·sis·tor
tran·sis·tor·ize
tran·sit
tran·si·tion
tran·si·tion·al
tran·si·tion·al·ly
tran·si·tive
tran·si·tive·ly
tran·si·to·ry
trans·lat·able
trans·late
trans·la·tion
trans·la·tor
trans·lit·er·ate
trans·lit·er·a·tion
trans·lu·cence
trans·lu·cent
trans·ma·rine
trans·mi·grate

trans·mi·gra·tion
trans·mi·gra·to·ry
trans·mis·si·ble
trans·mis·sion
trans·mit
  trans·mit·ted
  trans·mit·ting
trans·mit·ta·ble
trans·mit·tal
trans·mit·tance
trans·mit·ter
trans·mog·ri·fi·ca·tion
trans·mog·ri·fy
trans·mut·able
trans·mu·ta·tion
trans·mute
trans·oce·an·ic
tran·som
tran·son·ic
  also trans·son·ic

trans·pa·cif·ic
trans·par·en·cy
trans·par·ent
tran·spi·ra·tion
tran·spire
trans·plant
trans·plant·able
trans·po·lar
tran·spon·der
trans·port
trans·por·ta·tion
trans·port·er
trans·pos·able
trans·pose

trans·po·si·tion
trans·ship
  trans·shipped
  trans·ship·ping
trans·ship·ment
tran·sub·stan·ti·a·tion
trans·val·u·a·tion
trans·val·ue
trans·ver·sal
trans·verse
trans·verse·ly
trap
  trapped
  trap·ping
trap·door
tra·peze
tra·pe·zi·um
trap·e·zoid
trap·per
trap·pings
trap·shoot·ing
tra·pun·to
  pl tra·pun·tos

trash·i·ness
trashy
trau·ma
  pl trau·ma·ta *or*
  trau·mas

trau·mat·ic
trau·mat·i·cal·ly
trau·ma·tize
tra·vail
trav·el
  trav·eled
    or trav·elled

trav·el·ing
  or trav·el·ling

trav·el·er
  or trav·el·ler

trav·el·ogue
  also trav·el·og

tra·vers·able
tra·verse
trav·er·tine
trav·es·ty
trawl·er
treach·er·ous
treach·ery
trea·cle
tread
  trod
    also tread·ed

  trod·den
    or trod

  tread·ing
trea·dle
tread·mill
trea·son
trea·son·able
trea·son·ous
trea·sur·able
trea·sure
trea·sur·er
trea·sury
treat·able
trea·tise
treat·ment
trea·ty
tre·ble
tre·bly

tree
  treed
  tree·ing
tree·less
tree·nail
  also tre·nail

tree·top
tre·foil
treil·lage
trek
  trekked
  trek·king
trel·lis
trel·lis·work
trem·ble
trem·bly
tre·men·dous
trem·o·lo
  pl trem·o·los

trem·or
trem·u·lous
tren·chant
tren·cher
Tren·ton
tre·pan
  tre·panned
  tre·pan·ning
trep·i·da·tion
tres·pass
tres·pass·er
tres·tle
  also tres·sel

tres·tle·work
tri·able
tri·ad

tri·al
tri·an·gle
tri·an·gu·lar
tri·an·gu·late
tri·an·gu·la·tion
trib·al
trib·al·ism
trib·al·ly
tribes·man
trib·u·la·tion
tri·bu·nal
trib·une
trib·u·tary
trib·ute
trice
tri·ceps
  pl tri·ceps·es *also*
  tri·ceps

tri·chi·na
  pl tri·chi·nae *also*
  tri·chi·nas

trich·i·no·sis
tri·chot·o·mous
tri·chot·o·my
tri·chro·mat·ic
trick·ery
trick·i·ly
trick·i·ness
trick·le
trick·ster
tricky
tri·col·or
tri·cor·nered
tri·cot
tri·cus·pid
tri·cy·cle

tri·dent
tri·di·men·sion·al
tri·en·ni·al
tri·er
tri·fle
tri·fler
tri·fling
tri·fo·cal
tri·fur·cate
trig·ger
trig·o·no·met·ric
  also trig·o·no·met·
  ri·cal

trig·o·nom·e·try
tri·lat·er·al
tri·lin·gual
tril·lion
tril·lionth
tril·o·gy
trim
  trimmed
  trim·ming
tri·ma·ran
tri·mes·ter
trim·e·ter
trim·mer
tri·month·ly
Trin·i·dad
Trin·i·dad and
  To·ba·go
Trin·i·da·di·an
Trin·i·ty
trin·ket
tri·no·mi·al
trio
  pl tri·os

tri·ode
trip
  tripped
  trip·ping
tri·par·tite
trip-ham·mer
triph·thong
tri·ple
tri·ple-space
trip·let
tri·plex
trip·li·cate
tri·ply
tri·pod
trip·tych
tri·sect
trite
trit·u·rate
tri·umph
tri·um·phal
tri·um·phant
tri·um·vir
tri·um·vi·rate
triv·et
triv·ia
triv·i·al
triv·i·al·i·ty
triv·i·al·ly
tri·week·ly
tro·cha·ic
tro·che
  lozenge

tro·chee
  poetic meter

trof·fer

trog·lo·dyte
troi·ka
troll
trol·ley
  or trol·ly

trol·lop
trom·bone
trom·bon·ist
troop
  soldiers (see troupe)

troop·er
troop·ship
tro·phy
trop·ic
trop·i·cal
tro·pism
tro·po·sphere
trot
  trot·ted
  trot·ting
trot·line
trot·ter
trou·ba·dour
trou·ble
trou·ble·mak·er
trou·ble·shoot·er
trou·ble·some
trough
trounce
troupe
  stage company (see
  troop)

troup·er
trou·sers

trous·seau
  pl trous·seaux *or*
  trous·seaus

trout
  pl trout *also* trouts

tro·ver
trow·el
  trow·eled
  or trow·elled

  trow·el·ing
  or trow·el·ling

tru·an·cy
tru·ant
truck·age
truck·er
truck·ing
truck·le
truck·line
truck·load
truc·u·lence
truc·u·lent
trudge
true
  trued
  true·ing
  also tru·ing

true-blue
true·heart·ed
true-life
true·love
true·ness
truf·fle
tru·ism
tru·ly
trumped-up

trum·pery
trum·pet
trum·pet·er
trun·cate
trun·ca·tion
trun·cheon
trun·dle
truss
truss·ing
trust·ee
  guardian (see
  trusty)

trust·ee·ship
trust·ful
trust·ful·ly
trust·ful·ness
trust·i·ness
trust·wor·thi·ly
trust·wor·thi·ness
trust·wor·thy
trusty
  dependable (see
  trustee)

truth·ful
truth·ful·ly
truth·ful·ness
try
  tried
  try·ing
try·out
tryst
T-shirt
tsar
  var of czar

tsu·na·mi
tub

tubbed
tub·bing
tu·ba
tub·by
tube·less
tu·ber
tu·ber·cle
tu·ber·cu·lar
tu·ber·cu·late
  or tu·ber·cu·lat·ed

tu·ber·cu·lin
tu·ber·cu·lo·sis
tu·ber·cu·lous
tube·rose
tu·ber·ous
tub·ing
tu·bu·lar
tu·bule
tuck·er
Tuc·son
Tues·day
tu·fa
tug
  tugged
  tug·ging
tug·boat
tug-of-war
  pl tugs-of-war

tu·ition
tu·la·re·mia
tu·lip
tulle
Tul·sa
tum·ble
tum·ble·down

tum·bler
tum·ble·weed
tum·bling
tum·brel
  or tum·bril
tu·mes·cence
tu·mes·cent
tu·mid
tu·mid·i·ty
tu·mor
tu·mor·i·gen·ic
tu·mor·ous
tu·mult
tu·mul·tu·ous
tun
  cask, measure (see
   ton)

tu·na
  pl tu·na *or* tu·nas

tun·able
  also tune·able

tun·dra
tune·ful
tune·ful·ly
tune·less
tun·er
tune-up
tung·sten
tu·nic
Tu·ni·sia
Tu·ni·sian
tun·nel
  tun·neled
   or tun·nelled

  tun·nel·ing
   or tun·nel·ling

tun·ny
  pl tun·nies *also*
   tun·ny

tu·pe·lo
  pl tu·pe·los

tuque
tur·ban
tur·bid
tur·bine
tur·bo
  pl tur·bos

tur·bo·fan
tur·bo·jet
tur·bo·prop
tur·bot
  pl tur·bot *also*
   tur·bots

tur·bu·lence
tur·bu·lent
tu·reen
turf
  pl turfs *or* turves

tur·gid
tur·gid·i·ty
Tur·key
tur·key
Turk·ish
tur·mer·ic
tur·moil
turn·about
turn·around
turn·buck·le
turn·coat
turn·down
turn·er
turn-in

turn·ing
tur·nip
turn·key
turn·off
turn·out
turn·over
turn·pike
turn·spit
turn·stile
turn·ta·ble
tur·pen·tine
tur·pi·tude
tur·quoise
  also tur·quois

tur·ret
tur·tle
tur·tle·back
  or tur·tle-backed

tur·tle·dove
tur·tle·neck
tusk·er
tus·sle
tus·sock
tu·te·lage
tu·te·lary
tu·tor
tu·to·ri·al
tu·tu
Tu·va·lu
tux·e·do
  pl tux·e·dos *or*
  tux·e·does

tv
twad·dle
twain
twang

tweak
tweed·i·ness
tweedy
tweet·er
tweez·ers
twelfth
twelve
twelve·month
twen·ti·eth
twen·ty
twice-told
twid·dle
twig·gy
twi·light
twi·lit
twill
twin
  twinned
  twin·ning
twinge
twi-night
twin·kle
twin·kler
twin·kling
twirl·er
twist·er
twit
  twit·ted
  twit·ting
twitch
twit·ter
two-bit
two-by-four
two-di·men·sion·al
two-faced

two-fist·ed
two·fold
two-hand·ed
two-ply
two-sid·ed
two·some
two-step
two-time
two-way
ty·coon
tyke
tym·pan·ic
tym·pa·num
  pl tym·pa·na *also*
  tym·pa·nums

type·able
type·cast
type·face
type·found·ry
type·script
type·set
  type·set·ting
type·set·ter
type·write
  type·wrote
  type·writ·ten
  type·writ·ing
type·writ·er
ty·phoid
ty·phoon
ty·phus
typ·i·cal
typ·i·cal·ly
typ·i·fy
typ·ist

ty·po
pl ty·pos

ty·pog·ra·pher
ty·po·graph·ic
ty·po·graph·i·cal
ty·po·graph·i·cal·ly
ty·pog·ra·phy
ty·po·log·i·cal
ty·po·log·i·cal·ly
ty·pol·o·gy
ty·ran·ni·cal
also ty·ran·nic

ty·ran·ni·cal·ly
tyr·an·nize
tyr·an·niz·er
tyr·an·nous
tyr·an·ny
ty·rant
ty·ro
pl ty·ros

tzar
var of czar

U

ubiq·ui·tous
ubiq·ui·ty
U-boat
ud·der
Ugan·da
Ugan·dan
ug·li·ness
ug·ly
ukase

Ukraine
Ukrai·ni·an
uku·le·le
ul·cer
ul·cer·ate
ul·cer·ation
ul·cer·ous
ul·lage
ul·ster
ul·te·ri·or
ul·ti·mate
ul·ti·mate·ly
ul·ti·ma·tum
pl ul·ti·ma·tums *or*
ul·ti·ma·ta

ul·ti·mo
ul·tra
ul·tra·cen·tri·fuge
ul·tra·con·ser·va·tive
ul·tra·fash·ion·able
ul·tra·high
ul·tra·ism
ul·tra·ma·rine
ul·tra·mi·cro
ul·tra·mi·cro·scope
ul·tra·min·ia·ture
ul·tra·mod·ern
ul·tra·mon·tane
ul·tra·na·tion·al·ism
ul·tra·pure

ul·tra·short
ul·tra·son·ic
ul·tra·sound
ul·tra·vi·o·let
ul·tra vi·res
ul·u·late
ul·u·la·tion
um·bel
um·bel·late
um·ber
um·bil·i·cal
um·bi·li·cus
pl um·bi·li·ci *or*
um·bi·li·cus·es

um·bra
pl um·bras *or*
um·brae

um·brage
um·bra·geous
um·brel·la
umi·ak
um·laut
um·pire
ump·teen
un·abashed
un·abat·ed
un·able
un·abridged
un·ac·com·pa·nied
un·ac·count·able
un·ac·count·ably
un·ac·count·ed
un·ac·cus·tomed
un·adorned
un·adul·ter·at·ed

un·ad·vised
un·af·fect·ed
un·aligned
un·al·loyed
un·al·ter·able
un·al·ter·ably
un-Amer·i·can
una·nim·i·ty
unan·i·mous
un·an·swer·able
un·ap·peal·ing
un·armed
un·asked
un·as·sail·able
un·as·sail·ably
un·as·sum·ing
un·at·tached
un·avail·ing
un·avoid·able
un·avoid·ably
un·aware
un·awares
un·bal·anced
un·bar
un·bear·able
un·bear·ably
un·beat·able
un·beat·en
un·be·com·ing
un·be·known
   or un·be·knownst

un·be·lief
un·be·liev·able
un·be·liev·ably
un·be·liev·er

un·be·liev·ing
un·bend
  un·bent
un·bend·ing
un·bi·ased
un·bid·den
   also un·bid

un·bind
un·blush·ing
un·bod·ied
un·bolt
un·born
un·bo·som
un·bound·ed
un·bowed
un·braid
un·bri·dled
un·bro·ken
un·buck·le
un·bur·den
un·but·ton
un·cage
un·called-for
un·can·ni·ly
un·can·ny
un·cap
un·ceas·ing
un·cer·e·mo·ni·
  ous
un·cer·tain
un·cer·tain·ty
un·chain
un·change·able
un·change·ably
un·char·i·ta·ble

un·char·i·ta·bly
un·chart·ed
un·chris·tian
un·churched
un·cial
un·civ·il
un·civ·i·lized
un·clasp
un·clas·si·fied
un·cle
un·clean
un·clean·li·ness
un·clench
Un·cle Sam
un·cloak
un·clothe
un·coil
un·com·fort·able
un·com·fort·ably
un·com·mit·ted
un·com·mon
un·com·mu·ni·
  ca·tive
un·com·pro·mis·
  ing
un·con·cern
un·con·cerned
un·con·di·tion·al
un·con·di·tion·al·
  ly
un·con·for·mi·ty
un·con·quer·able
un·con·scio·na·
  ble
un·con·scio·na·
  bly

un·con·scious
un·con·sti·tu·
  tion·al
un·con·sti·tu·
  tion·al·i·ty
un·con·sti·tu·
  tion·al·ly
un·con·trol·la·ble
un·con·trol·la·bly
un·con·ven·tion·
  al
un·con·ven·tion·
  al·i·ty
un·con·ven·tion·
  al·ly
un·cork
un·count·ed
un·cou·ple
un·couth
un·cov·er
un·crit·i·cal
un·crit·i·cal·ly
un·cross
unc·tion
unc·tu·ous
un·curl
un·cut
un·daunt·ed
un·de·mon·stra·
  tive
un·de·ni·able
un·de·ni·ably
un·der
un·der·achiev·er
un·der·act
un·der·age

un·der·arm
un·der·bel·ly
un·der·bid
un·der·brush
un·der·car·riage
un·der·charge
un·der·class·man
un·der·clothes
un·der·cloth·ing
un·der·coat
un·der·coat·ing
un·der·cov·er
un·der·cur·rent
un·der·cut
un·der·de·vel·
  oped
un·der·dog
un·der·done
un·der·es·ti·mate
un·der·es·ti·ma·
  tion
un·der·ex·pose
un·der·ex·po·sure
un·der·foot
un·der·gar·ment
un·der·gird
un·der·glaze
un·der·go
  un·der·went
  un·der·gone
  un·der·go·ing
un·der·grad·u·ate
un·der·ground
un·der·growth
un·der·hand
un·der·hand·ed

un·der·hung
un·der·lay
  un·der·laid
  un·der·lay·ing
un·der·lie
  un·der·lay
  un·der·lain
  un·der·ly·ing
un·der·line
un·der·ling
un·der·lip
un·der·ly·ing
un·der·mine
un·der·most
un·der·neath
un·der·nour·ished
un·der·paid
un·der·pants
un·der·part
un·der·pass
un·der·pin·ning
un·der·play
un·der·priv·i·
  leged
un·der·pro·duc·
  tion
un·der·rate
un·der·score
un·der·sea
un·der·sec·re·
  tary
un·der·sell
  un·der·sold
  un·der·sell·ing
un·der·sexed
un·der·shirt

un·der·shoot
  un·der·shot
  un·der·shoot·
    ing
un·der·shorts
un·der·side
un·der·signed
  pl un·der·signed

un·der·sized
  also un·der·size

un·der·skirt
un·der·slung
un·der·stand
  un·der·stood
  un·der·stand·
    ing
un·der·stand·able
un·der·stand·ably
un·der·stand·ing
un·der·state
un·der·state·ment
un·der·stood
un·der·study
un·der·sur·face
un·der·take
  un·der·took
  un·der·tak·en
  un·der·tak·ing
un·der·tak·er
un·der·tak·ing
un·der-the-count·
  er
un·der·tone
un·der·tow
un·der·trick

un·der·val·u·a·
  tion
un·der·val·ue
un·der·wa·ter
un·der·way
un·der·wear
un·der·weight
un·der·world
un·der·write
  un·der·wrote
  un·der·writ·ten
  un·der·writ·ing
un·der·writ·er
un·de·sir·able
un·de·sir·ably
un·de·vi·at·ing
un·dies
un·do
  un·did
  un·done
  un·do·ing
un·doubt·ed
un·drape
un·dress
un·due
un·du·lant
un·du·late
un·du·la·tion
un·du·ly
un·dy·ing
un·earned
un·earth
un·eas·i·ly
un·eas·i·ness
un·easy
un·em·ploy·able

un·em·ployed
un·em·ploy·ment
un·end·ing
un·equal
un·equaled
un·equal·ly
un·equiv·o·cal
un·e·quiv·o·cal·ly
un·err·ing
un·es·sen·tial
un·even
un·event·ful
un·ex·am·pled
un·ex·cep·tion·
  able
un·ex·pect·ed
un·fail·ing
un·fair
un·faith·ful
un·faith·ful·ly
un·fa·mil·iar
un·fa·mil·iar·i·ty
un·fas·ten
un·fa·vor·able
un·fa·vor·ably
un·feel·ing
un·feigned
un·fet·ter
un·fit
un·flap·pa·ble
un·flinch·ing
un·fold
un·for·get·ta·ble
un·for·get·ta·bly
un·formed
un·for·tu·nate

un·found·ed
un·fre·quent·ed
un·friend·li·ness
un·friend·ly
un·frock
un·fruit·ful
un·furl
un·gain·li·ness
un·gain·ly
un·gen·er·ous
un·gird
un·god·li·ness
un·god·ly
un·gov·ern·able
un·grace·ful
un·grace·ful·ly
un·gra·cious
un·grate·ful
un·grate·ful·ly
un·guard·ed
un·guent
un·gu·late
un·hand
un·hap·pi·ly
un·hap·pi·ness
un·hap·py
un·healthy
un·heard
un·heard-of
un·hinge
un·hitch
un·hook
un·horse
un·hur·ried
uni·cam·er·al
uni·cel·lu·lar

uni·corn
uni·cy·cle
uni·di·rec·tion·al
uni·fi·able
uni·fi·ca·tion
uni·fi·er
uni·form
uni·for·mi·ty
uni·fy
uni·lat·er·al
uni·lat·er·al·ly
un·im·peach·able
un·im·peach·ably
un·in·hib·it·ed
un·in·tel·li·gent
un·in·tel·li·gi·ble
un·in·tel·li·gi·bly
un·in·ten·tion·al
un·in·ten·tion·al·
  ly
un·in·ter·rupt·ed
union
union·ism
union·iza·tion
union·ize
Union of So·vi·et
  So·cial·ist Re·
  pub·lics
unique
uni·sex
uni·son
unit
uni·tar·i·an
uni·tary
unite
unit·ed

Unit·ed Ar·ab
  Emir·ates
Unit·ed King·dom
Unit·ed Na·tions
Unit·ed States of
  Amer·i·ca
uni·ty
uni·ver·sal
Uni·ver·sal·ist
uni·ver·sal·i·ty
uni·ver·sal·ize
uni·ver·sal·ly
uni·verse
uni·ver·si·ty
un·just
un·kempt
un·kind
un·know·ing
un·known
un·lace
un·lade
un·latch
un·law·ful
un·law·ful·ly
un·learn
un·learned
un·leash
un·less
un·let·tered
un·like
un·like·li·hood
un·like·li·ness
un·like·ly
un·lim·ber
un·lim·it·ed
un·list·ed

un·load
un·lock
un·looked-for
un·loose
un·loos·en
un·love·ly
un·luck·i·ly
un·luck·i·ness
un·lucky
un·make
  un·made
  un·mak·ing
un·man
un·man·ly
un·man·ner·ly
un·mask
un·men·tion·able
un·mer·ci·ful
un·mer·ci·ful·ly
un·mind·ful
un·mis·tak·able
un·mis·tak·ably
un·mit·i·gat·ed
un·moor
un·muf·fle
un·muz·zle
un·nail
un·nat·u·ral
un·nat·u·ral·ly
un·nec·es·sar·i·ly
un·nec·es·sary
un·nerve
un·num·bered
un·ob·tru·sive
un·oc·cu·pied
un·or·ga·nized

un·or·tho·dox
un·pack
un·par·al·leled
un·peg
un·per·son
un·pile
un·pin
un·pleas·ant
un·plumbed
un·pop·u·lar
un·pop·u·lar·i·ty
un·prec·e·dent·ed
un·pre·dict·abil·
  i·ty
un·pre·dict·able
un·pre·dict·ably
un·prej·u·diced
un·pre·ten·tious
un·prin·ci·pled
un·print·able
un·prof·it·able
un·prof·it·ably
un·prom·is·ing
un·qual·i·fied
un·ques·tion·able
un·ques·tion·ably
un·ques·tion·ing
un·quote
un·rav·el
un·read
un·read·i·ness
un·ready
un·re·al
un·re·al·is·tic
un·re·al·is·ti·cal·
  ly

un·re·al·i·ty
un·rea·son·able
un·rea·son·ably
un·rea·son·ing
un·re·con·struct·
  ed
un·reel
un·re·gen·er·ate
un·re·lent·ing
un·re·mit·ting
un·re·served
un·rest
un·re·strained
un·rid·dle
un·righ·teous
un·ripe
un·ri·valed
  or un·ri·valled

un·robe
un·roll
un·ruf·fled
un·rul·i·ness
un·ruly
un·sad·dle
un·sat·u·rat·ed
un·sa·vory
un·scathed
un·schooled
un·sci·en·tif·ic
un·sci·en·tif·i·
  cal·ly
un·scram·ble
un·screw
un·scru·pu·lous
un·seal

un·search·able
un·sea·son·able
un·sea·son·ably
un·seat
un·seem·ly
un·seen
un·seg·re·gat·ed
un·self·ish
un·set·tle
un·set·tled
un·shack·le
un·shaped
un·sheathe
un·shod
un·sight·ly
un·skilled
un·skill·ful
un·sling
  un·slung
  un·sling·ing
un·snap
un·snarl
un·so·phis·ti·cat·
  ed
un·sought
un·sound
un·spar·ing
un·speak·able
un·speak·ably
un·spot·ted
un·sta·ble
un·stead·i·ly
un·stead·i·ness
un·steady
un·stop
un·strap

un·stressed
un·string
  un·strung
  un·string·ing
un·stud·ied
un·sub·stan·tial
un·suc·cess·ful
un·suc·cess·ful·ly
un·suit·able
un·suit·ably
un·sung
un·tan·gle
un·taught
un·think·able
un·think·ing
un·thought
un·ti·dy
un·tie
  un·tied
  un·ty·ing
  or un·tie·ing

un·til
un·time·li·ness
un·time·ly
un·ti·tled
un·to
un·told
un·touch·abil·i·ty
un·touch·able
un·to·ward
un·tried
un·true
un·truth
un·truth·ful
un·truth·ful·ly

un·tu·tored
un·twist
un·used
un·usu·al
un·usu·al·ly
un·ut·ter·able
un·ut·ter·ably
un·var·nished
un·veil
un·voiced
un·war·rant·able
un·wary
un·washed
un·weave
  un·wove
  or un·weaved

  un·wo·ven
  or un·weaved

  un·weav·ing
un·well
un·whole·some
un·wield·i·ness
un·wieldy
un·will·ing
un·wind
  un·wound
  un·wind·ing
un·wise
un·wit·ting
un·world·li·ness
un·world·ly
un·wor·thi·ly
un·wor·thi·ness
un·wor·thy
un·wrap

un·writ·ten
un·yield·ing
un·yoke
un·zip
up-and-down
up·beat
up·braid
up·bring·ing
up·com·ing
up-coun·try
up·date
up·draft
up·end
up·grade
up·growth
up·heav·al
up·hill
up·hold
  up·held
  up·hold·ing
up·hol·ster
up·hol·ster·er
up·hol·stery
up·keep
up·land
up·lift
up·most
up·on
up·per
up·per·case
up·per-class
up·per·class·man
up·per·cut
up·per·most
Up·per Vol·ta
Up·per Vol·tan

up·pish
up·pi·ty
up·right
up·ris·ing
up·roar
up·roar·i·ous
up·root
up·set
  up·set
  up·set·ting
up·shot
up·side down
up·stage
up·stairs
up·stand·ing
up·start
up·state
up·stream
up·stroke
up·surge
up·swept
up·swing
up·take
up-tem·po
up·thrust
up·tight
up-to-date
up·town
up·trend
up·turn
up·ward
  or up·wards
up·wind
ura·ni·um
ur·ban
  of the city

ur·bane
  polished

ur·ban·ism
ur·ban·ite
ur·ban·i·ty
ur·ban·iza·tion
ur·ban·ize
ur·chin
urea
ure·mia
ure·ter
ure·thra
  pl ure·thras *or*
  ure·thrae

urge
ur·gen·cy
ur·gent
uric
uri·nal
uri·nal·y·sis
uri·nary
uri·nate
uri·na·tion
urine
urn
uro·log·ic
  or uro·log·i·cal

urol·o·gist
urol·o·gy
ur·sine
Ur·u·guay
Uru·guay·an
us·abil·i·ty
us·able
  also use·able

us·age
use
  used
  us·ing
use·ful
use·ful·ly
use·less
us·er
ush·er
usu·al
usu·al·ly
usu·fruct
usu·rer
usu·ri·ous
usurp
usur·pa·tion
usurp·er
usu·ry
Utah
uten·sil
uter·ine
uter·us
  pl uteri *also*
    uter·us·es

utile
util·i·tar·i·an
util·i·tar·i·an·
  ism
util·i·ty
uti·liz·able
uti·li·za·tion
uti·lize
ut·most
uto·pia
uto·pi·an
ut·ter

ut·ter·ance
ut·ter·most
uvu·la
  pl uvu·las *or*
    uvu·lae

ux·o·ri·ous

V

va·can·cy
va·cant
va·cate
va·ca·tion
va·ca·tion·er
vac·ci·nate
vac·ci·na·tion
vac·cine
vac·il·late
vac·il·la·tion
vac·il·la·tor
va·cu·ity
vac·u·ole
vac·u·ous
vac·u·um
  pl vac·u·ums *or*
    vac·ua

vac·u·um-packed
va·de me·cum
  pl va·de me·cums

vag·a·bond
vag·a·bond·age
va·ga·ry
va·gi·na
  pl va·gi·nae *or*
    va·gi·nas

va·gran·cy

va·grant
vague
vague·ly
vail
  let fall (see vale, veil)

vain
  futile, conceited
    (*see* vane, vein)

vain·glo·ri·ous
vain·glo·ry
va·lance
  drapery (see
    valence)

vale
  valley (see vail, veil)

vale·dic·tion
vale·dic·to·ri·an
vale·dic·to·ry
va·lence
  chem (see valance)

Va·len·ci·ennes
val·en·tine
va·let
val·e·tu·di·nar·i·
  an
Val·hal·la
val·iant
val·id
val·i·date
val·i·da·tion
va·lid·i·ty
va·lise
val·ley
  pl val·leys

val·or
val·o·ri·za·tion

val·o·rize
val·or·ous
val·u·able
val·u·ably
val·u·a·tion
val·ue
val·ued
val·ue·less
va·lu·ta
valve
val·vu·lar
vam·pire
Van·cou·ver
van·dal
van·dal·ism
van·dal·ize
Van·dyke
vane
   wind indicator (see vain, vein)

van·guard
va·nil·la
van·ish
van·i·ty
van·quish
van·quish·able
van·tage
va·pid
va·pid·i·ty
va·por
va·por·iza·tion
va·por·ize
va·por·iz·er
va·por·ous
va·que·ro
vari·abil·i·ty

vari·able
vari·ably
vari·ance
vari·ant
vari·a·tion
vari·col·ored
var·i·cose
var·i·cos·i·ty
var·ied
var·ie·gate
var·ie·ga·tion
va·ri·etal
va·ri·etal·ly
va·ri·ety
var·i·o·rum
var·i·ous
var·mint
var·nish
var·si·ty
vary
vas·cu·lar
vas def·er·ens
   pl va·sa def·er·en·tia

va·sec·to·my
Vas·e·line
vaso·mo·tor
vas·sal
vas·sal·age
vast·ness
vat-dyed
Vat·i·can
vaude·ville
vaude·vil·lian
vault·ed
vault·ing

vaunt
V-day
vec·tor
veer
veg·e·ta·ble
veg·e·tal
veg·e·tar·i·an
veg·e·tate
veg·e·ta·tion
veg·e·ta·tive
ve·he·mence
ve·he·ment
ve·hi·cle
ve·hic·u·lar
V-8
veil
   screen (see vale, vail)

veil·ing
vein
   blood vessel, mood (see vain, vane)

vel·lum
ve·loc·i·pede
ve·loc·i·ty
ve·lour
   or ve·lours
   pl ve·lours

vel·vet
vel·ve·teen
vel·vety
ve·nal
   mercenary (see venial)

ve·nal·i·ty
ve·nal·ly
vend·ee

ven·det·ta
vend·ible
  or vend·able

ven·dor
ve·neer
ven·er·a·ble
ven·er·ate
ven·er·a·tion
ve·ne·re·al
ven·ery
Ven·e·zu·e·la
Ven·e·zu·e·lan
ven·geance
venge·ful
venge·ful·ly
ve·nial
  excusable (see
  venal)

ve·ni·re
ve·ni·re·man
ven·i·son
ven·om
ven·om·ous
ve·nous
ven·ti·late
ven·ti·la·tion
ven·ti·la·tor
ven·tral
ven·tral·ly
ven·tri·cle
ven·tril·o·quism
ven·tril·o·quist
ven·ture
ven·ture·some
ven·tur·ous
ven·ue

ve·ra·cious
  truthful (see
  voracious)

ve·rac·i·ty
ve·ran·da
  or ve·ran·dah

ver·bal
ver·bal·iza·tion
ver·bal·ize
ver·bal·ly
ver·ba·tim
ver·be·na
ver·biage
ver·bose
ver·bos·i·ty
ver·bo·ten
ver·dant
ver·dict
ver·di·gris
ver·dure
verge
ver·i·fi·able
ver·i·fi·ca·tion
ver·i·fi·er
ver·i·fy
ver·i·ly
veri·si·mil·i·tude
ver·i·ta·ble
ver·i·ta·bly
ver·i·ty
ver·meil
ver·mi·cel·li
ver·mi·form
ver·mi·fuge
ver·mil·ion
  or ver·mil·lion

ver·min
  pl ver·min

Ver·mont
ver·mouth
ver·nac·u·lar
ver·nal
ver·ni·er
ver·sa·tile
ver·sa·til·i·ty
ver·si·cle
ver·si·fi·ca·tion
ver·si·fy
ver·sion
ver·so
  pl ver·sos

ver·sus
ver·te·bra
  pl ver·te·brae *or*
  ver·te·bras

ver·te·bral
ver·te·brate
ver·tex
  pl ver·ti·ces *also*
  ver·tex·es

ver·ti·cal
ver·ti·cal·ly
ver·ti·cil·late
ver·tig·i·nous
ver·ti·go
  pl ver·ti·goes

ver·vain
verve
very
ves·i·cant
ves·i·cle
ve·sic·u·lar

ves·per
ves·pers
ves·sel
ves·tal
ves·ti·bule
ves·tige
ves·ti·gial
ves·ti·gial·ly
vest·ment
vest-pock·et
ves·try
ves·try·man
ves·ture
vetch
vet·er·an
vet·er·i·nar·i·an
vet·er·i·nary
ve·to
   pl ve·toes
ve·to·er
vex
   vexed
   also vext
   vex·ing
vex·a·tion
vex·a·tious
vi·a·bil·i·ty
vi·a·ble
vi·a·bly
vi·a·duct
vi·al
   small bottle (see
   vile, viol)
vi·and
vi·bran·cy
vi·brant

vi·bra·phone
vi·brate
vi·bra·tion
vi·bra·to
   pl vi·bra·tos

vi·bra·tor
vi·bra·to·ry
vi·bur·num
vic·ar
vic·ar·age
vi·car·i·al
vi·car·i·ate
vi·car·i·ous
vice
   depravity (see vise)

vice-chan·cel·lor
vice-con·sul
vice-pres·i·den·cy
vice-pres·i·dent
vice·roy
vice ver·sa
vi·chys·soise
vi·chy
vi·cin·i·ty
vi·cious
vi·cis·si·tude
vic·tim
vic·tim·iza·tion
vic·tim·ize
vic·tim·iz·er
vic·tor
Vic·to·ria
Vic·to·ri·an
vic·to·ri·ous
vic·to·ry

vict·ual
vi·cu·ña
   or vi·cu·na

vi·de
vid·eo
vid·eo·tape
vie
   vied
   vy·ing
vi·er
Viet·nam
Viet·nam·ese
   pl Viet·nam·ese

view·er
view·point
vig·il
vig·i·lance
vig·i·lant
vig·i·lan·te
vig·i·lan·tism
vi·gnette
vig·or
vig·or·ous
vile
   repulsive (see vial,
   viol)

vile·ly
vil·i·fi·ca·tion
vil·i·fi·er
vil·i·fy
vil·la
vil·lage
vil·lag·er
vil·lain
vil·lain·ous
vil·lainy

vil·lous
covered with villi

vil·lus
pl vil·li
hairlike projection

vin·ai·grette
vin·ci·ble
vin·di·ca·ble
vin·di·cate
vin·di·ca·tion
vin·di·ca·tor
vin·di·ca·to·ry
vin·dic·tive
vin·dic·tive·ly
vin·e·gar
vin·e·gary
vine·yard
vi·ni·cul·ture
vi·nous
vin·tage
vint·ner
vi·nyl
vi·ol
musical instrument
(see vial, vile)

vi·o·la
vi·o·la·ble
vi·o·late
vi·o·la·tion
vi·o·la·tor
vi·o·lence
vi·o·lent
vi·o·let
vi·o·lin
vi·o·lin·ist
vi·o·list

vi·o·lon·cel·list
vi·o·lon·cel·lo
vi·os·ter·ol
VIP
vi·per
vi·per·ous
vi·ra·go
pl vi·ra·goes *or*
vi·ra·gos

vi·ral
vir·eo
pl vir·e·os

vir·gin
vir·gin·al
vir·gin·al·ly
Vir·gin·ia
Vir·gin·ia Beach
vir·gin·i·ty
vir·gule
vir·ile
vi·ril·i·ty
vi·rol·o·gist
vi·rol·o·gy
vir·tu
objets d'art (see
virtue)

vir·tu·al
vir·tu·al·ly
vir·tue
goodness (see virtu)

vir·tu·os·i·ty
vir·tu·o·so
pl vir·tu·o·sos *or*
vir·tu·o·si

vir·tu·ous

vir·u·lence
or vir·u·len·cy

vir·u·lent
vi·rus
vi·sa
vi·saed
vi·sa·ing
vis·age
vis-à-vis
pl vis-à-vis

vis·cer·al
vis·cer·al·ly
vis·cid
vis·cid·i·ty
vis·co·elas·tic
vis·cose
vis·cos·i·ty
vis·cous
thick

vis·cus
pl vis·cera
body organ

vise
clamp (see vice)

vis·i·bil·i·ty
vis·i·ble
vis·i·bly
vi·sion
vi·sion·ary
vis·it
vis·i·tant
vis·i·ta·tion
vis·i·tor
vi·sor
vis·ta

vi·su·al
vi·su·al·iza·tion
vi·su·al·ize
vi·su·al·iz·er
vi·su·al·ly
vi·ta
   pl vi·tae
vi·tal
vi·tal·i·ty
vi·tal·iza·tion
vi·tal·ize
vi·tal·ly
vi·tals
vi·ta·min
vi·ti·ate
vi·ti·a·tion
vi·ti·a·tor
vi·ti·cul·ture
vit·re·ous
vit·ri·fi·ca·tion
vit·ri·fy
vit·ri·ol
vit·ri·ol·ic
vit·tles
vi·tu·per·ate
vi·tu·per·a·tion
vi·tu·per·a·tive
vi·va
vi·va·ce
vi·va·cious
vi·vac·i·ty
vi·va vo·ce
vi·var·i·um
   pl vi·var·ia *or*
   vi·var·i·ums
viv·id

viv·i·fi·ca·tion
viv·i·fi·er
viv·i·fy
vi·vip·a·rous
vivi·sect
vivi·sec·tion
vix·en
viz·ard
vi·zier
vo·ca·ble
vo·cab·u·lary
vo·cal
vo·cal·ic
vo·cal·ist
vo·cal·ize
vo·cal·ly
vo·ca·tion
voc·a·tive
vo·cif·er·ate
vo·cif·er·ous
vod·ka
vogue
vogu·ish
voiced
voice·less
void·able
void·er
voile
vol·a·tile
vol·a·til·i·ty
vol·ca·nic
vol·ca·nism
vol·ca·no
   pl vol·ca·noes *or*
   vol·ca·nos
vo·li·tion

vol·ley
vol·ley·ball
volt·age
vol·ta·ic
vol·ta·me·ter
volt-am·pere
volt·me·ter
vol·u·bil·i·ty
vol·u·ble
vol·u·bly
vol·ume
vol·u·met·ric
vo·lu·mi·nous
vol·un·ta·ri·ly
vol·un·tary
vol·un·teer
vo·lup·tu·ary
vo·lup·tuous
vo·lute
vom·it
voo·doo
vo·ra·cious
   insatiable (see
   veracious)
vo·rac·i·ty
vor·tex
   pl vor·ti·ces *also*
   vor·tex·es
vor·ti·cal
vo·ta·ry
vot·er
vo·tive
vouch·er
vouch·safe
vow·el

vox po·pu·li
voy·age
voy·ag·er
voy·eur
vul·ca·ni·za·tion
vul·can·ize
vul·can·iz·er
vul·gar
vul·gar·i·an
vul·gar·ism
vul·gar·i·ty
vul·gar·iza·tion
vul·gar·ize
vul·gar·iz·er
vul·ner·a·bil·i·ty
vul·ner·a·ble
vul·ner·a·bly
vul·ture
vul·tur·ous
vul·va
   pl vul·vae

W

wad
  wad·ded
  wad·ding
wad·able
  or wade·able

wad·ding
wad·dle
wad·er
wa·di
wa·fer
waf·fle
waft

wag
  wagged
  wag·ging
wa·ger
wa·ger·er
wag·gery
wag·gish
wag·gle
wag·gly
wag·on
wag·on·ette
wa·gon-lit
  pl wa·gons-lits *or*
    wa·gon-lits

wa·hi·ne
wa·hoo
  pl wa·hoos

waif
wail
  cry (see wale, whale)

wain·scot
  wain·scot·ed
   or wain·scot·ted

  wain·scot·ing
   or wain·scot·ting

wain·wright
waist
  middle (see waste)

waist·band
waist·coat
waist·line
wait·er
wait·ress
waive
  give up (see wave)

waiv·er
wake
  waked
   or woke

  waked
   or wo·ken

  wak·ing
wake·ful
wak·en
wale
  ridge, texture (see
   wail, whale)

walk·away
walk·er
walk·ie-talk·ie
walk-in
walk-on
walk·out
walk·over
walk-up
walk·way
wal·la·by
wall·board
wal·let
wall·eye
wall·flow·er
wal·lop
wal·lop·ing
wal·low
wall·pa·per
wal·nut
wal·rus
  pl wal·rus *or*
   wal·rus·es

waltz
wam·pum

wan
  wanned
  wan·ning
wan·der
wan·der·lust
wan·gle
wan·i·gan
  or wan·ni·gan
want·ing
wan·ton
wan·ton·ness
wa·pi·ti
  pl wa·pi·ti *or*
  wa·pi·tis

wap·per-jawed
war
  warred
  war·ring
war·ble
war·bler
war·bon·net
war·den
ward·er
ward·robe
ward·room
ware·house
war·fare
war·head
war-horse
wari·ly
wari·ness
war·like
war·lock
war·lord
warm-blood·ed
warmed-over

warm·heart·ed
war·mon·ger
warmth
warm-up
warn·ing
warp
war·path
war·plane
war·rant
war·rant·able
war·ran·tor
war·ran·ty
war·ren
war·rior
war·ship
wart
war·time
wary
wash·able
wash·ba·sin
wash·board
wash·bowl
wash·cloth
washed-out
wash·er
wash·er·wom·an
wash·house
wash·ing
Wash·ing·ton
wash·out
wash·room
wash·stand
wash·tub
washy
wasp·ish
was·sail

wast·age
waste
  refuse (see waist)

waste·bas·ket
wast·ed
waste·ful
waste·ful·ly
waste·land
waste·pa·per
wast·rel
watch·band
watch·case
watch·dog
watch·ful
watch·ful·ly
watch·mak·er
watch·mak·ing
watch·man
watch·tow·er
watch·word
wa·ter
wa·ter·borne
Wa·ter·bury
wa·ter·col·or
wa·ter-cool
wa·ter·course
wa·ter·craft
wa·ter·cress
wa·ter·fall
wa·ter-fast
wa·ter·fowl
wa·ter·front
wa·ter·i·ness
wa·ter·leaf
  pl wa·ter·leafs

wa·ter·less
wa·ter·line
wa·ter·logged
wa·ter·loo
   pl wa·ter·loos

wa·ter·mark
wa·ter·mel·on
wa·ter·pow·er
wa·ter·proof
wa·ter-re·pel·lent
wa·ter-re·sis·tant
wa·ter·scape
wa·ter·shed
wa·ter·side
wa·ter-ski
wa·ter-ski·er
wa·ter-soak
wa·ter·spout
wa·ter·tight
wa·ter·way
wa·ter·wheel
wa·ter·works
wa·ter·worn
wa·tery
watt·age
watt-hour
wat·tle
watt·me·ter
wave
   flutter, sea swell
   (see waive*)*

wave·length
wave·let
wa·ver
wav·i·ly
wav·i·ness

wavy
wax·en
wax·i·ness
wax·ing
wax·wing
wax·work
waxy
way
   route, method (see
   weigh, whey*)*

way·bill
way·far·er
way·far·ing
way·lay
   way·laid
   way·lay·ing
way-out
way·side
way·ward
weak·en
weak·fish
weak·heart·ed
weak-kneed
weak·ling
weak·ly
weak·mind·ed
weak·ness
weal
   well-being, welt (see
   wheal, wheel*)*

wealth·i·ly
wealth·i·ness
wealthy
wean
weap·on
weap·on·ry

wear
   wore
   worn
   wear·ing
wear·able
wear·er
wea·ri·ly
wea·ri·ness
wea·ri·some
wea·ry
wea·sel
weath·er
   atmospheric
   conditions (see
   whether*)*

weath·er·abil·i·ty
weath·er-beat·en
weath·er·board
weath·er-bound
weath·er·cock
weath·er·glass
weath·er·ing
weath·er·man
weath·er·proof
weath·er-strip
weath·er-wise
weath·er·worn
weave
   wove
    or weaved

   wo·ven
    or weaved

   weav·ing
weav·er
web
   webbed

web·bing
web-foot·ed
wed
   wed·ded
    also wed

   wed·ding
wedge
Wedg·ies
wed·lock
Wednes·day
weed·er
weedy
week·day
week·end
week·ly
wee·ny
   also ween·sy

weep
   wept
   weep·ing
weep·er
weepy
wee·vil
weigh
   measure weight
    (see way, whey)

weight·i·ly
weight·i·ness
weight·less
weighty
weird
wel·come
weld·er
weld·ment
wel·fare
wel·far·ism

well
   bet·ter
   best
well-ad·vised
well-ap·point·ed
well-be·ing
well-be·loved
well·born
well-bred
well-con·di·tioned
well-de·fined
well-dis·posed
well-done
well-fa·vored
well-fixed
well-found·ed
well-groomed
well-ground·ed
well-han·dled
well·head
well-heeled
well-knit
well-known
well-mean·ing
well-nigh
well-off
well-or·dered
well-read
well-set
well-spo·ken
well·spring
well-thought-of
well-timed
well-to-do
well-turned
well-wish·er

well-worn
wel·ter
wel·ter·weight
welt·schmerz
wench·er
were·wolf
   pl were·wolves

wes·kit
west·bound
west·er·ly
west·ern
West·ern·er
west·ern·iza·tion
west·ern·ize
West·ern Sa·moa
West Vir·gin·ia
wet
   moist (see whet)

   wet·ter
   wet·test
wet
   wet
    or wet·ted

   wet·ting
wet·back
wet·land
wet·ness
wet·tish
whale
   sea animal (see
    wail, wale)

whale·back
whale·boat
whale·bone
whal·er

wharf
   pl **wharves** *also*
      wharfs

wharf·age
wharf·in·ger
what·ev·er
what·not
what·so·ev·er
wheal
   skin welt (see
      weal, wheel)

wheat
whee·dle
wheel
   disk (see weal, wheal)

wheel·bar·row
wheel·base
wheel·chair
wheel·er
wheel·er-deal·er
wheel·horse
wheel·house
wheel·wright
wheeze
wheez·i·ly
wheez·i·ness
wheezy
whelp
whence
when·ev·er
when·so·ev·er
where·abouts
   also where·about

where·as
where·at
where·by

where·fore
where·from
where·in
where·of
where·on
where·so·ev·er
where·to
where·up·on
wher·ev·er
where·with
where·with·al
wher·ry
whet
   sharpen (see wet)

whet·ted
whet·ting
wheth·er
   if (see weather)

whet·stone
whey
   watery part of milk
      (see way, weigh)

which·ev·er
which·so·ev·er
whiff
while
   time (see wile)

whim
whim·per
whim·si·cal
whim·si·cal·i·ty
whim·si·cal·ly
whim·sy
   or whim·sey

whine
   cry (see wine)

whin·er
whin·ny
whip
   whipped
   whip·ping
whip·cord
whip·lash
whip·per·snap·
   per
whip·pet
whip·poor·will
whip·saw
whip·stitch
whip·stock
whip·worm
whir
   also whirr

   whirred
   whir·ring
whirl
whirl·i·gig
whirl·pool
whirl·wind
whirly·bird
whisk
whisk·er
whis·key
   or whis·ky

whis·per
whis·tle
whis·tler
whis·tle-stop
whis·tling
whit
   bit (see wit)

white·bait
white·cap
white-col·lar
white·face
white-faced
white·fish
White·hall
white-hot
white-liv·ered
whit·en·er
white·ness
whit·en·ing
white·wall
white·wash
whith·er
   where (*see* wither)

whith·er·so·ev·er
whit·ing
whit·ish
whit·tle
whiz
   or whizz

   whizzed
   whiz·zing
whiz
   or whizz
   pl whiz·zes

whiz·zer
who·dun·it
   or who·dun·nit

who·ev·er
whole·heart·ed
whole·ness
whole·sale
whole·sal·er

whole·some
whol·ly
whom·ev·er
whom·so·ev·er
whoop-de-do
   or whoop-de-doo

whoop·ee
whoop·la
whop·per
whop·ping
whore
whorl
who·so·ev·er
Wich·i·ta
Wich·i·ta Falls
wick·ed
wick·er
wick·er·work
wick·et
wick·i·up
wide-an·gle
wide-awake
wide-eyed
wid·en
wide-mouthed
wide·spread
wid·geon
   also wi·geon

wid·get
wid·ish
wid·ow
wid·ow·er
width
wield
wieldy

wie·ner
wife
   pl wives

wife·less
wife·li·ness
wife·ly
wig·an
wig·gle
wig·gly
wig·let
wig·mak·er
wig·wag
wig·wam
wil·co
wild·cat
   wild·cat·ted
   wild·cat·ting
wild·cat·ter
wil·de·beest
wil·der·ness
wild-eyed
wild·fire
wild·fowl
wild·life
wild·wood
wile
   trick (*see* while)

wil·i·ly
wil·i·ness
will·ful
   or wil·ful

will·ful·ly
wil·lies
will·ing
wil·li·waw

will-o'-the-wisp
wil·low
wil·low·ware
wil·lowy
will·pow·er
wil·ly-nil·ly
wily
wim·ple
win
  won
  win·ning
wince
wind
  detect by scent, rest

  wind·ed
  wind·ing
wind
  blow, sound

  wind·ed
   or wound

  wind·ing
wind
  bend

  wound
   also wind·ed

  wind·ing
wind·age
wind·bag
wind·blown
wind·break
wind·burn
wind·er
wind·fall
wind·i·ly
wind·i·ness

wind·ing-sheet
wind·jam·mer
wind·lass
  machine

wind·less
  without wind

wind·mill
win·dow
win·dow-dress
win·dow·pane
win·dow-shop
win·dow-shop·per
win·dow·sill
wind·pipe
wind·proof
wind·row
wind·shield
Wind·sor
wind·storm
wind·swept
wind·up
wind·ward
wind-wing
windy
wine
  beverage (see whine)

wine·glass
wine·grow·er
wine·press
win·ery
wine·shop
wine·skin
wing·back
wing·ding
wing-foot·ed

wing·span
wing·spread
win·kle
win·na·ble
win·ner
win·ning
Win·ni·peg
win·now
win·some
Win·ston-Sa·lem
win·ter
win·ter·green
win·ter·iza·tion
win·ter·ize
win·ter·tide
win·ter·time
win·try
  or win·tery

wip·er
wir·able
wire·draw
wire·hair
wire·haired
wire·less
Wire·pho·to
wire-pull·er
wir·er
wire·tap
wire·work
wire·worm
wir·i·ness
wir·ing
wiry
Wis·con·sin
wis·dom

wise·acre
wise·crack
wise·ly
wish·bone
wish·ful
wish·ful·ly
wishy-washy
wispy
wis·te·ria
  or wis·tar·ia

wist·ful
wist·ful·ly
wit
  ingenuity (see whit)

witch·craft
witch·ery
witch-hunt
witch·ing
with·al
with·draw
  with·drew
  with·drawn
  with·draw·ing
with·draw·al
with·drawn
with·er
  dry up (see whither)

with·ers
with·hold
  with·held
  with·hold·ing
with·in
with·out
with·stand
  with·stood

with·stand·ing
wit·less
wit·ness
wit·ti·cism
wit·ti·ly
wit·ti·ness
wit·ty
wiz·ard
wiz·ard·ry
wiz·en
wob·ble
wob·bly
woe·be·gone
woe·ful
  also wo·ful

woe·ful·ly
wolf
  pl wolves *also*
    wolf

wolf·hound
wol·ver·ine
wom·an
  pl wom·en

wom·an·hood
wom·an·ish
wom·an·kind
wom·an·li·ness
wom·an·ly
womb
wom·en·folk
  also wom·en·folks

won
  pl won
  currency

won·der
won·der·ful

won·der·ful·ly
won·der·land
won·der·ment
won·der-work·er
won·drous
wood·bin
wood·bine
wood-carv·er
wood·chuck
wood·cock
wood·craft
wood·cut
wood·cut·ter
wood·ed
wood·en
wood·en·head
wood·en·ware
wood·land
wood·peck·er
wood·pile
wood·shed
woods·man
woodsy
wood·wind
wood·work
woody
woo·er
woof·er
wool·en
  or wool·len

wool·gath·er·ing
wool·li·ness
wool·ly
  also wooly

wool·ly-head·ed

wool·pack
woo·zi·ly
woo·zi·ness
woo·zy
Worces·ter
word·age
word·book
word·i·ly
word·i·ness
word·ing
word·less
word·mon·ger
word-of-mouth
word·play
wordy
work
  worked
   or wrought
  work·ing
work·abil·i·ty
work·able
work·a·day
work·bas·ket
work·bench
work·book
work·day
work·er
work·horse
work·house
work·ing·man
work·man
work·man·like
work·man·ship
work·out
work·room
work·shop

work·ta·ble
work·week
world-beat·er
world·li·ness
world·ly
world·ly-wise
world-shak·ing
world-wea·ri·ness
world·wide
worm-eat·en
worm·hole
worm·wood
worn-out
wor·ri·er
wor·ri·ment
wor·ri·some
wor·ry
wor·ry·wart
worse
wors·en
wor·ship
  wor·shiped
   or wor·shipped

  wor·ship·ing
   or wor·ship·ping

wor·ship·er
wor·ship·ful
wor·ship·ful·ly
worst
wor·sted
wor·thi·ly
wor·thi·ness
worth·less
worth·while
wor·thy

would-be
wound
wound·wort
wrack
wraith
wran·gle
wran·gler
wrap
  cover (see rap)

  wrapped
  wrap·ping
wrap·around
wrap·per
wrap·ping
wrap-up
wrath·ful
wrath·ful·ly
wreak
  inflict (see reek)

wreath
  noun

wreathe
  verb

wreck·age
wreck·er
wren
wrench
wrest
wres·tle
wres·tler
wres·tling
wretch
  miserable person (see
  retch)

wretch·ed

wrig·gle
wrig·gler
wring
   squeeze (see ring)

wrung
wring·ing
wring·er
wrin·kle
wrin·kly
wrist·band
wrist·let
wrist·lock
wrist·watch
writ
write
   wrote
   writ·ten
   also writ

   writ·ing
write-down
write-in
write-off
writ·er
write-up
writhe
wrong·do·er
wrong·do·ing
wrong·ful
wrong·ful·ly
wrong·head·ed
wrong·ly
wrought
wrung
   past of wring *(see rung)*

wry
   contorted (see rye)

wry·ly
Wy·o·ming

X

x
   x-ed
     also x'd *or* xed

   x-ing
     or x'ing

x-ax·is
X-dis·ease
xe·bec
xe·no·phobe
xe·no·pho·bia
xe·ric
xe·ro·graph·ic
xe·rog·ra·phy
xe·roph·i·lous
xe·roph·thal·mia
xe·ro·phyte
Xmas
x-ray
   verb

X ray
   noun

xy·lo·phone
xy·lo·phon·ist

Y

yacht
yacht·ing

yachts·man
ya·hoo
   pl ya·hoos

yam·mer
Yan·kee
yap
   yapped
   yap·ping
yard·age
yard·arm
yard·bird
yard·man
yard·mas·ter
yard·stick
yarn-dye
yar·row
yawl
yawn
yaws
y-ax·is
yea
year·book
year·ling
year·long
year·ly
yearn
year-round
yeasty
yel·low
yel·low-dog
yel·low·ish
yelp
Ye·men
Ye·me·ni
Ye·men·ite

yen
pl yen
currency

yen
pl yens
longing

yeo·man

ye·shi·va
or ye·shi·vah
pl ye·shi·vas *or*
ye·shi·voth

yes-man

yes·ter·day

yes·ter·year

yew
tree (see ewe)

yield

yield·ing

yo·del
yo·deled
or yo·delled

yo·del·ing
or yo·del·ling

yo·del·er

yo·ga

yo·gi
or yo·gin

yo·gurt
or yo·ghurt

yoke
couple (see yolk)

yo·kel

yolk
yellow of eggs (see
yoke)

Yom Kip·pur

yon·der

Yon·kers

youn·ger

young·ish

young·ster

Youngs·town

your·self

your·selves

youth·ful

youth·ful·ly

yowl

yo-yo
pl yo-yos

yu·an
pl yu·an

yuc·ca

Yu·go·slav

Yu·go·sla·via

Yu·go·sla·vi·an

Yu·kon

yule·tide

Z

Zaire

Zam·bia

Zam·bi·an

za·ni·ly

za·ni·ness

zany

zar·zue·la

z-ax·is

zeal

zeal·ot

zeal·ous

ze·bra
pl ze·bras *also* ze·bra

zeit·geist

Zen

ze·nith

ze·o·lite

zeph·yr

zep·pe·lin

ze·ro
pl ze·ros *also* ze·roes

zest·ful

zest·ful·ly

zig·zag
zig·zagged
zig·zag·ging

zil·lion

Zim·bab·we Rho·
de·sia

zinc
zinced
or zincked

zinc·ing
or zinck·ing

zin·nia

Zi·on·ism

zip
zipped
zip·ping

zip·per

zip·py

zir·con

zith·er

zlo·ty
pl zlo·tys *also* zlo·ty

zo·di·ac

zo·di·a·cal

zom·bie
    also zom·bi

zon·al

zon·al·ly

zoo

zoo·ge·og·ra·pher

zoo·ge·o·graph·ic
    or zoo·ge·o·graph·i·
    cal

zoo·ge·o·graph·i·
    cal·ly

zoo·ge·og·ra·phy

zoo·log·i·cal
    also zoo·log·ic

zoo·log·i·cal·ly

zo·ol·o·gist

zo·ol·o·gy

zoy·sia

zuc·chet·to

zuc·chi·ni
    pl zuc·chi·ni *or*
    zuc·chi·nis

zwie·back

zy·gote

zy·mase

zy·mol·o·gy

zy·mot·ic

zy·mur·gy

ABBREVIATIONS

Most of the abbreviations included in this list have been normalized to one form. Variation in the use of periods, in typeface, and in capitalization is frequent and widespread (as *mph*, mph, MPH, m.p.h., Mph).

a acre, alto, answer
A ace, argon, assists
AA Alcoholics Anonymous, associate in arts
AAA American Automobile Association
A and M agricultural and mechanical
ab about
AB able-bodied seaman, at bats, bachelor of arts
ABA American Bar Association
abbr abbreviation
ABC American Broadcasting Company
abl ablative
abp archbishop
abr abridged, abridgment
abs absolute
abstr abstract
ac account
Ac actinium
AC alternating current, ante Christum (*Latin*, before Christ), ante

cibum (*Latin*, before meals)
acad academic, academy
accel accelerando
acct account
ack acknowledge, acknowledgment
act active, actual
A.C.T. Australian Capital Territory
actg acting
A.D. after date, anno Domini (*Latin*, in the year of our Lord)
addn addition
addnl additional
ad int ad interim
adj adjective, adjutant
ad loc ad locum (*Latin*, to [at] the place)
adm admiral
admin administration
adv adverb, advertisement
ad val ad valorem (*Latin*, according to value)
advg advertising

advt advertisement

AEF American Expeditionary Force

aeq aequales (*Latin*, equal)

aet, aetat aetatis (*Latin*, of age)

AF air force, audio frequency

AFB air force base

afft affidavit

AFL-CIO American Federation of Labor and Congress of Industrial Organizations

Afr Africa, African

Ag argentum (*Latin*, silver)

AG adjutant general, attorney general

agcy agency

agric, agr agricultural, agriculture

agt agent

AID Agency for International Development

AK Alaska

Al aluminum

AL Alabama

Ala Alabama

ALA American Library Association, Automobile Legal Association

alc alcohol

ald alderman

alg algebra

alk alkaline

alt alternate, altitude

Alta Alberta

alter alteration

a.m. ante meridiem (*Latin*, before noon)

Am America, American, americium

AM amplitude modulation, master of arts

AMA American Medical Association

amb ambassador

amdt amendment

AME African Methodist Episcopal

Amer America, American

amp ampere

amt amount

anal analogy, analysis, analytic

anat anatomy

anc ancient

and andante

ann annals, annual

anon anonymous

ans answer

ant antonym

anthrop anthropology

a/o account of

ap apothecaries'

AP additional premium, Associated Press

APO army post office

app   apparatus, appendix
appl   applied
appnt   appointment
approx   approximate,
   approximately
appt   appoint,
   appointment
Apr   April
apt   apartment
aq   aqueous
ar   arrival, arrive
Ar   Arabic, argon
AR   Arkansas
ARC   American Red
   Cross
arch   architecture
archeol   archeology
archit   architecture
arith   arithmetic
Ariz   Arizona
Ark   Arkansas
arr   arranged, arrival,
   arrive
art   article, artificial,
   artillery
ARV   American Revised
   Version
As   arsenic
AS   Anglo-Saxon,
   antisubmarine
assn   association
assoc   associate,
   association
ASSR   Autonomous
   Soviet Socialist Republic
asst   assistant

astrol   astrology
astron   astronomer,
   astronomy
ASV   American Standard
   Version
At   astatine
Atl   Atlantic
atm   atmosphere,
   atmospheric
att   attached, attention,
   attorney
attn   attention
attrib   attributive
atty   attorney
Au   aurum (*Latin*, gold)
aud   audit, auditor
Aug   August
AUS   Army of the United
   States
Austral   Australian
auth   authentic, author,
   authorized
aux   auxiliary
av   avenue, average,
   avoirdupois
AV   ad valorem (*Latin*,
   according to value);
   audiovisual, Authorized
   Version
avdp   avoirdupois
ave   avenue
avg   average
AZ   Arizona

b   bass, book; born
B   bachelor, bishop, boron

Ba barium
BA bachelor of arts
bal balance
bar barometer
Bart baronet
BB bases on balls, best of breed
BBA bachelor of business administration
BBB Better Business Bureau
BBC British Broadcasting Corporation
bbl barrel
B.C. before Christ, British Columbia
BCS bachelor of commercial science
bd board, bound
BD bachelor of divinity, bank draft, bills discounted, brought down
bdl bundle
Be beryllium
BE bill of exchange
BEF British Expeditionary Force
Belg Belgian, Belgium
bet between
bf boldface
BF brought forward
bg bag
bhd bulkhead
Bi bismuth

bib Bible, biblical
bibliog bibliographer, bibliography
BID bis in die (*Latin*, twice a day)
biochem biochemistry
biog biographical, biography
biol biologic, biological, biology
bk bank, book
Bk berkelium
bkg banking
bkgd background
bkt basket, bracket
bl bale, blue
B/L bill of lading
bldg building
bldr builder
blk black, block
blvd boulevard
BM basal metabolism, bowel movement
B/M bill of material
BMR basal metabolic rate
BO body odor, branch office, buyer's option
BOD biochemical oxygen demand
BOQ bachelor officers' quarters
bor borough
bot botanical, botany
bp bishop, boiling point
BP bills payable, blood

pressure, British
Pharmacopoeia
bpl birthplace
BPOE Benevolent and
Protective Order of Elks
br branch, brass, brown
Br British, bromine
BR bills receivable
brig brigade, brigadier
Brit Britain, British
bro brother
bros brothers
BS bachelor of science,
balance sheet, bill of sale
BSA Boy Scouts of
America
BSc bachelor of science
bskt basket
Bt baronet
Btu British thermal unit
bu bushel
bull bulletin
bur bureau
bus business
BV Blessed Virgin
BWI British West Indies
bx box
BX base exchange

c cape, carat, cent,
centimeter, century,
chapter, circa, copyright,
cup
C carbon, centigrade
ca circa
Ca calcium

CA California, chartered
accountant, chief
accountant,
chronological age
CAF cost and freight
cal calendar, caliber,
calorie
calc calculating
Calif, Cal California
Can Canada, Canadian
Canad Canada, Canadian
canc canceled
C and F cost and freight
cap capacity, capital,
capitalize, capitalized
caps capitals, capsule
capt captain
card cardinal
CARE Co-operative for
American Remittances
to Everywhere
cat catalog
CATV community
antenna television
CBC Canadian
Broadcasting
Corporation
CBD cash before delivery
CBS Columbia
Broadcasting System
CBW chemical and
biological warfare
cc cubic centimeter
CC carbon copy
CCC Civilian
Conservation Corps

CCTV closed-circuit television
ccw counterclockwise
cd cord
Cd cadmium
cdr commander
Ce cerium
CE chemical engineer, civil engineer
cen central
cent centigrade, central, century
cert certificate, certification, certified, certify
cf confer (*Latin*, compare)
Cf californium
CF carried forward, cost and freight
CFI cost, freight, and insurance
cg, cgm centigram
CG coast guard, commanding general
ch chain, champion, chapter, church
CH clearinghouse, courthouse, customhouse
chap chapter
chem chemical, chemist, chemistry
chg change, charge
Chin Chinese
chm, chmn chairman

chron chronicle, chronological, chronology
Chron Chronicles
CI cost and insurance
cía compañía (*Spanish*, company)
cie compagnie (*French*, company)
CIF cost, insurance, and freight
C in C commander in chief
cir circle, circular
circ circular
cit citation, cited, citizen
civ civil, civilian
ck cask, check
cl class
Cl chlorine
CL carload
cld called, cleared
clk clerk
clo clothing
clr clear
cm centimeter
CM Congregation of the Mission
cml commerical
CN credit note
CNO chief of naval operations
CNS central nervous system
co company, county
c/o care of

Co cobalt
CO cash order, Colorado, commanding officer, conscientious objector
COD cash on delivery, collect on delivery
C of C Chamber of Commerce
C of S chief of staff
cog cognate
col colonel, colony, column
Col Colossians
coll college
collat collateral
colloq colloquial
Colo Colorado
com commander, commerce, commissioner, committee, common
comb combination, combining
comdg commanding
comdr commander
comdt commandant
coml commercial
comm commission, commonwealth
commo commodore
comp comparative, compiled, compiler, composition, compound
compar comparative
comr commissioner

con consul, contra (*Latin*, against)
conc concentrated
conf conference
Confed Confederate
cong congress
conj conjunction
Conn Connecticut
cons consonant
consol consolidated
const constant, constitution, constitutional
constr construction
cont containing, contents, continent, continental, continued, control
contd continued
contg containing
contr contract, contraction
contrib contribution, contributor
cor corner
Cor Corinthians
CORE Congress of Racial Equality
corp corporal, corporation
corr corrected, correction, correspondence, corresponding, corrugated
cos companies, counties
COS cash on shipment, chief of staff

cp compare, coupon
CP chemically pure, Communist party
CPA certified public accountant
cpd compound
CPFF cost plus fixed fee
cpl corporal
CPO chief petty officer
CPS cycles per second
CQ charge of quarters
cr credit, creditor, crown
Cr chromium
cresc crescendo
crit critical, criticism
cryst crystalline
cs case, cases
c/s cycles per second
Cs cesium
CS chief of staff, civil service
CSA Confederate States of America
C SS R Congregatio Sanctissimi Redemptoris (*Latin*, Congregation of the Most Holy Redeemer)
CST Central standard time
ct carat, cent, count, court
CT Central time, Connecticut
ctge cartage
ctn carton
ctr center

cu cubic
Cu cuprum (*Latin*, copper)
cum cumulative
cur currency, current
cw clockwise
CWO cash with order, chief warrant officer
cwt hundredweight
cyc cyclopedia
cycl cyclopedia
cyl cylinder
CYO Catholic Youth Organization
CZ Canal Zone

d date, daughter, day, degree, died, penny
D Democrat, Democratic, diameter, doctor, dollar, Dutch
DA days after acceptance, deposit account, district attorney, don't answer
Dan Daniel, Danish
DAR Daughters of the American Revolution
dat dative
dau daughter
db decibel
dbl double
DC da capo (*Italian*, from the beginning), decimal classification, direct current, District of

Columbia, doctor of chiropractic, double crochet

DD days after date, demand draft, dishonorable discharge, doctor of divinity

DDD direct distance dialing

DDS doctor of dental science, doctor of dental surgery

DE Delaware

dec deceased, decrease

Dec December

def definite, definition

deg degree

del delegate, delegation

Del Delaware

dely delivery

Dem Democrat, Democratic

Den Denmark

dep depart, departure, deposit, deputy

depr depreciation

dept department

deriv derivation, derivative

det detached, detachment, detail

Deut Deuteronomy

dev deviation

DEW distant early warning

DF damage free

DFC distinguished flying cross

DFM distinguished flying medal

DG Dei gratia (*Late Latin*, by the grace of God), director general

dia diameter

diag diagonal, diagram

dial dialect

diam diameter

dict dictionary

diff difference

dig digest

dil dilute

dim dimension, diminished, diminutive

dir director

disc discount

dist distance, district

distn distillation

distr distribute, distribution, distributor

div divided, dividend, division

dk dark, deck, dock

DLit doctor of letters, doctor of literature

DLitt doctor of letters, doctor of literature

DLO dead letter office

DMD doctor of dental medicine

dn down

do ditto

DOA dead on arrival

doc document
dol dollar
dom domestic, dominant, dominion
doz dozen
DP domestic prelate, double play
dpt department
dr debit, debtor, dram, drive, drum
Dr doctor
DR dead reckoning, dining room
DS dal segno (*Italian*, from the sign), days after sight
DSC distinguished service cross, doctor of surgical chiropody
DSM distinguished service medal
DSO distinguished service order
dsp decessit sine prole (*Latin*, died without issue)
DST daylight saving time
Du Dutch
dup, dupl duplicate
DV Deo volente (*Latin*, God willing), Douay Version
DVM doctor of veterinary medicine
dwt pennyweight
DX distance

dz dozen

E east, eastern, einsteinium, English, errors, excellent
ea each
E and OE errors and omissions excepted
EC east central
eccl ecclesiastic, ecclesiastical
Eccles Ecclesiastes
Ecclus Ecclesiasticus
ecol ecological, ecology
econ economics, economist, economy
Ecua Ecuador
ed edited, edition, editor, education
EDT Eastern daylight time
educ education, educational
EE electrical engineer
eff efficiency
e.g. exempli gratia (*Latin*, for example)
Eg Egypt, Egyptian
ehf extremely high frequency
el elevation
elec electric, electrical, electricity
elect electric, electrical, electricity
elem elementary

elev elevation
embryol embryology
emer emeritus
EMF electromotive force
emp emperor, empress
emu electromagnetic unit
enc enclosure
encl enclosure
ency encyclopedia
encyc encyclopedia
ENE east-northeast
eng engine, engineer, engineering
Eng England, English
engr engineer, engraved, engraving
enl enlarged, enlisted
ens ensign
entom entomology
entomol entomology
env envelope
EOM end of month
Eph Ephesians
eq equal, equation
equip equipment
equiv equivalent
ER earned runs
ERA earned run average
erron erroneous
Es einsteinium
ESE east-southeast
esp especially
ESP extrasensory perception
esq esquire

est established, estimate, estimated
EST Eastern standard time
Esth Esther
ET Eastern time
ETA estimated time of arrival
et al et alii (*Latin*, and others)
etc et cetera (*Latin*, and so forth)
ETD estimated time of departure
ethnol ethnology
et seq et sequens (*Latin*, and the following one), et sequentes *or* et sequentia (*Latin*, and those that follow)
ety etymology
Eu europium
Eur Europe, European
EV electron volt
EVA extravehicular activity
evap evaporate
ex example, express, extra
exc excellent, except
exch exchange, exchanged
ex div without dividend
exec executive, executor
Exod Exodus
exor executor

exp expense, export, exported, express
expt experiment
exptl experimental
ext extension, exterior, external, extra, extract
Ezek Ezekiel

f female, feminine, filly, focal length, folio, following, forte, frequency
F Fahrenheit, fair, false, fellow, fluorine, French, Friday, furlong
fac facsimile, faculty
FAdm fleet admiral
Fahr Fahrenheit
FAO Food and Agricultural Organization of the United Nations
FAS free alongside
fath fathom
FB freight bill
FBI Federal Bureau of Investigation
fcp foolscap
fcy fancy
FDIC Federal Deposit Insurance Corporation
Fe ferrum (*Latin*, iron)
Feb February
fec fecit (*Latin*, he [she] made it)
fed federal, federation

fedl federal
fedn federation
fem feminine
FEPC Fair Employment Practices Commission
ff folios, following
FICA Federal Insurance Contributions Act
FIFO first in, first out
fig figurative, figuratively, figure
fin finance, financial, finish
Finn Finnish
FIO free in and out
fisc fiscal
fl flourished, fluid
FL Florida
Fla Florida
Flem Flemish
fm fathom
Fm fermium
FM frequency modulation
fn footnote
fo folio
FOB free on board
FOC free of charge
fol folio
for foreign, forestry
FOR free on rail
FOS free on steamer
FOT free on truck
fp freezing point
FPC fish protein concentrate

fpm feet per minute
FPO fleet post office
fr father, friar, from
Fr francium, French, Friday
freq frequent, frequently
Fri Friday
front frontispiece
FRS Federal Reserve System
frt freight
frwy freeway
FSLIC Federal Savings and Loan Insurance Corporation
ft feet, foot, fort
fur furlong
furn furnished, furniture
fut future
fwd forward
FYI for your information

g acceleration of gravity, gauge, gram, gravity
G German, good
ga gauge
Ga gallium, Georgia
GA general agent, general assembly, general average, Georgia
Gael Gaelic
gal gallon
Gal Galatians
galv galvanized
gar garage

GAR Grand Army of the Republic
GAW guaranteed annual wage
gaz gazette, gazetteer
GB games behind, Great Britain
GCA ground-controlled approach
GCT Greenwich civil time
Gd gadolinium
gds goods
Ge germanium
gen general, genitive
Gen Genesis
genl general
geog geographic, geographical, geography
geol geologic, geological, geology
geom geometrical, geometry
ger gerund
Ger German, Germany
GHQ general headquarters
gi gill
GI general issue, government issue
Gk Greek
gloss glossary
gm gram
GM general manager
Gmc Germanic

GNP gross national product
GOP Grand Old Party (Republican)
Goth Gothic
gov governor
govt government
gox gaseous oxygen
gp group
GP general practitioner
GPO general post office, Government Printing Office
GQ general quarters
gr grade, grain, gram, gravity, gross
grad graduate
gram grammar
gro gross
GSA Girl Scouts of America
gt great, gutta (*Latin*, drop)
GT gross ton
Gt Brit Great Britain
gtd guaranteed
GU Guam

h hard, hardness, hour, husband
H hits, hydrogen
ha hectare
Hab Habakkuk
Hag Haggai
handbk handbook
Hb hemoglobin

HBM Her Britannic Majesty, His Britannic Majesty
HC Holy Communion, House of Commons
HCL high cost of living
hd head
HD heavy-duty
hdbk handbook
hdkf handkerchief
hdqrs headquarters
hdwe, hdwre hardware
He helium
HE high explosive, His Eminence, His Excellency
Heb Hebrew, Hebrews
hf half, high frequency
Hf hafnium
Hg hydrargyrum (*Latin*, mercury)
HG High German
hgt height
HH Her Highness, His Highness, His Holiness
hhd hogshead
HI Hawaii
hist historian, historical, history
HJ hic jacet (*Latin*, here lies) — used in epitaphs
HL House of Lords
HM Her Majesty, His Majesty
HMS Her Majesty's Ship, His Majesty's Ship

Ho holmium
hon honor, honorable, honorary
hor horizontal
hort horticultural, horticulture
Hos Hosea
hosp hospital
hp horsepower
HP high pressure
HQ headquarters
hr hour
HR home run, House of Representatives
HRH Her Royal Highness, His Royal Highness
HS high school, house surgeon
hse house
ht height
HT high-tension
Hung Hungarian, Hungary
HV high voltage
hvy heavy
hwy highway
hyp, hypoth hypothesis, hypothetical

I iodine, island, isle
Ia Iowa
IA Iowa
ib, ibid ibidem (*Latin*, in the same place)
IBM intercontinental ballistic missile
ICBM intercontinental ballistic missile
ICJ International Court of Justice
id idem (*Latin*, the same)
ID Idaho, identification
i.e. id est (*Latin*, that is)
IE Indo-European
IF intermediate frequency
IGY International Geophysical Year
IHP indicated horsepower
IHS Iesus Hominum Salvator (*Latin*, Jesus, Savior of Men)
IL Illinois
ill illustrated, illustration
Ill Illinois
illus, illust illustrated, illustration
ILS instrument landing system
imit imitative
imp imperative, imperfect, imperial, import, imported
imperf imperfect
in inch
In indium
IN Indiana
inc incorporated, increase
incl including, inclusive

incog incognito
incr increase
ind independent, index, industrial, industry
Ind Indiana
indef indefinite
indic indicative
inf infantry, infinitive, information
infl influenced
INP International News Photo
INRI Iesus Nazarenus Rex Iudaeorum (*Latin*, Jesus of Nazareth, King of the Jews)
ins inches, insurance
insol insoluble
insp inspector
inst instant, institute, institution
instr instructor, instrument
int interest, interior, internal, international
interj interjection
interrog interrogative
intl international
intrans intransitive
introd introduction
inv invoice
IOOF Independent Order of Odd Fellows
IP innings pitched
IPA International Phonetic Alphabet

i.q. idem quod (*Latin*, the same as)
IQ intelligence quotient
Ir iridium, Irish
IRBM intermediate range ballistic missile
Ire Ireland
irreg irregular
IRS Internal Revenue Service
Isa Isaiah
isl island
Isr Israel, Israeli
It Italian
ital italic, italicized
Ital Italian
IUCD intrauterine contraceptive device
IUD intrauterine device
IV intravenous
IWW Industrial Workers of the World

J jack, journal
Jam Jamaica
Jan January
Jap Japan, Japanese
Jas James
JCC Junior Chamber of Commerce
JCS joint chiefs of staff
jct junction
Je June
Jer Jeremiah
jg junior grade
Jn John

jnt, jt   joint
Josh   Joshua
jour   journal
JP   jet propulsion, justice of the peace
jr   junior
JRC   Junior Red Cross
Judg   Judges
Jul   July
jun   junior
Jun   June
junc   junction
juv   juvenile
JV   junior varsity

k   karat, knit
K   kalium (*Latin*, potassium), king
Kans   Kansas
kc   kilocycle
KC   king's counsel, Knights of Columbus
kc/s   kilocycles per second
KD   kiln-dried, knocked down
kg   kilogram
kgm   kilogram
KKK   Ku Klux Klan
km   kilometer
kn   knot
K of C   Knights of Columbus
KS   Kansas
kt   karat, knight
kw   kilowatt
Ky   Kentucky

KY   Kentucky

l   left, length, line, liter
L   lake, large, Latin, libra (*Latin*, pound)
La   Louisiana
LA   law agent, Los Angeles, Louisiana
Lab   Labrador
lam   laminated
Lam   Lamentations
lang   language
lat   latitude
Lat   Latin
lb   pound
LC   letter of credit, Library of Congress
LCD   lowest common denominator
lcdr   lieutenant commander
LCL   less than carload
LCM   least common multiple
ld   load, lord
LD   lethal dose
ldg   landing, loading
lect   lecture
leg   legal, legislative, legislature
legis   legislative, legislature
LEM   lunar excursion model
Lev   Leviticus
lf   low frequency

lg large
LG Low German
lge large
LGk Late Greek
LH left hand, lower half
li link
Li lithium
LI Long Island
lib liberal, librarian,
  library
lieut lieutenant
LIFO last in, first out
lin lineal, linear
liq liquid, liquor
lit liter, literal, literally,
  literary, literature
LitD doctor of letters,
  doctor of literature
lith, litho lithography
LittD doctor of letters,
  doctor of literature
Lk Luke
ll lines
LL Late Latin
LLD doctor of laws
LOB left on bases
loc cit loco citato (Latin,
  in the place cited)
log logarithm
Lond London
long longitude
loq loquitur (Latin, he
  [she] speaks)
LP low pressure
LS left side, letter signed,
  locus sigilli (Latin,

place of the seal)
lt lieutenant, light
LT long ton, low-tension
ltd limited
LTL less than truckload
ltr letter
lub lubricant, lubricating
lv leave

m male, mare, married,
  masculine, meridian,
  meridies (Latin, noon),
  meter, mile, mill,
  minute, month, moon
M master, medium, mille
  (Latin, thousand),
  Monday, monsieur
MA Massachusetts,
  master of arts, mental
  age
mach machine,
  machinery, machinist
mag magazine,
  magnetism, magneto,
  magnitude
maj major
Mal Malachi
man manual
Man Manitoba
manuf manufacture,
  manufacturing
mar maritime
Mar March
masc masculine
Mass Massachusetts
math mathematical,

mathematician, mathematics
MATS Military Air Transport Service
max maximum
mc megacycle
MC master of ceremonies, member of congress
Md Maryland
MD doctor of medicine, Maryland, months after date
mdnt midnight
mdse merchandise
Me Maine
ME Maine, mechanical engineer, Middle English, mining engineer
meas measure
mech mechanical, mechanics
med medical, medicine, medieval, medium
mem member, memoir, memorial
mer meridian
Messrs messieurs
met metropolitan
meteorol meteorology
MEV million electron volts
Mex Mexican, Mexico
mf medium frequency
MF Middle French

mfd manufactured
mfg manufacturing
mfr manufacture, manufacturer
mg milligram
Mg magnesium
MG machine gun, military government
MGk Middle Greek
mgr manager, monseigneur, monsignor
mgt management
mi mile, mill
MI Michigan, military intelligence
MIA missing in action
Mic Micah
Mich Michigan
mid middle
mil military
min minimum, mining, minister, minor, minute
mineral mineralogy
Minn Minnesota
misc miscellaneous
Miss Mississippi
mixt mixture
mk mark
Mk Mark
ML Middle Latin
MLD minimum lethal dose
Mlle mademoiselle
mm millimeter
MM Maryknoll Missioners, messieurs

Mme madame
Mn manganese
MN Minnesota
mo month
Mo Missouri,
    molybdenum
MO mail order, medical
    officer, Missouri, money
    order
mod moderate, modern
modif modification
mol molecular, molecule
mol wt molecular weight
MOM middle of month
Mon Monday
Mont Montana
mos months
mp melting point
MP member of
    parliament, metropolitan
    police, military police,
    military policeman
mpg miles per gallon
mph miles per hour
Mr mister
Mrs mistress
MS manuscript, master
    of science, Mississippi,
    motor ship
msg message
msgr monseigneur,
    monsignor
MSgt master sergeant
msl mean sea level
MSS manuscripts

MST Mountain standard
    time
mt mount, mountain
Mt Matthew
MT metric ton, Montana,
    Mountain time
mtg, mtge mortgage
mtl metal
mtn mountain
mun, munic municipal
mus museum, music
MV mean variation,
    motor vessel
mythol mythology

n net, neuter, new, noon,
    note, noun, number
N knight, nitrogen,
    normal, north,
    northern
Na natrium (*Latin*,
    sodium)
NA no account
NAACP National
    Association for the
    Advancement of Colored
    People
Nah Nahum
NAS naval air station
nat national, native,
    natural
natl national
NATO North Atlantic
    Treaty Organization
naut nautical

nav naval, navigable, navigation

Nb niobium

NB Nebraska, nota bene (*Latin*, note well)

N.B. New Brunswick

NBC National Broadcasting Company

NBS National Bureau of Standards

NC no charge, North Carolina

N.C. North Carolina

NCE New Catholic Edition

NCO noncommissioned officer

Nd neodymium

ND no date, North Dakota

N.D. North Dakota

N.Dak. North Dakota

Ne neon

NE New England, northeast

Neb Nebraska

NEB New English Bible

Nebr Nebraska

NED New English Dictionary

neg negative

Neh Nehemiah

NEI not elsewhere included, not elsewhere indicated

NES not elsewhere specified

Neth Netherlands

neurol neurology

neut neuter

Nev Nevada

NF no funds

Nfld Newfoundland

NG National Guard, no good

NGk New Greek

NH New Hampshire

N.H. New Hampshire

NHG New High German

NHI national health insurance (*Brit.*)

Ni nickel

NJ New Jersey

N.J. New Jersey

nk neck

NL New Latin, night letter, non liquet (*Latin*, it is not clear)

NLT night letter

NM nautical mile, New Mexico, night message, no mark, not marked

N.M. New Mexico

N.Mex. New Mexico

NNE north-northeast

NNW north-northwest

no north, northern, nose, number

No nobelium

NOIBN not otherwise

indexed by name

nol pros nolle prosequi (*Latin*, to be unwilling to prosecute)

nom nominative

non seq non sequitur

Norw Norway, Norwegian

NOS not otherwise specified

Nov November

Np neptunium

NP no protest, notary public

NPN nonprotein nitrogen

nr near, number

NS not specified

N.S. Nova Scotia

NSF not sufficient funds

N.S.W. New South Wales

NT New Testament

N.T. Northern Territory

NTP normal temperature and pressure

nt wt net weight

NU name unknown

Num Numbers

numis numismatic, numismatics

NV Nevada

NW northwest

NWT Northwest Territories

NY New York

N.Y. New York

NYC New York City

N.Z. New Zealand

o ocean, ohm

O oxygen

o/a on account

OAS Organization of American States

ob obiit (*Latin*, he [she] died)

Obad Obadiah

obj object, objective

obl oblique, oblong

obs obsolete

obv obverse

OC overcharge

occas occasionally

OCS officer candidate school

oct octavo

Oct October

o/d on demand

OD officer of the day, olive drab, overdraft, overdrawn

OE Old English

OED Oxford English Dictionary

OES Order of the Eastern Star

OF Old French

ofc office

off office, officer, official

OFM Order of Friars Minor

O.F.S. Orange Free State

OG original gum

OH Ohio
OK Oklahoma
Okla Oklahoma
ON Old Norse
Ont Ontario
op opus, out of print
OP Order of Preachers
op cit opere citato (*Latin*, in the work cited)
opp opposite
opt optical, optician, optional
OR Oregon, owner's risk
orch orchestra
ord order, ordnance
Oreg, Ore Oregon
org organization, organized
orig original, originally
ornith ornithology
o/s out of stock
Os osmium
OS ordinary seaman
OS and D over, short, and damaged
OSB Order of St. Benedict
OT Old Testament, overtime
OTS officers' training school
oz ounce

p page, participle, past, penny, per, pint, purl

P pawn, phosphorus, pressure
pa per annum
Pa Pennsylvania
PA passenger agent, Pennsylvania, power of attorney, press agent, private account, public address, purchasing agent
Pac Pacific
paleon paleontology
pam pamphlet
Pan Panama
P and L profit and loss
par paragraph, parallel, parish
parl parliament, parliamentary
part participial, participle, particular
pass passenger, passive
pat patent
path, pathol pathology
payt payment
Pb plumbum (*Latin*, lead)
pc percent, percentage, piece, postcard, post cibum (*Latin*, after meals)
PC petty cash, privy council, privy councillor
pct percent
pd paid, pond
Pd palladium

PD per diem, potential difference
PE professional engineer, Protestant Episcopal
ped pedal
P.E.I. Prince Edward Island
pen peninsula
penin peninsula
Penn Pennsylvania
Penna Pennsylvania
per period
Per Persian
perf perfect, perforated
perh perhaps
perm permanent
perp perpendicular
pers person, personal
Pers Persia, Persian
pert pertaining
Pet Peter
pf preferred
pfc private first class
pfd preferred
pg page
PG postgraduate
pharm pharmaceutical, pharmacist, pharmacy
PhD doctor of philosophy
Phil Philippians
Phila Philadelphia
Philem Philemon
philos philosopher, philosophy
phon phonetics

photog photographic, photography
phr phrase
phys physical, physician, physics
physiol physiologist, physiology
P.I. Philippine Islands
pinx pinxit (*Latin*, he [she] painted it)
pk park, peak, peck
pkg package
pkt packet
pkwy parkway
pl place, plate, plural
pm premium
p.m. post meridiem (*Latin*, afternoon)
Pm promethium
PM paymaster, police magistrate, postmaster, postmortem, prime minister, provost marshal
pmk postmark
pmt payment
PN promissory note
pnxt pinxit (*Latin*, he [she] painted it)
Po polonium
PO petty officer, postal order, post office, putouts
POC port of call
POD pay on delivery
POE port of embarkation, port of entry

Pol Poland, Polish
polit political, politician
polytech polytechnic
pop popular, population
POR pay on return
Port Portugal, Portuguese
pos position, positive
poss possessive
POW prisoner of war
pp pages, past participle, pianissimo
PP parcel post, post position
PPC pour prendre congé (*French*, to take leave)
ppd postpaid, prepaid
PPS post postscriptum (*Latin*, an additional postscript)
ppt precipitate
pptn precipitation
PQ Province of Quebec
pr pair, price
Pr praseodymium
PR payroll, public relations, Puerto Rico
prec preceding
pred predicate
pref preface, preference, preferred, prefix
prelim preliminary
prem premium
prep preparatory, preposition
pres present, president

prev previous
prf proof
prim primary, primitive
prin principal
PRN pro re nata (*Latin*, for an occasion that has arisen, as occasion arises)
PRO public relations officer
prob probable, probably, problem
proc proceedings
prod production
prof professor
pron pronoun, pronounced, pronunciation
prop propeller, property, proprietor, proposition
pros prosody
Prot Protestant
prov province, provincial, provisional
Prov Proverbs
prp present participle
Ps Psalms
PS postscriptum (*Latin*, postscript), public school
pseud pseudonym
psi pounds per square inch
PST Pacific standard time
psych psychology

psychol psychologist, psychology

pt part, payment, pint, point, port

Pt platinum

PT Pacific time, physical therapy, physical training

PTA Parent-Teacher Association

pte private (*Brit.*)

ptg printing

PTO please turn over

PTV public television

Pu plutonium

pub public, publication, published, publisher, publishing

publ publication, published

pvt private

PW prisoner of war

PX post exchange

q quart, quarto, query, question, quire

Q queen

QC Queen's Counsel

qd quaque die (*Latin*, daily)

qda quantity discount agreement

QED quod erat demonstrandum (*Latin*, which was to be demonstrated)

QEF quod erat faciendum (*Latin*, which was to be done)

QEI quod erat inveniendum (*Latin*, which was to be found out)

QID quater in die (*Latin*, four times a day)

Q'land Queensland

Qld Queensland

QM quartermaster

QMC quartermaster corps

QMG quartermaster general

qq v quae vide (*Latin*, which [pl] see)

qr quarter, quire

qt quart

q.t. quiet

qto quarto

qty quantity

quad quadrant

Que Quebec

quot quotation

q.v. quod vide (*Latin*, which see)

qy query

r rare, right, river, roentgen

R rabbi, radius, Republican, resistance, rook, runs

Ra radium

RA regular army, royal academy

RAAF Royal Australian Air Force

rad radical, radio, radius

RAdm rear admiral

RAF Royal Air Force

R and D research and development

Rb rubidium

RBC red blood cells, red blood count

RBI runs batted in

RC Red Cross, Roman Catholic

RCAF Royal Canadian Air Force

RCMP Royal Canadian Mounted Police

rd road, rod, round

RD rural delivery

re reference, regarding

Re rhenium

REA Railway Express Agency

rec receipt, record, recording, recreation

recd received

recip reciprocal, reciprocity

rec sec recording secretary

rect rectangle, rectangular, receipt, rectified

ref referee, reference, referred, reformed, refunding

refl reflex, reflexive

refr refraction

refrig refrigerating, refrigeration

reg region, register, registered, regular, regulation

regt regiment

rel relating, relative

relig religion

rep report, reporter, representative, republic

Rep Republican

repl replace, replacement

rept report

req require, required, requisition

res research, reserve, residence, resolution

resp respective, respectively

retd retained, retired, returned

rev revenue, reverend, reverse, review, reviewed, revised, revision, revolution

Rev Revelation

RF radio frequency

RFD rural free delivery

Rh rhodium

RH right hand

RI Rhode Island

R.I. Rhode Island

RIP requiescat in pace (*Latin*, may he [she] rest in peace)

riv river

rm ream, room

RMA Royal Military Academy (Sandhurst)

RMS root mean square

Rn radon

RN registered nurse, Royal Navy

rnd round

RNZAF Royal New Zealand Air Force

ROG receipt of goods

Rom Roman, Romance, Romania, Romanian, Romans

ROTC Reserve Officers' Training Corps

rpm revolutions per minute

RPO railway post office

rps revolutions per second

rpt repeat, report

rr rear

RR railroad, rural route

RS recording secretary, revised statutes, right side, Royal Society

RSV Revised Standard Version

RSVP répondez s'il vous plaît (*French*, please reply)

RSWC right side up with care

rt right, route

RT radiotelephone

rte route

Ru ruthenium

Rum Rumania, Rumanian

Russ Russia, Russian

RW radiological warfare, right worshipful, right worthy

rwy railway

ry railway

s second, section, semi, series, shilling, singular, son, soprano

S sacrifice, saint, Saturday, senate, small, south, southern, sulfur, Sunday

Sa Saturday

SA Salvation Army, sex appeal, sine anno (*Latin*, without date), South Africa, subject to approval

S.A. South Australia

SAC Strategic Air Command

Sam Samuel

sanit sanitary, sanitation

SAR Sons of the American Revolution

Sask Saskatchewan

sat saturate, saturated, saturation

Sat Saturday

S. Aust South Australia

sb substantive

SB bachelor of science, stolen base

sc scale, scene, science, scilicet (*Latin*, that is to say), small capitals

Sc scandium, Scots

SC South Carolina

S.C. South Carolina

Scand Scandinavia, Scandinavian

ScD doctor of science

ScGael Scottish Gaelic

sch school

sci science, scientific

scil scilicet (*Latin*, that is to say)

Scot Scotland, Scottish

script scripture

sctd scattered

sculp, sculpt sculpsit (*Latin*, he [she] carved it), sculptor, sculpture

SD sea-damaged, sine die, South Dakota, special delivery

S.D. South Dakota

S. Dak South Dakota

Se selenium

SE southeast

SEATO Southeast Asia Treaty Organization

sec second, secondary, secretary, section, secundum (*Latin*, according to)

sect section

secy secretary

sel select, selected, selection

sem seminary

sen senate, senator, senior

sep separate

sepn separation

Sept, Sep September

seq sequens (*Latin*, the following [singular])

seqq sequentia (*Latin*, the following [plural])

ser serial, series

serg sergeant

sergt sergeant

serv service

sf science fiction

SF sacrifice fly

sfc sergeant first class

sg senior grade, singular, specific gravity

SG solicitor general, surgeon general

sgd signed

sgt sergeant

sh share, show

Shak Shakespeare

shpt, shipt shipment

shr share

sht sheet

shtg shortage
Si silicon
S.I. Sandwich Islands, Staten Island (N.Y.)
sig signal, signature
sigill sigillum (*Latin*, seal)
sing singular
SJ Society of Jesus
Skt Sanskrit
SL salvage loss
s.l.a.n. sine loco, anno, vel nomine (*Latin*, without place, year, or name)
sld sailed, sealed
sm small
Sm samarium
SM master of science, Society of Mary
Sn stannum (*Late Latin*, tin)
so south, southern
SO seller's option, strikeouts
soc social, society
sociol sociology
sol solicitor, soluble, solution
Sol Solomon
soln solution
sop soprano
SOP standard operating procedure
soph sophomore
sp special, species, specimen, spelling, spirit

Sp Spain, Spanish
SP shore patrol, sine prole (*Latin*, without issue)
Span Spanish
SPCA Society for the Prevention of Cruelty to Animals
SPCC Society for the Prevention of Cruelty to Children
spec special, specialist
specif specific, specifically
sp. gr. specific gravity
spp species (plural)
sq squadron, square
sr senior
Sr sister, strontium
SR shipping receipt
SRO standing room only
SS saints, steamship, Sunday school, sworn statement
SSE south-southeast
SSgt staff sergeant
ssp subspecies
SSR Soviet Socialist Republic
SSS Selective Service System
SSW south-southwest
st saint, stanza, start, state, stitch, stone, straight, strait, street
ST short ton

sta   station
stat   statute
stbd   starboard
std   standard
STOL   short takeoff and
   landing
STD   doctor of sacred
   theology
stg, ster   sterling
stk   stock
STP   standard
   temperature and
   pressure
str   stretch
stud   student
subj   subject, subjunctive
suff   sufficient, suffix
suffr   suffragan
Sun   Sunday
sup   superior,
   supplement,
   supplementary, supply,
   supra (*Latin*, above)
superl   superlative
supp, suppl   supplement,
   supplementary
supt   superintendent
surg   surgeon, surgery,
   surgical
surv   survey, surveying,
   surveyor
SV   sub verbo *or* sub voce
   (*Latin*, under the word)
SW   shipper's weight,
   shortwave, southwest
S.W.A.   South-West Africa

Switz   Switzerland
syll   syllable
sym   symbol, symmetrical
syn   synonym,
   synonymous, synonymy
syst   system

t   teaspoon, temperature,
   tenor, ton, troy
T   tablespoon, Thursday,
   true, Tuesday
Ta   tantalum
tan   tangent
Tas, Tasm   Tasmania
taxon   taxonomy
Tb   terbium
TB   trial balance,
   tuberculosis
tbs, tbsp   tablespoon
TC   teachers college
TD   touchdown
Te   tellurium
tech   technical,
   technically, technician,
   technological,
   technology
tel   telegram, telegraph,
   telephone
teleg   telegraphy
temp   temperature,
   temporary, tempore
   (*Latin*, in the time of)
ten   tenor
Tenn   Tennessee
ter   terrace, territory
terr   territory

Tex Texas
Th thorium, Thursday
ThD doctor of theology
theat theatrical
theol theological, theology
therm thermometer
Thess Thessalonians
thou thousand
Thu Thursday
Thur Thursday
Thurs Thursday
Ti titanium
TID ter in die (*Latin*, three times a day)
Tim Timothy
tinct tincture
Tit Titus
tk tank, truck
TKO technical knockout
tkt ticket
Tl thallium
TL total loss
TLC tender loving care
Tm thulium
TM trademark
TMO telegraph money order
tn ton, town
TN Tennessee
tnpk turnpike
TO telegraph office, turn over
topog topography
tot total
tp title page, township

tpk turnpike
tr translated, translation, translator, transpose
trans transaction, transitive, translated, translation, translator, transportation, transverse
transl translated, translation
transp transportation
treas treasurer, treasury
trib tributary
trig trigonometry
TSgt technical sergeant
tsp teaspoon
Tu Tuesday
Tue Tuesday
Tues Tuesday
Turk Turkey, Turkish
TV television
TVA Tennessee Valley Authority
TX Texas

u unit
U university, uranium
UAR United Arab Republic
UFO unidentified flying object
UH upper half
uhf ultrahigh frequency
UK United Kingdom
ult ultimate

UMT Universal Military Training

UN United Nations

UNESCO United Nations Educational, Scientific, and Cultural Organization

univ universal, university

UNRWA United Nations Relief and Works Agency

UPI United Press International

u.s. ubi supra (*Latin*, where above [mentioned]), ut supra (*Latin*, as above)

US United States

USA United States Army, United States of America

USAF United States Air Force

USCG United States Coast Guard

USES United States Employment Service

USIA United States Information Agency

USM United States mail, United States Marines

USMA United States Military Academy

USMC United States Marine Corps

USN United States Navy

USNA United States Naval Academy

USNG United States National Guard

USNR United States Naval Reserve

USO United Service Organizations

USP United States Pharmacopeia

USS United States Ship

USSR Union of Soviet Socialist Republics

usu usual, usually

UT Utah

UV ultraviolet

UW underwriter

v vector, velocity, verb, verse, versus, vide (*Latin*, see), voice, volume, vowel

V vanadium, victory, volt, voltage

Va Virginia

VA Veterans Administration, vice admiral, Virginia

VAdm vice admiral

val value

var variable, variant, variation, variety, various

vb verb

VC vice-chancellor, vice-consul

VD venereal disease

veg vegetable

vel vellum, velocity
ven venerable
vert vertical
vet veterinarian, veterinary
VF video frequency, visual field
VFD volunteer fire department
VFW Veterans of Foreign Wars
VG very good, vicar-general
vhf very high frequency
vi verb intransitive, vide infra (*Latin*, see below)
VI Virgin Islands
vic vicinity
Vic Victoria
vil village
VIP very important person
vis visibility, visual
viz videlicet (*Latin*, namely)
VL Vulgar Latin
vlf very low frequency
VNA Visiting Nurse Association
VOA Voice of America
voc vocative
vocab vocabulary
vol volume, volunteer
vou voucher
VP vice-president
vs verse, versus, vide

supra (*Latin*, see above)
vss verses, versions
V/STOL vertical short takeoff and landing
vt verb transitive
Vt Vermont
VT Vermont
VTOL vertical takeoff and landing
Vulg Vulgate
vv verses, vice versa

w water, watt, week, weight, wide, width, wife, with
W Wednesday, Welsh, west, western, wolfram
WA Washington
war warrant
Wash Washington
W. Aust. Western Australia
WB water ballast, waybill
WBC white blood cells, white blood count
WC water closet, west central, without charge
WCTU Women's Christian Temperance Union
Wed Wednesday
wf wrong font
wh which
whf wharf
WHO World Health Organization

whol wholesale
whs, whse warehouse
whsle wholesale
WI Wisconsin
W.I. West Indies
wid widow, widower
Wis Wisconsin
Wisc Wisconsin
wk week, work
WL wavelength
wmk watermark
WNW west-northwest
w/o without
WO warrant officer
wpm words per minute
wrnt warrant
WSW west-southwest
wt weight
WV West Virginia
W. Va. West Virginia
WW World War
WY Wyoming
Wyo Wyoming

X experimental
xd without dividend
x div without dividend
Xe xenon
x in, x int without interest
XL extra large
Xn Christian

Xnty Christianity

y yard, year
Y YMCA, yttrium
Yb ytterbium
yd yard
yld yield
YMCA Young Men's
  Christian Association
YMHA Young Men's
  Hebrew Association
YO yarn over, year-old
yr year, your
yrbk yearbook
Yt yttrium
YT Yukon Territory
YW Young Women's
  Christian Association
YWCA Young Women's
  Christian Association
YWHA Young Women's
  Hebrew Association

z zero
Zech Zechariah
Zeph Zephaniah
ZIP Zone Improvement
  Plan
Zn zinc
zool zoological, zoology
Zr zirconium

PUNCTUATION

.	period	—	dash
?	question mark	( )	parentheses
!	exclamation point	[ ]	brackets
,	comma	-	hyphen
;	semicolon	" "	quotation marks
:	colon	'	apostrophe

PERIOD
- A period is used to mark the end of a sentence that is not a question and that is not an exclamation.
- A period may be used following an abbreviation — U.S.A.; 7 a.m., Dr. John H. Doe.
- Periods usually follow common contractions formed by leaving out letters within a word. — secy.; mfg.; recd.
- A period is necessary before a decimal and between dollars and cents in figures. — .72 pounds; 16.6 feet; $12.95.

QUESTION MARK
- A question mark is used at the end of an interrogative sentence. — Will you be here on Thursday?
- A question mark, usually enclosed in parentheses, is often used after a word, phrase, or date to indicate uncertainty of its accuracy. — John Doe, the new secretary(?); James Doe began as an office boy in 1952(?); Richard Doe (1883-1918?).
- A question mark is *not* used after a sentence expressed as a question out of courtesy. — Will you kindly fill out the enclosed form and return it to this office.

EXCLAMATION POINT
- An exclamation point follows an expression or statement that is an exclamation. — Oh no! Not that! Hurry! We need help!

COMMA

- Commas are used to set off words, phrases, and other sentence elements that are parenthetical or independent. Items of this sort are contrasting expressions, prefatory exclamations, the names of persons directly addressed, and expressions like *he said* in direct quotations. — More work, not words, is what is needed. The monthly figures, though not entirely to our liking, are better than we expected. "Don't go to Chicago," he said. George, you must improve the efficiency of your department.
- A comma usually sets off appositional or modifying words, phrases, or clauses that do not limit or restrict the main idea of a sentence. — George, his own brother, turned against him. John, whom we saw yesterday, is away today. We leave at 3 p.m., when the bell rings, and return at 3:30. The formation is of great interest to geologists, although most of us would hardly notice it.
- Commas set off transitional words and expressions when they are subordinate. Such words and expressions include *on the contrary, on the other hand, consequently, furthermore, moreover, nevertheless, therefore.* — The question, however, remains unanswered. On the contrary, under the rules a report is due monthly.
- A comma usually separates words, phrases, or clauses that occur in a series. — The estate is to be divided among his wife, his son, and his daughters. He opened the carton, removed the contents, and replaced the lid.
- A comma is often used before *and* or *or* introducing the final item in a closed series. — Scientific, technical, and academic periodicals are important sources. He ordered blue, yellow, green, and white cards.
- A comma separates statements or clauses joined by a coordinating conjunction. — He seemed unhappy, but he said nothing. We know very little about him, and he has volunteered no information.
- Commas are used without conjunctions to separate brief and closely related statements or clauses. — He delivered his report,

then left the meeting. He will always remember, the experience is now part of him. Don't bother, it doesn't make any difference.

- A comma is used to separate items in dates and addresses. — She was born on January 16, 1937. Send your order directly to the Superintendent of Documents, Washington, D.C.
- A comma is used to separate expressions such as *namely, that is, i.e., e.g., viz.* from what follows. — There are two ways to do the job: namely, a right way and a wrong way. He forbade future forays; that is, there were to be no more raids.
- A comma usually indicates the place of an omitted word or group of words. — The yellow forms are for reporting sick days; the green, for vacation days.
- A comma usually separates a direct quote from the rest of a sentence. — He asked abruptly, "Where is the report?"
- In numbers, a comma is used to separate thousand, millions, and other groups of three digits except in dates, page numbers, street numbers, and in numbers of four digits. — More than 2,643,762 were registered. We received 67,413 replies.
- A comma is used to set off titles, degrees, etc., from names. — John Doe, M.D. Richard Doe, president. Henry Doe, M.A., Ph.D.
- A comma is customary after the salutation in personal letters and after the complimentary close in all letters. — Dear Joe, . . . Sincerely yours,. . . .
- A comma may always be used to avoid ambiguity. — To Ruth, James was always a good worker. In 1972, 25% of the districts reported higher sales.

SEMICOLON

- A semicolon usually separates independent statements or clauses joined together in one sentence without a conjunction. Such statements are usually closely related. — Make no terms; insist on full restitution.
- A semicolon separates two statements or clauses when the second begins with a sentence connector or conjunctive adverb such as *accordingly, also, consequently, furthermore, hence, however, indeed, moreover, nevertheless, otherwise, so, still,*

then, therefore, thus, yet. — His performance has been satisfactory; nevertheless he will not be promoted. You have recommended him highly; therefore we will give him a trial.

- A semicolon is used to separate phrases or clauses that are themselves broken up by punctuation. — The country's resources include large oil deposits; lumber, waterpower, and good soils; and a literate, active work force.
- A semicolon sometimes is used to separate items in lists of names with addresses, titles, or figures where a comma alone would not clearly separate the items. — Genesis 3:1–19; 4:1–16. John Doe, treasurer; Richard Doe, secretary.

COLON

- A colon is used to link two parts of a sentence. The second part, after the colon, usually balances, supplements, defines, restates, sums up, enumerates, or lists the idea expressed in the first part. — The same space appears on the statement: the buyer must express approval. His ambition must be stirred: his interest must be aroused. The following items are required: a valid passport, inoculation certificate, and visa. Representatives of four departments presented reports: advertising, customer service, sales, and shipping.
- Colons function as dividers in set formulas such as those expressing ratios, time, volume and page references, Biblical citations, and place and publisher. — We need a 3:5 ratio. It will be at 3:30. Check *Encyclopædia Britannica* 18:643. See Luke 2:12. Springfield: Merriam-Webster Inc.
- A colon is used after a formal salutation in a letter. — Dear Mr. Doe:. . . .
- A colon is used to introduce an extended quotation. — We quote from your letter: "The statement received on 23 May did not include all items."
- A colon is used to separate a title from a subtitle when the subtitle is not otherwise set off. — Monthly Report: June 1973.

DASH

- A dash usually marks an abrupt change or suspension in the thought or structure of a sentence. — He was — how shall I put it — unhappy with the results.
- A dash often makes parenthetic or explanatory matter stand out clearly or emphatically. — Two of our men — John and George — made a good showing. He is willing to discuss all operations — those that are efficient and the trouble spots.
- A dash often occurs before a summarizing statement. — Oil, steel, and transportation — these are the basis of development.
- A dash is used to precede the name of an author or source at the end of a quotation. — "In the beginning God created the heavens and the earth" — Genesis 1:1.
- A long dash often indicates the omission of a word or of letters in a word. — Mr. M ——, our department head. I don't really give a d——.
- A dash is used to indicate extent or duration. — See pages 124–127. The New York–Chicago flight was late. The period 1962–1971 was exceptional.

PARENTHESES

- Parentheses set off supplementary material that is not part of the main statement or not a structural element of the sentence. — Our long-range goals (I think you have set them out clearly) are sound. The chart (Fig. 3) indicates the problem.
- Parentheses are used to set off parenthetic material when the interruption is more marked than that usually indicated by commas. — Three older lines (now all out of production) will be eliminated. He is hoping (as we all are) that it will succeed.
- Parentheses are used to enclose numbers in a series. — We must look at (1) advertising, (2) publicity, and (3) our customer relations.
- Parentheses enclose an arabic number confirming a number written out. — Delivery will be made in thirty (30) days.

BRACKETS
- Brackets serve as parentheses within parentheses. — Local regulations (City Ordinance 46 [sec. 5]) prohibit it.
- Brackets set off a word or phrase that is extraneous or incidental, or explanatory. — The department head [Richard Doe] must approve all requests.

HYPHEN
- A hyphen marks the separation of a word at the end of a line. — He will be here on Tues- [*end of line*] day, the 14th.
- A hyphen suspends the second part of a hyphenated compound when used with another hyphenated compound. — There will be ten- and twenty-year notes.
- A hyphen is used to link two or more words used as a single modifying term. — We do not accept larger-than-life material. Newly-produced items must be tested.

QUOTATION MARKS
- Quotation marks are used before and after a direct quote. In long quotations, repeat the double quotation marks at the beginning of each paragraph as well as at the beginning and end of the entire passage quoted. — He repeated his instructions, "We cannot accept exchanges."
- Single quotation marks enclose a quotation within a quote. — The witness said, "I heard him say, 'I'll be back,' before he left."
- Quotation marks are used to enclose the title of a short poem, an article, or a chapter or part of a book. The title of a book or play is usually set in italics, or underlined in typing. — See his remarks in "Tomorrow's Goals," in *Thirty Years of Progress.*
- Quotation marks are sometimes used to emphasize a particular word or to set off a technical or unfamiliar word. — We will test your "unshrinkable" fabric. An "em" is a unit of measure used by printers.

APOSTROPHE

- An apostrophe is used to indicate possession. — John's; everyone's.
- An apostrophe may be used to indicate omission of letters within a word. — sec'y.

CAPITALIZATION

- A capital letter is used for the first letter of the first word of a sentence.
- A capital letter is used to begin a direct quote within a sentence. — He said, "Now is the time."
- A capital letter begins proper names and many of their derivatives. — All employees there must learn Spanish. A new branch in New York will open soon. The style shows a distinct French influence.
- A capital begins titles placed before the name of the holder. It is not usually used when the title follows the name. — Treasurer John Doe; John Doe, treasurer, ...
- Capitals begin all the words in a title, except for articles, conjunctions, and short prepositions. — United States of America; *Webster's Dictionary of Proper Names.*
- Capital letters are used throughout in the abbreviated form of the names of many organizations. — UNESCO; IBM.

WEIGHTS AND MEASURES

Unit	Equivalents in Other Units of Same System	Metric Equivalent
length		
mile	5280 feet 320 rods 1760 yards	1.609 kilometers
rod	5.50 yards 16.5 feet	5.029 meters
yard	3 feet 36 inches	0.914 meters
foot	12 inches 0.333 yards	30.480 centimeters
inch	0.083 feet 0.027 yards	2.540 centimeters
area		
square mile	640 acres 102,400 square rods	2.590 square kilometers
acre	4840 square yards 43,560 square feet	0.405 hectares 4047 square meters
square rod	30.25 square yards 0.006 acres	25.293 square meters
square yard	1296 square inches 9 square feet	0.836 square meters
square foot	144 square inches 0.111 square yards	0.093 square meters
square inch	0.007 square feet 0.00077 square yards	6.451 square centimeters
volume		
cubic yard	27 cubic feet 46,656 cubic inches	0.765 cubic meters
cubic foot	1728 cubic inches 0.0370 cubic yards	0.028 cubic meters
cubic inch	0.00058 cubic feet 0.000021 cubic yards	16.387 cubic centimeters
weight *avoirdupois*		
ton		
short ton	20 short hundredweight 2000 pounds	0.907 metric tons
long ton	20 long hundredweight 2240 pounds	1.016 metric tons

hundredweight		
short hundredweight	100 pounds 0.05 short tons	45.359 kilograms
long hundredweight	112 pounds 0.05 long tons	50.802 kilograms
pound	16 ounces 7000 grains	0.453 kilograms
ounce	16 drams 437.5 grains	28.349 grams
dram	27.343 grains 0.0625 ounces	1.771 grams
grain	0.036 drams 0.002285 ounces	0.0648 grams

troy

pound	12 ounces 240 pennyweight 5760 grains	0.373 kilograms
ounce	20 pennyweight 480 grains	31.103 grams
pennyweight	24 grains 0.05 ounces	1.555 grams
grain	0.042 pennyweight 0.002083 ounces	0.0648 grams

apothecaries'

pound	12 ounces 5760 grains	0.373 kilograms
ounce	8 drams 480 grains	31.103 grams
dram	3 scruples 60 grains	3.887 grams
scruple	20 grains 0.333 drams	1.295 grams
grain	0.05 scruples 0.002083 ounces 0.0166 drams	0.0648 grams

capacity
(U.S. liquid measure)

gallon	4 quarts (231 cubic inches)	3.785 liters
quart	2 pints (57.75 cubic inches)	0.946 liters
pint	4 gills (28.875 cubic inches)	0.473 liters
gill	4 fluidounces (7.218 cubic inches)	118.291 milliliters
fluidounce	8 fluidrams (1.804 cubic inches)	29.573 milliliters

| fluidram | 60 minims
(0.225 cubic inches) | 3.696 milliliters |
| minim | 1/60 fluidram
(0.003759 cubic inch) | 0.061610 milliliters |

(U.S. dry measure)

bushel	4 pecks (2150.42 cubic inches)	35.238 liters
peck	8 quarts (537.605 cubic inches)	8.809 liters
quart	2 pints (67.200 cubic inches)	1.101 liters
pint	1/2 quart (33.600 cubic inches)	0.550 liters

**British imperial
liquid and
dry measure**

bushel	4 pecks (2219.36 cubic inches)	0.036 cubic meters
peck	2 gallons (554.84 cubic inches)	0.009 cubic meters
gallon	4 quarts (277.420 cubic inches)	4.545 liters
quart	2 pints (69.355 cubic inches)	1.136 liters
pint	4 gills (34.678 cubic inches)	568.26 cubic centimeters
gill	5 fluidounces (8,669 cubic inches)	142.066 cubic centimeters
fluidounce	8 fluidrams (1,7339 cubic inches)	28.416 cubic centimeters
fluidram	60 minims (0.216734 cubic inches)	3.5516 cubic centimeters
minim	1/60 fluidram (0.003612 cubic inches)	0.059194 cubic centimeters

NOTES

NOTES